Lecture Notes in Com

Commenced Publication in 1973
Founding and Former Series Editors:
Gerhard Goos, Juris Hartmanis, and Jan van Leeuwen

Yale N. Patt   Pierfrancesco Foglia
Evelyn Duesterwald   Paolo Faraboschi
Xavier Martorell (Eds.)

High Performance Embedded Architectures and Compilers

5th International Conference, HiPEAC 2010
Pisa, Italy, January 25-27, 2010
Proceedings

 Springer

Volume Editors

Yale N. Patt
The University of Texas at Austin
Department of Electrical and Computer Engineering
1 University Station C0803, Austin, TX 78712-0240, USA
E-mail: pattyn@austin.utexas.edu

Pierfrancesco Foglia
Università di Pisa, Dipartimento di Ingegneria della Informazione
Via Diotisalvi 2, 56100 Pisa, Italy
E-mail: foglia@iet.unipi.it

Evelyn Duesterwald
IBM T.J.Watson Research Center
19 Skyline Drive, Hawthorne, NY 10532, USA
E-mail: duester@us.ibm.com

Paolo Faraboschi
Hewlett-Packard
Cami de Can Graells 1-21, Sant Cugat del Vallés, 08174 Barcelona, Spain
E-mail: paolo.faraboschi@hp.com

Xavier Martorell
Technical University of Catalunya (UPC), Computer Architecture Department
c/Jordi Girona 1-3, 08034 Barcelona, Spain
E-mail: xavim@ac.upc.edu

Library of Congress Control Number: 2009942994

CR Subject Classification (1998): B.2, C.1, D.3.4, B.5, C.2, D.4

LNCS Sublibrary: SL 1 – Theoretical Computer Science and General Issues

ISSN   0302-9743
ISBN-10   3-642-11514-4 Springer Berlin Heidelberg New York
ISBN-13   978-3-642-11514-1 Springer Berlin Heidelberg New York

springer.com

© Springer-Verlag Berlin Heidelberg 2010
Printed in Germany

Typesetting: Camera-ready by author, data conversion by Scientific Publishing Services, Chennai, India
Printed on acid-free paper   SPIN: 12838325   06/3180   5 4 3 2 1 0

Preface

Message from the General Co-chairs

It is our honor and pleasure as General Co-chairs to welcome you to the proceedings of HiPEAC 2010 which was held in Pisa. This was the fifth HiPEAC conference, following in the strong tradition of the first conference in Barcelona in 2005 and the subsequent conferences in Ghent (2007), Goteborg (2008), and Paphos (2009).

HiPEAC 2010 offered a rich and diverse set of technical and non-technical activities. The technical activities included most importantly another strong technical program, and in addition, eight workshops and five tutorials, all central to the HiPEAC network roadmap. The workshops explored multi-cores, simulation and performance evaluation, compiler and optimizations, design reliability, reconfigurable computing, interconnection networks, operating system and computer architecture codesign. The tutorials dealt with statistical methodology to evaluate program speed-ups, design for reliability, how to teach introductory computer architecture and programming, programming FPGA-based accelerators and adaptability.

We were particularly fortunate to have two keynote addresses, one by Bob Iannucci, formerly from Nokia, on how data center thinking can be effectively ushered into the embedded system domain, and one by Roger Espasa from Intel on the Larrabee Architecture.

The non-technical activities reflected the academic, historical, and cultural charm of Pisa, a major center of Tuscany, and we hope the participants took advantage of our scheduled guided tour of historical Pisa and the conference banquet in a historic villa.

The planning of every conference starts well in advance, and HiPEAC 2010 was no exception. Were it not for the unselfish and hard work of a large number of devoted individuals, this conference could not have been successful. First, we thank the Program Co-chairs Evelyn Duesterwald and Paolo Faraboschi for putting together an outstanding Technical Program, which is the sine qua non of every conference, and we are looking forward to this one. Special thanks to Alessandro Bardine from the University of Pisa, who helped us with the local organization and the team from the CARGO group in Pisa for their support. We would also like to thank Sandro Bartolini (Siena) for putting together an attractive pre–conference program; Wouter De Raeve (Ghent), our Finance Chair for running the books; Roberto Giorgi (Siena) for timely publicity campaigns; Xavier Martorell (BSC) for the hard work in putting together the proceedings; Michiel Ronsse (Ghent) for administering the submission and review system; and Klaas Millet (Ghent) for administering the website. We are pleased to acknowledge the advice of Antonio Prete and of our senior mentors from HiPEACs past, Per Stenström and Koen De Bosschere, chair of the HiPEAC2 network. Thanks to you all.

Finally, we would like to gratefully acknowledge the Seventh Framework Programme of the European Union, represented by project officer Panagiotis Tsarchopoulos, for sponsoring the event, and for providing both needed moral support and the money for travel grants.

November 2009   Yale N. Patt
                                                             Pierfrancesco Foglia

Message from the Program Co-chairs

We are pleased to present the proceedings of the HiPEAC 2010 Conference. In the call for papers we emphasized HiPEAC's focus on the convergence of the challenges faced by the high–performance general–purpose and embedded worlds. Not long ago, the computational requirements of today's embedded devices were of concern only in the supercomputing realm. Conversely, the energy and cost consideration traditionally associated with embedded computing have become key design criteria for high-performance and general-purpose computing.

The Program Committee selected 23 papers among the 94 submissions to appear at the conference. The selection process required 365 reviews, with 275 from PC members and 90 from an external review committee of 47 experts individually selected by the Program Co-chairs. All papers received at least three reviews with an average of 3.9 reviews per paper. All papers, regardless of their standing, were considered for general discussion and final selection at the PC meeting.

The PC meeting was held on September 12, 2009 at the UPC facilities in Barcelona, with 13 of the 27 PC members attending the meeting in person, and several others by telephone. At the close of each paper discussion, the recommendations of the PC members who had reviewed the paper were followed by an advisory vote from the entire committee and a final binding decision by the Program Co-chairs. PC members left the room during the discussion of any paper they had a conflict with.

We were also honored to have two excellent keynote speakers this year. Bob Iannucci, former CTO of Nokia and CEO and Co–founder of Sensaré LLC, enlightened us about "Embedded Systems as Datacenters." Roger Espasa, principal engineer at Intel, presented "Larrabee: A Many-Core Intel Architecture for Visual Computing."

It takes the enthusiasm of many people to put together a successful program and we would like to mention some of them here. Michiel Ronsse spent endless hours administering the web system for paper submissions and reviews. Per Stenström and Koen De Bosschere offered valuable suggestions for the program and committee selection process. We would also like to thank the PC members who put enormous effort into reviewing the papers and selecting the final program, as well as all the members of the external review committee who graciously agreed to lend their expertise.

November 2009

Evelyn Duesterwald
Paolo Faraboschi

Organization

Executive Committee

General Co-chairs	Yale N. Patt (UT Austin, USA)
	Pierfrancesco Foglia (Università di Pisa, Italy)
Program Co-chairs	Evelyn Duesterwald (IBM T.J. Watson Research Center, USA)
	Paolo Faraboschi (HP Labs, Spain)
Workshop/Tutorials Chair	Sandro Bartolini (Università di Siena, Italy)
Local Arrangements Chair	Alessandro Bardine (Università di Pisa, Italy)
Finance Chair	Wouter De Raeve (Ghent University, Belgium)
Publicity Chair	Roberto Giorgi (Università di Siena, Italy)
Publications Chair	Xavier Martorell (BSC, Spain)
Submissions Chair	Michiel Ronsse (Ghent University, Belgium)
Web Chair	Klaas Millet (Ghent University, Belgium)

Program Committee

Erik Altman	IBM T.J. Watson Research Center, USA
Albert Cohen	INRIA Saclay, France
Jesus Corbal	Intel Labs, Barcelona, Spain
Jack Davidson	University of Virginia, USA
Koen De Bosschere	Ghent University, Belgium
Jim Dehnert	Google, Inc., USA
Giuseppe Desoli	STMicroelectronics, Italy
Pedro C. Diniz	Technical University of Lisbon (IST)/INESC–ID, Portugal
Carol Eidt	Microsoft Corporation, USA
Babak Falsafi	EPFL Lausanne, Switzerland
Georgi Gaydadjiev	TU Delft, The Netherlands
Thomas Gross	ETH Zurich, Switzerland
Rajiv Gupta	University of California, Riverside, USA
Mary Jane Irwin	Penn State University, USA
Wolfgang Karl	Karlsruhe Institute of Technology (KIT), Germany
Josep Llosa	Universitat Politènica de Catalunya, Spain
Scott Mahlke	University of Michigan, USA
Sally A. McKee	Chalmers University of Technology, Sweden
Avi Mendelson	Microsoft Corporation, Israel
Michael O'Boyle	University of Edinburgh, UK
Daniel Ortega	HP Labs, Barcelona, Spain

Emre Ozer	ARM Cambridge, UK
Keshav Pingali	UT Austin, USA
Milos Prvulovic	Georgia Tech, USA
Cristina Silvano	Politecnico di Milano, Italy
David Whalley	Florida State University, USA
Donald Yeung	University of Maryland, USA

External Review Committee

Eduardo Argollo	Roberto Gioiosa	Luigi Raffo
Hans Boehm	Wei Hsu	Partha Ranganathan
Rajesh Bordawekar	Michael Huang	Erven Rohou
Greg Bronevetsky	Robert Hundt	Yannakis Sazeides
Anton Chernoff	Paolo Ienne	Andre Seznec
Bruce Childers	Ravi Iyer	Uma Srinivasan
Dave Christie	Mahmut Kandemir	Per Stenström
Tom Conte	Steve Keckler	John Stratton
Al Davis	Mikko Lipasti	Olivier Temam
Chen Ding	Gabriel Loh	Osman Unsal
Amer Diwan	Grant Martin	Manish Vachharajani
Jose Duato	Frank Mueller	Neil Vachharajani
Lieven Eeckhout	Walid Najjar	Sami Yehia
Ayose Falcon	Nacho Navarro	Cliff Young
Hubertus Franke	Kevin O'Brien	Antonia Zhai
Maria Garzaran	David Penry	

Steering Committee

Anant Agarwal	MIT, USA
Koen De Bosschere	Ghent University, Belgium
Joel Emer	Intel, USA
Wen–mei W. Hwu	UIUC, USA
Margaret Martonosi	Princeton University, USA
Michael O'Boyle	University of Edinburgh, UK
Andr Seznec	IRISA, France
Per Stenström	Chalmers University, Sweden
Theo Ungerer	University of Augsburg, Germany
Mateo Valero	UPC, Spain

Table of Contents

Invited Program

Architectural Support for Concurrency

Compilation and Runtime Systems

Reconfigurable and Customized Architectures

Multicore Efficiency, Reliability, and Power

Memory Organization and Optimization

Programming and Analysis of Accelerators

Embedded Systems as Datacenters
(Keynote)

Bob Iannucci

CEO and Co–founder, Sensaré LLC

Abstract. Designing embedded systems the way we did 20 years ago is still alive and well. As expected, with declining costs, embedded systems are appearing in more and more applications. Advances to the state of the art in creating such systems, where memory and processor are precious resources, have continued, and this work is to be applauded. But just as interestingly, embedded systems are taking on not only problems that require loosening the memory and processor constraints but also those problems that push us into the domain of datacenter design. Datacenter design is where system thinking about heterogeneous parallel processing, data archiving, mission-critical connectivity, and energy management are first-order concerns. In this talk I will illustrate the latter case with some recent explorations and give some attention to how datacenter thinking can be effectively ushered into this new domain.

Biography of Bob Iannucci

Bob is co-founder and CEO of Sensaré LLC, a startup pursuing opportunities in mobile sensing. Formerly, Bob was senior vice president and CTO of Nokia. There, he played a defining role in reshaping the company's long-term R&D strategy. Challenging traditional management thinking, he brought open innovation to Nokia and built a research environment suited to Internet ways of working and systems-level thinking. With three decades in the IT industry, first at IBM during the mainframe days, then at Digital with its minis, and next at Compaq in the 1990s, plus three startups, he brings insights in reshaping mature businesses into growth businesses and tackling the so-called Innovator's Dilemma. Bob holds a PhD in Electrical Engineering and Computer Science from the Massachusetts Institute of Technology, and is the author and co-author of two books and several academic papers. He holds five patents.

Y.N. Patt et al. (Eds.): HiPEAC 2010, LNCS 5952, p. 1, 2010.

Larrabee: A Many-Core Intel Architecture for Visual Computing
(Keynote)

Roger Espasa

Principal Engineer, Intel Corporation

Abstract. This talk will describe a many-core visual computing architecture code named Larrabee. Larrabee uses multiple in-order x86 CPU cores that are augmented by a wide vector processor unit, as well as some fixed function logic blocks. The talk will go into an overview of the Larrabee architecture and will cover the LRB Vector ISA in detail. We'll then cover the Larrabee programming model and finally close with how one would target Larrabee for high performance 3D graphics.

Biography of Roger Espasa

Roger Espasa got his Ph.D. in 1997 at the Universitat Politècnica de Catalunya. In 1999-2001 he worked for the Alpha Microprocessor Group (Compaq at the time) on a vector extension to the Alpha architecture. The project, codenamed Tarantula, never shipped, but was an 8-way SMT EV8 coupled to a large vector unit. In 2002, the Alpha team, and the tiny subsidiary that we had created in Barcelona to work on Tarantula was acquired by Intel. Since then Roger has been working at Intel, where he currently is a Principal Engineer. At Intel, Roger worked first on a vector extension for Nehalem, which again did not ship and later applied the vector concept to Larrabee. Since 2005, Roger has worked on the Larrabee architecture, where he is responsible for the vector instruction set and the texture sampler.

Y.N. Patt et al. (Eds.): HiPEAC 2010, LNCS 5952, p. 2, 2010.

Remote Store Programming
A Memory Model for Embedded Multicore

Henry Hoffmann, David Wentzlaff, and Anant Agarwal

Tilera Corporation
hank@alum.mit.edu, wentzlaf@tilera.com, agarwal@tilera.com

Abstract. This paper presents remote store programming (RSP), a programming paradigm which combines usability and efficiency through the exploitation of a simple hardware mechanism, the remote store, which can easily be added to existing multicores. The RSP model and its hardware implementation trade a relatively high store latency for a low load latency because loads are more common than stores, and it is easier to tolerate store latency than load latency. This paper demonstrates the performance advantages of remote store programming by comparing it to cache-coherent shared memory (CCSM) for several important embedded benchmarks using the TILEPro64 processor. RSP is shown to be faster than CCSM for all eight benchmarks using 64 cores. For five of the eight benchmarks, RSP is shown to be more than 1.5× faster than CCSM. For a 2D FFT implemented on 64 cores, RSP is over 3× faster than CCSM. RSP's features, performance, and hardware simplicity make it well suited to the embedded processing domain.

1   Introduction

Due to the scaling limitations of uniprocessors, multicore architectures, which aggregate multiple processing cores onto a single chip, have become ubiquitous in many disciplines of computing. One of the key design features of a multicore architecture is its programming model, which must handle inter-core communication. Cache-coherent shared memory is a popular programming model that is supported by several commercial multicores including those from Intel, Cavium, RMI, and Tilera.

In the cache-coherent shared memory (CCSM) model processes communicate by reading and writing a globally accessible address space. This model is popular as it is generally considered easy-to-use, and the ease of use derives from the fact that communication in the CCSM model is accomplished using familiar load and store instructions. In addition, CCSM communication is one-sided and fine-grain, which is easy to schedule and overlap with computation. However, reliance on the abstraction of global, uniformly accessible shared memory makes it difficult for programmers to determine when their code will result in communication, and how much that communication will cost.

The CCSM model also makes it difficult to exploit locality for performance in regularly structured applications, like those typically found in video, image and

Y.N. Patt et al. (Eds.): HiPEAC 2010, LNCS 5952, pp. 3–17, 2010.

signal processing. Locality can be especially important for performance on CCSM architectures which distribute the shared cache using directory protocols [1]. Locality will become more important as more cores are integrated onto a single chip because both the probability and penalty of non-local access increases with increasing numbers of cores.

This paper presents the remote store programming (RSP) model, which combines some of the features that make CCSM easy to use while still allowing programmers to control locality in software for performance. In addition, RSP requires only a small set of hardware features and is incrementally supportable in multicore architectures that support standard load and store instructions. Significantly, RSP requires less hardware support than the CCSM model but can achieve higher performance executing regular computations on multicores with a large number of cores. The RSP model can complement cache-coherent architectures by providing an alternative for performance-critical code where locality is an issue. Alternatively, RSP can be implemented as the only programming model on an architecture which may be attractive for multicore architectures targeting regular application domains.

In the RSP model processes have private address spaces by default, but they can give other processes write access to their local memory. Once a producer has write access to a consumer's memory, it communicates directly with the consumer using the standard store instruction to target remote memory, hence the name "remote store programming." Communication in the RSP model is one-sided and fine-grain making it easy to schedule. In addition, consumer processes are guaranteed to read physically close, or local, memory.

The performance of the RSP model is evaluated by emulating it using the TILEPro64 processor. This study demonstrates that the RSP paradigm can achieve efficient parallel implementations on important multicore applications like video, image, and digital signal processing. An RSP implementation of an H.264 encoder for HD video achieves a speedup of 30.5x using 40 processes, while a 2D FFT achieves a speedup of 60x using 64 processes. Additionally, the TILEPro64 allows comparison of RSP to CCSM. While CCSM is generally faster or equivalent to RSP using a small number of cores, RSP achieves anywhere from 1.25× to over 3× the performance of CCSM using 64 cores. The speedup relative to shared memory is due to RSP's emphasis on locality-of-reference, as RSP programs always access physically close memory and minimize load latencies. Furthermore, RSP achieves this performance with less hardware support.

The RSP model is similar to some existing programming models like the partitioned global address space (PGAS) model [2], Digital Equipment Corporation's memory channels (MC) model [3], and virtual memory mapped communication (VMMC) as implemented on the SHRIMP processor [4]. All these models combine features of CCSM while allowing users to manage locality in software. The RSP model differs in that it is designed specifically for multicore by including only mechanisms that can be incrementally supported in existing multicore architectures.

This paper makes the following contributions:

- It identifies the RSP model which is supportable with a small set of hardware features that can be incrementally added to a multicore architecture supporting loads and stores. This model includes features based on existing distributed shared memory models and is particularly suited to embedded processing.
- It describes the high-level features required to support RSP and argues that this model needs less support than CCSM.
- It presents a detailed performance comparison of the RSP and CCSM models using eight embedded benchmarks and finds that RSP out-performs CCSM using large numbers of cores.

The remainder of this paper is organized as follows. Section 2 describes the RSP model. Section 3 discusses the hardware and system software support required to implement the model. Section 4 discusses the methodology used to evaluate RSP and compare it to CCSM using the TILEPro64 multicore processor. Section 5 presents the comparison of RSP and CCSM performance. Related work is discussed in Section 6. Finally, the paper concludes in Section 7.

2   The Remote Store Programming Model

This section discusses programming using the RSP model. The term *process* refers to the basic unit of program execution. This work assumes that there is a one-to-one mapping between processes and processor cores, but that restriction is easily relaxed. A parallel programming paradigm is distinguished by three features: *process model*, *communication* mechanism, and *synchronization* mechanism.

The process model. RSP presents a system abstraction where each process has its own local, private memory. However, a process can explicitly give a subset of other processes write access to regions of its private memory. These regions of memory are referred to as *remotely writable*. The system abstraction for RSP is illustrated in Figure 1. The key idea of the remote store paradigm is that programmers ensure that a process always reads local memory.

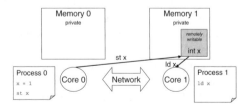

Fig. 1. Illustration of the remote store programming model. There are two cores, each of which executes a process. Process 1 allocates a remotely-writable region of memory to hold the integer x. Process 0 writes a new value into x, and this new data travels from Process 0's registers to Process 1's cache.

The communication mechanism. In an RSP application, processes communicate by writing directly into other processes' memory using the store instruction as the communication primitive. A process that wants to consume data uses a special memory allocation function to allocate remotely writable memory. The consumer process then makes the address of this memory available to the data producer. The producer uses the standard store instruction to write to the remote memory. Once the data is stored remotely, the consumer uses standard load instructions to read the data generated by the producer; however, load instructions are not allowed to target remote memory.

The synchronization mechanism. Processes in an RSP program synchronize using atomic synchronization operations, like test-and-set or fetch-and-add. These synchronization operations are allowed to access remote memory and are the one class of operations that are allowed to read remote memory. One can easily build more advanced synchronization primitives from these operations, so high level synchronization features like mutexes, condition variables, and barriers are available as part of the RSP model.

Given this description, RSP has the following features:

- Familiarity of shared memory programming. Like CCSM, RSP uses standard load and store instructions to communicate.
- Emphasis on locality of reference. RSP encourages programmers to write code in such a way that loads always target local, physically close memory.
- One-sided communication. In RSP programs, data is pushed from the producer to the consumer. Unlike two-sided communication schemes that require a *send* to be accompanied by a *receive*, remote stores do not require acknowledgement in this model. One-sided communication leads to code that is both easier to write and higher performing than a two-sided model.
- No explicit support for bulk transfers. The RSP model does not support a special *put* operation like SHMEM [5] and UPC [6][1]. This omission is designed to encourage programmers to store data remotely as it is produced so that data is transferred from the registers of the producer to the cache of the consumer with no extra buffering or copying.
- No support for remote reads. The RSP model does not support remote loads or *get* operations. This omission is designed to encourage users to structure code such that all reads target local memory, ensuring that loads have minimum latency. RSP focuses on minimizing load latency for two reasons. First, loads are more common than stores. Second, it is easier to tolerate store latency than load latency. One can overlap communication and computation with simple hardware support using remote stores, but such overlap would be hard to achieve for remote loads without more hardware support, like a direct memory access (DMA) engine or hardware prefetching.

---

[1] The C function `memcpy` can provide the semantics of a bulk transfer function in the RSP model, but the RSP model does not assume any additional bulk data movement mechanisms.

3   Implementation of the RSP Model

The RSP model is designed specifically to be incrementally achievable in multicore architectures that support loads and stores using a small set of hardware features that have a large impact on program performance. In the RSP model data is transfered from the registers of a producer into the cache of a consumer as illustrated in Figure 2(a). The data is not buffered on the producer to be transferred in bulk, but ideally each datum is sent as it is produced. This model results in many small messages and does not attempt to amortize the cost of communication by bundling many messages into a small number of large messages. In trade, RSP programs exhibit good locality of reference, have lower load latencies, and outperform CCSM on highly parallel multicores.

RSP needs hardware and operating system support for the following mechanisms: allocating remotely-writable data, executing store instructions targeting remotely-writable data, maintaining memory consistency, and executing synchronization operations targeting remotely-writable data. These features are discussed in turn.

Allocation of remotely writable data. Processes must be capable of allocating data that can be written by other processes. Such data should be both readable and writable by the allocating process.

Store instructions targeting remote data. Processes may execute store instructions where the destination register specifies an address in remotely writable memory. The processor executing such a store should not allocate the cache-line, but forward the operation to the consumer processor that allocated the data. This forwarding should be handled in hardware and requires that a message be sent to the consumer containing both the datum and the address at which it is to be stored. The consumer receives this message and handles it as it would any other write. In RSP, data that is allocated as remotely writable can only be cached in the allocating processor. This protocol preserves locality of reference by guaranteeing that reads are always local, ensuring minimal load latency.

Support for managing memory consistency. After a producer process writes data to remote memory, it needs to signal the availability of that memory to the consumer. To ensure correctness, the hardware must provide sequential consistency, or a memory fence operation so that the software can ensure correct execution.

Synchronization instructions may read and write remote data. RSP allows atomic synchronization operations, such as test-and-set or fetch-and-add, to both read and write remote data. This allows one to allocate locks, condition variables, and other synchronization structures in remotely writable memory.

With support for these features a multicore architecture can efficiently implement remote store programs. This set of features represents a small, incremental change over the set of features that would be required on any multicore architecture. On an architecture supporting loads and stores, a core must be able to

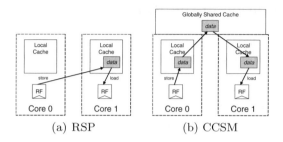

Fig. 2. Communication mechanisms in multicore. The figure illustrates two different mechanisms for sending data from Core 0 to Core 1. RSP transfers data directly from the sender's registers (the box labeled "RF") to the receiver's local memory (cache or scratch-pad). CCSM transfers data through the global address space.

send a message to a memory controller to handle cache misses. To support RSP, this capability is augmented so that write misses to remotely allocated data are forwarded not to the memory controller, but to the core that allocated the data. The RSP implementation can use the same network that communicates with the memory controller. The additional hardware support required is logic to determine whether to send a write miss to the memory controller or to another core. Unlike RSP, CCSM hardware transfers data from registers to a local cache and then to a globally shared cache or memory as illustrated in Figure 2(b). To support CCSM one could implement either a snoopy or a directory-based coherence protocol. A snoopy protocol would require a centralized structure which would be difficult to scale to large numbers of cores. Directory-based schemes provide better scalability, but require additional $O(P)$ bits (where P is the number of processors) to store directory information [7] and possibly another network that is dedicated to coherence messages. In addition to the extra hardware structures, a cache coherence protocol requires additional design and verification complexity.

4   Evaluation Methodology

This section presents the approach used to evaluate the remote store paradigm on the TILEPro64 processor. To begin, the TILEPro64 and its implementation of the RSP model are described. Next the eight benchmarks and the parameters used in this evaluation are discussed.

4.1   The TILEPro64

The TILEPro64 processor is a 64 core multicore processor with hardware support for cache-coherent shared memory. Each of the 64 cores is an identical three-wide VLIW capable of running SMP Linux. Each core has a unified 64KB L2 cache, and the L2 caches can be shared among cores to provide an effective 4MB of shared, coherent, and distributed L3 cache. Cores are connected through six low-latency, two-dimensional mesh interconnects [8]. Two of these networks carry user data, while the other four handle memory, I/O and cache-coherence traffic. The TILEPro64 can run off-the-shelf POSIX threads programs under SMP Linux.

The TILEPro64 uses a directory-based cache-coherence scheme with full-map directories. Loads and stores to shared memory which miss in the local L2 cache generate coherence messages that are handled by a directory on a remote core. The latency of these coherence messages is proportional to twice the distance between the accessing core and the core that contains the directory for that memory location. Clearly, if the directory is physically close, the latency is less than if the directory is physically far away. Ideally, one wants to access directories that are physically close to minimize latency.

In addition to standard cache-coherent shared memory, the TILEPro64 allows users to allocate shared memory that is *homed* on the allocating core. On this home core, reads and writes function as usual. However, when cores write remotely homed memory, no cache line is allocated on the remote core. Instead, these writes stream out of the writing core to the home cache without generating any other coherence traffic. This homed memory is used to implement remotely writable memory for remote store programs.

4.2   Benchmark Applications

Table 1 presents the application benchmarks used to compare RSP to CCSM. These benchmarks include representatives from image, video, and digital signal processing. For each benchmark optimized implementations are developed for a single core and then for both the CCSM and RSP paradigms.

For both paradigms, several common optimizations are used. Cache-blocking is used to reduce the number of data cache misses. Flags are used instead of locks whenever applicable (one exception is the histogram benchmark described below) to reduce contention. All stacks and read-only data are allocated as private for both paradigms, meaning that stack accesses and accesses to global constant data will not result in coherence traffic.

In the *bitonic sort* benchmark, a list of integers is sorted by dividing it among processes. Each process sorts its assigned integers independently using quicksort

Table 1. Benchmark applications used to compare RSP to CCSM

Application	Input
Bitonic Sort	Integer list of length 128k
Convolution	1920×1080 Image
Error Diffusion	4096×2048 Image
2D FFT	256×256 matrix of complex 16-bit fixed-point values
Histogram	4096×2048 Image
Matrix Multiply	Two 512×512 matrices of 16-bit fixed-point values
Transpose	1024×1024 matrix of integers
H.264	Raw 1280×720 video

and locally sorted lists are combined through a series of merge steps. Each merge requires a process to exchange data with a partner. In the CCSM implementation the array is stored in global shared memory and all updates are done in place. In the RSP implementation, each process allocates remotely writable memory and data is copied into the partner's address space using remote stores. Barriers synchronize both implementations.

The *convolution* benchmark convolves an input image with a 3×3 mask. Each process is responsible for producing separate rows of the output image. In the CCSM implementation both the input and output arrays are stored in global shared memory. In the RSP implementation, each process allocates remotely writable memory to store its assigned rows of both the input and output images. The RSP implementation requires allocation of additional memory to hold input values on the border of processes' assigned regions. Barrier synchronization is used in both implementations.

The *error diffusion* benchmark performs Floyd-Steinberg Error Diffusion on an input image. Each process is responsible for performing computation on separate columns of pixels, and the computation is done in place. Pixels on the border between processes are shared and these values are both read and written by neighboring processes. In the CCSM implementation, the image is stored in global memory and flags (also stored in global shared memory) are used to synchronize access to the image. In the RSP implementation, each process allocates private memory to store its assigned regions of the image. In addition, each process allocates remotely writable regions of memory to store the shared pixels and flags. When a process produces a value that is to be shared, it stores one copy locally, then stores another copy, and sets a flag in remotely writable memory.

The *FFT* benchmark performs a two-dimensional Fast Fourier Transform (2DFFT) on an input matrix. The benchmark first performs an FFT on each row and then performs an FFT on each column. Both implementations use out-of-place computation for both the row and column FFTs. Before executing the column FFTs, data is transposed in memory so that the consecutive elements in a column are unit distance apart. Each process is assigned a set of row FFTs and a set of column FFTs. In the CCSM implementation, the input, temporary, and output matrices are all stored in global shared memory. In the RSP implementation, each process allocates remotely writable memory to store results of the row FFTs, and other data is stored in private, local memory. As the row FFTs are computed, their results are written directly into this remotely writable memory.

The *histogram* benchmark computes a histogram representing the tonal distribution of an input image. Each process is assigned a separate region of the image. In the CCSM implementation, the image and the histogram are both allocated in global shared memory. As a process works on its part of the input image, it updates the histogram. Each bin of the histogram is guarded by a separate lock. In the RSP implementation, the histogram is distributed across processes. Each process allocates remotely writable memory to store temporary results from other processes. Then, the processes all compute the histogram of their assigned region of the image. Once these local histograms are completed, each process writes the appropriate local values to a remote process which performs a reduction on the local data. In the RSP implementation, a barrier is used to synchronize.

The *matrix multiplication* benchmark multiplies two input matrices to compute an output matrix. Each process is responsible for computing a separate region of the output matrix. In the CCSM implementation all matrices are allocated in global shared memory. In the RSP implementation, each process allocates remotely writable memory to store the rows and columns of the input matrix that are needed to compute the assigned region of the output. In both implementations barriers are used to synchronize.

The *transpose* benchmark performs the transpose of an input matrix. Each process is responsible for producing a separate region of the output matrix. In the SM implementation, both the input and output matrices are allocated in globally addressable shared memory. In the RSP implementation each process allocates remotely writable memory to hold a region of the output matrix. Each process performs its part of the transpose by reading local values and writing them to the appropriate location in remotely writable memory.

The *H.264* benchmark performs Baseline profile H.264 encoding on raw high-definition video. Both implementations attempt to minimize latency by partitioning the encoding of a frame among multiple processes. Each process is responsible for encoding its assigned region of the frame. To perform this encoding each process needs data from those processes that are assigned neighboring regions of the frame. In the CCSM implementation frames and associated meta-data are stored in global shared memory. In the RSP implementation, each process allocates remotely writable memory to store its assigned part of the frame and the overlapping regions assigned to neighboring processes. These overlapping regions of data are stored locally in the process that created them and then copied to neighboring processes using remote stores. Both implementations synchronize using a combination of flags and barriers. Additionally, both implementations are limited to a maximum of 40 processes.

5   Performance Evaluation

This section evaluates the performance of remote store programming. First, the speedup of RSP implementations of each benchmark is shown and compared to the speedup achieved with CCSM implementations. Next, the load-latency of each of the benchmarks is evaluated.

5.1   Speedup Evaluation

Figure 3 illustrates the performance of both the CCSM and RSP implementations of each of the eight benchmarks as the number of cores is varied from 2 to 64. These results all use one process per core. All speedups are computed

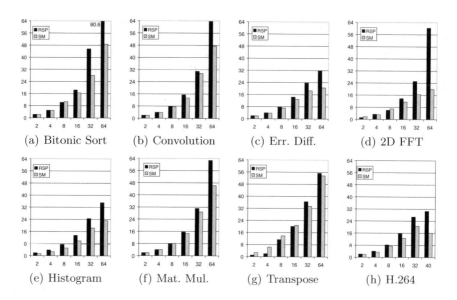

Fig. 3. Speedup of RSP and CCSM implementations of eight benchmarks. Speedup is shown on the y-axis while number of cores is on the x-axis. (The RSP implementation of bitonic sort achieves a speedup of 80.6 on 64 cores.)

relative to an optimized single core implementation. Higher bars represent greater speedup and greater performance.

For these benchmarks, RSP achieves greater performance than CCSM using large numbers of cores. Using 16 cores or fewer, RSP is generally higher perform-ing, but there are some exceptions and overall the approaches achieve similar performance. However, using 32 or more cores, RSP begins to clearly out perform CCSM as shown in Figure 4.

Figure 4 shows the ratio of RSP to CCSM performance for each of the eight benchmarks using 2 to 64 cores. Ratios of less than one indicate that RSP is slower while ratios greater than one indicate that RSP is faster (higher bars are better). Figure 4 shows that the performance benefits of RSP are greater for large numbers of cores. When using more than 32 cores, RSP achieves speedup over CCSM for each of the eight benchmarks. When using 64 cores, RSP achieves greater than 1.25x the performance of CCSM for 7 of the 8 benchmarks and greater than 1.5x the performance of CCSM for 5 of 8. For H.264 on 40 cores, RSP achieves greater than 1.8x the performance of CCSM. For the FFT on 64 cores, RSP achieves greater than 3x the performance of CCSM.

The transpose benchmark defies the general trend in that the RSP and SM implementations achieve comparable performance for all numbers of cores. The reason for the similar speedup numbers is that the transpose benchmark consists of loads of input values followed by stores which put the transposed matrix in place. The benchmark time includes the time required for all stores to complete, so the transpose represents one benchmark where store latency is critical. In this

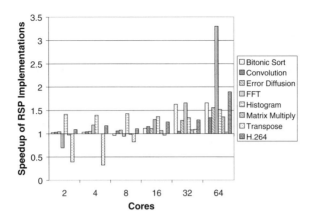

Fig. 4. Performance comparison of RSP and CCSM benchmarks. The speedup of RSP compared to CCSM is shown as a function of the number of cores. Speedups of less than 1 indicate RSP is slower. Speedups of more than 1 indicate RSP is faster. (The H.264 speedup listed for 64 represents the value measured using 40 cores.)

case the low load latency of the RSP implementation is cancelled out by its high store latency.

The relative performance gain of RSP increases with an increasing number of cores. Locality becomes a larger factor in performance with large core count and RSP allows software to control locality while CCSM does not. When using a large number of cores, a cache miss in a CCSM application can result in accessing a cache-coherence directory that is physically far away. In this case many of the distant accesses are loads, and the resulting high load latency has a dramatic effect on performance. However, in the RSP implementation loads do not generate coherence traffic to remote cores and load latency is lower.

5.2 Locality Evaluation

As discussed in Section 2 and Section 3 the RSP model and its implementation emphasize the use of physically close memory with the goal of minimizing load latency. The Tilera simulator allows one to measure the latency of load instructions that access the L2 cache. This statistic keeps track of the time it takes to service an L1 data cache miss.

The average L2 load latency is recorded for each of the eight benchmarks. Figure 5 shows this data expressed as the ratio of RSP load latency to CCSM load latency for each of the eight benchmarks on 2 to 64 cores. A ratio of 1 indicates that both implementations achieve the same load latency. A ratio of less than 1 indicates that the RSP load latency is lower than that of CCSM (lower bars are better).

The L2 load latency generally follows the same trend as the speedup results. Latencies are similar for both implementations when using a small number of cores, but the RSP latency tends to be much lower using large numbers of cores. Using 64 cores, RSP load latency is lower for 6 of the 8 applications.

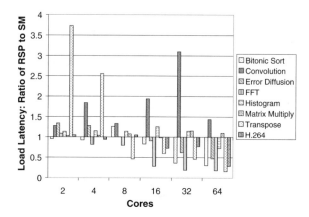

Fig. 5. Ratio of L2 load latency for RSP and CCSM benchmarks. The ratio of the load latencies for RSP and CCSM implementations is shown as a function of the number of cores. Ratios less than 1 indicate RSP is lower latency than CCSM, while ratios greater than 1 indicate RSP load latency is higher.(The H.264 load-latency listed for 64 represents the value measured using 40 cores.)

The two applications for which RSP load latency is higher with 64 cores are the convolution and matrix multiplication. Figure 4 shows that the RSP implementations of these benchmarks out perform CCSM despite the higher load latency.

The difference in performance for the convolution is the result of an increased number of data TLB misses on the part of the CCSM implementation. In fact, the CCSM implementation of the convolution produces almost 9 times more data TLB misses than the RSP implementation. The profiling tool does not count time spent in the TLB miss towards load latency (it is accounted for as a separate statistic). This TLB behavior is not an inherent aspect of the CCSM programming model, but rather a random effect due to the combination of the input image size and the way in which processes in this application access globally addressable shared memory. However, page misses are not an issue in the RSP implementation of this application because each process allocates data locally and the amount of local data easily fits in the TLB.

For matrix multiplication the difference in performance is explained by the worst case load latency. To compute average load latency, the latency of all loads on all cores is averaged; however, for the CCSM matrix multiplication one core has a consistently higher load latency than the others. In the CCSM implementation, Core 0 has an average load latency of 13 cycles, while the average for all cores is 10.1. This difference is due to the fact that core 0 accesses directories that are, on average, farther away than those accessed by other cores. In contrast, the RSP implementation has a maximum per-core load latency of 11.5 cycles with an average of 11.1. Although the CCSM matrix multiply has a lower average load latency, the maximum is higher and the performance of the application is determined by the slowest core.

On the whole, RSP fulfills its promise of exploiting locality to minimize load latency. The predictability of load latency and TLB behavior under RSP is an advantage in embedded systems that tend to require repeatable performance to meet real-time requirements.

6   Related Work

Both the partitioned global address space (PGAS) model and RSP combine the familiarity of CCSM with explicit control over locality for performance[2]. The PGAS model is designed to be implemented in high-level languages such as Unified Parallel C [6], Titanium [9], and Co-Array Fortran (CAF) [10]. The RSP model is designed to be implemented in hardware and can serve as the lowest-level communication primitive for an architecture. In this sense, the two approaches are complementary. A PGAS implementation can benefit from targeting RSP to achieve higher performance than would be available through standard CCSM mechanisms. A high-level PGAS language targeting RSP would make the efficiency of RSP available to a greater number of programmers.

Despite the similarities, there are some differences in the way programs are written using the PGAS and RSP models. While the PGAS model can target multicore, it was designed for multichip parallel computers with physically distributed, non-uniform memory access (NUMA) memory architectures like clusters and supercomputers. On these architectures programs typically perform best when total communication is reduced, the remaining communication is bundled into a small number of large messages, and communication and computation is overlapped. These optimization techniques affect the interface as most PGAS implementations include *put* and *get* (or similar) operations that are used to transfer large buffers between local and remote DRAMs and efficient programs are structured to make such infrequent, large transfers.

In contrast, the RSP model targets multicore architectures which support shared address spaces built using relatively powerful on-chip networks to connect physically distributed caches on the same chip. The network makes it possible for processors to transfer data from cache to cache (e.g. IBM Cell [11]), registers to cache (e.g. TILEPro64 as described above [8]), or even from registers to registers (e.g. Raw [12]). The RSP model is designed to support fine-grained communication on these types of multicore architectures. Specifically, RSP is designed to encourage programmers to structure code so that data is transferred from registers to cache as data is produced without buffering or bulk transfer.

The reflective memory model also combines the familiarity of CCSM with mechanisms that allow users to control locality [13]. This multichip model supports a paradigm in which writes in one process' address space appear (or are "reflected") in another address space. Unlike the PGAS model, reflective memory systems are designed to efficiently support individual writes as a communication primitive. The two reflective memory implementations that share the most in common with RSP are virtual memory mapped communication (VMMC) [14] as implemented on the SHRIMP processor [4] and DEC's Memory Channels [3].

Like RSP, VMMC [14] uses writes to transfer data between processors' virtual address spaces. Using the "automatic update" option of VMMC, both the producer and the consumer allocate a data buffer to communicate. The producer writes its local copy of the memory, the data is stored locally, and the writes are put on a system bus. The consumer snoops this bus and intercepts writes that also map to its address space. Unlike VMMC, the RSP implementation uses messages and can be implemented on a mesh network without requiring a snoopy protocol or a centralized bus. Furthermore, RSP does not require the producer to keep a separate copy of the data in its own local memory.

The most significant difference between Memory Channels (MC) and RSP is that MC allows pages of the shared address space to be mapped to a processor for read or write access, but not read/write. RSP allows read/write mappings for home nodes. All 8 benchmarks discussed in this paper make use of read/write mappings, and disallowing this, as in MC, would add code complexity, copy operations, or both to RSP applications. Unlike RSP, MC requires the OS to "pin" shared pages to communicating processors. This restriction limits the number of sharers to the size of the page table limiting scalability and may effectively waste a page table entry for processes that communicate infrequently. Furthermore, RSP can be implemented on heterogeneous cores while MC is restricted to homogeneous clusters. Finally, MC has hardware support for broadcast/multicast. While RSP lacks this support, it does not require the additional hardware and only 2 of the 8 applications could make use of multicast.

Leverich et al. performed a similar study comparing CCSM to streaming memory for multicore [15]. This study found similar performance for the two models even though stream programming allows a user to explicitly control locality. In contrast, the results presented here show that allowing a user to control locality can have significant benefits for large numbers of cores. There are two major differences in the approaches that may account for the different findings. First, the Leverich study uses a snooping, bus-based coherence protocol, while the study presented here uses a directory scheme built on a mesh network. The bus-based scheme may provide better performance for small numbers of cores, but has limited scalability to large multicores. Second, and perhaps most importantly, the Leverich study limits the comparison to a maximum of sixteen core chips, where the study presented here includes performance using 32 and 64 core processors. In fact, for RSP the most significant performance gains are found when using 32 or more cores.

7   Conclusion

The RSP model is designed to provide high performance and ease-of-use while requiring only incremental hardware support in multicore architectures. As demonstrated, RSP implementations of eight benchmarks exhibit better performance than shared memory for large numbers of cores. RSP can augment directory-based cache-coherence schemes for multicores with many processors. Standard shared memory techniques can be used for code that is highly dynamic in its memory access patterns, while RSP could be used for performance critical sections of regularly structured code. Alternatively, RSP can be used as the only paradigm to provide a convenient and efficient programming model on multicore DSPs.

References

1. Shan, H., Singh, J.P.: A comparison of MPI, SHMEM and cache-coherent shared address space programming models on a tightly-coupled multiprocessors. Int. J. Parallel Program. 29(3), 283–318 (2001)
2. Carlson, W., El-Ghazawi, T., Numric, R., Yelick, K.: Programming with the PGAS model. In: IEEE/ACM SC 2003 (2003)
3. Gillett, R.B.: Memory channel network for PCI. IEEE Micro 16(1), 12–18 (1996)
4. Blumrich, M.A., Dubnicki, C., Felten, E.W., Li, K.: Protected, user-level dma for the shrimp network interface. In: Proceedings of the Second IEEE Symposium on High-Performance Computer Architecture, pp. 154–165 (1996)
5. Quadrics: SHMEM Programming Manual. Quadrics Supercomputers World Ltd., Bristol (2001)
6. Chauvin, S., Saha, P., Cantonnet, F., Annareddy, S., El-Ghazawi, T.: UPC Manual (May 2005), http://upc.gwu.edu/downloads/Manual-1.2.pdf
7. Hennessy, J.L., Patterson, D.A.: Computer Architecture: A Quantitative Approach. Morgan Kaufmann, San Mateo
8. Wentzlaff, D., Griffin, P., Hoffmann, H., Bao, L., Edwards, B., Ramey, C., Mattina, M., Miao, C.C., Brown III, J.F., Agarwal, A.: On-chip interconnection architecture of the Tile Processor. IEEE Micro 27(5), 15–31 (2007)
9. Yelick, K., Semenzato, L., Pike, G., Miyamoto, C., Liblit, B., Krishnamurthy, A., Hilfinger, P., Graham, S., Gay, D., Colella, P., Aiken, A.: Titanium: A high-performance Java dialect. In: ACM, pp. 10–11 (1998)
10. Numrich, R.W., Reid, J.: Co-array Fortran for parallel programming. SIGPLAN Fortran Forum 17(2), 1–31 (1998)
11. Kistler, M., Perrone, M., Petrini, F.: Cell multiprocessor communication network: Built for speed. IEEE Micro 26(3), 10–23 (2006)
12. Taylor, M.B., Lee, W., Miller, J., Wentzlaff, D., Bratt, I., Greenwald, B., Hoffmann, H., Johnson, P., Kim, J., Psota, J., Saraf, A., Shnidman, N., Strumpen, V., Amarasinghe, S., Agarwal, A.: Evaluation of the Raw Microprocessor: An Exposed-Wire-Delay Architecture for ILP and Streams. In: International Symposium on Computer Architecture (June 2004)
13. Jovanovic, M., Milutinovic, V.: An overview of reflective memory systems. IEEE Concurrency 7(2), 56–64 (1999)
14. Dubnicki, C., Iftode, L., Felten, E., Li, K.: Software support for virtual memory-mapped communication, April 1996, pp. 372–381 (1996)
15. Leverich, J., Arakida, H., Solomatnikov, A., Firoozshahian, A., Horowitz, M., Kozyrakis, C.: Comparing memory systems for chip multiprocessors. SIGARCH Comput. Archit. News 35(2), 358–368 (2007)

Low-Overhead, High-Speed Multi-core Barrier Synchronization

John Sartori and Rakesh Kumar

Coordinated Science Laboratory
University of Illinois at Urbana-Champaign

Abstract. Whereas efficient barrier implementations were once a concern only in high-performance computing, recent trends in core integration make the topic relevant even for general-purpose CMPs. While the nature of CMP applications requires low-latency, the cost of low-latency barrier implementations using hardware-based techniques can be prohibitive for CMPs, where die area represents opportunities for throughput and yield. Similarly, whereas traditional multiprocessor barrier implementations were developed primarily for dedicated environments, scheduling and multi-programming on CMPs require more adaptable barrier implementations.

In this paper, we present and evaluate three barrier implementations that are hybrids of software and dedicated hardware barriers and are specifically tailored for CMPs. The implementations leverage the unique characteristics of CMPs and provide low latency comparable to that of dedicated hardware networks at a fraction of the cost. The implementations also support adaptability, enabling efficient multi-programming and dynamic remapping of the barrier network.

1 Introduction

Barrier synchronization has been a well-studied problem for large-scale, traditional multiprocessors [1, 2, 3, 4]. A wide variety of barrier implementations have been proposed, ranging from software-based [2,5,6,7,8] to fully hardware-based [3,9,10,11,12]. Several of these implementations have been used in the context of large-scale parallel applications with large data sizes, coarse-grained parallelism, and high computation to communication ratios.

Requirements for barrier synchronization for CMPs are different, however. In contrast to typical multiprocessor applications which target coarse-grained parallelism, multi-core applications tend to exploit fine-grained parallelism, making low-latency synchronization a primary concern. Consequently, multi-core applications can be highly sensitive to barrier performance. For example, Figure 1 shows the performance of three OpenMP NAS benchmarks [13] that exploit inner-loop parallelism. As the granularity of parallelism decreases, the overhead of barrier synchronization becomes relatively larger, and performance degrades. As the results show, performance can be very sensitive to barrier latency for applications with fine-grained parallelism. So, a barrier implementation for multi-cores should have low latency.

Also, low latency barrier implementations have traditionally been achieved through dedicated hardware support. For CMPs, however, the high area and power overheads

Y.N. Patt et al. (Eds.): HiPEAC 2010, LNCS 5952, pp. 18–34, 2010.

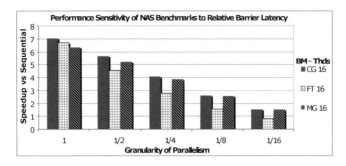

Fig. 1. The performance of three NAS parallel benchmarks degrades as the granularity of parallelism becomes finer and relative barrier latency increases on a 16-threaded workload. When relative barrier latency becomes high, as can be the case for software barrier implementations, taking advantage of fine-grained parallelism has little or no benefit.

of hardware barrier implementations are particularly taxing. Figure 2 shows how the area overhead of additional dedicated links scales with the number of cores for a dedicated hardware barrier tree implementation in 65nm technology. The area cost of dedicated links is determined by the thickness (dependent on metal layer) and length of the wires [14], and may represent a considerable fraction of the precious die area for CMPs (up to 16% assuming a $400mm^2$ die). Since die area is a precious resource for CMPs (as it can translate into higher throughput – saved area can be used for more cache or cores – or higher yield – yield varies inversely with die area), a barrier implementation for multi-cores cannot afford to ignore the area/power costs of providing low latency.

Finally, while applications for high-performance systems are typically run in a dedicated system mode, multi-core applications are often expected to run in shared environments with scheduling and multi-programming. So, barrier implementations for multi-cores should be adaptable for various levels of participation and dynamically configurable based on the mapping of threads to cores.

In this paper, we revisit barrier synchronization for CMPs and present three CMP platforms that achieve barrier latencies close to those of dedicated hardware barrier

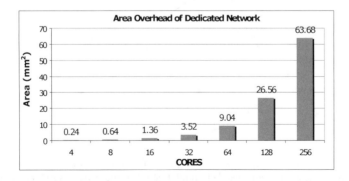

Fig. 2. A dedicated network adds considerable area overhead to the chip. The plot above shows the area overhead of a dedicated tree network in terms of additional wiring cost for 65nm technology.

networks at a fraction of the cost. The implementations support adaptability, enabling efficient multi-programming and dynamic remapping of the barrier network.

2 Hardware-Supported Mapping of Virtual Barrier Topologies

Our first CMP-specific optimization accelerates software-based barrier implementations. One way to reduce the performance overhead of software-based barrier synchronization while keeping area overhead low is to form a virtual hierarchical network atop the physical mesh. In terms of topologies, a butterfly network can potentially achieve the lowest latency for global barrier synchronization. However, for this study, we consider a virtual tree network due to the high connectivity/area and messaging costs of the butterfly ($(N/2) \cdot log_2 N$ and $N \cdot log_2 N$, respectively) as compared to the tree ($N-1$ and $2 \cdot (N-1)$). We assume that the existing topology of the network-on-chip for general purpose communication is a mesh. The following section describes our first platform for providing low-overhead, accelerated barrier support.

2.1 Implementation

When a group of cores that will perform synchronization is mapped into a virtual barrier tree, we can reduce the software overhead of synchronization by adding a simple state machine to each router to control routing of intermediate barrier notifications in the interconnect, without involving the cores.

The state machine in each router (Figure 3) contains three registers and three notification bits. The registers store the location of the parent, left child, and right child of a node in the network. The notification bits record whether a node has received an arrival notification from left child, right child, and self. When a thread reaches the barrier, it sends a notification to itself. When all notification bits are set, the last arriving notification is forwarded to the parent node. When the barrier has been satisfied at the root, completion notices are propagated back down to the leaves of the tree.

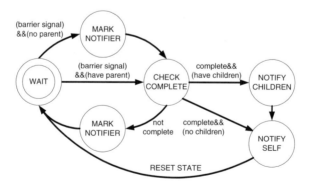

Fig. 3. This state machine describes the routing logic for barrier notifications in the virtual network. Arrival notifications are forwarded up the tree when the barrier is satisfied at the current level. Completion notifications are propagated down the tree after the barrier is satisfied at the root level.

Since propagation of the intermediate signals in the virtual barrier network can be performed in hardware, a node only needs to perform the initial arrival notification and the final check for barrier completion. Moreover, all of the notification details (such as neighbors, size, etc.) are determined and stored in the routers when the virtual network is configured. Therefore, rather than using a high overhead, generalized software procedure to send and receive notifications, we allocate a memory mapped address for use in barrier algorithms such that a store to the address sends an arrival notification to the network, and a load from the address stalls until the barrier completion notification is received at the node.

2.2 Benefits and Overheads

Adding hardware support for virtual networks reduces barrier latency by minimizing the software overhead of barrier management. Additional cost at routers consists only of a few registers and a small state machine. This approach adds no additional area overhead for communication links.

2.3 Map Optimization

While hardware support for virtual barrier networks improves the performance of barriers without adding much overhead, the performance gains are constrained if a naive strategy is used to map the virtual network onto the physical interconnect. In this section, we consider the benefits of intelligent mapping.

Determination of the optimal virtual to physical mapping involves finding the minimum depth spanning tree of the graph represented by the CMP cores (vertices) and mesh links (edges), where depth represents the longest distance from root to leaf. In general, this problem is NP-complete [15], and the goodness of a solution may depend on several factors, including the amount of time spent in computation. This may not be a problem for a statically assigned tree, but for the case of multicore processors, in which thread-to-core mappings are assigned dynamically at runtime and may change depending on availability of nodes and number of threads in a thread group, a static mapping will likely be inadequate.

The algorithm used to determine virtual to physical mappings is described in Figure 4. When a thread group will utilize barrier synchronization, this algorithm is executed by the processor's software runtime at the time a thread-to-core mapping is

```
NodeList.append(root); hasParent[root] = true
while NodeList not empty do
    POP Node i from NodeList with minimum depth
    for child in {left,right} do
        child = node with min distance(i, child) AND hasParent(child) = false
        NodeList.append(child); hasParent[child] = true
    end for
end while
```

Fig. 4. The virtual to physical mapping algorithm bears some similarities to Prim's algorithm for minimum spanning trees. The goal of the algorithm is to find the spanning tree with minimum root-to-leaf depth.

assigned for the task. Once the involved routers are configured by the runtime, no additional runtime support is needed during barrier execution. The algorithm selects a root near the center of the selected mesh nodes to maximize opportunities for fanout as the tree expands. Exhaustive testing over all possible tree roots confirms that the algorithm achieves minimum global barrier latency by minimizing the depth of the tree. Figure 5 gives examples of a naive mapping and an optimized mapping for a 16-core CMP.

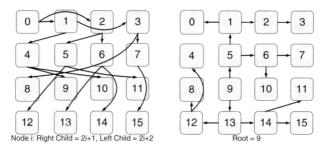

Fig. 5. In the figure on the left, an obvious (but naive) mapping strategy is used to assign tree neighbors. In this strategy, node i's children are at indices $2i + 1$ and $2i + 2$, and the resulting tree depth and aggregate hops of the mapping are 8 and 34. In an optimized approach to assigning the tree structure, a search is performed to find the best tree root, and each node's children are determined dynamically to minimize tree depth. The network on the right has a depth of 4 and an aggregate hop count of 17 – **half that of the naive mapping.**

2.4   Platform Adaptability

The support for virtual barrier networks described above is easily adaptable to support semi-global synchronization of dynamic thread groups. When a processor's runtime schedules a group of threads, it may assign to them a dynamically computed virtual barrier tree if they will be performing barrier synchronization. In this case, the runtime selects a group of cores for the threads to use, computes a virtual to physical mapping for the graph represented by the cores and mesh links, and configures the state of the routers to connect and initialize the virtual network.

3   Barrier Implementation Using Hybrid Networks

While the previous CMP-specific barrier implementation accelerates software-based barrier implementations by providing hardware support for mapping virtual barrier topologies to physical topologies, in this section, we discuss a CMP-specific barrier implementation that tries to get the benefits of both software and hardware-based barrier implementations by creating a hybrid network.

A dedicated barrier network includes a dedicated link between two nodes that are neighbors in the topology. However, for a good mapping strategy, a direct connection may already exist between the two nodes in the form of a regular mesh link. Thus, adding an extra dedicated link does not buy additional performance in several cases. However, there *can* be a benefit for placing a dedicated link when there is not already a mesh link connecting two virtual neighbors in the barrier topology. This is the basis of a technique we call *barrier bolstering*.

3.1   Implementation

In an attempt to create a perfect barrier tree, with one hop between each level of the tree for all paths (each node is directly connected to all tree neighbors), we can add a dedicated physical link between two virtual neighbors any time a single-hop path does not exist between the nodes in the physical network. With this approach, the latency of the hybrid network would be very close to that of the dedicated network, and presumably, the cost would be lower, since some virtual links correspond directly to single physical links in the mesh. However, since wire delay depends on wire length, the effectiveness of this technique in reducing latency would be somewhat limited, since long wires (even long *dedicated* wires) would incur multiple-cycle delays. Also, due to limited connectivity at each switch in the mesh, the overhead of this strategy approaches that of a dedicated network as the number of nodes increases.

The previously mentioned approach to barrier bolstering can incur high area overheads when the number of cores is large. Also, perceived benefits may in reality be limited, since long wires require multiple cycle delays. Thus, for our actual implementation of barrier bolstering, we choose a more cost-effective technique for adding dedicated links, and we assume that link latency is proportional to link length in hops. Under this assumption, replacing long virtual links with dedicated links does not buy much performance relative to the cost.

While it may be unrealistic to assume substantial reduction in latency by replacing all multi-hop links with dedicated links, it is certainly possible to equalize the latency of links that have similar latencies by replacing the longer virtual link with a dedicated link. We define *barrier slack* as the difference in delay between two virtual links that connect sibling nodes in the topology. When barrier slack is present, the critical path of a virtual tree will be limited by the longer of the virtual links at a given level of the tree. Thus, we can reduce the critical path of the tree by adding a dedicated link to short circuit the longer path and equalize the latencies of the paths to the siblings. Figure 6 demonstrates how barrier bolstering can reduce the depth of a barrier tree

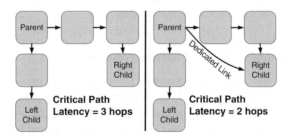

Fig. 6. This figure demonstrates how dedicated links can be selectively added to reduce the critical path of a tree. When two virtual links in the same level of the tree differ in length (in hops), barrier slack exists between the two links. Under certain circumstances, adding a dedicated link can eliminate the slack and equalize the latencies of the links to that of the shorter link, reducing the critical path of the tree network.

by selectively adding dedicated links to equalize the latency of paths to two sibling nodes. This reduction in latency is mostly attributed to the reduced routing cost on the dedicated link.

3.2 Benefits and Overheads

Barrier bolstering produces a very low latency barrier implementation, with performance close to that of a dedicated network (results in section 6) by selectively adding dedicated links to reduce the depth of the tree network. Different approaches to bolstering affect the number and lengths of dedicated links that are added, which determines the area overhead of the bolstering technique.

Figure 7 compares various approaches to barrier bolstering in terms of their wiring overhead costs. Even if possible to implement with acceptable link latencies, the cost of the first mentioned technique (with single-hop links for every link) approaches the cost of a dedicated network for large number of cores. This cost can be reduced somewhat by realizing that permitting a certain number of two-hop links does not increase the latency of the barrier. However, in our actual implementation of barrier bolstering, the wiring cost remains low (less than 1% die area) even for large number of cores.

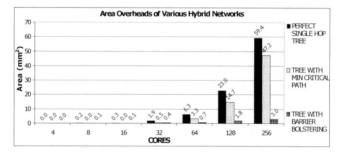

Fig. 7. This figure compares the area overheads for various hybrid network configurations. Whereas the cost of a perfect single-hop tree (where every node is directly connected to its neighbors) approaches that of a dedicated tree for high core integration (compare to Figure 2), the cost of slack elimination via barrier bolstering remains low.

3.3 Mapping Considerations for Barrier Bolstering

In the case of barrier bolstering, the virtual to physical mapping algorithm from the previous implementation (Figure 4) is modified to minimize the slack between sibling nodes in the virtual tree. Figure 8 shows the new algorithm, which is used during network design to determine the locations of supplemental dedicated links in the network for optimal global barrier performance. Although the network is optimized for global barriers, semi-global barriers can also achieve good performance, since they can be mapped to optimized subtrees of the global tree. During dynamic mapping, the final *if* statement of Figure 8 is ignored, since the locations of dedicated links are statically assigned.

```
NodeList.append(root); hasParent[root] = true
while NodeList not empty do
    POP Node i from NodeList with minimum depth
    select children with: min(max(distance(i,left),distance(i,right))) AND min(|distance(i,left)-distance(i,right)|) AND
    hasParent(left,right) = false
    NodeList.append(left,right); hasParent[left,right] = true
    if |distance(i,left)-distance(i,right)| < max correctable slack then
        mark longer link as dedicated
    end if
end while
```

Fig. 8. The virtual to physical mapping algorithm for barrier bolstering attempts to minimize slack between siblings. This algorithm is used to select the locations of dedicated links for best global barrier performance.

3.4   Platform Adaptability

Since some dedicated links are used in barrier bolstering, the adaptability of the platform for dynamic thread mapping is somewhat lessened. For semi-global synchronization, the best case is when a thread group can be mapped to a subtree of the originally mapped tree. In this case, the threads receive the full benefits of the bolstering. In the worst case, the virtual to physical mapping for a thread group may not be able to use any of the dedicated links. In this case, the performance of the bolstered network is equivalent to that of the unbolstered virtual network.

4   Reducing Virtual Link Latency with Router Bypassing

While the first technique (hardware-supported mapping of virtual barrier topologies) required no additional link area overhead, the previous technique (barrier bolstering) allowed closer approximation of the performance of a dedicated hardware barrier network. In this section, we discuss a way to get most of both benefits by allowing direct virtual connections instead of physical connections in the case of bolstering.

4.1   Implementation

Using a well-mapped virtual topology in conjunction with barrier state machines at the routing nodes significantly reduces the latency of barrier synchronization. Note, however, that for a virtual link in a virtual tree, there may be multiple hops between successive levels of the tree. This occurrence adds latency to the critical path of the tree, and a significant portion of this latency is due to the packet being routed at multiple routers along its path between tree levels. A recent work suggests the use of *express virtual channels* [16] to mitigate the cost of routing packets that travel multiple hops.

Figure 9 explains the concept of an express virtual channel (EVC). When the downstream destination of a packet is further than one hop away, an EVC may be allocated, spanning all intermediate routers so that the packet can continue on the same virtual channel without being routed at the intermediate nodes. Routing only needs to be performed again when the packet reaches the terminus of the EVC.

We use EVCs as a way to set up virtual connections between nodes that are logical neighbors in the virtual barrier topology. Since the set of routing paths to be accelerated

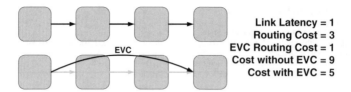

Fig. 9. An EVC has a source and sink node and spans multiple hops along a routing path. When a packet allocates an EVC, it skips the routing stage at intermediate routers and a routing decision only needs to be made again once the packet exits the EVC.

for a given tree mapping are fixed, EVCs can be planned and allocated efficiently according to the state of the configuration registers in the routers. When configured by the runtime for a specific virtual topology, the registers store the location of virtual neighbor nodes, describing the parameters for an EVC between the nodes.

4.2   Benefits and Overheads

Using EVCs to enhance routing between virtual neighbors maintains all the benefits of the virtual network platform and also adds the benefit of reduced routing latency for some multi-hop virtual links. The extent to which this benefit can improve performance depends on how well EVCs can be utilized.

The costs incurred to obtain this additional benefit are increased router complexity to add support for EVCs and potential degradation of other network traffic, since EVCs suppress communication on intermediate routers when they are allocated until they are freed. Use of EVCs does not add any area/power cost in terms of communication links.

4.3   Mapping Considerations

The use of EVCs adds a new dimension to the virtual to physical topology mapping problem. Since EVCs are only allowed to travel along a single routing dimension [16], the selection criteria for choosing the children of a node when forming a virtual tree are somewhat different. Whereas in the original algorithm, children were chosen to minimize the number of hops between successive tree levels, they are now selected to simultaneously minimize both the number of hops and the number of directional changes. This implies a different distance function that accounts for the relative costs of link traversal and routing latency in EVCs. Because the cost of routing is higher than the cost of link traversal, situations arise in which it is more efficient to travel more hops in a single direction than fewer hops in multiple directions.

When an EVC flow passes through a router, any other traffic at that router is suppressed. This situation reveals a tradeoff for EVCs. While they exhibit potential to expedite communication along the EVC path, they also potentially slow down other traffic that uses any of the routers in the EVC path. We account for this by minimizing the occurrence of crossing paths in the same level of the tree whenever possible. This means that if multiple potential children are located at the same distance, children are selected to avoid crossing paths in the same tree level. Figure 10 gives the EVC-aware virtual to physical mapping algorithm.

```
let distance(i,j) = (link latency)·hops(i,j)+(routing latency)·dirChanges(i,j)
NodeList.append(root); hasParent[root] = true
while NodeList not empty do
    POP node i from NodeList with min depth
    select children with: min distance(i,child) AND hasParent(child) = false
    if multiple potential children with min distance then
        select children to minimize crossing paths
    end if
    NodeList.append(children); hasParent[children] = true
end while
```

Fig. 10. The EVC-aware virtual to physical mapping algorithm minimizes directional changes and same-level crossing paths, features that inhibit the utilization or performance of EVCs.

Figure 11 demonstrates that a mapping algorithm that is aware of the tradeoffs inherent in the use of EVCs can produce a different mapping than the normal mapping algorithm, which considers the cost of all hops along a virtual path to be the same, independent of the directional implications.

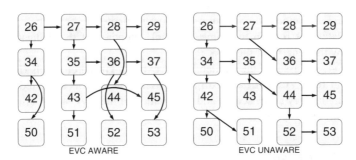

Fig. 11. The figure above compares the same subsection of a 64-core mesh for two mapping strategies – one that considers EVC tradeoffs during the mapping phase (left) and one that does not (right). When EVC tradeoffs are considered, virtual paths that change directions are less desirable.

4.4 Platform Adaptability

Since EVCs are allocated dynamically, not statically like the dedicated links in barrier bolstering, this platform shares all adaptability features of the original virtual network platform.

5 Methodology

To obtain our experimental results, we use a modified version of the M5 simulator [17] that has been adapted to support communication over a network-on-chip (NoC) rather than a shared bus. In our baseline architecture, the NoC has a rectangular mesh topology, with link latency equal to 1 cycle and routing latency equal to 4 cycles. Routers are pipelined for increased throughput. Table 1 lists some additional details about the simulated architecture.

Table 1. Architectural Details

Clock	2GHz	Mem Latency	300 cyc	Execution	In-order
L1 Icache	32KB	L1 Dcache	64KB	L2	4MB/CORE, 10 cyc

To model a dedicated hardware barrier network, we add an extra set of physical links to the chip and arrange them in a tree topology. Routing for the dedicated network is simple, deterministic, and suffers no resource contention. Thus, we specify single cycle latency for routing on the dedicated network. Link latencies for the dedicated links are assigned based on the Manhattan distance between the connected nodes.

For virtual barrier configurations, described in section 2, we model routers with supplemental routing logic equivalent to the state diagram of Figure 3. The state machine logic requires only a few latches and gates. For an N-core processor, the additional state required at each router is composed of $3 \cdot log N$ bits to store the indices of the parent, left child, and right child, and 3 bits to track whether arrival notifications have been received from left child, right child, and self.

In section 3, we model the addition of select dedicated links to the regular mesh. All routing latencies remain the same, and link latencies of the dedicated links are determined by the lengths of the links.

In section 4, we assume the availability of express virtual channels (EVCs). Necessary support for EVCs is described in [16]. When an EVC is allocated, we assume normal routing latency at the source and termination of the EVC and routing latency of 1 cycle for intermediate routers.

6   Analysis of Results

In this section, we first reinforce the point made in section 1 that barrier synchronization mechanisms for CMPs need to be different from those for traditional multi-processors. Then we compare the performance of the various CMP-specific barrier implementations presented in this paper. Finally, we discuss the implication of new barrier implementations on performance and design of parallel applications.

6.1   Traditional Barrier Mechanisms in the Context of CMPs

In our revisitation of barrier mechanisms for CMPs, we looked at three categories of software barrier implementations, categorized based on their communication patterns – centralized barriers, decentralized barriers, and hierarchical barriers.

Centralized barriers are most commonly found in cache coherent shared memory systems. In this style of barrier, all participating threads communicate with a central entity to make known their arrival at the barrier. When the centralized entity receives notifications from all threads, it responds in turn by sending barrier completion notifications to the participants. While this type of barrier is simple to implement, obvious performance and scalability detriments are inherent in the design.

Decentralized barrier algorithms differ from centralized algorithms in that all threads determine completion of the barrier locally. Thus, decentralized algorithms perform notification and completion phases in parallel, at the expense of extra communication between participants. An example of a decentralized barrier that we evaluated is a broadcast barrier.

In a **hierarchical barrier** algorithm, each participant synchronizes with some subset of the global nodes and subsequently propagates the local synchronization state to a higher level until global synchronization can be determined. Some example implementations of this type are tree and butterfly barriers [2].

Figure 12 shows the performance of various standard software barrier implementations on multi-core architectures with different number of cores.

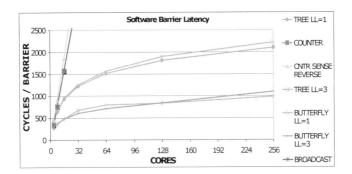

Fig. 12. This figure shows the latency of different software barrier implementations for varying number cores. While the hierarchical software implementations show some promise, the other approaches are constrained by software overheads on the critical path. For implementations that are sensitive to link latency, LL=X denotes the link latency.

Figure 12 demonstrates a few key CMP-specific points. First, there is no difference between the performance of the centralized and decentralized software barriers on the CMP due to the relative expense of barrier management in software as compared to the relatively low cost of communication between cores. Essentially, notifications arrive faster than the software is able to process them.

Another observation is that changing the latency of the communication links for a multi-core architecture has almost no effect on the performance of centralized and decentralized barriers. This further demonstrates that these implementations are constrained by software overhead and shared resource constraints and are unsuitable for use in CMPs. On the other hand, the hierarchical barriers do respond to changing link latency, with a more pronounced effect as the depth of the hierarchy grows. This is because the critical paths of these algorithms depend more directly on link latency. Since notifications do not always queue up for threads, they must spend time waiting for notifications to travel from one level of the hierarchy to the next.

The final observation to be drawn from the figure is that even though some software approaches are not completely dominated by software overhead, the barrier synchronization overhead is still unacceptably high for all software barrier implementations in scenarios where medium to fine grain synchronization is desirable. So, barriers for CMPs should preferably not be implemented in software and should have low latency. We also investigated using dedicated hardware barrier tree networks.

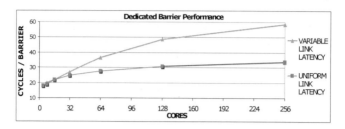

Fig. 13. Dedicated barrier networks achieve very low latency synchronization. The two curves represent different assumptions about the routing and latency determination for network links. In one, uniform link latency is assumed. For the other curve, we assume link latency proportional to link length.

Figure 13 shows performance scalability for dedicated tree barrier networks. The two curves represent different assumptions about link latencies. The lower curve corresponds to the situation where routing can be done through different metal layers to normalize the link latency. For the upper curve we assume pipelined links where the length determines the number of latches necessary and thus the end-to-end latency of the link. As the latter assumption represents a more realistic scenario, we use this approach for comparison in the rest of our discussion.

Comparison of Figure 12 and Figure 13 demonstrates that dedicated hardware barrier implementations have much smaller performance overhead than software implementations. In fact, compared to the dedicated barrier tree implementation, the best performing software implementation exhibits up to **22.82x increased latency**. However, dedicated hardware barrier networks have prohibitive area overhead (see section 1). So, new CMP-specific implementations are needed.

6.2 Performance Benefits of CMP-Specific Barriers

Figure 14 compares the latencies of the efficient barrier techniques to those of the dedicated hardware barrier network. The results demonstrate that with efficient barrier notifications and minimal support in the NoC, we can achieve close to dedicated performance at a greatly reduced cost.

There are several sources of benefits for each of the three barrier implementations. For example, our first technique (hardware-supported mapping of virtual barrier topologies to physical topologies) uses loads/stores instead of sends/receives. The formula for latency of the tree barrier has the form $X + Y \cdot log_2 N$, where X and Y represent the notification/completion cost and the inter-level traversal latency, respectively. Thus, adding load/store support for barrier notifications reduces latency by cutting down the value of X.

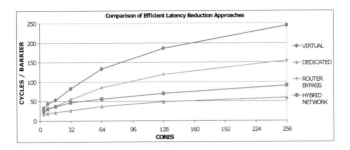

Fig. 14. The efficient latency reduction techniques all represent ways to approach the performance of a dedicated network without paying the associated overhead cost. The hybrid approach comes very close to matching the performance of a dedicated synchronization network with a sizable reduction in overhead.

Similarly, optimizing the virtual to physical mapping for a synchronization network can significantly affect performance. Figure 15(a) compares the latency of a naively mapped virtual tree, in which children are located at the obvious node indices, to an optimized virtual mapping, in which the children of each node in the tree are selected intelligently based on the algorithm outlined in Figure 4.

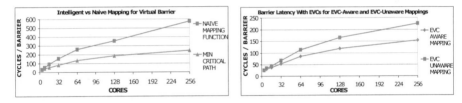

Fig. 15. Mapping strategies for virtual barrier networks should be intelligent (a), and should consider how to best utilize available network features, such as EVCs (b).

Figure 15(b) shows that if EVCs are employed to expedite routing on virtual links, then it becomes necessary to consider the limitations of virtual channels when deciding on the optimal virtual to physical mapping. Mappings that are unaware of these considerations are not able to make the most efficient use of available EVCs. As Figure 15(b) demonstrates, the benefit of adding EVC capability to the NoC is small unless an EVC-aware mapping policy is used.

6.3 Implications for Performance and Design of Parallel Applications

To further validate the usefulness of our barrier techniques, we demonstrate how fast barriers enable large-scale CMPs to exploit fine-grained parallelism and achieve speedups on challenging benchmark applications. As in [18], we evaluate the performance of our barrier techniques for two of the Livermore loops [19] and two benchmarks from the EEMBC suite [20]. Figure 16 compares the performance of parallel versions of the Livermore loops that employ software and hardware barrier techniques on a 128-core CMP against the sequential performance for varying vector lengths.

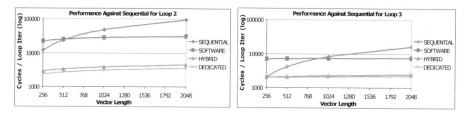

Fig. 16. Performance comparison of software, hybrid, and hardware barrier implementations for Livermore loops 2 and 3. Speedups are relative to sequential execution.

Although the granularity of parallelism is very fine, the efficient barrier techniques allow the large-scale CMP to achieve substantial speedups. For larger granularity of parallelism, software barriers can have benefits, but the benefits are very limited compared to those afforded by our efficient barrier techniques. These results demonstrate the need for low-overhead, CMP-specific barrier techniques.

Figure 17 shows the benefits of efficient barrier approaches for EEMBC Autocorrelation (32 lags, input=xspeech) and Viterbi decoder (input=getti.dat). The Autocorrelation results demonstrate that while software barriers leave performance on the table, virtual and hybrid approaches can nearly achieve the performance of a dedicated synchronization network. For the Viterbi decoder, using a software barrier implementation actually results in a slowdown with respect to sequential, while hybrid approaches achieve modest gains. For these benchmarks, performance variation between our efficient techniques was small. This variation increases with increased application dependence on barriers and increased number of cores performing synchronization.

In a nutshell, using CMP-specific barrier implementations allows existing parallel applications to exploit fine-grained parallelism more effectively. It also allows applications to be parallelized at a finer granularity, potentially resulting in significant application speedups.

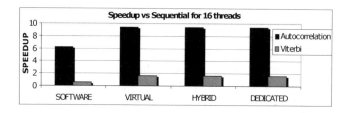

Fig. 17. Performance comparison of software, hybrid, and hardware barrier implementations for EEMBC Autocorrelation and Viterbi decoder. Speedups are relative to sequential execution.

7   Related Work

Barrier synchronization in the context of large scale multiprocessors has been a well-studied problem [1, 2, 3, 4]. Several approaches target efficient software algorithms [2, 5, 6, 7, 8], but dedicated hardware synchronization networks have also been deployed in some systems. Notably, IBM's Bluegene/L [9] contains multiple interconnect networks, each with a dedicated purpose. Both the global interrupt network and the collective communication networks of BG/L can be used to achieve low latency barrier synchronization [3]. Targeting low latency synchronization, other systems have also used dedicated networks, including the AND-tree barrier synchronization circuits of the Cray T3D [10], the network-supported fetch-and-add approach of the NYU Ultracomputer [11], and the barrier register proposed by Beckmann, et al. [12]. While we evaluate the performance of a dedicated hardware barrier network, we do so in the context of a CMP, where we observe a different set of constraints and design considerations than those found in previous large-scale multiprocessors.

More recent works have looked at the topic of synchronization in CMPs. Zhu, et al. propose a synchronization state buffer [21] for reducing the overhead of fine-grain synchronization support by tracking only actively synchronized data. Sampson, et al., suggest the use of barrier filters [18] that are implemented in the memory controllers of a shared memory processor. These efforts both represent centralized, memory-based approaches, whereas our techniques are inherently decentralized in nature and focus on support in the NoC.

Another recent work [22] evaluates barrier performance in CMPs with the intent of determining how well various barrier algorithms perform on different NoC topologies. This is similar to the way in which we map virtual topologies onto disparate physical topologies, however, the mapping strategies used in [22] are naive, leading to a different set of conclusions. Another Cray multiprocessor, the T3E [23], uses configurable routers, equipped with barrier synchronization units to map a virtual topology onto a separate physical topology.

Our optimization of virtual barrier networks through the use of express virtual channels (EVCs) is based on the work of Kumar, et al. [16], who propose EVCs as a technique for approaching an ideal interconnect fabric for NoCs.

8   Conclusion

In this research, we have revisited the subject of barrier synchronization for many-core CMPs. First, we established that the unique characteristics and constraints of CMPs dictate that software-only barrier implementations perform poorly relative to implementations that utilize a dedicated synchronization network. Then we observed that the overhead of adding a dedicated synchronization network to a chip can be high, especially as core integration continues to increase. Based on these observations, we suggested several techniques that utilize the existing network on chip with slight modifications to allow dramatically increased barrier performance without paying the price of a dedicated network. Our techniques allow us to achieve near-dedicated barrier performance for minimal cost.

References

1. Shang, S., Hwang, K.: Distributed hardwired barrier synchronization for scalable multiprocessor clusters. IEEE Trans. Parallel Distrib. Syst. 6(6), 591–605 (1995)
2. Hoefler, T.: A survey of barrier algorithms for coarse grained supercomputers. Chemnitzer Informatik-Berichte (2004)

3. Almási, G., et al.: Optimization of MPI collective communication on Bluegene/L systems. In: ICS 2005, pp. 253–262 (2005)
4. Ramakrishnan, V., Scherson, I.D.: Efficient techniques for nested and disjoint barrier synchronization. J. Parallel Distrib. Comput. 58(2), 333–356 (1999)
5. Chen, J., Watson, W.: Software barrier performance on dual quad-core Opterons. In: NAS 2008, pp. 303–309 (2008)
6. Nikolopoulos, D., Papatheodorou, T.: Fast synchronization on scalable cache-coherent multiprocessors using hybrid primitives. In: IPDPS 2000, p. 711 (2000)
7. Lee, J.B., Jhon, C.S.: Reducing coherence overhead of barrier synchronization in software DSMs. In: ICS 1998, pp. 1–18 (1998)
8. Mellor-Crummey, J.M., Scott, M.L.: Algorithms for scalable synchronization on shared-memory multiprocessors. ACM Trans. Comput. Syst. 9(1), 21–65 (1991)
9. Coteus, P., et al.: Packaging the BlueGene/L supercomputer. IBM Journal of Research and Development 49(2-3), 213–248 (2005)
10. Adams, D.: Cray T3D system architecture overview manual (1993), ftp://ftp.cray.com/product-info/mpp/T3D_Architecture_Over/T3D.overview.html
11. Freudenthal, E., Peze, O.: Efficient synchronization algorithms using fetch-and-add on multiple bitfield integers. Ultracomputer Note 148 (1988)
12. Beckmann, C., Polychronopoulos, C.: Fast barrier synchronization hardware. In: ICS 1990, pp. 180–189 (1990)
13. Biswas, R.: NAS parallel benchmarks (2009), http://www.nas.nasa.gov
14. Kumar, R., Zyuban, V., Tullsen, D.: Interconnections in multi-core architectures: Understanding mechanisms, overheads, and scaling. In: ISCA 2005 (2005)
15. Althaus, E., Funke, S., Har-peled, S., Knemann, J.: Approximating k-hop minimum-spanning trees. Operations Research Letters 33, 120 (2005)
16. Kumar, A., et al.: Express virtual channels: Towards the ideal interconnection fabric. SIGARCH Comput. Archit. News 35(2), 150–161 (2007)
17. Binkert, N.L., et al.: The M5 simulator: Modeling networked systems. MICRO 26(4), 52–60 (2006)
18. Sampson, J., et al.: Exploiting fine-grained data parallelism with chip multiprocessors and fast barriers. MICRO 39, 235–246 (2006)
19. McMahon, F.: Livermore loops coded in C (1992), http://www.netlib.org/benchmark/livermorec
20. E.M.B. Consortium: EEMBC (2009), http://www.eembc.org
21. Zhu, W., et al.: Synchronization state buffer: Supporting efficient fine-grain synchronization on many-core architectures. In: ISCA 2007, pp. 35–45 (2007)
22. Villa, O., Palermo, G., Silvano, C.: Efficiency and scalability of barrier synchronization on NOC based many-core architectures. In: CASES 2008, pp. 81–90 (2008)
23. Scott, S.L.: Synchronization and communication in the T3E multiprocessor. SIGOPS Oper. Syst. Rev. 30(5), 26–36 (1996)

Improving Performance by Reducing Aborts in Hardware Transactional Memory

Mohammad Ansari[1,*], Behram Khan[2], Mikel Luján[2], Christos Kotselidis[2],
Chris Kirkham[2], and Ian Watson[2]

[1] Department of Computer Science, Umm Al-Qura University
mmansari@uqu.edu.sa
[2] School of Computer Science, University of Manchester
{bkhan,mlujan,ckotselidis,ckirkham,iwatson}@cs.manchester.ac.uk

Abstract. The optimistic nature of Transactional Memory (TM) systems can lead to the concurrent execution of transactions that are later found to conflict. Conflicts degrade scalability, and may lead to aborts that increase wasted work, and degrade performance. A promising approach to reducing conflicts at run-time is dynamically, and transparently, reordering the execution of transactions upon discovery of conflicts. This approach has been explored in Software TMs (STMs), but not in Hardware TMs (HTMs). Furthermore, STM implementations of this approach cannot be ported to HTMs easily.

This paper investigates the feasibility of such reordering in HTMs, and presents two designs that are scalable, independent of the on-chip interconnect, require only minor modifications to each core, and add no execution overhead if no conflicts occur. The evaluation takes LogTM-SE as a base line and considers benchmarks with different levels of contention (transactional conflicts). The results show that the preferred design increases HTM performance by up to 17% when contention is low, 57% when contention is high, and never degrades performance. Finally, the designs are orthogonal to LogTM-SE; they require no modification to cache structures, and continue to support transaction virtualization, open and closed unbounded nesting, paging, thread suspension, and thread migration.

1 Introduction

Traditionally, locks have been used to provide synchronization between threads that access shared data concurrently. Locks are known to be challenging to use, with well-documented challenges such as deadlocks, race conditions, convoying, and debugging. Transactional Memory (TM) [1] proposes a programming model to simplify safe access to shared data, which is achieved by providing *implicit synchronization*; the programmer marks, as transactions, those blocks of code that access shared data, and TM ensures correct synchronization when those blocks of code execute concurrently.

TM provides implicit synchronization by checking, at runtime, whether accesses by concurrently executing transactions intersect, i.e., conflict. If a transaction completes

---

[*] A large part of this work was conducted while the author was with the School of Computer Science, University of Manchester.

Y.N. Patt et al. (Eds.): HiPEAC 2010, LNCS 5952, pp. 35–49, 2010.

executing and detects no conflict, it commits, but if a conflict is detected, one of the conflicting transactions is usually aborted. TM implementations may detect conflicts eagerly (upon access to a data element), or lazily (when the transactional code block has been completely executed). TM implementations write to shared data, i.e., perform version management, eagerly (write to shared data in place), or lazily (write to a buffer). The former has a fast commit phase, but a slower abort phase as it requires the transaction to undo all its updates to shared data, while the latter has a fast abort phase, but a slower commit phase as it must copy updates from the buffer to the shared data.

TM has been implemented in hardware (HTM) [2,3,4,5,6,7], software (STM) [8,9, 10,11,12,13], or a hybrid of the two (HyTM) [14,15,16,17]. The advantage of HTMs is a low overhead in performing transactional conflict detection, but at the cost of limiting the total accesses of each transaction to the size of the L1 or L2 cache. STMs remove this limitation, but at the cost of increased conflict detection overhead. Research in TM has focused on reducing the overhead of conflict detection, but also on understanding TM behavior [18], and even on adapting to dynamic workload characteristics [19,20]. This paper focuses on HTMs.

As the number of cores on a chip multiprocessor (CMP) rises, efficiently exploiting the cores to achieve high speedup becomes more challenging, even with TM. TM applications that scale ideally up to, say, 16 cores, may well find that they scale poorly when executed on 128 cores due to more and more transactions conflicting and aborting. To make matters worse, TM implementations have often tried to optimize the execution of a committing transaction at the cost of penalizing aborts, for example, by using eager version management.

Steal-on-Abort (SOA) [21] is our technique to improve the performance of TM when noticeable contention (i.e., transactional conflicts) occurs. SOA targets a pathological interaction between conflicting transactions called *repeat conflicts*. This occurs when a specific transaction A conflicts with, and is aborted by, a specific transaction B. Transaction A is restarted after its abort, but performs an access that causes it to *repeat* its conflict with transaction B, and then transaction A aborts again. This scenario may repeat a number of times. SOA proposes that transaction A not be restarted, and instead be stolen by transaction B, to prevent it from being re-executed until transaction B commits. Once B commits, A is made available for execution. By not executing transaction A again, a potential repeat conflict and abort is avoided, which could have wasted cycles, power, and degraded application performance. Additionally, on SOA-enabled STMs [21], the thread on which transaction A was running acquires a new, third, transaction C, to execute. If transaction C commits, application performance may improve.

However, implementations of SOA exist only in STMs [21]. Furthermore, they have used dynamic data structures such as double-ended queues (deques) that make it difficult to perform a straightforward port of SOA to HTMs. As a result, the feasibility of implementing SOA in HTMs remains unexplored.

This paper is the first to investigate implementing SOA in HTMs, and presents two designs: SOA-HTM-PURE, and SOA-HTM-UTLZN. The former guarantees repeat conflicts are eliminated, but implements a restricted form of SOA compared to STMs. The latter implementation is less restricted, but permits repeat conflicts in certain scenarios. Notably, both implementations require only simple modifications to each core, are independent of the on-chip interconnect, and highly scalable. For evaluation, the designs are implemented in LogTM-SE [7], and continue to offer all the advantages of LogTM-SE such as unmodified cache structures, and support for transaction virtualization, open and closed unbounded nesting, paging, thread suspension, and thread migration. Results show that the benefit of SOA seen in STMs extends to HTMs; improving speedup up to 57%, reducing processor usage up to 26%, and reducing the number of aborts up to 54%. In addition, the HTM designs of SOA also improve performance in low contention benchmarks, and, promisingly, improve speedup by increasing margins as the number of cores rises.

The remainder of this paper is organized as follows. Section 2 presents the designs of SOA for HTM, and Section 3 discusses how they impact other structures. Section 4 evaluates the designs by implementing them in LogTM-SE, and executing a range of benchmarks. Section 5 discusses related work, and Section 6 concludes the paper.

2   Steal-on-Abort Hardware Implementation

SOA abstractly consists of the three following actions:

1. Upon abort, a transaction is stolen, and hidden, by its opponent.
2. Upon commit, a transaction makes available for execution any transactions it stole.
3. Optionally, another transaction is acquired and executed in place of the stolen one.

The first two actions are enough to support SOA: they prevent repeat conflicts between two transactions by preventing them from executing concurrently. The third action attempts to increase speedup (if the new transaction commits).

However, these actions are non-trivial to support in hardware. For example, transactions are often tightly-coupled to the threads on which they are executing, as threads maintain the execution state of an application. It may be impossible for a core to steal an opponent transaction without stealing the thread on which it is executing. Assuming transactions can be stolen, storing them in hardware is another challenge as there is no limit to the number of steals that may be performed by a transaction. Thus, it may become necessary to overflow stolen transactions to memory, which could significantly slow down an executing transaction, and increase interconnect bandwidth usage. Nevertheless, promising results from SOA on STMs give incentive for exploring if an efficient design for SOA on HTMs can be achieved.

This paper proposes two carefully constructed designs that aim to minimise performance degradation, interconnect traffic, and modifications to cores and cache structures. The latter is particularly important for keeping the designs practically feasible. The first proposal is called SOA-HTM-PURE, which supports only the first two actions mentioned above, and the second is called SOA-HTM-UTLZN, which implements all three actions.

2.1   SOA-HTM-PURE

A single register, called SOA_AMAP (SOA abort map), is added to each core, and has one bit for each core in the CMP. If a core aborts another, it sets the relevant bit in

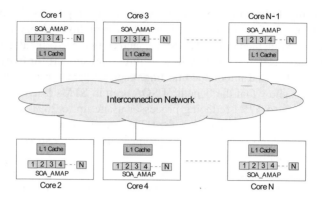

Fig. 1. Architecture for SOA on HTM. Only one additional register per-core needed, called SOA_AMAP.

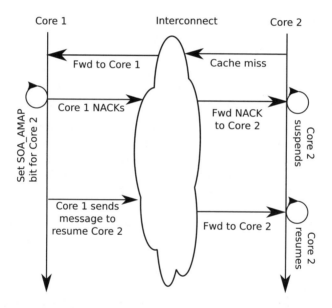

Fig. 2. SOA example. Core 2 has a (data) cache miss, and makes a request to the interconnect that is forwarded to Core 1. Core 1 responds with a NACK, and records the NACK in its SOA_AMAP. Core 2 receives the NACK, aborts, and suspends. Upon commit, Core 1 notifies all cores recorded in its SOA_AMAP to resume.

SOA_AMAP. Since aborting an opponent requires communicating over the interconnect, setting a bit in the register adds negligible overhead. Cores that are aborted stall indefinitely, and are restarted later by their opponents. For now we assume threads do not migrate; we address this issue later.

Once a core commits, it checks if any bits are set in its SOA_AMAP. If all the bits are clear, the core commits as normal. In this way, SOA-HTM-PURE adds no overhead when there is no contention. If one or more bits are set, the corresponding cores are resumed by sending a message across the interconnect. The exact mechanism for sending such a message is architecture specific. In Section 4.3, the messaging mechanism is described for our implementation using LogTM-SE, and results in a single outgoing message from a committing core, and a single multi-cast message from a directory. In this way, commit overhead is kept low by only adding a single, non-broadcast, message.

SOA should reduce communication traffic if repeat conflicts exist as fewer data requests will be received from cores that restart aborted transactions, and fewer abort messages will be sent to them in reply. Furthermore, it may be possible to power down stalled cores to save energy.

The design can feasibly scale to 2048 cores, requiring only a 2048 bit register per core (existing HTM implementations, for example, have suggested implementing 2048 bit signatures per core [7]), easily exceeding the number of cores expected on CMPs in the near future.

2.2 SOA-HTM-UTLZN

SOA-HTM-UTLZN is an acronym for "SOA on HTM for utilization", and extends SOA-HTM-PURE to add the last action of SOA. SOA-HTM-UTLZN piggybacks on hardware thread context support that is common in CMPs [22]. Hardware context support allows a core to store several thread contexts in hardware registers, and swap execution between them quickly, primarily to hide memory latency. SOA-HTM-UTLZN extends SOA-HTM-PURE by swapping threads in hardware contexts if the currently executing thread is stalled (due to executing a transaction that has been aborted). For now we assume thread contexts do not migrate; we address this issue later.

SOA-HTM-UTLZN adds a single bit, called CTXT_SOA, to each hardware thread context, which is set if the transaction being executed by the thread is aborted. A core does not switch to any context that has its CTXT_SOA bit set. When a core sends a resumption message to another core, the other core clears the CTXT_SOA bit in all its thread contexts. This reintroduces the chance of repeat conflicts as the resumption message will have been sent for only one of the contexts on the other core, and waking up all contexts prematurely allows them to repeat their conflict with their respective opponents. However, the benefit of this approach is that it leaves the SOA_AMAP register unchanged; one bit per core, maintaining the scalability of the design. To support resuming specific contexts SOA_AMAP must map one bit per context, which requires either the register to increase in size, or the the potential scalability to be reduced.

It should be noted that using hardware contexts to increase utilization has its limits; if all contexts on a core are stalled due to transactional conflicts, then that core can no longer execute transactions until a resumption message is received. One option may be to swap contexts with another core, but there are several design trade-offs involved with such a mechanism, and we leave it for future work.

3 Impact of SOA

The previous sections described two proposals for implementing SOA in HTM. This section explores the impact of those designs on processor architecture, transactional execution, and the operating system.

3.1   Processor Architecture

Each core is extended with a single register called SOA_AMAP. A simple messaging protocol is also required to resume cores, requiring the interconnect to simply forward the necessary messages to predefined destinations. A strength of the SOA designs proposed is that no other change is required. No other hardware modifications are needed, and in particular the pipeline, private caches, and shared caches of the core are left unchanged. This significantly reduces the impact on design verification, making the SOA proposals attractive for practical implementation.

3.2   Transactional Execution

SOA is only applicable to eager conflict detection, as lazy conflict detection only detects conflicts with transactions that have committed, which rules out repeat conflicts. The use of eager version management may increase the benefit of SOA, as it should reduce the overhead of roll backs if it reduces the number of aborts. The benefit of SOA may also increase if it is used in conjunction with signature-based conflict detection, as they may lead to false-positives, which may increase the number of repeat conflicts.

A committing core incurs an overhead of sending messages to resume other cores if any bits in its SOA_AMAP are set. In our implementation, only a single message is sent by a committing core. There is no increase in overhead on aborting cores. Nested transactions, both open and closed, are orthogonal to SOA, and work in harmony with it. For example, the Deque benchmark used in the evaluation executes nested transactions.

3.3   OS Context Migration

Earlier, the SOA designs were restricted to prevent threads from leaving their cores, because a stalled thread expects to receive a resumption message from the core of the opponent thread, and the opponent core holds only enough information to send a resumption message to the core that it aborted, not the stalled thread itself. This restriction is simple to remove. First, a stalled thread that is removed from a core needs to be marked as active, and not stalled. No change is needed in SOA_HTM_PURE, and in SOA_HTM_UTLZN the CTXT_SOA bit should be cleared for the thread context in question.

However, removing this restriction reintroduces repeat conflicts, as the migrated thread is no longer stalled waiting for its opponent, and could begin re-executing immediately. Furthermore, cores may send resumption messages that are no longer needed, possibly resuming threads that are not their opponents, which further increases the chance of repeat conflicts. Nevertheless, earlier work with SOA on STMs suggested SOA is highly effective even when the implementation reintroduced repeat conflicts, and contention was already high [21]. Thus, not only is it possible to override the above restriction, but past results have shown that it may be an acceptable decision.

3.4   OS Virtual Memory Paging

The SOA designs do not peek at memory addresses, and as such are compatible with support for paging. Furthermore, the modifications required to implement the SOA designs do not impact HTM-specific support for paging.

4 Evaluation

SOA-HTM-PURE and SOA-HTM-UTLZN are evaluated using full-system simulations with a range of benchmarks, and results compared with a "Base" implementation that has SOA disabled. The evaluation shows that the designs improve speedup, and reduce aborts, although performance of SOA-HTM-UTLZN is mixed; in some cases it improves performance, while in others it degrades it.

4.1 Methodology

SOA-HTM-PURE and SOA-HTM-UTLZN are implemented in LogTM-SE built on Simics 3.0.31 [23], and GEMS 2.1 [24] Ruby pipeline and memory timing model. The simulated platform uses simple in-order SPARC ISA cores running an unmodified Solaris 9. Experiments are executed with 1, 4, 8, and 16 cores (and corresponding benchmark threads). Each benchmark thread is bound to an individual processor, using Solaris' pset_bind(). As a result, OS thread migration and context switching are implicitly disabled. The architecture of the evaluated CMP is described in Section 4.3.

SOA-HTM-UTLZN is executed with four hardware contexts per processor, and consequently each benchmark is launched with four times as many threads. In order to isolate the performance benefit of hardware context switching to SOA-HTM-UTLZN alone, hardware context switching is only permitted when a thread stalls due to SOA, i.e., cannot be used to hide memory latency.

4.2 Workloads

The microbenchmarks Deque and Btree, and the non-trivial benchmarks Kmeans and Vacation (from the the STAMP benchmark suite [17]), are used to evaluate SOA-HTM. In deque, transactions attempt to push or pop a double-ended queue. Transactions in Btree insert, delete, or lookup items in a B-tree. Kmeans is a clustering algorithm, and contention is controlled by the number of clusters to which objects are assigned. We experiment with 1, 5, and 15 clusters, which lead to progressively lower contention. Finally, Vacation is a travel database simulating multiple customers concurrently booking flights, hotels, and cars.

4.3 Evaluated CMP Configurations

SOA-HTM-PURE and SOA-HTM-UTLZN are implemented in the LogTM-SE HTM that is provided with GEMS 2.1. LogTM-SE and the SOA are a complementary union. LogTM-SE aims to keep cache structures unmodified as this improves the chances of adoption. Similarly, the SOA designs require minimal changes for each core. LogTM-SE attempts to achieve high scalability by using a non-broadcast commit phase, and directory coherency. The SOA designs add no overhead to the commit phase if conflicts do not occur, and is agnostic of the interconnect or coherency protocol. LogTM-SE uses eager validation, which is a requirement for SOA.

LogTM-SE is configured to use eager version management, eager conflict detection, and a conflict resolution policy of self-abort, with exponential backoff (increase backoff

Table 1. Benchmark parameters

Benchmark	Parameters
Btree	tx:5000, inserts:20%
Deque	tx:1024, bkoff:32
Kmeans C1	m:1, n:1, threshold:0.05,
	input_file:random-n2048-d16-c16.txt
Kmeans C5	m:5, n:5, threshold:0.05,
	input_file:random-n2048-d16-c16.txt
Kmeans C15	m:15, n:15, threshold:0.05,
	input_file:random-n2048-d16-c16.txt
Vacation	tx:1024, n:8, q:10, u:80, r:65536

on retry). Note that this choice should reduce the benefit of SOA-HTM, as choosing to abort the opponent is likely to generate more repeat conflicts, and exponential backoff also reduces repeat conflicts, but at the risk of backing off for too long and harming performance. A 2048 bit H_3 signature is used for conflict detection [25].

Figure 3 presents a block diagram of the 16 core CMP architecture. Further configurations include 1, 4, and 8 core CMPs. In each case, the number of L2 banks is equal to the number of cores. Cores are connected by a packet-switched interconnect in a grid topology using 64-byte links and adaptive routing. On-chip memory controllers connect to standard DRAM banks. A MESI directory protocol enforces inclusion at L2. Each

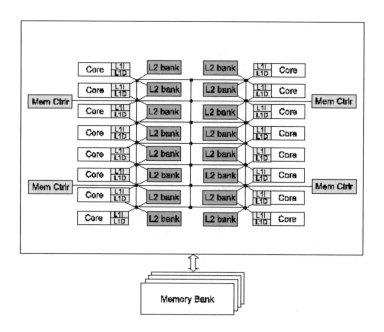

Fig. 3. Base Log-TM-SE CMP configuration

Table 2. Simulation parameters for SOA-HTM

Feature	Description
L1 cache	32KB 4-way split, 64-byte blocks, 1-cycle access.
L2 cache	8MB 8-way unified, 64 byte blocks, 34-cycle access.
Memory	16GB, 500 cycle off-chip access.
L2-Directory	Full-bit vector sharer list; 6-cycle latency.
Interconnect	grid, 64-byte links, 3-cycle link latency.

L2 tag contains a bit-vector of the L1 sharers and a pointer to the exclusive copy, if it exists. Table 2 summarizes system parameters that remain fixed for each configuration.

The SOA communication protocol is as follows. Upon commit, a core checks its SOA_AMAP register, and if any bit is non-zero, it sends a single CORE_RESUME_REQ message to its local directory, containing the complete value of SOA_AMAP. The directory sends a single multi-cast DIR_RESUME_REQ message out to each core for which the corresponding bit is set in the received SOA_AMAP value. The design creates minimal overhead; a core only needs to send a single message if any bit is set in SOA_AMAP. If transactions are committing in the common case, then there is little or no overhead of SOA as NACKs will be rare, and CORE_RESUME_REQ/DIR_RESUME_REQ messages will also be rare, as they are only sent if there is a waiting core. Similarly, if commits are common then there is little change in traffic for the directory. If aborts occur, then the design will increase commit overhead, and stall cores, but should compensate by leading to a net increase in performance.

On its own, this protocol is susceptible to deadlock; two transactions may signal each other to abort, and consequently never restart. However, LogTM-SE itself is susceptible to such deadlocks, and thus includes a multi-stage abort mechanism that detects and prevents deadlock cycles. Our extensions to LogTM-SE do not interfere with this mechanism, and therefore only abort (and stall) transactions when doing so will not lead to a deadlock. Consult the LogTM [6] and LogTM-SE [7] papers for further details.

4.4 Results

The evaluation explores the impact of SOA on three scenarios: low contention, high contention with low repeat conflicts, high contention with high repeat conflicts. The first scenario should trigger SOA rarely, and is used to illustrate the minimal impact of SOA on performance when aborts are negligible. The second scenario should trigger SOA often, but provide little performance improvement since there are few repeat conflicts, and may even degrade performance due to SOA overhead. The third scenario should trigger SOA often, and could result in larger performance improvements.

Figures 4a-4f illustrate speedup. A cursory look reveals two important findings. First, SOA-HTM-PURE gives similar or better performance than Base in all cases. Second, SOA-HTM-UTLZN improves upon SOA-HTM-PURE in Kmeans C1, but in most other cases it degrades performance compared to Base.

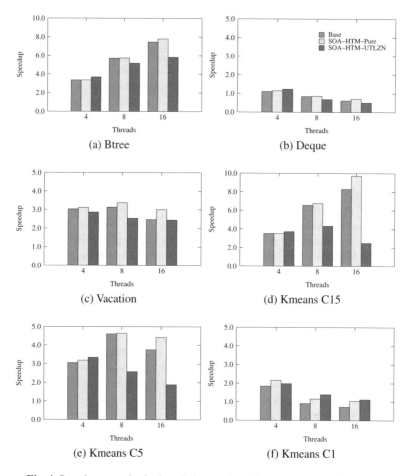

Fig. 4. Speedup over single-threaded execution. Note different y-axis ranges.

Btree and Kmeans C15 have low contention, aborting on average 10% and 20% of transactions with 16 cores. In these benchmarks both Base and SOA-HTM-PURE scale similarly, which is indicative of the low overhead of SOA when aborts are rare. SOA-HTM-UTLZN degrades performance in both, and the degradation is more severe in Kmeans C15, which also has a higher percentage of aborts. Profiling data reveals that SOA-HTM-UTLZN is thrashing local caches by context switching. In Kmeans C15 with 16 cores, we find that the number of L1 data misses increases 10 to 15 fold over Base and SOA-HTM-PURE.

Deque and Kmeans C5 are benchmarks with a large amount of contention, but few transactional retries, and thus little scope for repeat conflicts. At 16 cores, Kmeans C5 aborts 65% of its transactions, but retries on average only 1.9 times. However, SOA-HTM-PURE still improves performance by 16%. In deque an almost identical situation arises at 16 cores; 78% contention, and 3.5 retries on average increases the scope for repeat conflicts. The scalability of Deque is limited by transactions accessing either end of the deque structure, making repeat conflicts highly likely, and this is confirmed by the 16% performance improvement with SOA-HTM-PURE. For SOA-HTM-UTLZN the cache misses due to context switching are 1.5 to 2 times higher than Base and SOA-HTM-PURE at 16 cores, degrading performance by 18% over Base in Deque, and 50% in Kmeans C5.

Vacation and Kmeans C1 are benchmarks with a large amount of contention, and a high number of retries. In Vacation, this occurs at 8 and 16 cores, where 77% and 90% of transactions abort, and the average number of retries is 3.2 and 9.0, respectively. Modest performance improvements of 6% and 21% are observed with SOA-HTM-PURE. In Kmeans C1 there is little exploitable parallelism, as all transactions update a single cluster. By 16 cores, Kmeans C1 aborts 96% of transactions, and its average number of retries is 24.4. SOA-HTM-PURE results in a performance improvement of 44%, while SOA-HTM-UTLZN, in one of the few cases where it improves performance, does so by 57%. Kmeans' larger performance improvement than Vacation at 16 cores, despite having a lower number of retries, is indicative of repeat conflicts representing a smaller number of retries in the latter. It is worth noting that contention is rising in these benchmarks as the number of cores increases, and SOA-HTM-PURE provides correspondingly larger performance improvements. Thus we would expect even larger performance improvements if the benchmarks were executed using a larger number of cores.

SOA-HTM-UTLZN improved performance in a limited number of cases, and in all those cases SOA-HTM-PURE improved performance similarly. However, SOA-HTM-PURE results in better performance in many cases that SOA-HTM-UTLZN does not. Thus, for brevity we limit further analysis to Base and SOA-HTM-PURE.

Table 3. Average number of retries

Benchmark	Base			SOA-HTM-PURE		
	4 cores	8 cores	16 cores	4 cores	8 cores	16 cores
Btree	0	0	0.15	0	0	0.10
Kmeans C15	0	0.1	1.6	0	0.1	0.2
Deque	0	1.6	4.2	0	1.3	3.3
Kmeans C5	0.1	1.9	7.5	0.1	0.6	5.5
Vacation	0.4	3.2	9.0	0.2	1.5	4.1
Kmeans C1	2.0	19.5	24.4	0.7	14.0	16.6

Table 3 illustrates the impact of SOA-HTM-PURE on the average number of transactional retries. For the scalable benchmarks (Btree, Kmeans C15) there are marginal differences in retries. Only Kmeans C15 at 16 cores is significant, and likely to be responsible for the performance improvement seen earlier. The remaining benchmarks all see marked reductions in the number of retries, which increase with the number of cores, suggesting again that SOA may provide even better results with larger numbers of cores.

Table 4 shows the number of cycles saved by SOA-HTM-PURE, which is the difference between Base and SOA-HTM-PURE in the number of cycles spent stalling.

Recall that SOA-HTM-PURE stalls cores upon abort, and those cycles spent stalling are effectively saved. These saved cycles could be used for executing other applications, or SOA-HTM-PURE could be extended to sleep cores on abort, and resume upon notification from the opponent core, thus saving energy. The cycles are not wasted in executing transactions that abort. The table shows that 8-26% of cycles can be saved in the high contention experiments, while maintaining or improving speedup over Base. In some cases SOA-HTM-PURE uses more cycles than Base (shown with negative numbers). Although the increase represents a small fraction of the total execution cycles, small variations can occur since stall cycles also include stalling for cache misses.

Table 4. Average reduction in number of cycles used to execute the benchmarks using SOA-HTM-PURE. In parenthesis: as a percentage of Base total execution cycles.

Benchmark	4 cores	8 cores	16 cores
Btree	-597 (-0.03)	-922 (-0.09)	-6,793 (-0.84)
Kmeans C15	-662 (-0.03)	-3,863 (-0.3)	-17,701 (-1.72)
Deque	800 (0.12)	49,191 (5.7)	99,876 (8.51)
Kmeans C5	16,265 (1.1)	13 (0)	166,329 (13.81)
Vacation	-32,990 (-0.53)	455,190 (7.61)	1,766,740 (23.34)
Kmeans C1	-20,462 (-1.3)	388,982 (12.2)	1,061,083 (26.44)

5   Related Work

SOA was first implemented in an STM [26, 21] by adding two dynamically sized deques to each thread: one that held ready-to-execute work, and one which held stolen transactions. Transaction stealing was performed by abstracting transactions into job objects that held sufficient metadata to enable any thread to execute the transaction. The implementation resulted in a pseudo thread pool framework for executing transactions. This implementation permitted repeat conflicts, and performance results revealed it to be highly effective at reducing repeat conflicts, unlike SOA-HTM UTLZN, which suffered due to increased cache misses. The difficulties in implementing SOA on HTM using the STM-based solution inspired the work in this paper.

Little other work exists on automatically reducing the impact of contention, or attempting to improve performance when contention occurs. Early work on contention management [27, 28] developed intricate backoff and work-estimation metrics to try and resolve conflicts. Recently, CAR-STM [29] implemented a similar framework to SOA [21] for a different STM. Additionally, CAR-STM allows users can define a routine to serialize transactions they expect to conflict, although such functionality is similar to that presented by Bai *et al.* [30].

Our earlier work [31, 19] on dynamically adapting to available parallelism in an STM application, by changing the number of threads permitted to execute transactions (in a thread pool), reduced the number of aborts, and reduced wasted work. Yoo and Lee [32] implemented a STM transaction scheduling framework that queues threads onto a global queue if they greater than a user-specified threshold of aborts over a history window of transactions, which resulted in similar functionality to our adaptive work, although our solution has the ability to be more responsive in certain cases. In contrast, the STM transaction scheduling framework of Yoo and Lee is more amenable to an HTM implementation.

6   Conclusions

This paper has presented the first proposals for SOA in HTM. The two proposed implementations are scalable, require minimal architectural modifications, and independent of the on-chip interconnect. The two implementations were seamlessly integrated into LogTM-SE [7], and were evaluated using a range of benchmarks and contention scenarios. The results showed SOA-HTM-PURE to be consistently well performing. Although SOA-HTM-UTLZN outperforms SOA-HTM-PURE in two cases, in most other cases it provides the worst performance. In scenarios where the benchmark was highly scalable, SOA-HTM-PURE resulted in no observable performance degradation, and in one case a performance improvement of 17%. When contention rose, performance began to improve more consistently, ranging from 16% to 44% with 16 cores, suggesting that SOA-HTM-PURE may benefit applications with even low contention. Performance improvements increased with the number of cores, strongly suggesting that larger improvements may be observed with larger numbers of cores. Finally, SOA-HTM-PURE reduced the average number of retries (i.e., aborts) by 54%, and saving up to 26% of the execution cycles.

References

1. Larus, J.R., Rajwar, R.: Transactional Memory. Morgan and Claypool, San Francisco (2006)
2. Ananian, C.S., Asanovic, K., Kuszmaul, B.C., Leiserson, C.E., Lie, S.: Unbounded transactional memory. In: HPCA 2005: Proceedings of the 11th International Symposium on High-Performance Computer Architecture (February 2005)
3. Bobba, J., Goyal, N., Hill, M.D., Swift, M.M., Wood, D.A.: Tokentm: Efficient execution of large transactions with hardware transactional memory. In: ISCA 2008: Proceedings of the 35th Annual International Symposium on Computer Architecture (June 2008)
4. Hammond, L., Wong, V., Chen, M., Carlstrom, B.D., Davis, J.D., Hertzberg, B., Prabhu, M.K., Wijaya, H., Kozyrakis, C., Olukotun, K.: Transactional memory coherence and consistency. In: ISCA 2004: Proceedings of the 31st Annual International Symposium on Computer Architecture (2004)
5. Khan, B., Horsnell, M., Rogers, I., Luján, M., Dinn, A., Watson, I.: An object-aware hardware transactional memory system. In: HPCC 2008: Proceedings of the 2008 10th IEEE International Conference on High Performance Computing and Communications (2008)
6. Moore, K.E., Bobba, J., Moravan, M.M., Hill, M.D., Wood, D.A.: Logtm: Log-based transactional memory. In: HPCA 2006: Proceedings of the 12th International Symposium on High-Performance Computer Architecture (2006)
7. Yen, L., Bobba, J., Marty, M.M., Moore, K.E., Volos, H., Hill, M.D., Swift, M.M., Wood, D.A.: Logtm-se: Decoupling hardware transactional memory from caches. In: HPCA 2007: Proceedings of the 13th International Symposium on High-Performance Computer Architecture (2007)
8. Dice, D., Shalev, O., Shavit, N.N.: Transactional Locking II. In: Dolev, S. (ed.) DISC 2006. LNCS, vol. 4167, pp. 194–208. Springer, Heidelberg (2006)

9. Harris, T., Fraser, K.: Language support for lightweight transactions. In: OOPSLA 2003: Proceedings of the 18th Annual ACM SIGPLAN conference on Object-Oriented Programing, Systems, Languages, and Applications (2003)
10. Herlihy, M., Luchangco, V., Moir, M.: A flexible framework for implementing software transactional memory. In: OOPSLA 2006: Proceedings of the 21st Annual Conference on Object-Oriented Programming Systems, Languages, and Applications (October 2006)
11. Lev, Y., Luchangco, V., Marathe, V., Moir, M., Nussbaum, D., Olszewski, M.: Anatomy of a scalable software transactional memory. In: TRANSACT 2009: Fourth ACM SIGPLAN Workshop on Transactional Computing (February 2009)
12. Marathe, V., Spear, M., Herio, C., Acharya, A., Eisenstat, D., Scherer III, W., Scott, M.L.: Lowering the overhead of software transactional memory. In: TRANSACT 2006: First ACM SIGPLAN Workshop on Transactional Computing (June 2006)
13. Saha, B., Adl-Tabatabai, A.-R., Hudson, R.L., Minh, C.C., Hertzberg, B.: McRT-STM: a high performance software transactional memory system for a multi-core runtime. In: PPoPP 2006: Proceedings of the 11th ACM SIGPLAN Symposium on Principles and Practice of Parallel Programming (March 2006)
14. Baugh, L., Neelakantam, N., Zilles, C.: Using hardware memory protection to build a high-performance, strongly atomic hybrid transactional memory. In: ISCA 2008: Proceedings of the 35th Annual International Symposium on Computer Architecture (June 2008)
15. Damron, P., Fedorova, A., Lev, Y., Luchangco, V., Moir, M., Nussbaum, D.: Hybrid transactional memory. In: ASPLOS-XII: Proceedings of the 12th International Conference on Architectural Support for Programming Languages and Operating Systems (2006)
16. Lev, Y., Moir, M., Nussbaum, D.: PhTM: Phased transactional memory. In: TRANSACT 2007: Second ACM SIGPLAN Workshop on Transactional Computing (2007)
17. Minh, C.C., Trautmann, M., Chung, J., McDonald, A., Bronson, N., Casper, J., Kozyrakis, C., Olukotun, K.: An effective hybrid transactional memory system with strong isolation guarantees. In: ISCA 2007: Proceedings of the 34th Annual International Symposium on Computer Architecture (June 2007)
18. Bobba, J., Moore, K.E., Volos, H., Yen, L., Hill, M.D., Swift, M.M., Wood, D.A.: Performance pathologies in hardware transactional memory. In: ISCA 2007: Proceedings of the 34th annual international symposium on Computer architecture (June 2007)
19. Ansari, M., Kotselidis, C., Jarvis, K., Luján, M., Kirkham, C., Watson, I.: Advanced concurrency control for transactional memory using transaction commit rate. In: EUROPAR 2008: Fourteenth European Conference on Parallel Processing (August 2008)
20. Marathe, V., Scherer III, W., Scott, M.L.: Adaptive software transactional memory. In: Fraigniaud, P. (ed.) DISC 2005. LNCS, vol. 3724. Springer, Heidelberg (2005)
21. Ansari, M., Kotselidis, C., Jarvis, K., Luján, M., Kirkham, C., Watson, I.: Steal-on-abort: Dynamic transaction reordering to reduce conflicts in transactional memory. In: Seznec, A., Emer, J., O'Boyle, M., Martonosi, M., Ungerer, T. (eds.) HiPEAC 2009. LNCS, vol. 5409, pp. 4–18. Springer, Heidelberg (2009)
22. Kongetira, P., Aingaran, K., Olukotun, K.: Niagara: A 32-way multithreaded sparc processor. IEEE Micro 25(2) (April 2005)
23. Magnusson, P.S., Christensson, M., Eskilson, J., Forsgren, D., Hållberg, G., Högberg, J., Larsson, F., Moestedt, A., Werner, B.: Simics: A full system simulation platform. IEEE Computer 35(2) (2002)
24. Martin, M.M.K., Sorin, D.J., Beckmann, B.M., Marty, M.R., Xu, M., Alameldeen, A.R., Moore, K.E., Hill, M.D., Wood, D.A.: Multifacet's general execution-driven multiprocessor simulator (gems) toolset. SIGARCH Computer Architecture News 33(4) (2005)
25. Yen, L., Draper, S.C., Hill, M.D.: Notary: Hardware techniques to enhance signatures. In: MICRO 2008: Proceedings of the 41st IEEE/ACM International Symposium on Microarchitecture (November 2008)

26. Ansari, M., Luján, M., Kotselidis, C., Jarvis, K., Kirkham, C., Watson, I.: Steal-on-abort: Dynamic transaction reordering to reduce conflicts in transactional memory. In: SHCMP 2008: First Workshop on Software and Hardware Challenges of Manycore Platforms (June 2008)
27. Scherer III, W., Scott, M.L.: Contention management in dynamic software transactional memory. In: CSJP 2004: Workshop on Concurrency and Synchronization in Java Programs (July 2004)
28. Scherer III, W., Scott, M.L.: Advanced contention management for dynamic software transactional memory. In: PODC 2005: Proceedings of the 24th Annual Symposium on Principles of Distributed Computing (July 2005)
29. Dolev, S., Hendler, D., Suissa, A.: Car-stm: Scheduling-based collision avoidance and resolution for software transactional memory. In: PODC 2008: Proceedings of the 27th annual ACM symposium on Principles of distributed computing (August 2008)
30. Bai, T., Shen, X., Zhang, C., Scherer, W.N., Ding, C., Scott, M.L.: A key-based adaptive transactional memory executor. In: IPDPS 2007: Proceedings of the 21st International Parallel and Distributed Processing Symposium (March 2007)
31. Ansari, M., Kotselidis, C., Jarvis, K., Luján, M., Kirkham, C., Watson, I.: Adaptive concurrency control for transactional memory. In: MULTIPROG 2008: First Workshop on Programmability Issues for Multi-Core Computers (January 2008)
32. Yoo, R.M., Lee, H.-H.S.: Adaptive transaction scheduling for transactional memory systems. In: SPAA 2008: Proceedings of the twentieth annual symposium on Parallelism in algorithms and architectures, New York, NY, USA (2008)

Energy and Throughput Efficient Transactional Memory for Embedded Multicore Systems

Cesare Ferri[1], Samantha Wood[1,2], Tali Moreshet[3,*],
Iris Bahar[1,**], and Maurice Herlihy[4,***]

[1] Division of Engineering, Brown University, Providence, RI 02912
[2] Computer Science Department, Bryn Mawr College, Bryn Mawr, PA 19010
[3] Engineering Department, Swarthmore College, Swarthmore, PA 19081
[4] Computer Science Department, Brown University, Providence, RI 02912

Abstract. We propose a new design for an energy-efficient hardware transactional memory (HTM) system for power-aware embedded devices. Prior hardware transactional memory designs proposed a small, fully-associative transactional cache at the same level as the L1 cache. We propose an alternative design that unifies the transactional and L1 caches, and provides a small victim cache to reduce effects of capacity and conflict evictions. We evaluate our new HTM scheme on a variety of benchmarks, both in terms of energy and performance. We show that the victim cache scheme can provide up to a 4X improvement in energy-delay product, compared to a traditional HTM scheme that uses a separate transactional cache.

1 Introduction

High-end embedded systems such as smart phones, game consoles, GPS-enabled automotive systems, and home entertainment centers are becoming increasingly important in everyday life. Like their general-purpose counterparts, high-end embedded systems are multicore architectures subject to dynamic and unpredictable loads, increasingly called upon to manage substantial resources in the form of memory, connectivity, and access to devices. Because many embedded devices run on batteries, *energy efficiency* is perhaps the single most important criterion for evaluating hardware and software effectiveness in embedded devices.

Multicore architectures must provide ways for concurrent threads to synchronize access to shared memory. Prior work, for example [1], suggests that hardware transactional memory (HTM) can provide both energy and performance benefits over more conventional approaches such as locking. While hardware transactional memory makes fewer resource demands than software transactional memory, limitations on cache size and associativity bound the size of transactions that can be run efficiently. For most embedded systems, such limitations are not

---

* Supported by NSF Grant CCF-0903295.
** Supported by NSF Grant CCF-0903384.
*** Supported by NSF Grant CCF-0811289.

Y.N. Patt et al. (Eds.): HiPEAC 2010, LNCS 5952, pp. 50–65, 2010.

a major concern, because applications' resource requirements are typically well-understood, and transactions that exceed those expectations are likely to be rare. Nevertheless, these observations suggest the following research question: how can we design caches for HTM in embedded systems to maximize transaction sizes without compromising performance or increasing energy consumption?

In this paper, we investigate how a variety of cache designs affects the performance and energy consumption of a multicore embedded system that supports HTM. (A direct comparison of HTM and locking appears in prior work [1].) Prior work on HTM has focused on a simple cache architecture [1, 2] in which non-transactional data was stored in a large direct-mapped cache, and a smaller, fully associative *transactional cache* was used to store all data accessed within a transaction. This architecture has drawbacks. Namely, since the transactional cache is the only place to store transactional data, any transaction that exceeds the size of this cache will overflow, forcing transactions to serialize, even if no data conflicts exist between them. So, although a small transactional cache is desirable for energy purposes, making it too small could hurt throughput significantly.

Here, we consider an alternative design suitable for embedded systems in which both caches are unified into a single L1 cache holding both transactional and non-transactional entries. A unified cache eliminates the need to maintain coherence across two same-level caches, but introduces the problem that the direct-mapped nature of the cache causes more transactions to overflow because of conflict misses. To compensate, we introduce two levels of defense: we make the L1 cache 4-way associative, and we introduce a small victim cache to catch transactional entries evicted from the main cache by conflict misses. Although we are back to a two-cache architecture, the victim cache is needed only when the main cache overflows, so a simple, small, direct-mapped victim cache will suffice.

We test variations of this scheme against a number of benchmarks. We find that our more sophisticated cache architecture improves the power/performance profile of most benchmarks relative to previously proposed HTM implementations. In particular, for 8 core embedded platforms, the energy-delay product can improve by up to a factor of 4X. These results confirm that ignoring energy considerations can lead to non-optimal design choices, particularly for resource constrained embedded platforms.

2   Background and Previous Work

There are many mechanisms for synchronizing access to shared memory. Today, the two most prominent are locks and transactions. While most of the literature evaluates these proposals with respect to performance and ease of use, we focus here on a third criterion important for embedded devices: energy efficiency.

Prior work includes techniques for increasing the efficiency of lock-based synchronization for real-time embedded systems. Tumeo *et al.* [3] proposed new techniques for efficient lock-based synchronization in FPGA-based multiprocessor system-on-chips (MPSoCs) for real-time applications. Lee *et al.* [4] improved the real-time performance of embedded Linux by monitoring the lock hold times.

Other researchers have investigated the energy implications of locks for multi-processor systems-on-a-chip. Loghi *et al.* [5] evaluated power-performance trade-offs in lock implementations. Monchiero *et al.* [6] proposed a *synchronization-operation buffer* as a high-performance yet energy-efficient spin lock implementation that reduces memory references and network traffic. Yu *et al.* introduced energy-efficient producer-consumer communication by compiler-inserted write-through store insertions to update a cached memory location before exiting a synchronization region [7].

Others have investigated lock-free synchronization for embedded systems. Cho *et al.* considered the benefits of lock-free synchronization for the multi-writer/multi-reader problem in embedded real-time systems [8]. Yang *et al.* showed how to exploit access pattern regularity in a single producer/single consumer synchronization to implement a light-weight synchronization mechanism that encodes dependence information within each memory access [9].

Transactional memory has been extensively investigated as an alternative means of synchronization in general-purpose systems. The principle behind the transactional memory working model is simple: each transaction is speculatively executed by the CPU, and, if no conflicts with another transaction are detected, its effects become permanent (that is, the transaction commits). Otherwise, if conflicts are detected, its effects are discarded (that is, the transaction aborts), and the transaction is restarted. Transactional memory can be implemented in hardware (e.g. [2, 10, 11]), in software (e.g., [12, 13]), or via hybrid mechanisms that combine hardware and software (e.g, [14, 15]). A survey of transactional memory is provided in [16]. Because previous transactional memory proposals targeted general-purpose systems, they focused mainly on performance and ease-of-programming. In our work we target embedded systems, which are resource and energy constrained. Therefore, we focus on simple hardware transactional memory, which has minimal demand on resources, and our main design goal is energy efficiency.

Ferri *et al.* [1] showed that hardware transactional memory can be implemented in embedded systems with minimal, energy-efficient hardware support. Their scheme, like all pure HTM systems, is limited to running transactions whose data sets fit in the hardware cache. Transactions that overflow the cache are run in a less-efficient serial mode. In this paper, we consider alternative cache architectures for HTM in embedded systems, architectures designed to reduce the likelihood of cache overflow with the additional goal of reducing overall energy consumption. Specifically, we proposed the use of the L1 cache as the primary storage space for holding transactional data (along with non-transactional data). In addition, we use a small victim cache to hold transactional data evicted from the L1 cache due to conflict misses, thereby reducing the occurrence of transactional overflows that force transactions to be serialized. While our proposed scheme has similarities to other transactional memory proposals that use a victim cache (most notably [17]), our work is distinct in that prior work did not fully evaluate the impact of the victim cache itself on either energy or performance. In addition, since we are focusing on embedded platforms rather than general-purpose systems, our findings are driven to a large extent by the resource constraints existing within these embedded systems.

Unbounded (or virtualized) transactional memory [10,18,19,20] proposals include additional hardware structures to allow transactions to continue after overflowing the L1 cache, and even to migrate from processor to processor. While some of these proposals may be attractive for general-purpose systems, they are too complex for today's embedded systems.

The *permissions-only cache* (PO cache) of Blundell et al. [21] addresses the same problem as our victim cache: minimizing transaction overflow. On an overflow, speculative data is written back to memory, and the original values are logged in thread-local storage, but the (much smaller) permission bits are kept in the cache, allowing the cache coherence protocol to continue to detect conflicts. (If the the PO cache itself overflows, then an additional serialization mechanism is called into play.)

While the PO cache scheme may be attractive for general-purpose architectures, it is incompatible with our goal of minimizing changes to the underlying embedded architecture. Maintaining the undo-log, in fact, would require not only non-trivial changes to the CPU pipeline (since a write operation should be monitored and properly propagated into the log), but also cost extra cycles even for the case of non-conflicting transactions (since logging is not a cycle-free operation). Moreover, when a transaction aborts, the PO cache scheme must restore the original memory state from the log, blocking (or perhaps restarting) any concurrent transactions that attempt to access that data while recovery is in progress. This functionality would require substantial changes to the base architecture, tracking more synchronization state, and adding new states, messages, and behaviors to the standard cache coherence protocols. These changes go far beyond those needed to support a victim cache.

3   Energy-Efficient HTM for Embedded Systems

All our experiments are conducted using the MPARM multi-processor simulation framework [22,23]. We chose this embedded system simulator because we can accurately model both performance and power at the cycle level. The performance and power models are based mostly on data obtained from a 0.13μm technology provided by STMicroelectronics [24], and the energy model for the fully associative caches is based on [25]. MPARM also provided the flexibility necessary to do extensive design space exploration. Here, we model a system with up to 8 cores, containing a complex memory hierarchy, that supports caches, scratchpad memories, and multiple types of interconnects.

The baseline configuration allows for a variable number of ARM7 cores (each with an 8KB L1 cache, evenly split into 4KB of instruction cache and 4KB of data cache), a set of private memories (256KB each), a single shared memory bank (256KB), and one bank (16KB) of memory-mapped registers serving as hardware semaphores. The interconnect is an AMBA-compliant communication architecture [26]. A cache-coherence protocol (MESI) is also provided by snoop

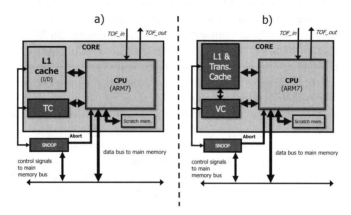

Fig. 1. a) Architectural configuration to support hardware transactional memory. Note the transactional cache holds all transactional data. b) New architectural configuration to support hardware transactional memory using a victim cache (VC). Note that the primary storage structure for transactional data is now the L1 cache. In case of conflict evictions, transactional data can be held in the VC.

devices connected to the master ports. Platforms featuring such cache-coherency subsystems are not uncommon (e.g., the ARM11 MPCore Multiprocessor [27]). Note that while the private and shared memories are sized arbitrarily large (256KB each), they do not significantly impact the performance or power of our system (as will be shown in Section 4). Next we describe the implementation for an embedded HTM platform used in prior work.

In the original HTM proposal [2], each core had a *transactional cache* (TC) in addition to its L1 cache (see Figure 1a)). In the embedded HTM platform [1], to start a transaction, the CPU creates a local checkpoint by saving its registers to a small Scratchpad Memory [28]. The scratchpad memory must be large enough to hold the entire set of CPU registers.

Each transaction stores two copies of accessed data in the TC: a working copy and a back up copy. If the data is found in the L1 cache, it must be invalidated there before being placed in the TC. The transaction modifies the working copy. If there is no data conflict, the transaction completes successfully, invalidates the backup copies of the data, and the working copies become visible. On a data conflict, the snoop device notifies the CPU, invalidating the working copies, and restoring the back up copies. The CPU enters a low-power mode, and after a random backoff, re-executes the transaction. Note that in our model we also considered a realistic state-switching overhead (i.e., idle to active), as described in Section 4.

When reading/writing data from memory, the TC is always accessed first. In case of a TC miss, the rest of the memory hierarchy (starting with the L1 cache) may be accessed. This decision to serialize accesses to the caches is made for power reasons and since most requested data is located in the TC, this scheme has a negligible impact on performance.

Note that it is not strictly necessary to keep valid data in the TC once a transaction commits. Earlier work [1] shows that it is often advantageous in terms of energy efficiency to write back the modified lines to the traditional cache hierarchy after the commit, allowing the transactional cache to be powered down when not in use. This approach is called *aggressive shutdown* mode. In order to flush the TC of its contents, the CPU is stalled and no new instructions are allowed to execute until flushing is complete. Turning the TC back on at the start of a new transaction incurs a $0.2\mu s$ (40 cycles) overhead. Shutting down the TC may not be the best choice in case of back-to-back transactions, since it often results in unnecessarily moving data back and forth between the TC and the rest of the memory hierarchy.

The embedded HTM platform uses an "eager" type of conflict detection and resolution scheme. That is, the system detects and resolves a conflict when a transaction accesses a location, rather than waiting until a transaction is ready to commit. This strategy is used since it requires fewer modifications to the original MESI protocol. In particular, neither new bus states nor new coherence signals are needed. For example, in a MESI protocol, a CPU wanting to write to an address that another CPU has modified must broadcast an *invalidate* signal on the bus. By monitoring the invalidate signal, all the other snoop devices may easily detect the data conflict, and instantaneously forward the information to the CPU. By forwarding the data to the requester, the responder effectively aborts its own transaction, allowing the requester to always win the conflict. While this type of conflict management does not always yield the best throughput, we can see that it is particularly lightweight, and fits quite well with the hardware restrictions of an embedded platform. Also, the fact that the hardware modifications are rather limited not only helps the design verification process, but also increases significantly the portability of such method to other invalidation-based cache coherence schemes (e.g., MOESI, MSI).

While prior embedded HTM implementations provided simple hardware solutions that led to good performance benefits, there are two ways that they can fall short. A transaction triggers an overflow if its data footprint is too large to fit in the TC, or if one of its entries is evicted from the TC because of a line conflict. To avoid conflict evictions, transactional cache designs have typically been fully associative, even though a fully associative transactional cache can consume a significant amount of energy [1]. We face a dilemma: a larger TC means we can run larger transactions, but substantially increases power consumption.

In this paper, our goal is two-fold. First, we investigate power-efficient alternative cache architectures with the objective of reducing the number of transactions aborted by cache overflows or evictions. Second, we describe an architecture that can handle larger transactions without requiring a larger, more energy-hungry TC.

If a transaction overflows the TC, the system switches to serial mode, which stops all other processors executing transactions (this is handled exclusively by dedicated hardware). The overflowing transaction runs by itself, using the entire memory hierarchy, and the other CPUs will wait for the overflowing transaction to commit before continuing their own transactions. Unless a conflict is detected, no abort is required.

The problem is, running transactions in serial mode provides no concurrency. This absence of concurrency is not important for conflicting transactions, which must execute serially no matter what, but it does matter for large, non-conflicting concurrent transactions.

It seems wasteful to require transactions to fit in the smaller TC when the L1 cache, which is normally much larger than the transactional cache, may have plenty of room. Instead, we propose a new scheme that uses the L1 cache for both transactional and non-transactional data. This approach yields much more memory to hold transactional data, reducing the likelihood of overflow. However, because it is impractical to make the L1 cache highly associative (especially in a power-constrained embedded platform), we have introduced a new danger: transactions may be serialized by conflict evictions.

We make two more changes to reduce the likelihood of conflict evictions. First, we propose a *victim cache* (VC) between the L1 cache and main memory to catch transactional items evicted from the L1. Although victim caches have been proposed for different purposes (e.g., [17, 29, 30]), our work is distinct in that we are the first to analyze its energy-performance impact specifically for implementing HTM.

We use the L1 cache as our primary storage structure for holding transactional data, and only in case of conflict misses do we resort to storing data in the victim cache. Therefore, our strategy is to access the L1 cache first on a data request and only after an L1 miss is the VC accessed. As with the TC scheme, by serializing the cache accesses we save power without hampering performance since most accesses will hit in the L1 cache.

Transactions continue to execute concurrently while the VC is in use. If, despite everything, the VC overflows, then the transaction asks the system to continue in serial mode. Because the combination of the L1 and victim caches provides much more room than the conventional transactional cache, overflows should be rarer in the victim cache scheme. The second change is to further reduce conflict evictions by giving the L1 cache a modest level of associativity (say, 4-way). Our new architectural configuration is shown in Figure 1b).

Note that unlike the TC, the L1 and VC caches do not hold a backup copy of the transactional data. In case of an abort, the CPU needs to refill the line from the main memory, thus increasing bus traffic, which is bad for performance and energy efficiency. However, this cost should be acceptable if the abort rate is reasonably low. Also, since the VC is only utilized in those cases where transactions do not fit in the L1 cache, it makes sense to keep the VC powered down unless needed. Similar to the TC, the penalty to reactivate the VC is on the order of tens of cycles (i.e., 40 cycles).

4   Experimental Results

In this section we evaluate our proposed HTM platform using a mix of applications. We first describe the benchmarks used in our experiments as well as our experimental setup, followed by a detailed discussion of our results.

4.1   Software

To test our ideas, we chose a range of different applications. Three of these applications were taken from the STAMP benchmark suite [31]:

- **Vacation** (STAMP): implements a non-distributed travel reservation system. Each thread interacts with the database via the system's transaction manager. The application features large critical sections.
- **K-means** (STAMP): a partition-based program (commonly found in image filtering applications). The number of objects to be partitioned is equally subdivided among the threads. Barriers and short critical sections are both used to obtain concurrency.
- **Genome** (STAMP): a gene sequencing program. A gene is reconstructed by matching DNA segments of a larger gene. The application has been parallelized through barriers and large critical sections.
- **RBTree, SList**: applications operating on special data structures (i.e., redblack-trees and skip-lists). The workload is composed of a certain number of atomic operations (i.e., inserts, deletes and lookups) to be performed on these two data structures. Redblack-trees and skip-lists constitute the fundamental blocks of many memory management applications found in embedded applications.

For each set of applications we also considered an average of the results, called the "Application Mix".

4.2   Hardware

For convenience, in Table1 we report the principal system parameters and relative configurations.

Table 1. Overview of the system configurations

Parameter	Configuration(s)
CPU	ARMv7, 3-stage in-order pipeline, 200Mhz
L1 cache	4KB 4-way Icache, 4KB 4-way Dcache
Cores	{1,4,8}
Tx Policies	vanilla-TM, TM-aggressive-L1WB, TM-victim
TC, VC	{1-way, 4-way, Fully Associative}, {64B,512B}
Bus	Amba AHB

We considered the following alternative HTM implementations.

- **vanilla-TM:** the original transactional memory implementation [2, 1], consisting of an additional transactional cache (TC). The transactional data resides exclusively in the TC. The TC is never turned off. While prior works fixed the TC to be fully associative, we vary this associativity in our experiments.
- **TM-aggressive-L1WB:** same as vanilla TM, except that the TC is aggressively shut down after each commit, as described in Section 3. Before turning off the TC, the CPU writes back the modified TC lines into the L1 cache. The overhead of turning the TC back on is $0.2\mu s$ (i.e., the CPU will stall for 40 cycles when reactivating the TC). In our experimental results, this configuration is referred to as *TM-aggressive-L1WB*.
- **TM-victim:** the new victim cache configuration. The VC contains the lines that were evicted from the (transactional) L1 cache because of conflict misses. Similar to TM-aggressive-L1WB, the VC is shut down at the end of each transaction. The modified VC lines will be written back into the main memory (i.e., SRAM). As with the other configurations, we vary the associativity of the VC in our experiments.

We also varied two key architectural parameters: the number of cores (i.e., 1, 4 or 8 cores), and the size of the caches (i.e., 64Bytes and 512Bytes).

All three TM configurations incur a penalty of $2\mu s$ whenever a core wakes up from the power-idle state because of an abort due to a data conflict. This specific value was chosen since it is consistent with that found in real embedded systems (e.g., [32, 33]).

As mentioned in Section 3, while prior work used the TC along with a *direct-mapped* L1 cache, in this study we increased the associativity of the L1 to *4-way* (which is a common degree for the associativity of data caches in embedded platforms, e.g., [32]). Our initial experiments showed this configuration to be the best in terms of energy-delay product for all benchmarks. Therefore, all experimental results shown in this paper assume the 4-way configuration for the L1 cache.

4.3   Experimental Data

For each application run, we measured both the total execution cycles and the consumed energy. Then we quantified the energy/ performance tradeoff by considering the Energy-Delay Product (EDP).

Figure 2 shows five graphs, each reporting the EDP data for a different application: RBtree, SkipList, Genome, Vacation, and Kmeans. Note that the scale for the energy-delay values on the y-axis are different for each benchmark.

First, we see that higher associativity for the VC in the *TM-victim* configuration does not translate to improvements in energy-delay product. This is because most transactional data already fits into the L1 data cache, and even a small direct-mapped VC is enough to take care of almost all conflict misses in the L1.

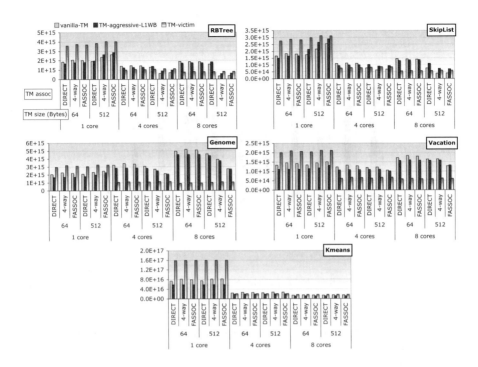

Fig. 2. Energy-Delay Product for the STAMP suite, RBtree, and SkipList benchmarks. Units are pJ · cycles. Note that the scale for the energy-delay values on the y-axis are different for each benchmark.

Next, we analyze the *TM-victim* configuration relative to *vanilla-TM* and *TM-aggressive-L1WB*. In most cases, the *TM-victim* configuration offers the best EDP when more than 1 core is available. For example, for the Genome benchmark, we see that *TM-victim* has a 4X improvement in EDP compared to *vanilla-TM* for the 8 core 64B configuration. Using the *TM-aggressive-L1WB* scheme improves EDP a little relative to *vanilla-TM*, mainly by avoiding accesses to the TC when not executing transactional code. However, since the *TM-aggressive-L1WB* scheme does not address the problem of overflows, it will not be sufficient in the case of large transactions. In a 1 core system the *TM-victim* configuration is penalized in terms of cycles because of 1) the overhead incurred when flushing the VC to main memory, and 2) the VC wake up time. For K-means, we found that the time spent within transactions is quite low (i.e., about 5%); the only potential benefit of using a victim configuration over a TC is mainly due to the energy saving when shutting down the VC.

For RBtree and SList, *TM-victim* offers good EDP; however, it is not the best option compared to the fully-associative *vanilla-TM* with a 512 Byte TC. In this case, the entire data set fits within the TC so no overflow occurs, allowing the system's throughput to reach its maximum. The *vanilla-TM* configuration has the additional advantage of dissipating less power per data access, on average,

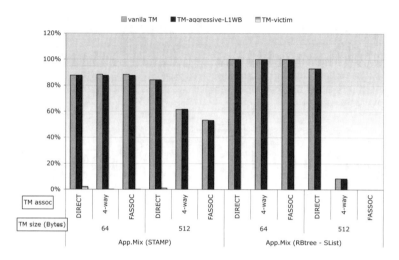

Fig. 3. Transaction Overflow Rate for the STAMP and RBtree-SkipList Application Mixes with 4 cores

since the larger L1 data cache is only accessed in case of a miss to the TC. In contrast, the *TM-victim* always accesses the L1 data cache first. *vanilla-TM* has the additional advantage of dissipating less power per data access, on average, compared with *TM-victim*, which always accesses the L1 data cache first. Even *TM-aggressive-L1WB* offers no advantage over *vanilla-TM* since this scheme only leads to increased data transfers between TC and L1 caches.

The general trend to note here is that when a system is executing large non-conflicting transactions, the victim configuration can often lead to a significantly better energy-delay product compared to a *vanilla-TM* configuration, even with a very small direct mapped VC. To further appreciate these results, we next consider how a specific configuration may impact the transaction overflow rate and transaction abort rate.

Figure 3 shows the transaction overflow rate when running with 4 cores for the STAMP Application Mix and RB-SkipList Application Mix, for various sizes and associativities. As expected, we see that 1) the overflow rate is very high for *vanilla-TM* and *TM-aggressive-L1WB*, except when the TC is large and highly associative, and 2) the number of overflowing transactions is drastically reduced to almost zero with a victim configuration.

We can also notice that EDP and overflow rates are correlated; usually better EDP corresponds to low overflow rates. For example, as shown in Figure 2 for the STAMP benchmarks, *TM-victim* offers the best EDP for a 64 Byte VC configuration. For the same VC size, Figure 3 shows overflow rate dropping by the largest absolute amount when switching from a *vanilla-TM* to a *TM-victim* configuration.

As mentioned earlier, another important parameter affecting the performance of a transactional memory system is the transaction abort rate. Recall that when

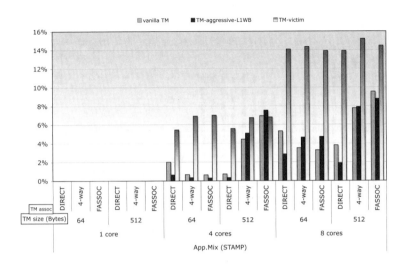

Fig. 4. Transaction Abort Rate for the STAMP application mix. No aborts were detected in RBtree and Skip-list.

a transaction detects a data conflict with another transaction, one of the transactions needs to abort, causing the core executing that transaction to go into a low-power state for some random backoff period while the other transaction continues to execute. Eventually, the core executing the aborted transaction is woken up so it can attempt to re-execute that transaction. This whole process consumes extra energy and cycles, but is required in order to properly synchronize the two transactions. As with the overflow case, the overall effect on the system is to serialize the execution.

Figure 4 reports the abort rate for the STAMP Application Mix. The equivalent data for RBtree and SkipList is omitted since no aborts were detected for any configuration. In STAMP, we see that *TM-victim* is affected by a slightly higher abort rate than *vanilla-TM*. This is expected; in *vanilla-TM* the transactions overflow most of the time, and hence avoid conflict because of the serialization. Still, the abort rate is quite acceptable under *TM-victim*, therefore leading to overall improvements in EDP for the STAMP benchmarks.

Recall that the RBtree and SkipList do not incur aborts or overflows using the *TM-victim* configuration. This type of scenario can be classified as an ideal case for *TM-victim*. In fact, we see a very significant improvement in EDP of about 80% with an 8 core configuration. In summary, if applications requiring a lot of synchronization still have high inherent parallelism (i.e., incur few data conflicts), then a *TM-victim* scheme offers a substantial advantage over *vanilla-TM*. If data conflicts are common, then it's best to let the transaction overflow as soon as possible and resort to serialized execution, so *TM-victim* would offer no advantage over *vanilla-TM* or *TM-aggressive-L1WB*.

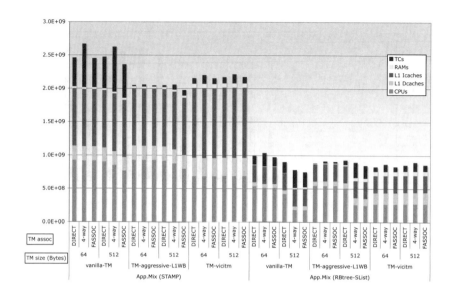

Fig. 5. Energy Distribution of an 8 core system for the STAMP and RBtree-Slist application mixes. Energy values are given in nJ.

Finally, Figure 5 shows the energy distribution of an 8 core system for the two types of application mixes. Note that in our model we include power numbers for a 0.13μm technology, where the dynamic power is dominant; hence, leakage has not been taken into consideration.

In general, we see that the CPUs and caches consume most of the energy in the system and the small on-chip SRAMs contribute a negligible amount to total energy consumption. In addition, we see that while the *TM-victim* configuration causes the L1 energy consumption to increase. This is due to the fact that now the L1 is used for both transactional and non-transactional data, and also because of increased abort rates as the system tries to execute more transactions in parallel. However, this increased L1 energy consumption is more than compensated for by the drop in energy consumption in both the CPUs and VCs. Again, this is expected since the TM-victim configuration doesn't need to spend as many CPU cycles executing overflowing transactions serially. The *TM-aggressive-L1WB* scheme can help reduce the energy consumption in the TC, but cannot reduce CPU energy consumption significantly since it still has to spend about the same amount of time handling overflow transactions as the *vanilla-TM* scheme. In the end, even though the *TM-aggressive-L1WB* scheme can have lower overall energy consumption than the *TM-victim* scheme (as in the case of the STAMP mix), it is not better in terms of EDP since performance is still hampered by high overflow rates.

5 Conclusions

We have seen how cache architecture design can increase the size of transactions that can be executed directly in an energy-aware hardware transactional memory scheme. Some design decisions that individually consume more energy than their simpler alternatives yield overall energy savings. For example, the additional energy consumed by making the L1 cache 4-way associative is more than compensated by the reduced number of conflict evictions resulting in cache overflows. We also show that only a small, direct-mapped victim cache is sufficient in order to drastically reduce the number of overflow cases, compared to a traditional HTM scheme. Given a limited amount of storage capacity, overall, the *TM-victim* scheme is the better way to go since it is more flexible in how it makes use of the available memory. Again, this is particularly important in resource-constrained embedded systems.

There are still open questions. We switch to serial mode both for transactions that overflow the hardware cache, and for transactions that repeatedly abort due to data conflicts. Further work is needed to evaluate strategies for switching aborted transactions: should one switch right away, on the grounds that data conflicts probably prevent the current transaction mix from executing concurrently, or is it more sensible to try several times, hoping that the conflicts are transient? Can we exploit the observation that in many embedded systems, the transaction mix is often, but not always, known in advance, and configure the cache and overflow policies accordingly?

References

1. Ferri, C., Bahar, R.I., Moreshet, T., Viescas, A., Herlihy, M.: Energy efficient synchronization techniques for embedded architectures. In: ACM/IEEE Great Lakes International Symposium on VLSI (May 2008)
2. Herlihy, M., Moss, J.E.B.: Transactional memory: Architectural support for lock-free data structures. In: International Symposium on Computer Architecture (May 1993)
3. Tumeo, A., Pilato, C., Palermo, G., Ferrandi, F., Sciuto, D.: HW/SW methodologies for synchronization in FPGA multiprocessors. In: International Symposium on Field Programmable Gate Arrays (2009)
4. Lee, J., Park, K.H.: Delayed locking technique for improving real-time performance of embedded linux by prediction of timer interrupt. In: IEEE Real Time and Embedded Technology and Applications Symposium (2005)
5. Loghi, M., Poncino, M., Benini, L.: Cache coherence tradeoffs in shared-memory MPSoCs. ACM Transactions on Embedded Computing Systems 5(2), 383–407 (2006)
6. Monchiero, M., Palermo, G., Silvano, C., Villa, O.: Power/performance hardware optimization for synchronization intensive applications in MPSoCs. In: Design Automation and Test in Europe Conference (April 2006)
7. Yu, C., Petrov, P.: Latency and bandwidth efficient communication through system customization for embedded multiprocessors. In: Design Automation Conference (2008)

8. Cho, H., Ravindran, B., Jensen, E.D.: Lock-free synchronization for dynamic embedded real-time systems. In: Design Automation and Test in Europe Conference (2006)
9. Yang, C., Orailoglu, A.: Light-weight synchronization for inter-processor communication acceleration on embedded MPSoCs. In: International Conference on Compilers, Architecture and Synthesis for Embedded Systems (2007)
10. Moore, K.E., Bobba, J., Moravan, M.J., Hill, M.D., Wood, D.A.: LogTM: Log-based transactional memory. In: International Symposium on High-Performance Computer Architecture (February 2006)
11. Hammond, L., Carlstrom, B.D., Wong, V., Hertzberg, B., Chen, M., Kozyrakis, C., Olukotun, K.: Programming with transactional coherence and consistency (TCC). ACM SIGOPS Operating Systems Review 38(5), 1–13 (2004)
12. Shavit, N., Touitou, D.: Software transactional memory. Distributed Computing Special issue(10), 99–116 (1997)
13. Herlihy, M., Koskinen, E.: Transactional boosting: A methodology for highly-concurrent transactional objects. In: Principles and Practice of Parallel Programming, PPOPP (2008)
14. Damron, P., Fedorova, A., Lev, Y., Luchangco, V., Moir, M., Nussbaum, D.: Hybrid transactional memory. In: International Conference on Architectural Support for Programming Languages and Operating Systems (2006)
15. Shriraman, A., Dwarkadas, S., Scott, M.L.: Flexible decoupled transactional memory support. In: Proceedings of the 35th International Symposium on Computer Architecture (2008)
16. Larus, J., Rajwar, R.: Transactional Memory (Synthesis Lectures on Computer Architecture). Morgan & Claypool Publishers, San Francisco (2007)
17. Waliullah, M.M., Stenstrom, P.: Starvation-free commit arbitration policies for transactional memory systems. ACM SIGARCH Computer Architecture News 35(1), 39–46 (2007)
18. Ananian, C.S., Asanovic, K., Kuszmaul, B.C., Leiserson, C.E., Lie, S.: Unbounded transactional memory. In: International Symposium on High-Performance Computer Architecture (February 2005)
19. Ceze, L., Tuck, J., Cascaval, C., Torrellas, J.: Bulk disambiguation of speculative threads in multiprocessors. In: International Symposium on Computer Architecture (June 2006)
20. Rajwar, R., Herlihy, M., Lai, K.: Virtualizing Transactional Memory. In: International Symposium on Computer Architecture (June 2005)
21. Blundell, C., Devietti, J., Lewis, E.C., Martin, M.: Making the fast case common and the uncommon case simple in unbounded transactional memory. In: International Symposium on Computer Architecture (June 2007)
22. Angiolini, F., Ceng, J., Leupers, R., Ferrari, F., Ferri, C., Benini, L.: An integrated open framework for heterogeneous MPSoC design space exploration. In: Design Automation and Test in Europe Conference (DATE), pp. 1145–1150 (2006)
23. Loghi, M., Angiolini, F., Bertozzi, D., Benini, L., Zafalon, R.: Analyzing on-chip communication in a MPSoC environment. In: Design Automation and Test in Europe Conference (DATE), February 2004, pp. 752–757 (2004)
24. STMicroelectronics: Nomadik platform, http://www.stm.com
25. Efthymiou, A., Garside, J.D.: An adaptive serial-parallel cam architecture for low-power cache blocks. In: International Symposium on Low Power Electronics and Design (2002)
26. AMBA: ARM Ltd. The advanced microcontroller bus architecture (AMBA), http://www.arm.com/products/solutions/AMBAHomePage.html

27. Goodacre, J., Sloss, A.N.: Parallelism and the ARM instruction set architecture. IEEE Computer 38(7) (July 2005)
28. Banakar, R., Steinke, S., Lee, B.S., Balakrishnan, M., Marwedel, P.: Scratchpad memory: design alternative for cache on-chip memory in embedded systems. In: Symposium on Hardware/Software Codesign, pp. 73–78 (2002)
29. Jouppi, N.P.: Improving direct-mapped cache performance by the addition of a small fully-associative cache and prefetch buffers. In: International Symposium on Computer Architecture (May 1990)
30. Bahar, R.I., Albera, G., Manne, S.: Power and performance tradeoffs using various caching strategies. In: International Symposium on Low Power Electronics and Design, August 1998, pp. 64–69 (1998)
31. Minh, C.C., Chung, J., Kozyrakis, C., Olukotun, K.: STAMP: Stanford transactional applications for multi-processing. In: IISWC 2008: Proceedings of The IEEE International Symposium on Workload Characterization (September 2008)
32. STMicroelectronics-Cortex: STMicroelectronics Cortex-M3 CPU, http://www.st.com/mcu/inchtml-pages-stm32.html
33. Freescale-QE: Freescale low-power QE family processor, http://www.freescale.com/files/microcontrollers/

Split Register Allocation: Linear Complexity Without the Performance Penalty

Boubacar Diouf[1], Albert Cohen[1], Fabrice Rastello[2], and John Cavazos[3]

[1] ALCHEMY Group, INRIA Saclay and Paris-Sud University
[2] LIP, École Normale Supérieure de Lyon
[3] University of Delaware

Abstract. Just-in-time compilers are becoming ubiquitous, spurring the design of more efficient algorithms and more elaborate intermediate representations. They rely on continuous, feedback-directed (re-)compilation frameworks to adaptively select a limited set of hot functions for aggressive optimization. To date, (quasi-)linear complexity has remained a driving force in the design of just-in-time optimizers.

This paper describes a *split register allocator* showing that linear complexity does not imply reduced code quality. We present a *split compiler* design, where more expensive ahead-of-time analyses guide lightweight just-in-time optimizations. A split register allocator can be very aggressive in its offline stage, producing a semantic summary through bytecode annotations that can be processed by a lightweight online stage. The challenges are fourfold: (sub-)linear-size annotation, linear-time online processing, minimal loss of code quality, and portability of the annotation.

We propose a split register allocator meeting these challenges. A compact annotation derived from an optimal integer linear program (ILP) formulation of register allocation drives a linear-time algorithm near optimality. We study the robustness of this algorithm to variations in the number of physical registers. Our method is implemented in JikesRVM and evaluated on standard benchmarks.

1 Introduction

Just-In-Time (JIT) compilers rely on continuous, feedback-directed (re-)compilation frameworks to select hot functions (frequently executed) for online optimizations. These online optimizations must make important trade-offs in terms of reducing compilation time for decreased generated code performance. Reducing compilation overhead has two main benefits, low-complexity algorithms simultaneously increase the amount of code being optimized while reducing the compilation time for hot functions. In practice, (quasi-)linear complexity is the rule for JIT compilation. This severely impacts what kind of optimizations are admissible and how aggressive they may be.

1.1 A Case for Split Compilation

Traditional bytecode language tool chains distribute the roles among offline and online compilers. Verification and code compaction are typically assigned to

Y.N. Patt et al. (Eds.): HiPEAC 2010, LNCS 5952, pp. 66–80, 2010.

offline compilation, while target-specific optimizations are performed by online compilation. *Split compilation* reconsiders this notion: it allows *a single optimization algorithm* to be split into *an offline and an online stage*, transferring the semantic information between those stages through carefully designed bytecode annotations.

Split compilation has the potential to combine the advantages of offline and online compilation: running expensive analyses offline to prune the optimization space, deferring a more educated optimization decision to the online stage, when the precise execution context is known. Many JIT compilation efforts tried to leverage the accuracy of dynamic analysis to outperform native compilers; but split compilation is a concrete path to get the best of both worlds.

To make a concrete case for split compilation, we selected the (spill-everywhere) register allocation problem [1,2]. Register allocation is an ideal candidate to demonstrate how split compilation impacts the design of future bytecode languages and compilers, and how it differs from plain annotation-enhanced JIT compilation [3]. Indeed:

- the principles of register allocation are reasonably well understood;
- it is one of the most important components of all JIT compilers;
- it is challenging to design an offline analysis that would improve online register allocation, while ignoring the exact register count of the target.

1.2   Outline of the Paper

This paper makes two important contributions.

1. We design bytecode annotations enabling a linear-time online algorithm to achieve high-quality register allocation, with negligible impact on the size of the bytecode.
2. We demonstrate how such annotations are robust to variations in the number of registers. With additional provisions in the offline stage, it is even possible to accommodate radical changes in the instruction set target architecture.

Our method is implemented in the JikesRVM open source JIT compiler for Java [4], and evaluated on x86. We do believe that it would be easy to port it to multi-language JIT frameworks like the ECMA-335 CLI standard.[1]

The paper is organized as follows. Section 2 presents the split register allocation flow and algorithms. Section 3 evaluates split register allocation, with coverage of performance improvements as well as annotation compaction and portability. Section 4 explores more complex compilation scenarios. Finally, Section 5 discusses related work on annotation-enhanced just-in-time compilation.

2   Split Register Allocation

We first introduce some terminology. An interval characterizing the entire lifetime of a local variable or temporary may contain some *idle holes*. The live range

---

[1] http://www.ecma-international.org/publications/standards/Ecma-335.htm

of a variable x is the set of program points where x is live; it corresponds to a union of basic intervals. When linearising the control flow (e.g., when generating code), the basic interval of a given live range are interleaved with holes. Those holes correspond either to program points dominated by a redefinition of the variable (the variable is effectively dead at those points), or to a hole resulting from the order in which the basic blocks are numbered (a control-flow artifact). *Register pressure* refers to the amount of locally living variables. Considering that a variable is not alive during its idle holes can help in reducing the register pressure. JikesRVM takes advantage of this.

2.1   Optimization Problem and Baseline Algorithm

Since our primary focus is to illustrate the split compilation concept, we limit ourselves to the most basic register allocation and assignment problem:

– Spill everywhere allocation: spill the whole live range.
– Single-color assignment: when such a live range is allocated, all its basic intervals must be assigned to the same register. Some live ranges may be preassigned due to function call conventions and operand restrictions of some target instructions;

Throughout the paper, we handle register allocation in different register classes separately (e.g., general purpose, floating point), and call R the number of registers in the current class of interest.

Algorithm 1 recalls the main steps of the linear scan algorithm, as implemented in JikesRVM. Every time a basic interval i becomes active, Algorithm 1 calls the function ASSIGNORSUGGESTSPILLCANDIDATE($V(i)$), where $V(i)$ is the live range corresponding to i. According to the allocation that has been performed up to this point, function ASSIGNORSUGGESTSPILLCANDIDATE($V(i)$) returns, either a live range or $\perp$ (bottom): if it returns a live range, it is the one to be spilled in order to continue allocation; if it returns $\perp$ it was possible to assign $V(i)$ without spilling. These algorithms are the basic framework upon which the offline and online phases of our split register allocation are constructed.

Algorithm 1. LINEARSCAN

Input: *list*: the list of basic intervals ordered by increasing start point
1: **foreach:** $i \in list$ **do**
2:     $toSpill \leftarrow$ ASSIGNORSUGGESTSPILLCANDIDATE($V(i)$)
3:     **if** $toSpill \neq \perp$ **then**
4:         **if** $toSpill \neq V(i)$ **then**
5:             Assign $V(i)$ to the register freed by $toSpill$
6:         **end if**
7:         Spill $toSpill$
8:     **end if**
9: **end for**
Return: sets of spilled live ranges and register assignments

Algorithm 2. ASSIGNORSUGGESTSPILLCANDIDATE

Input: v: a live range
1: **if** v was previously assigned to a register r **then**
2:     **if** r is free **then**
3:         Continue with this assignment
4:         Return $\bot$
5:     **else if** v can be assigned to another register r' **then**
6:         Assign v to r'
7:         Return $\bot$
8:     **else**
9:         Let v' be the live range assigned to r
10:        Return the live range with the minimum cost among v and v'
11:    **end if**
12: **else if** v can be assigned to a free register r **then**
13:     Assign v to r
14:     Return $\bot$
15: **else**
16:     Return v' with the lowest cost among v and the other live ranges at the current point
17: **end if**
Return: a live range to spill or $\bot$

2.2   The ILP Model

Here, we discuss our formulation of spilling in register allocation as an ILP problem. We obtain spilling decisions offline and pass this information to the online compilation phase using annotations. Considering a set S of live ranges, a *spill set* of S is any subset S' of S such that $S \setminus S'$ can be allocated over the R registers (without spilling). We also consider a function which assigns to each live range in S the cost of spilling it. The cost of a spill set is the sum of the costs of live ranges within that set. An optimal register allocation is associated with a spill set with the minimal cost.

We build an ILP model that is optimal among spill-everywhere, single-color allocations, for a given cost model.

We model register allocation as a $\{0, 1\}$ linear program, the objective function being the cost of the spill set. We support multiple classes of registers, each register class is further decomposed into 2 subclasses: caller-saved (scratch register) and callee-saved (non-scratch register). Live ranges are partitioned according to register classes, and can be of the *volatile*, *non-volatile* or *preassigned* kinds: a *non*-volatile live range can only be assigned to some callee-saved register, and a preassigned live range can only be assigned to a specific physical register.

We create a $\{0, 1\}$ variable l_r for each live range l and register r that l may be assigned to (considering class and volatility constraints):

$$l_r = 1 \text{ if and only if } l \text{ is assigned to } r.$$

These variables are constrained by 3 kinds of (in)equalities.

1. At most one register per live range (single color assignment):

$$\sum_{1 \le r \le R} l_r \le 1.$$

2. Interfering live ranges cannot be assigned to the same register: $l_r + l'_r \le 1$.
3. The third constraint states that if a live range l interferes with a live range l' preassigned to r, then $l_r = 0$.

2.3   Annotation Semantics

The offline stage generates annotations that can be used by an online stage to characterize important properties of some live ranges. The online stage may run on a target that may not match what was used to generate the annotations in the offline stage. This triggers portability problems: we address register count variations in this section, and defer the discussion of other problems to Section 4.

In the context of register allocation, the most specific portability issue is related to variations in the number of registers. To define portable annotations, it would be ideal to prove a general result about the inclusion of an optimal spill set for a given number of physical registers into one of the optimal spill sets for a lower number of registers. Unfortunately, this is not true in general. Figure 1 shows a counter example on the allocation of 5 live ranges — the horizontal bars. Every number on top of a horizontal bar denotes the cost of spilling the corresponding live range. Dashed black lines correspond to spilled live ranges. For the left graph, we assume $R = 2$ registers. For the graph on the right, $R = 1$ register only. When $R = 2$, we may optimally spill i_3 to assign i_1 and i_4 to one register and to assign i_2 and i_5 to the another one. When $R = 1$, the single optimal allocation is to spill i_2 and i_4 and to assign i_1, i_3 and i_5 to the single register. In this example we see clearly that an optimal spill set for two registers is not included in the optimal spill set for one register.

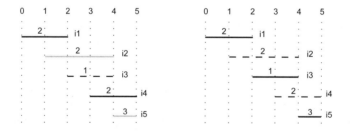

Fig. 1. Counter example to spill set inclusion

Although such an inclusion property does not always hold, we experimentally validated that only few live ranges should be spilled for $R + 1$ registers but allocated for R registers. For example, considering the x86 instruction-set architecture, when moving incrementally by one register from the minimum number of registers, to a spill-free[2] number of registers for each method, inclusion property was violated for only 0.13% of the live ranges over the whole SPEC JVM

---

[2] Until we reach a number of register for which allocation can be done without spilling.

suite. This validates the intuition that the semantics of an allocate/spill-oriented annotation is portable across variations in the register count.

2.4 The Offline Procedure

Our split register allocation procedure derives from three key observations.

1. First, once the ILP solver finds an optimal spill set, it would be possible to directly annotate the code with the best spill set. This can lead to annotation bloat (although linear), with total annotation size potentially larger than the bytecode itself. Jones and Kamin do not address the problem [5].
2. Second, the more detailed the annotation, the more sensitive it is to low-level decisions on instruction selection and scheduling that may happen after register allocation. To make the annotation portable, it is important to focus it on semantic properties that preserve the essence of the offline optimization while maximizing independence w.r.t. post-pass optimizations in the online compilation stage. The idea here is to focus the annotation on long live ranges whose interferences do not vary much w.r.t. post-register allocation instruction selection and scheduling. Indeed, short live ranges are likely to be allocated due to their limited interferences and high-rate register usage.
3. Third, notice that a greedy allocation algorithm is typically too conservative, allocating a live range that should have been spilled or assigning an inappropriate register/color. This means that annotations should only pertain to "must-spill" information.

With those three observations in mind, we devised Algorithm 3. The intuition behind this algorithm is natural: why store annotations for live ranges on which a greedy, linear procedure can readily make the right decision?

The algorithm uses an oracle-driven version of the linear scan. Every time the greedy heuristic wishes to spill a live range which does not belong to the annotations, the algorithm forces it to spill a live range which is currently active and which belongs to the annotations. By doing so, we discover live ranges in the optimal spill set that the linear scan *cannot* find on its own.

Considering Algorithm 3, at a step where live range $V(i)$ is active (according to the allocation performed since the beginning of the method being allocated), function ASSIGNORSUGGESTSPILLCANDIDATE($V(i)$) returns, either a live range or $\perp$ (bottom): if it returns a live range, it is the one to be spilled in order to continue allocation; if it returns $\perp$ it was possible to assign i without spilling. Function FINDACTIVELIVERANGE(*optimalSpills*) returns a currently active live range that is in the set *optimalSpills*, and set *annotation* records live ranges that will not be found by the linear scan.

The algorithm returns live ranges that will not be optimally allocated by the linear scan and keeps those as the constituents for the compressed annotations.

The final step consists of pairing the live ranges returned by Algorithm 3 with a "must-spill" tag. This pairing should be as economical as possible to represent, but it should also make sense across different targets and carry relevant allocation

---

Algorithm 3. COMPRESSANNOTATION

Input: *list*: the list of basic intervals ordered by increasing start point
Input: *optimalSpills*: the set of live ranges to be spilled as decided by the optimal allocator
1: *annotation* ← ⊥
2: **foreach:** $i \in list$ **do**
3:     *toSpill* ← ASSIGNORSUGGESTSPILLCANDIDATE($V(i)$)
4:     **if** *toSpill* ≠ ⊥ **then**
5:         **if** *toSpill* ∉ *optimalSpills* **then**
6:             *toSpill* ← FINDACTIVELIVERANGE(*optimalSpills*)
7:             *annotation* ← *annotation* ∪ *toSpill*
8:         **end if**
9:         **if** *toSpill* ≠ $V(i)$ **then**
10:             Assign $V(i)$ to the register freed by *toSpill*
11:         **end if**
12:         Spill live range *toSpill*
13:     **end if**
14: **end for**
Return: *annotation*: the compressed annotations

---

information. For each live range l, we compute the maximal value of R for which l must be spilled, denoting it as $R_{\max}(l)$. We do not care much about offline compilation time in this study: the computation thus boils down to iterating the ILP model over decreasing values of R, pre-spilling live ranges spilled at the previous step (for $R + 1$ register) to guarantee inclusion.

Finally, annotated live ranges need to be stored in a compact persistent format, together with the bytecode program. Rather than storing every pair $(i, R_{\max}(l))$, we cluster live ranges with the same value of $R_{\max}(l)$, sort those clusters, and serialize the list of live ranges in every cluster, prepending each cluster's list with the corresponding value of $R_{\max}(l)$. We end up with separate strings, one for each size s of the register set, listing the live ranges that must be spilled for s registers and that were *not* already listed in a string associated with size s' greater than s. This way, most of the space is used to store live range names, for which we conservatively count up to 4 bytes per live range.

2.5   The Online Procedure

The online stage performs allocation based on a compact spill set collected by the offline stage, and carried as bytecode annotations.

Our online algorithm follows the steps of Algorithm 1. In addition, at every basic interval beginning, it checks whether the corresponding live range is present in the annotation. *If so, then spill it* (if the live range was not previously spilled).

This algorithm takes its roots in the decoupled allocation/assignment approach. As our experiments will confirm, the annotation-enhanced linear scan algorithm results in a much better quality allocation. Yet it does not optimally preserve the information available in the annotation and may yield spurious spill code. The reason is simple: register *assignment* on a colorable (spill-free) graph is equivalent to a graph coloring decision problem, which is NP-complete on live ranges [1]. It is *not* NP-complete with sufficient live-range splitting: linear complexity can be achieved on SSA form following a perfect elimination order — a greedy reverse post-order traversal of the SSA graph [6]. It is clearly the way to

---

Algorithm 4. ONLINEALLOCATION

Input: *list*: the list of basic intervals sorted in increasing start point
Input: *annotation*: a set of annotated live ranges
1: **foreach:** $i \in list$ **do**
2: **if** $V(i)$ is not spilled **then**
3:    **if** $V(i) \in annotation$ **then**
4:      Spill $V(i)$
5:    **else**
6:      ASSIGNORSUGGESTSPILLCANDIDATE($V(i)$)
7:    **end if**
8: **end if**
9: **end for**
Return: sets of spilled live ranges and register assignments

---

go for optimality preservation, but it also implies a major engineering endeavor that has not yet been undertaken in a full-scale JIT compiler. Fortunately, the interference graphs that arise in non-SSA code are "mostly" chordal [7], which guarantees the existence of a perfect elimination order in most cases; this motivates the decoupled approach and explains the observed quality of our online algorithm.

3   Experimental Evaluation

We implemented split register allocation in JikesRVM version 3.0.1 [4], relying on CPLEX[3] for the offline resolution of optimal allocation problems.

3.1   Methodology

To assess the cost of a spill, we need to define the optimal solution we are aiming for. The cost model of the spill-everywhere problem is implemented in JikesRVM; it combines dynamic edge profiling, static use count and instruction type.

We illustrate split register allocation on SPEC JVM benchmarks. Experiments on the DaCapo benchmarks [8] could not be included at the time of the submission, but we are working hard on it. We target a 2.67GHz Intel Core 2 Quad, running in 32-bit mode, in a PC platform. This configuration is favorable to register allocation experiments due to the low number of registers, although the cost of spilling is often marginal due to out-of-order execution and to the sophisticated memory hierarchy.

Each figure was obtained from 100 individual runs of the benchmark, eliminating the 10% best and 10% worst performing points. We did not conduct a systematic statistical study of the performance distribution. Instead, we eliminated the largest source of variation by selecting a non-adaptive, aggressive (maximal optimization), profile-directed strategy (with embedded replay), using the following compilation flags:

```
-Xmx1024M -Xms1024M -X:irc:O3 -X:aos:enable_recompilation=false -X:aos:initial_compiler=opt
-X:aos:enable_replay_compile=true -X:vm:edgeCounterFile=my_edge_counter_file
```

---

[3] http://www.ilog.com/products/cplex

Split compilation is of course compatible with adaptive optimization. This methodology differs from the standard practices in that we do not run an adaptive compilation scheme [8,9]. We claim our methodology is relevant in the context of split compilation:

- it eliminates the instability triggered by monitoring-based decisions, allowing to focus on the effect of the register allocation itself;
- an adaptive execution methodology is needed to compare the relative contributions of JIT-compilation, monitoring, garbage collection, and the effect of the optimizations themselves [9]; our methodology allows for a fair comparison nonetheless, since the online stage of the split allocation does not introduce significant overhead w.r.t. the original linear scan implementation.

Thanks to its Java API, it was easy to connect CPLEX to our framework. The total resolution time for the optimal register allocation of all SPEC JVM benchmarks — running with aggressive optimization including inlining and unrolling — takes less than 4 minutes on a Core 2 Quad processor at 2.67GHz with 4GB of RAM.

3.2   Performance Results

Table 1 illustrates the effectiveness of the annotation compression scheme: it shows the total number of live ranges (*Live ranges*); the effective number of live ranges within the annotations (*Annotations*); the *Annotations/Live ranges* ratio (*Compression*, in percentage); the number of live ranges within the optimal spill sets (*Optimal spill set*); the *Annotations/Optimal Spill set* ratio (*Remaining spills*, in percentage); and the size overhead w.r.t. the bytecode itself (*Bytecode*, in percentage, counting 4 bytes per annotation).

Table 1. Annotation compression

Benchmark	check	compress	jess	raytrace	db	javac	mpegaudio	mtrt	jack
Live ranges	86672	86870	181396	122993	93055	406348	127847	122755	220871
Annotations	77	105	214	191	98	685	315	195	236
Compression %	0.09%	0.12%	0.12%	0.16%	0.11%	0.17%	0.26%	0.16%	0.11%
Optimal spill set	2950	2984	6408	3765	3210	16821	3830	3877	6400
Remaining spills %	2.60 %	3.51%	3.34%	5.07%	3.05%	4.07%	8.23%	5.03%	3.69%
Bytecode %	0.9%	6.9%	0.9%	6.9%	3.4%	0.5%	0.9%	1.1%	0.6%

Preserving the information collected in the offline stage requires at most 0.26% of the live ranges to be annotated. This is several orders of magnitude more effective than state-of-the-art approaches [5], and even comes with a formal guarantee about optimality. The addition compression row reports the benefits of Algorithm 3, and confirm its important role in making the annotation size negligible w.r.t. the bytecode size.

Table 2 Considers the analytical cost model of JikesRVM as a metric. *All live ranges annotation* correspond to annotation produced by Algorithm 3; LIR^4 *live*

---

[4] Low-level Intermediate Representation of JikesRVM, which does not include yet all the characteristics of the target architecture.

Table 2. Allocation cost penalty compared to optimal

Benchmark	check	compress	jess	raytrace	db	javac	mpegaudio	mtrt	jack	average
Original JikesRVM	1.31	1.38	1.16	1.19	1.59	1.41	1.39	1.14	1.27	1.32
All live ranges Annotation	1.02	1.30	1	1.17	1.01	1.25	1.03	1.19	1.03	1.11
LIR live ranges Annotation	1.02	1.30	1	1.17	1.01	1.25	1.03	1.19	1.03	1.11
Java local variables Annotation	1.25	1.44	1.02	1.19	1.59	1.36	1.32	1.13	1.18	1.28

Table 3. Wall-clock speedups of split register allocation

Benchmark	check	compress	jess	raytrace	db	javac	mpegaudio	mtrt	jack	average
All live ranges Annotation	0%	12.0%	-1.0%	0.9%	-0.4%	-0.6%	7.5%	1.2%	0.2%	2.2%
LIR live ranges Annotation	0%	12.1%	0.2%	1.0%	-0.3%	-0.7%	5.1%	1.1%	0.2%	2.1%
Java local variables Annotation	0%	5.1%	0.8%	0.0%	-0.3%	-0.2%	-1.4%	1.1%	-0.3%	0.4%

ranges annotation correspond to the intersection between the set of live ranges present in the LIR and *all live ranges annotation*; *Java local variables annotation* correspond the set of Java local variables present in *all live ranges annotation*. Table 2 shows the penalty of using the *Original JikesRVM* (linear scan), *All live ranges annotation*, *LIR live ranges annotation* and *Java local variable annotation* methods in terms of percentage of the optimal spill cost achieved by the ILP model. The JikesRVM linear-scan misses the optimal cost by 32% on average, whereas the split allocation only incurs a 11% average penalty. The case for annotation portability is validated by the very close figures for the full annotation (All live ranges) and the LIR-only annotation (*LIR live ranges*). However, when only annotating Java variables, the annotation loses its effectiveness. Using the LIR-only annotation appears as the best performance/portability trade-off.

Considering wall-clock execution time as a metric (JIT compilation plus execution time), Table 3 shows the speedup of split register allocation w.r.t. original JikesRVM's allocation algorithm. In most cases, the speedup is consistent between the optimal and split approaches. Nevertheless, the annotation does not help much on some benchmarks like javac. The strong improvement in the corresponding column in Table 2 indicates that the cost model itself misses the complex interplay between optimizations and important components of the target architecture.

3.3 Portability Across Variations of the Register Count

We showed there is no formal inclusion property among optimal spill sets in general. Nevertheless, for every method and among millions of live ranges, we varied R from a minimum equal to the number of pre-allocated physical registers for the method to the spill-free number of registers. Through all these allocation problems only 0.13% of the intervals spilled for $R + 1$ registers did not belong to the optimal spill set for R registers.

To make the annotation portable across variations in the register count, the compression algorithm must not eliminate a live interval that may be useless for a given number of registers but useful for a smaller number of registers. We thus run Algorithm 3 on $R = R_{\min}$ registers, where $R_{\min}$ is the minimal number of registers to enable code generation on the target.

4 Looking Forward

So far, we ignored important issues related with the practical applicability of split register allocation.

4.1 Portability of the Annotation

Let us first consider the portability of annotation names. The names of the annotated live ranges must remain consistent between the two stages. Some annotations may be missing or extraneous, but an annotation designating a live range during the offline stage must designate to the same live range during the online stage. There are practical solutions for most portability scenarios.

1. The majority of live ranges correspond to java variables, locations in the operand stack, and other live ranges synthesized in the intermediate, target-independent passes of JikesRVM (the LIR). For those live ranges, a non-ambiguous name can be crafted that is independent of the execution context when the JIT compiler is triggered.

2. A fraction of live ranges are synthesized along the target-dependent compilation flow: address computation temporaries, conditional predicates, etc. We discard annotations regarding those live ranges when compiling for another instruction-set architecture (ISA).[5] Fortunately, besides representing a small minority, these live ranges also feature a very short temporal locality and a low degree of interference with other live ranges. This reduces the chances of impacting an important allocation decision that would result in a significant performance difference. Indeed, we showed that annotation associated with target-dependent live ranges have negligible impact on performance.

Besides the live range names, annotation properties themselves need to be portable over multiple targets: liveness properties may vary significantly over the targets if no assumption is made on the optimization flow. To achieve portability, we thus make one important assumption: optimizations selected by different JIT compilers must not vary significantly *before* the pass where annotations are loaded and attached to the intermediate representation. This restriction does not impact target-specific, post-register allocation passes like instruction selection and local scheduling.

This restriction does not solve all portability problems: reusing annotations across ISAs remains an issue. There are multiple reasons to be optimistic. Some of these are due to the context in which JIT compilation is employed, and some to the nature of the optimizations being performed before register allocation:

– Embedded system designs value the code compression and safety benefits of bytecode languages, but do not stress portability to the extreme. Although many processors and hardware configurations may exist, Java or CLI applications are likely to run on some variant of the ARM instruction set. Varying

---

[5] Such annotations remain usable when varying the register count (or the calling convention) for a given ISA.

the number of registers is important to support the ARM's compact instruction encoding options, and to support extensions like vector instructions of ARM NEON. On general-purpose platforms, an analogous situation holds, with portability issues from the 32 and 64 bit variants of the x86 instruction set, different vector instruction sets and sizes, etc.

- Bytecode languages are important for link-time optimization. Complex software architectures built of thousands of independently designed components bring many opportunities for inter-module optimization at link-time. Again, the ISA portability issue is only secondary to many of these applications.
- Beyond ISA portability, bytecode languages are used for operating system portability. In this case, the JIT compiler is minimally impacted, and annotations are expected to be robust to changes to the underlying OS.
- Eventually, the software provider may easily specialize the offline stage to generate annotations for a particular family of targets and for a particular optimization flow, tagging the annotated bytecode accordingly. This consists of constructing a (lossless) union annotation considering all live ranges that occur when compiling to the different targets. Since many live ranges will remain the same (e.g., those associated with Java local variables and constant pool, as opposed to operand stack or target-specific temporaries), the union will not significantly increase the size of the annotation.

4.2   Separate Compilation

Realistic compilation scenarios will run the offline stage separately on the different modules of the application and on its library dependences. This raises a modularity problem for any annotation-based online compilation approach.

In the context of object-oriented and functional languages, function inlining is of utmost importance to reach performance levels on par with lower level imperative implementations. It raises the following dilemma:

- what is the point of annotating code in functions that will later be inlined, since the effective interference graph will only be known after inlining;
- what is the point of annotating functions whose calling context heavily influences the internal control flow, hence the spill costs?

Our approach to modular split compilation is twofold.

No performance regression. First of all, if one module depends on a module without annotations (such as a package form the Java Development Kit), only the code in the annotated module will benefit from split compilation. This is not ideal, but not worse than the usual penalty of separate compilation in offline, static compilers. Conversely, when optimizing a "library" module, it is always possible to run a *context-insensitive* split-compilation flow, relying on a representative execution profile; this again is consistent with the traditional way of optimizing libraries in static compilation.

Multiversioning for cross-boundary optimization. Nevertheless, JIT compilation opens many opportunities for *link-time optimization*, and JIT compilers for object-oriented and functional languages do implement such advanced techniques, effectively optimizing across module boundaries (e.g., across application-library boundaries). Split register allocation is possible in this context.

First of all, a *context-sensitive annotation* of the callee can be tuned according to the most frequent calling context(s). This is only impactful when the costs of the live ranges depend on the calling context, which may be the case when the callee contains complex, data-dependent control-flow.

A more aggressive approach consists in generating multiple versions of the annotations for the most frequent call trees. For example, if a library method m_2 is frequently called from an application method m_1, the offline stage of the split register allocation may inline m_2 into m_1, optimize the resulting new method, and generate the annotation for it. This specialized version of the inlined methods can later be checked for consistency with the dynamic execution context (indeed, the library code may have changed in the mean time, or dynamic class loading may have occurred), and used directly in favor of performing all the optimizations online and dropping the (irrelevant) per-method annotation. Practical ways to implement this scheme have been proposed in the QuickSilver project [10]. This scheme has all the benefits of running a JIT compiler offline (better optimizations, lower overhead) while preserving modularity (up to dynamic class loading) and the effectiveness of split compilation.

5   Related Work

Annotations are an optional part of the Java bytecode specification from the start and are part of the *class file attributes*. They have been used in debugging and integrated development environments. Syntactic support has been added in recent versions of Java. The same applies to the ECMA-335 CLI.

Interestingly, annotation-driven JIT compilation was first directed to register allocation, with the pioneering work of Azevedo et al. [11]. This work demonstrated how to achieve performance competitive with native priority-based graph coloring allocation. Jones and Kamin [5] extended their virtual register allocation approach, dealing with correctness, calling conventions and portability (addressing variations of the number of physical registers only).

The *split compilation* term was first coined in the context of JIT vectorization [12]. Split register allocation improves on Jones and Kamin's annotation-driven approach by leveraging the decoupled allocation (spilling) and assignment (coloring) phases of register allocation. Decoupled register allocation is the key to the compactness and the portability of our annotation. The intuition behind decoupled register allocation is that the assignment problem (mapping of variables to registers with no additional spill) is very easy, as long as the cost of live-range splitting (the introduction or register moves) is neglected. This intuition is backed by the important property that spill-free assignment is always possible if the maximal number of simultaneously live variables (MaxLive) is lower than the number of available registers. The online stage can rely on the colorability guarantee inherited from the offline stage through the annotation: these strong ties between the offline and online stages are specific to *split compilation* algorithms, as opposed to classical annotation-driven JIT compilation.

A fully decoupled approach has been used by Appel and George [13], and studied in the context of SSA-based register allocation [7,14,15]. Notice that recent versions of the linear scan algorithm are capable of live range splitting [16,17]; they are implicitly based on this decoupled approach. This is not the case for the linear scan implemented in JikesRVM, and leads in practice to spurious spills (to our disadvantage), as we confirmed in our evaluation.

Pominiville et al. [18] used annotations to mitigate the performance penalty of Java pointers and arrays, and designed a generic annotation-driven compilation framework (Soot). Eventually, Krintz and Calder [3] proposed a comprehensive method to reduce the compilation time overhead through bytecode annotations, enabling rapid method selection and optimization selection, and precomputing simple method statistics.

Several papers address two additional important questions related to register allocation in JIT compilers: is there any room for performance improvement, and is it important to use a linear-time allocation algorithm? Cavazos provides an original answer relying on adaptive optimization [19]. Annotation-enhanced versions of this method would be worth investigating.

When using annotations for optimization, safety issues immediately arise because of incorrect or malicious uses. Solutions can be found in proof-carrying code [20], encryption, or correct-by construction annotation designs. We choose the latter approach, relying on annotations whose misuse can at worst lead to performance degradations.

6 Conclusion

We designed a split compilation framework dedicated to register allocation. We experimentally validated the effectiveness of split register allocation and its portability with respect to register count variations, relying on annotations whose impact on the bytecode size is negligible. This combination of results is a strong improvement over the state of the art. It was made possible by revisiting the decoupling of the spilling and coloring (a.k.a. assignment) phases.

Nevertheless, the approach still depends on the stability of the upstream optimization flow in the JIT compiler. Although this restriction is acceptable in a majority of use cases, it would be useful to design a split register allocation framework that would be more robust to changes in the optimization flow. One direction of work consists in revisiting the context of pre-pass allocation to control register-pressure by inserting additional constraints in the data dependence graph [21]. This would accommodate for scheduling (local and global) changes, and possibly for code motion, redundancy elimination and hoisting as well. Beyond register allocation, we would like to investigate the potential of split compilation through the development, debugging and optimization cycle of software development.

References

1. Chaitin, G.J., Auslander, M.A., Cocke, A.K.C.J., Hopkins, M.E., Markstein, P.W.: Register allocation via coloring. Computer languages 6, 47–57 (1981)
2. Briggs, P., Cooper, K.D., Torczon, L.: Improvements to graph coloring register allocation. ACM Trans. Program. Lang. Syst. 16(3), 428–455 (1994)
3. Krintz, C., Calder, B.: Using annotations to reduce dynamic optimization time. In: PLDI 2001, pp. 156–167. ACM Press, New York (2001)
4. Alpern, B., et al.: The Jikes RVM project: Building an open source research community. IBM Systems Journal 44(2), 399–418 (2005)
5. Jones, J., Kamin, S.N.: Annotating java class files with virtual registers for performance. Concurrency – Practice and Experience 12(6), 389–406 (2000)
6. Bouchez, F., Darte, A., Rastello, F.: On the complexity of spill everywhere under ssa form. In: LCTES 2007, pp. 103–112 (2007)
7. Pereira, F.M.Q., Palsberg, J.: Register allocation via coloring of chordal graphs. In: Yi, K. (ed.) APLAS 2005. LNCS, vol. 3780, pp. 315–329. Springer, Heidelberg (2005)
8. Blackburn, S.M.: The dacapo benchmarks: java benchmarking development and analysis. In: OOPSLA 2006, pp. 169–190. ACM, New York (2006)
9. Georges, A., Eeckhout, L., Buytaert, D.: Java performance evaluation through rigorous replay compilation. SIGPLAN Not. 43(10), 367–384 (2008)
10. Serrano, M., Bordawekar, R., Midkiff, S., Gupta, M.: Quicksilver: A quasi-static compiler for java. In: OOPSLA 2000 (2000)
11. Azevedo, A., Nicolau, A., Hummel, J.: Java annotation-aware just-in-time (ajit) compilation system. In: Proc. ACM 1999 Conf. on Java Grande, pp. 142–151 (1999)
12. Lesnicki, P., Cohen, A., Cornero, M., Fursin, G., Ornstein, A., Rohou, E.: Split compilation: an application to just-in-time vectorization. In: GREPS 2007, Brasov, Romania (September 2007)
13. Appel, A.W., George, L.: Optimal spilling for CISC machines with few registers. In: PLDI 2001, Snowbird, Utah, USA, June 2001, pp. 243–253. ACM Press, New York (2001)
14. Hack, S., Grund, D., Goos, G.: Register allocation for program s in SSA-form. In: Mycroft, A., Zeller, A. (eds.) CC 2006. LNCS, vol. 3923, pp. 247–262. Springer, Heidelberg (2006)
15. Bouchez, F., Darte, A., Guillon, C., Rastello, F.: Register allocation: What does the NP-completeness proof of Chaitin et al. really prove? In: Almási, G.S., Caşcaval, C., Wu, P. (eds.) KSEM 2006. LNCS, vol. 4382, pp. 283–298. Springer, Heidelberg (2007)
16. Wimmer, C., Mössenböck, H.: Optimized interval splitting in a linear scan register allocator. In: VEE 2005, pp. 132–141. ACM, New York (2005)
17. Sarkar, V., Barik, R.: Extended linear scan: An alternate foundation for global register allocation. In: Krishnamurthi, S., Odersky, M. (eds.) CC 2007. LNCS, vol. 4420, pp. 141–155. Springer, Heidelberg (2007)
18. Pominville, P., Qian, F., Vallée-Rai, R., Hendren, L.J., Verbrugge, C.: A framework for optimizing java using attributes. In: Wilhelm, R. (ed.) CC 2001. LNCS, vol. 2027, pp. 334–354. Springer, Heidelberg (2001)
19. Cavazos, J., Moss, J.E.B., Boyle, M.F.O.: Hybrid optimizations: Which optimization algorithm to use? In: Mycroft, A., Zeller, A. (eds.) CC 2006. LNCS, vol. 3923, pp. 124–138. Springer, Heidelberg (2006)
20. Necula, G.: Proof-carrying code. In: PoPL 1997 (January 1997)
21. Touati, S., Eisenbeis, C.: Early periodic register allocation on ilp processors. Parallel Processing Letters 14(2) (June 2004)

Trace-Based Data Layout Optimizations for Multi-core Processors

Olga Golovanevsky[1], Alon Dayan[1], Ayal Zaks[1], and David Edelsohn[2]

[1] IBM Haifa Research Laboratory
{olga,alond,zaks}@il.ibm.com
[2] IBM Watson Research Center
edelsohn@us.ibm.com

Abstract. The focus of this paper is on cache-conscious data layout optimizations. Although these optimizations have already been adopted by industrial compilers, they were shown to be inefficient for multi-process[1] applications on multi-core platforms. Such factors as asymmetric distribution of processes over hardware resources (cores, cpus or hardware threads), along with their temporal migrations, unpredictably influence optimization results. Herein we present a new methodology that extends classical data layout optimizations to support multi-core architectures. Based on data trace collection that reflects actual interleaving of data accesses, this method aims to improve spatial locality of the data, while mitigating potential false sharing events. Introduction of architectural characteristics into an analysis phase further increases the accuracy of data affinity estimation. Feasibility study of this method, applied to multi-process webserver *lighttpd* on Power5 machine, not only showed performance improvement, but also proved its suitability for incorporation into an industrial compiler.

Keywords: Compiler optimizations, cache-conscious data layout, spatial locality, false sharing, data affinity.

1 Motivation

Prevalent number of data layout optimizations aim to increase data cache locality by fitting a data layout to the access pattern exposed in the program. Research studies on this subject already have a long history. Although numerous frameworks were developed [20], [21], [10], [24], [16], only a few of them found their place in modern industrial compilers, like IBM XL [4], [5], multi-backend GCC [6], [7], Open64 for x86 processors [8].

The analysis adopted in these compilers is mostly static, feedback directed and inter-procedural. They estimate the affinity of data accesses by mapping them against Control Flow Graph (CFG). Connected by the CFG edges, program data accesses form a directed graph, which can be weighted with execution

---

[1] The content of this paper is equally relevant for threads and processes, but in order to avoid repetitions, we usually mention only processes.

Y.N. Patt et al. (Eds.): HiPEAC 2010, LNCS 5952, pp. 81–95, 2010.

frequencies, received from profiling, or statically estimated. Shrinking this graph into a contracted graph, where nodes represent data objects or types, allows using its edges as numerical estimation of affinity between nodes. Optimal data layout is concluded directly from the contracted graph. Variations of this analysis consider only data accesses that happen in loops [8], [9], [10], other works count only hot accesses. In absence of profile information, execution frequencies can be estimated statically from branch prediction [30]. In addition, the data access cache miss rate can be used to weight graph edges, if provided in profile information [9].

Although data layout optimizations showed performance improvement on such benchmark suites as SPEC2000 [11] and SPEC2006 [12], the number of technical reports that justify their efficiency for real world applications is minor. This fact can be partially attributed to immaturity of inter-procedural analysis mechanism, such as GCC LTO [13] or SYZYGY [9], but apparently it indicates a discrepancy between these optimizations in their current state and combination of modern hardware and applications.

Our experience with a contemporary webserver application, *lighttpd* [2], presented in Section 3.1, confirms this assumption. When two data layout optimizations, namely structure peeling plus indexing [7] and structure reordering [15], [16], [6] were applied to *lighttpd* data structures, they showed improvement for single-process *lighttpd* (two leftmost bars on Fig. 4a), while for other *lighttpd* configurations their influence was mixed.

Evidently multi-core machines, running multi-threaded or multi-process applications, present a challenge for classical data layout optimizations. Leaving the transformation part of these optimizations intact, they significantly influence the method of data affinity estimation. The same statically estimated data access can belong to different processes, as well as run on different cpus, cores, or, in the presence of Simultaneous Multithreading (SMT), hardware threads. Scheduler decisions on distribution and migration of processes even further mix the order of data accesses. Additional complexity in the estimation of data affinity is introduced by the effect of false sharing, caused by cache coherence policy.

All these factors require modern data layout optimizations to capture and analyze the actual interleaving of data accesses ([27], [26]). Although the importance of collecting data traces was already recognized, we reconsider it with the following two requirements: (1) efficiency for multi-core processors, running multi-process applications, and (2) suitability for incorporation into a compiler. As a result, we developed a new methodology for data affinity estimation that satisfies both (1) and (2), and applied it to the *lighttpd* webserver.

(1) was achieved by extending data trace format and analysis with processor specific characteristics. In addition to the standard fields in the trace record, we introduced a *hardware thread id* field, indicating on which hardware thread the process was running when the record was written. We developed a data trace analysis algorithm that estimates the optimal data affinity by increasing spacial locality, while mitigating potential false sharing events. We extended this algorithm with such architectural parameters as the number

of CPUs, the number of cores per CPU, and the number of hardware threads per core. We incorporated this algorithm into the classical data layout optimization schema, described in Section 2.

(2) is guaranteed by small traces, collected by our method, relatively to the traces, even sampled [21], required for reuse distance [17], [18] and k-distance [19] analysis, as well as for heap optimization techniques [22], [29], [23]. Linearity of data trace analysis algorithm also contributes to (2).

Obviously other techniques have already targeted the problem of upgrading data layout optimizations to handle the multi-core, multi-process case. Raman et al. [25] suggested infusing basic blocks concurrency information, captured by a performance monitoring tool, into the static analysis model. In the area of objects pooling optimizations, Sarkar and Tullsen [23] extended the queue-based Temporal Relationship Graph, suggested by Calder et al. [29], to concurrent execution of applications. In comparison, our methodology requires no external tool assistance, and can be integrated into the compilation schema in the way similar to profiling.

Finally, we applied this methodology to the *lighttpd* webserver. We estimated affinity of two data structures, namely **server** and **connection**, and on the basis of the estimation results, applied to them a structure reordering data layout transformation. In spite of the fact that reordering is usually less effective than other structure layout transformations [9], and the *lighttpd* webserver is not a memory bound application, we received improvement in both L1 and L2 cache miss rates and the application run time on Power5 platform [3]. Moreover, this improvement persisted as we increased the number of *lighttpd* processes.

The rest of this paper presents our methodology (Section 2) and experimental results (Section 3). In Section 2.1 we describe an enriched trace format and its generation process. Trace Traversal Algorithm (Section 2.2) that comprises our methodology of architecture-specific affinity estimation (Section 2.4) occupies the rest of Section 2. Our experimental results are based on an implementation of this algorithm for Power5 architecture (Section 3.2). We draw conclusions and explain perspectives of this research work in Section 4.

2 Methodology

As described in Section 1, classical data layout optimizations are comprised of the following three stages:

For each data **type**[2]:

1. Estimate the affinity between accesses of **type** components.
2. Derive the affinity between **type** components from 1 above.
3. Derive the layout of the **type** from 2 above.

---

[2] Our methodology is equally relevant for data **objects** and data **types**, but for simplicity of description in the rest of this paper we mention only data **types**, or simply **types**. C-language *struct* construct is an example of data **type** and variable of **type** *struct* is an example of data **object**.

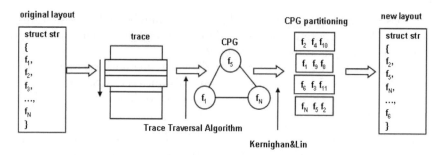

Fig. 1. Trace-based data layout optimization process

Our methodology follows the same schema, but implements it differently. In the classical schema, 1., sometimes combined with 2., is usually a static analysis, optionally enriched with profiling information. Hagog et al. [6] built Fields Reference Graph (FRG) that represents distances between fields references, measured in the number of statically estimated memory accesses that happen between them. Shen et al. [4] explored frequency-based affinity. Chakrabarti et al. [8] combined frequency of execution with loop-based affinity. Hundt et al. [9] also used loop-based affinity, but enhanced it with a number of factors, including even the cache miss rate.

Our methodology combines stages 1. and 2., and uses a trace of data accesses for their implementation. Using a data trace essentially simplifies the static analysis required for data layout optimizations, especially the complicated case of analyzing hierarchies of structures (though an analysis that guarantees the safety of data layout transformations, such as type-escape analysis [9],[7], is still required). Data trace is collected for each data type separately. Only records generated by accesses of the type under consideration are collected, bypassing all other data accesses in the program. Therefore it is by an order of magnitude smaller than traces collected for such techniques as reuse distance [17], [18], or k-distance analysis [19], which gather all data accesses in the program. A trace we collect expresses the mutual closeness between accesses of type components, without trying to simulate cache behavior, like in [29]. In addition, we extend the standard trace record format with the *hardware thread id* parameter to reflect multi-core architecture with SMT.

We build a graph, called Close Proximity Graph (CPG) in [6], with type components as its nodes. Its edges are weighted with pairwise affinity between the components they connect. We traverse the trace with time- or size-window. By comparing trace records, we increase or decrease affinity weights between the corresponding type components, depending on a number of factors, such as closeness of trace records in trace, kind of type under consideration (shared or private to process), location of execution (a processor/a cpu/a core/a hardware thread). *Examples 1-3* (Table 1) illustrate our trace record comparison principles for Power5 architecture[3](Fig. 3). This is different from the construction of the

---

[3] In our methodology we overlook an existence of L3 cache in Power5 architecture, because it is a victim cache.

Table 1. Examples of affinity estimation for Power5 architecture (Fig. 3). *str* is a structure type that might be shared by a number of processes. It contains fields f_1 and f_2 . r_1, r_2 are two trace records from the trace generated for the *str* type. The records r_1 and r_2 belong to different processes p_1, p_2, but access fields f_1 and f_2 of the same instance of the structure type *str*.

Example 1.	Suppose records r_1, r_2 represent two *read* accesses. The process p_1 runs on hardware thread 0 (*ht0*) and the process p_2 executing on hardware thread 1 (*ht1*). If we put f_1 close to f_2 so that they fit into a common cache line, then bringing f_1 to L1, will also bring there f_2. In this case, if f_2 was already in L1 cache, then first *read* access to f_1 does not influence the *read* access to f_2. However, if f_2 was only in L2 cache or, was not in any cache, then accessing f_1 brings f_2 into L1 cache, thus saving L1 or L2 miss correspondingly. Therefore as a result of comparing r_1, r_2 records, we increase the weight between f_1 and f_2 fields, thus increasing probability of their closeness in structure *str* layout.
Example 2.	Suppose we have *read* after *write* accesses. The processes p_1 and p_2 are running on two different cores of the same CPU, for example, on *ht0* and *ht2*. Suppose also that f_1 and f_2 are closely located and can get into the same cache line. If f_2 was already in L1 cache, then a *write* access to f_1 invalidates a L1 cache line that contains f_2, and *read* access to f_2 results in an L1 miss. (This scenario corresponds to L1 false sharing event.) However, if f_2 was in L2 cache, but was not in L1, then a *write* access to f_1 brings the new value of f_2 into L2, and the *read* access to f_2 results in L2 hit. Finally, if f_2 was not even in L2 cache, then the *write* access to f_1 causes a subsequent L2 hit, when the f_2 *read* happens. Since winning an L2 hit is more valuable from the latency point of view than losing an L1 hit, in this case we still increase the weight of the (f_1,f_2) edge in the CPG, causing f_1 and f_2 fields to be positioned close in a *str* layout.
Example 3.	Similarly, let us consider the same scenario as in *Example 2.*, with processes p_1 and p_2 running on two different cores of two different CPUs, for example, on *ht0* and *ht4*. If f_2 was already in L1 or L2 cache of *cpu1*, then a *write* access to f_1 on *cpu0* causes invalidation of this cache line in L1 or L2 cache respectively (i.e. L2 false sharing event). The *read* access to f_2 inevitably causes an L2 miss. Consequently, we reduce the probability of this situation by decreasing the weight of the (f_1,f_2) edge, and thus placing them further apart in the *str* layout.

FRG in [6], where only positive contributions into affinity weights are counted, without considering negative factors, like potential false sharing events.

Finally, in 3. we partition CPG using the Kernighan and Lin algorithm [1], into strongly connected components of a cache line size, combining them into the final type layout. Fig. 1 presents step-by-step trace-based data layout optimization process.

As any feedback-directed optimization, our proposed methodology fits into two-compilations-one-execution schema. During the first compilation, we instrument the program to generate the data access trace. Then, by executing program, we generate the data trace. During the second compilation, we analyze the trace, apply the selected data layout transformation, and proceed with the rest of compilation.

2.1   Trace Generation

We instrument the program to generate a trace record at each data access of a component of the **type** under consideration. The trace records are written to a single stream shared by all program processes. The instrumentation happens on inter-procedural level, when the compiler Intermediate Representation (IR) is close to the source, and source level data types are fully preserved. Although there may be differences, caused by compiler optimizations, between real data accesses and those reflected in a trace, they are usually local. In our experience, a window-based nature of our Trace Traversal Algorithm mostly neutralizes these differences. Table 2 presents our trace record format.

Table 2. Trace Record Format

Field Name	Description
access_type	corresponds to *read* or *write* access
pid	is the process id
ht_id	is the hardware thread id
name	is the **type** component name, such as field name for structure types
size	is the component size in bytes
instance_id	is an instance id, e.g. the index number in an array of structures

2.2   Trace Traversal Algorithm

Our Trace Traversal Algorithm (Fig. 2) receives a trace and a window size as input parameters. A window size can be measured in number of records in a window or in time unit, if the trace record format is extended with time information.

2.3   Records Comparison Characteristics

The key point of our methodology is the principle of comparison between two records:

r_1: $access\_type_1$: pid_1: ht_id_1: $name_1$: $size_1$: $instance\_id_1$ and
r_2: $access\_type_2$: pid_2: ht_id_2: $name_2$: $size_2$: $instance\_id_2$.

It allows to fully exploit the richness of our trace format. The `compare_two_records` function, in addition to `record` and `new_record` input parameters, utilizes such hardware specific characteristics as:

- *cpu_num*, number of CPUs;
- *cores_per_cpu*, number of cores per each CPU;
- *ht_per_core*, number of hardware threads per each core.

Combinations of these parameters with the *hd_id* allow calculating *cpu_id* and *core_id* for each record in a trace, i.e. if we define

$$ht\_per\_cpu = cores\_per\_cpu \cdot ht\_per\_core,$$

```
Input: trace; window size (in time units or in number of records)
Output: CPG
trace_traversal_algorithm {
    initialize empty window;
    while (trace) {
        get new_record;
        for each record in window {
            compare_two_records (record, new_record);}
        insert new_record into the bottom of the window;
        remove record(s) from the top of the window to fit window size;}}
```

```
Input: r1, r2
Output: Wc1,c2
compare_two_records {
    if(!eq_component && eq_instance) { (1)
        if (!eq_ht) {
            update affinity of Wc1,c2
            according to the affinity coefficients;}
        else {
            increase the affinity of Wc1,c2 according to the value
            of eq_cpu=1, eq_core=1 coefficient;}}}
```

Fig. 2. Trace Traversal Algorithm with implementation of compare_two_records function for shared data type. $W_{c1,c2}$ is a contribution for the affinity weight in CPG between $name_1$ and $name_2$ components.

then

$$cpu\_id = \lfloor ht\_id/ht\_per\_cpu \rfloor,$$
$$core\_id = \lfloor (ht\_id \pmod{} ht\_per\_cpu)/ht\_per\_core \rfloor.$$

For each pair of records (r_1, r_2), we also calculate:

$$eq\_cpu = \begin{cases} 1, & \text{if } cpu\_id_1 == cpu\_id_2 \\ 0, & \text{otherwise} \end{cases}$$

where cpu_id_i is a cpu_id on which a record r_i was taken. Similarly, we define the following characteristic of a pair of records (r_1, r_2): eq_ht, eq_core, eq_pid, $eq\_component$, $eq\_instance$.

As it was shown in *Examples 1-3* (Table 1), the order of accesses and their types are critical for the understanding of the contribution of a pair (r_1, r_2) to the affinity weight between $name_1$ and $name_2$ components. We define these characteristics as WW, WR, RW and RR where the letters W and R denote write and read access types correspondingly, and their order reflects the order of records in the pair (r_1, r_2).

Depending on these characteristics, we decide on positive or negative contribution for an affinity weight between $name_1$ and $name_2$ components.

2.4   Calculating Affinity Coefficients

First, let us consider different combinations of these characteristics. Suppose two records r_1 and r_2 belong to a trace of a shared data type, and satisfy the following conditions: $eq\_component = 0$, $eq\_instance = 1$ and $eq\_ht = 0$. Then we distinguish between the following groups of cases: records were taken on the same core; different cores of the same CPU; and different CPUs. For each group, depending on the combination of record access types, we estimate the effect of the sequence (r_1, r_2) according to the following heuristic. We assume, with equal probabilities, that before the sequence (r_1, r_2) took place, the component, referenced in the second record r_2, was in the L1 cache, or in the L2 cache, or

Table 3. The influence of the pair (r_1, r_2) on affinity between $name_1$ and $name_2$ components (shared data type, $eq\_component = 0$, $eq\_instance = 1$, $eq\_ht = 0$).

$eq\_cpu=1$, $eq\_core=1$	RR, RW, WR and WW	Suppose both $name_1$ and $name_2$ components are co-located in the memory so that they fit into the same cache line. Since both ht_1 and ht_2 belong to the same core, the first access, whether *read* or *write*, inevitable brings a cache line that contains both $name_1$ and $name_2$ components into an L1 cache. Then depending on an initial location of a component $name_2$, we win or nothing, or an L1 miss, or L2 miss.
$eq\_cpu=1$, $eq\_core=0$	RR and RW	In this case, if $name_1$ and $name_2$ components fit to the same cache line, then uploading one of them into an L1 cache only uploads the second into the common L2 cache. (It happens because two accesses belong to the same CPU, but different cores.) On the other hand, since a first access is a *read*, it does not displace the component $name_2$ from an L1 or an L2 cache, if it was there before. Thus the only winning situation is when the component $name_2$ was in the memory before the sequence (r_1, r_2) took place.
$eq\_cpu=1$, $eq\_core=0$	WR and WW	This case is similar to the previous one, but since the first access is a *write*, it invalidates the cache line, that contains the $name_2$ component in the L1 cache in case it was there before. Thus the subsequent second access results in an L1 cache miss.
$eq\_cpu=0$	RR and RW	It is clear that when two accesses belong to two different CPUs, the first *read* access to the component $name_1$ does not affect the second access, regardless of the location of the cache line containing both $name_1$ and $name_2$ components, whether it is in L1, or L2 cache of the second CPU, or in the memory.
$eq\_cpu=0$	WR and WW	In this case, a first *write* access to the component $name_1$ invalidates the cache line, which contains both $name_1$ and $name_2$ components, in the second CPU, independently of whether the line was in L1 or L2 cache.

in the memory. Starting from one of these assumptions, we estimate, in terms of cache misses, how the first access (record r_1) influences the second access (record r_2), if they are located closely, i.e. fit into the same cache line. If the influence is positive, i.e. we can win cache misses by co-locating the components $name_1$, $name_2$, then we increase the affinity weight between them; otherwise we decrease it. Tables 3 and 4 illustrate this heuristic for Power5 architecture.

Table 4. Affinity coefficients for a pair (r_1, r_2), measured in L1 and L2 cache misses (shared data type, $eq\_component = 0$, $eq\_instance = 1$, $eq\_ht = 0$). + represent potential win, - - potential loss. Three addenda of the affinity value correspond to the different assumptions about initial location of the component $name_2$: in an L1 cache (the first addendum), in an L2 cache (the second addendum), or in the memory (the third addendum).

combination	$eq\_cpu = 1, eq\_core = 1$	$eq\_cpu = 1, eq\_core = 0$	$eq\_cpu = 0$
	no effect	no effect	no effect
RR	+ L1 miss	no effect	no effect
	+ L2 miss	+ L2 miss	no effect
	no effect	no effect	no effect
RW	+ L1 miss	no effect	no effect
	+ L2 miss	+ L2 miss	no effect
	no effect	- L1 miss	- L2 miss
WR	+ L1 miss	no effect	- L2 miss
	+ L2 miss	+ L2 miss	no effect
	no effect	- L1 miss	- L2 miss
WW	+ L1 miss	no effect	- L2 miss
	+ L2 miss	+ L2 miss	no effect

Additional advantage of this estimation is in its numerical value. Knowing latencies of cache miss events for a specific architecture, and giving equal probability to the three initial positions of $component_2$, we can estimate it as:

$$latency = \frac{1}{3} \cdot (latency_1 + latency_2 + latency_3),$$

where $latency_i$ is the latency of event i, that happens as a consequence of the execution of sequence (r_1, r_2), when initially component $name_2$ was in the L1 cache, the L2 cache, or in the memory, respectively. We call these estimated latencies affinity coefficients. Table 5 exemplifies affinity coefficients for Power5 architecture.

The final algorithm for comparison between two records (Fig. 2) comprises all characteristics together. However, there is a difference between handling shared and non-shared (process-private) types of data. For non-shared data types we consider only records that belong to the same process, i.e. a condition $eq\_pid=1$ has to be added to (1) in Fig. 2, while for shared data we consider accesses

Table 5. Affinity coefficients for Power5 platform

combination	$eq\_cpu = 1, eq\_core = 1$	$eq\_cpu = 1, eq\_core = 0$	$eq\_cpu = 0$
RR	83	78	0
RW	83	78	0
WR	83	74	-156
WW	83	74	-156

from all processes. It can be noted, that for non-shared data the typical 'if' case in algorithm is when hardware threads are equal. Obviously, the second case represents process migration. For shared data algorithm, the situation is opposite. A case when hardware threads are different is frequent. Therefore the numerical estimation of affinity weights described above is especially important for shared data.

3   Experimental Results

In this section:

1 How to apply our methodology on Power5 machine.
2 Our experience with a lightweight webserver, *lighttpd*.
3 The performance results.

3.1   The *lighttpd* Webserver

lighttpd is a configurable multi-process webserver. It features explicit paralleliza-tion through usage of a *fork()* Linux function, so that most of a *lighttpd* code is executed in parallel, equally dividing its workload among its processes. In our runs, we used *lighttpd* version 1.4.19. http_load [14] was selected as a client application.

In the context of our methodology, a data type corresponds to a C-like struc-ture type, and its components are structure fields. Among numerous *lighttpd* structures, we selected the two most referenced. One, called server, represents server configuration. It is instantiated when *lighttpd* starts. The only instance of server is shared by all *lighttpd* processes. The structure has 51 fields, and its size is 696 bytes. Second structure, called *connection*, represent an individual connec-tion. Numerous connections are served by *lighttpd* simultaneously. Each *lighttpd* process allocates a private array of connections. Size of connection structure is 584 bytes, and it contains 49 fields.

3.2   Platform

For our experiments we used Power5 platform running SUSE Linux Enterprise Server (SLES) version 11. We found this platform appropriate for our purposes, since it is characterized by long cache lines (Fig. 3), that strengthen the effect

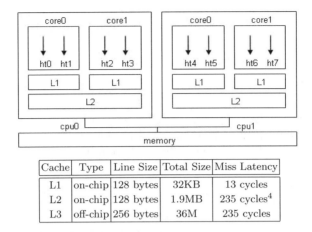

Cache	Type	Line Size	Total Size	Miss Latency
L1	on-chip	128 bytes	32KB	13 cycles
L2	on-chip	128 bytes	1.9MB	235 cycles[4]
L3	off-chip	256 bytes	36M	235 cycles

Fig. 3. Power5 2-cpus 4-cores architecture with cache subsystem characteristics

of false sharing [28]. All the runs were executed on a dedicated blade with two cpus, four cores, and eight hardware threads. We utilized *getcpu()* system call, supported in this version of SLES, to fetch the hardware thread id (ht_id) to be printed in each record. Alternatively, *sched_setaffinity()* Linux system call can be used for assigning processes to specific hardware threads and preventing all migrations.

Affinity coefficients for Power5 platform are presented in Table 5. They were calculated by substituting the miss latency values (last column of the table in Fig. 3) into the three addenda of the affinity estimation given in Table 4.

3.3   The Experimental Procedure

We instrumented *lighttpd* to generate data trace for connection and server. Linux POSIX semaphores guaranteed atomicity of record generation, without causing additional migration of *lighttpd* processes. For trace generation, we run an http_load request of size that is by an order of magnitude smaller than for performance measurements. For the Trace Traversal Algorithm we used window size equal to the cache line size (128 bytes). The size of partition in Kernighan and Lin [1] algorithm was selected similarly. Fields were divided into portions of equal size and, if needed, partitions were completed by dummy fields in order to guarantee the balance of the algorithm.

Although a field affinity, estimated by the CPG, can be used for a number of data layout optimizations, we decided to apply structure reordering. Being less effective than other data layout transformation [9], reordering requires neither safety analysis nor changes in data access sites and therefore can be easily

---

[4] Although an L2 miss can result in an L3 hit, for the context of this paper we presume that data is taken from the memory.

applied. To reorder lighttpd structures, we concatenated the partitions, generated by Kernighan and Lin algorithm, and aligned them on 128 bytes.

3.4   Performance Results

To measure influence of our methodology on *lighttpd*, we generated traces and
corresponding layouts for each *lighttpd* configuration separately. The number of
processes in each configuration was power of two. The results were based on fifty
runs for each configuration. Workload was randomized so that the size of the
input pool exceeded the size of an individual request by an order of magnitude.

The influence of server and connection reordering on *lighttpd* run time is presented on Fig. 4b. Although *lighttpd* is not a memory bound application, we
received a time improvement from connection (11-12%) and server (4-5%) reordering. As opposed to classical data layout optimizations, these results are
stable when the number of *lighttpd* processes is increased. Apparently, the connection reordering is more influential than server reordering because there are
many instances of connection in *lighttpd* and only one instance of server. This
proportion is also reflected in the size of the traces. Thus traces of server are two
orders of magnitude smaller than traces of connection.

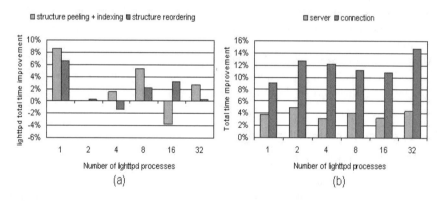

Fig. 4. Total time improvement obtained by applying (a) GCC data layout optimizations and (b) our methodology on *lighttpd*. The horizontal axis shows the number of
lighttpd processes, vertical — the improvement (in percents). (a) The results of applying
peeling plus indexing (*Light bars*) and reordering (*Dark bars*) to connection structure.
(b) The results of applying server reordering (*Light bars*) and connection reordering
(*Dark bars*) according to our methodology.

The L1 and L2 cache miss rates of loads and stores, received from server
reordering, are presented separately on Fig. 5. They prove that our methodology
was efficient in this case, but apparently its effect was not fully expressed in
lighttpd run time, since it was partly outweighed by heavy I/O operations.

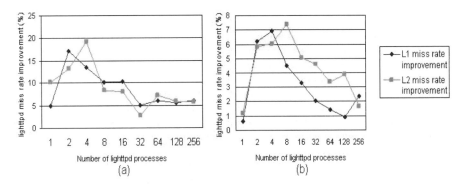

Fig. 5. Cache miss rate improvement obtained by applying our methodology on *lighttpd* server structure **types**. The chart (a) represents store misses, the chart (b) — load misses. *Dark line* shows L1 miss rate improvement, *Light line* — L2 miss rate improvement. The horizontal axis shows the number of *lighttpd* processes, the vertical — improvement (in percents).

4   Conclusions and Future Work

This paper presents a new methodology that allows extending the classical data layout optimizations to be efficient for multi-core processors. As part of this methodology, we developed a new technique for accurate numerical estimation of the data affinity, suitable for both multi- and single-core environments. We extended the classical data trace format with hardware-specific characteristics that allowed us to correctly identify the negative or positive contributions into the data affinity estimation. Finally, we showed how our methodology can be implemented for Power5 architecture, and applied it to real world application *lighttpd*. The performance results showed miss rate and total time improvements stable when the number of *lighttpd* processes was increased.

Our methodology fits the classical schema of feedback directed optimizations. The Trace Traversal Algorithm requires $O(T)$ time, where T is the trace length. Our traces are by an order of magnitude shorter, than those required for alternative techniques. Therefore we found our methodology suitable for incorporation into a compiler. In case the time required for trace analysis significantly exceeds overall compilation time, the trace analysis can be done off line. This option was already adopted by binary optimization tools [22].

Although, we successfully applied our methodology on the real world application *lighttpd*, checking it on the standard multi-threaded, multi-process suite of benchmarks is the part of our future plan.

References

1. Kernighan, B., Lin, S.: An efficient heuristic procedure for partitioning graphs. Bell sys. tech. J. 49, 291–308 (1970)
2. Lightweight open-source web server *lighttpd*, http://www.lighttpd.net/

3. Sinharoy, B., Kalla, R.N., Tendler, J.M., Eickemeyer, R.J., Joyner, J.B.: POWER5 system microarchitecure. IBM J. of Res. and Dev. 49(4/5), 505–522 (2005)
4. Shen, X., Gao, Y., Ding, C., Archambault, R.: Lightweight Reference Affinity Analysis. In: Proceedings of the 19th annual international conference on Supercomputing, pp. 131–140. ACM, New York (2005)
5. Curial, S., Zhao, P., Amaral, J.N., Gao, Y., Silvera, R., Archambault, R.: MPADS: Memory-Pooling-Assisted Data Splitting. In: Proceedings of the 7th international symposium on Memory management, pp. 101–110. ACM, New York (2008)
6. Hagog, M., Tice, C.: Cache Aware Data Layout Reorganization Optimization in GCC. In: Proceedings of the GCC Developers' Summit, pp. 69–92 (2005), http://www.gccsummit.org/
7. Golovanevsky, O., Zaks, A.: Struct-reorg: current status and future perspectives. In: Proceedings of the GCC Developers' Summit, pp. 47–56 (2007), http://www.gccsummit.org/
8. Chakrabarti, G., Chow, F.: Structure Layout Optimizations in the Open64 Compiler:design, Implementaton and Measurements. In: Open64 Workshop at the International Symposium on Code Generation and Optimization (2008), http://www.capsl.udel.edu/conferences/open64/2008
9. Hundt, R., Mannarswamy, S., Chakrabarti, D.: Practical Structure Layout Optimization and Advice. In: Proceedings of the International Symposium on Code Generation and Optimization, pp. 233–244. IEEE Computer Society, Washington (2006)
10. Zhao, P., Cui, S., Gao, Y., Silvera, R., Amaral, J.N.: Forma: A Framework for Safe Automatic array Reshaping. ACM Transactions on Programming Languages and Systems 30 (2007)
11. SPEC CPU2000, http://www.spec.org/cpu2000/
12. SPEC CPU2006, http://www.spec.org/cpu2006/
13. Link Time Optimizations, http://gcc.gnu.org/wiki/LinkTimeOptimization
14. http_load, multiprocessing http test client, http://www.acme.com/software/http_load/
15. Chilimbi, T.M., Davidson, B., Larus, J.R.: Cache-conscious structure definition. In: Proceedings of the ACM SIGPLAN 1999 Conference on Programming Language Design and Implementation, pp. 13–24. ACM, New York (1999)
16. Chilimbi, T.M., Davidson, B., Larus, J.R.: Efficient Representation and Abstractions for Quantifying and Exploiting Data Reference Locality. In: Proceedings of the ACM SIGPLAN 2001 Conference on Programming Language Design and Implementation, pp. 191–202. ACM, New York (2001)
17. Ding, C., Zhong, Y.: Predicting Whole-Program Locality through Reuse Distance Analysis. In: Proceedings of the ACM SIGPLAN 2003 Conference on Programming Language Design and Implementation, pp. 245–257. ACM, New York (2003)
18. Shen, X., Shaw, J., Meeker, B., Ding, C.: Locality Apploximation Using Time. In: Proceedings of the 34th annual ACM SIGPLAN-SIGACT symposium on Principles of programming languages, pp. 55–61. ACM, New York (2007)
19. Zhong, Y., Orlovich, M., Shen, X., Ding, C.: Array Regrouping and Structure Splitting Using Whole-Program Reference Affinity. In: Proceedings of the ACM SIGPLAN 2004 Conference on Programming Language Design and Implementation, pp. 255–266. ACM, New York (2004)
20. Jeon, J., Shin, K., Han, H.: Abstracting Access Patterns of Dynamic Memory Using Regular Expressions. ACM Transactions on Programming Languages and Systems 30 (2007)

21. Agarwal, A., Hennessy, J., Horowitz, M.: Cache Performance of Operating System and Multiprogramming Workloads. ACM Transactions on Computer Systems 431, 393–431 (1988)
22. Marathe, J., Mueller, F., Mohan, T., Mckee, S.A., De Suoinski, B.R., Yoo, A.: METRIC: Memory Tracing via Dynamic Binary Rewriting to Identify Cache Inefficiencies. ACM Transactions on Programming Languages and Systems 29, art.n.12 (2007)
23. Sarkar, S., Tullsen, D.M.: Compiler Techniques for Reducing Data Cache Miss Rate on a Multithreaded Architecture. In: Stenström, P., Dubois, M., Katevenis, M., Gupta, R., Ungerer, T. (eds.) HiPEAC 2007. LNCS, vol. 4917, pp. 353–368. Springer, Heidelberg (2008)
24. Rabbah, R.M., Palem, K.V.: Data Remapping for Design Space Optimization of Embedded Memory Systems. ACM Transactions on Embedded Computing Systems 2(2), 186–218 (2003)
25. Raman, E., Hundt, R., Mannarsway, S.: Structure Layout Optimization for Multithreaded Programs. In: Proceedings of the International Symposium on Code Generation and Optimization, pp. 271–282. IEEE Computer Society, Washington (2007)
26. Kandemir, M., Ramanujam, J.: Reducing False Sharing and Improving Spatial Locality in a Unified Compilation Framework. IEEE Transactions on Parallel and Distributed Systems 14, 337–354 (2003)
27. Ozturk, O., Chen, G., Kandemir, M.: Multi-Compilation: Capturing Interactions Among Concurrently-Executing Applications. In: Proceedings of the 3rd conference on Computing frontiers, pp. 157–170. ACM, New York (2006)
28. Woo, S.C., Ohara, M., Torrie, E., Singh, J.P., Gupta, A.: The SPLASH-2 Programs: Characterization and Methodological Considerations. In: Proceedings of the 22nd International Symposium on Computer Architecture, pp. 24-36. ACM, New York (1995)
29. Calder, B., Krintz, C., Austin, T.: Cache-Conscious Data Placement. In: Proceedings of the 8th International Conference on Architectural Support for Programming Languages and Operating Systems, pp. 139–149. ACM, New York (1998)
30. Youfeng, W., James, R.L.: Static Branch Frequency and Program Profile Analysis. In: Proceedings of the 27th International Symposium on Microarchitecture, pp. 1–11. ACM, New York (1994)

Buffer Sizing for Self-timed Stream Programs on Heterogeneous Distributed Memory Multiprocessors

Paul M. Carpenter, Alex Ramirez, and Eduard Ayguadé

Barcelona Supercomputing Center, C/Jordi Girona, 31, 08034 Barcelona, Spain
{paul.carpenter,alex.ramirez,eduard.ayguade}@bsc.es

Abstract. Stream programming is a promising way to expose concurrency to the compiler. A stream program is built from kernels that communicate only via point-to-point streams. The stream compiler statically allocates these kernels to processors, applying blocking, fission and fusion transformations. The compiler determines the sizes of the communication buffers, which affects performance since local memories can be small.

In this paper, we propose a feedback-directed algorithm that determines the size of each communication buffer, based on i) the stream program that has been mapped onto processors, ii) feedback from an earlier execution, and iii) the memory constraints. The algorithm exposes a trade-off between throughput and latency. It is general, in that it applies to stream programs with unstructured stream graphs, and it supports variable execution times and communication rates.

We show results for the StreamIt benchmarks and random graphs. For the StreamIt benchmarks, throughput is optimal after the first iteration. For random graphs with stochastic computation times, throughput is within 3% of optimal after four iterations. Compared with the previous general algorithm, by Basten and Hoogerbrugge, our algorithm has significantly better performance and latency.

1 Introduction

Many applications, including video, audio, 3D graphics, and radio, contain abundant task and data parallelism, but it is hard to extract from C source code. Stream programming represents the application as concurrent kernels, interacting only via point-to-point streams of data. This representation exposes concurrency to the compiler, is natural for signal processing, and easier to debug since it is deterministic. As the industry moves towards multiprocessors [1], there is increasing interest in portable, efficient, correct use of parallelism.

Much work on stream compilation has focused on blocking and allocation. Blocking unrolls kernels to amortise fixed costs. Allocation fuses one or more kernels, from the source program, into each task, in the executable, and maps these tasks onto processors, balancing loads on processors and buses.

This paper considers a problem that has received less attention: allocating memory for stream buffers, subject to memory constraints, when computation

Y.N. Patt et al. (Eds.): HiPEAC 2010, LNCS 5952, pp. 96–110, 2010.

times and communication rates are variable. This is an important problem, because it affects performance, as we explain in Section 2. The buffer sizes are constrained by the available memory, which may be small. On the Cell Broadband Engine [2], for example, code and data must fit in the 256KB local store.

The inputs to the algorithm are the *mapped stream program*, a *program trace* and the *machine description*, giving the target topology and memory budgets. A simple model of computation times and communication rates, such as independent normal distributions and Poisson arrivals, may be misleading, so the only options are simulation and real execution. We use coarse-grain simulation, but real execution could be used instead. The output is the buffer size for the producer and consumer on each stream, which may be different.

The main contributions of this paper are:

- In Section 3, we describe a feedback-driven method to allocate stream buffers in a distributed memory machine, when computation times and communication rates are variable.
- In Section 5.1, we describe two algorithms that analyse profiling information to find bottleneck cycles caused by undersized communication buffers. The first uses waiting times only; the second is more complex but more accurate.
- In Section 5.2, we describe an algorithm to allocate stream buffers using the above algorithms, which converges quickly to a close-to-optimal allocation.

2   Motivation

Double buffering is a well-known technique to overlap communication and computation. There are two situations, however, when a stream ought to be allocated more than two buffers. The first is when a stream covers a long latency or, equivalently, crosses more than one pipeline stage boundary. The second is when there are short-duration load imbalances due to variable computation times or communication rates.

The *chain8* benchmark illustrates the first situation, and is shown on the left of Figure 1. It has eight tasks in a pipeline, with streams between consecutive tasks, and another stream between the first and last tasks. Figure 1(a) shows the progress of the first and last tasks relative to the stream between them. The vertical axis is time, and the horizontal axis is the position in the stream. At any given time the producer is working on some interval of the stream, which it owns. It starts at the top left of the plot, at the beginning of both the stream and time, moving to the right when it sends data to the consumer, and continually downward through time. The figure also shows the progress of the consumer.

The periodic pattern of waiting is caused by the interaction between two dependencies. First, the consumer must wait for its data to arrive, which means that it waits for the producer, plus the latency of the pipeline. This gives a vertical dependency from producer to consumer. Second, the producer must wait for an empty consumer-side buffer in which to send its data, and this gives a horizontal dependency from consumer to producer.

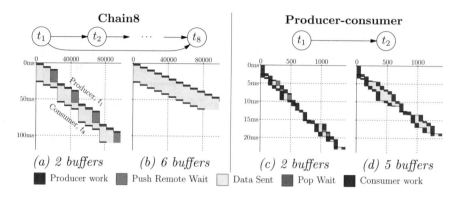

Fig. 1. Effect of consumer queue length on chain8 and producer-consumer

Figure 1(b) is for six consumer-side buffers, which increases throughput by 73%, and is sufficient for the producer to be always busy. This shows that double buffering was not sufficient, but also that the number of buffers can be less than one plus the difference in pipeline stage, which is the number of buffers allocated by StreamRoller [3] and SPIR [4]; in this case eight.

The second situation is illustrated using the *producer-consumer* example on the right of Figure 1. If the producer and consumer both have fixed computation times and communication rates, then double buffering is sufficient. Sometimes, single buffering at one or other end will be enough, even with good load balancing. Subfigure (c) shows the progress of this example, using double buffering, when computation times are normally distributed. Increasing the number of consumer buffers to five, as shown in subfigure (d), increases throughput by 20%.

The performance of the queue length assignment algorithm is quantified using the *utilisation*, which is the percentage of time that the most heavily loaded processor or bus is busy. Utilisation is proportional to throughput. If the stream graph is acyclic, at least one resource ought to be 100% busy. If any resource has utilisation less than 100%, it must be due to insufficient buffering.

The tradeoff between utilisation and the number of consumer buffers is illustrated in Figure 2. Chain has linearly increasing utilisation until it reaches 100%. Producer-consumer achieves 99% utilisation with 3 producer and 4 consumer buffers, and additional buffering yields diminishing returns.

3   The ACOTES Stream Compiler

This work is part of the ACOTES European project [5], which is developing an open source stream compiler for embedded systems. The compiler will map a portable stream program, written in the SPM [6], an annotated version of C, onto a heterogeneous multicore system, applying blocking and task fusion.

The compiler statically allocates tasks onto processors. Although a dynamic policy can achieve better load balance [7], it has greater overhead. On a distributed memory processor, instructions and state cannot be transferred on demand through caches, so a context switch requires all data to be transferred at once. A context switch on the Cell SPE requires about $30\mu s$ [8]. The techniques in this paper can be used to absorb small scale variation in complexity.

Figure 3 shows how the queue length assignment algorithm fits into this stream compiler. The blocking and partitioning stages transform the program as described in the introduction. The queue length assignment stage, which is the focus of this paper, then determines the optimal buffer allocation.

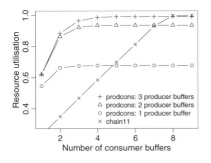

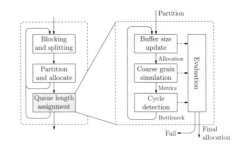

Fig. 2. Memory-performance tradeoff   **Fig. 3.** Mapping phase of the compiler

Our SPM language eliminates deadlock, so the objective function depends only on performance and latency. The interaction between bounded memory in process networks and deadlock, but not performance, has been explored in depth [9,10,11], and these techniques can determine the *minimum* buffer sizes.

The queue length assignment algorithm is iterative, and consists of a coarse-grain simulator, a *cycle detection algorithm*, a *buffer size update algorithm*, and an *evaluation algorithm*. The cycle detection algorithm analyses metrics from the simulator, and finds a bottleneck cycle. The buffer update algorithm chooses the initial buffer allocation, and adjusts buffer sizes to resolve the bottleneck. The evaluation algorithm monitors progress and decides when to stop, choosing the buffer allocation that achieved the best performance-latency tradeoff.

4   Formalisation of the Problem

Queue length assignment seeks to find an optimal tradeoff, subject to memory constraints, between throughput and latency We wish to find a close to Pareto optimal solution: that is, neither latency nor throughput can be improved without making the other one worse. We keep memory use within the constraints, but do not try to minimise it.

The stream program is represented as a connected, not necessarily acyclic, digraph, $\mathcal{P} = (T, S)$, where T is the set of vertices (tasks), and S is the set of edges (streams). Each stream s has a producer and consumer buffer size in bytes, $b_p(s)$ and $b_c(s)$, and a minimum number of buffers, sufficient to hold the working set and avoid deadlocks. If P is acyclic, as for ACOTES, deadlock is impossible; otherwise minimum sizes can be found using the references in Section 3. The algorithm determines the actual number of buffers, $n_p(s)$ and $n_c(s)$.

Each task has a trace, which is an alternating sequence of computation times and primitives. There are four communications primitives and a fire primitive, which marks the firing of a task; i.e. the calling of its work function inside an implicit loop. The communications primitives use a push model similar to the DBI variant of TTL [12]. They are described below, assuming, for simplicity, that the producer and consumer have the same buffer size, which is not required. A *block* is the contents of one buffer, and i and j count blocks, starting at zero. The first argument is the stream.

ProducerAcquire(s, k): Wait for the producer buffer for block $i + k$ to be available, meaning that the DMA transfer of block $i + k - n_p(s)$ has completed.

ProducerSend(s): Wait for the consumer buffer for block i to be available, meaning that the producer has received acknowledgement that block $i - n_c(s)$ has been discarded. Then send the block and increment i.

ConsumerAcquire(s, k): Wait for block $j + k$ to arrive in the consumer buffer.

ConsumerDiscard(s): Discard block j, send acknowledgement, and increment j.

The traces are interpreted using the ASM coarse-grain simulator, which takes a machine description that defines the target [13]. Queue length assignment needs only the memory constraints, which are represented using a bipartite graph, $\mathcal{H} = (R, E)$. The set of vertices, $R = P \cup M$, is a disjoint union of processors P and memories M, and the edges, E, connect processors to their local memories. Each memory has weight equal to the amount of memory available, in bytes, for stream buffers. Figure 4 shows the memory constraint graph for the Cell Broadband Engine; the memory weights depend on how much memory is already being used. We will later assume that each processor is connected to a single memory, but it may be shared with other processors.

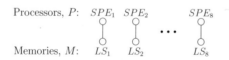

Fig. 4. Memory constraint graph for the Cell Broadband Engine

The evaluation algorithm and Section 6 of the paper require an estimate of latency. Since it is orthogonal to the rest of the paper, and only differences in latency matter, we use a scheme which ignores delays inside tasks.

Define $f_t(n)$ to be the time of firing, $n = 0, 1, \cdots, M_t - 1$ of task t, taken from the fire primitive. Since each task contributes to a common amount of real-world progress, normalise n to the interval $0 \leq x < 1$ by dividing it by M_t. Then $g_t(x) = f_t(\lfloor M_t x \rfloor)$ gives the time that task t was proportion $x \in [0, 1)$ through the calculation. The latency, $L(x)$, is the difference between the largest $g_t(x)$ for a sink and the smallest $g_t(x)$ for a source, which can, unfortunately, be negative when multiplicities are variable. We report the average value of $L(x)$.

5   Description of the Algorithms

In this section, we describe several algorithms for cycle detection and buffer size update. First we review the standard critical cycle detection algorithm, and explain when it is applicable. We introduce our *baseline* algorithm, which finds the bottleneck cycle by analysing the time each task is blocked on each stream. This data is easy to obtain, and the algorithm is quite effective. We then give an example that the baseline algorithm gets wrong, and propose the *token* algorithm, which requires extra bookkeeping but achieves better results. Finally, we describe several variants on the buffer update algorithm, which have different tradeoffs between speed of convergence and latency.

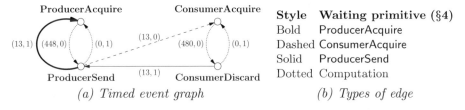

(a) *Timed event graph*   (b) *Types of edge*

Fig. 5. Example timed event graph used by the critical cycle algorithm

5.1   Cycle Detection Algorithms

Critical cycle algorithm: The *critical cycle* algorithm [14,15,16] solves the cycle detection problem for homogeneous Synchronous Data Flow (SDF) [17] with constant computation times and communications latencies. In homogeneous SDF, every time a producer or consumer fires, it pushes or pops a single buffer on each stream. All tasks therefore fire at the same rate. The algorithm can be extended to SDF, where each producer or consumer pushes or pops any fixed number of buffers, but it requires expanding the graph, which can make it much bigger [18].

Figure 5(a) shows how producer-consumer, assuming a single buffer at each end, is represented by this algorithm. Each vertex is the return from a communications primitive. The edges are distinguished, for the diagram but not the algorithm, using the convention in subfigure (b), which refers to the primitives in Section 4. Each edge has *weight*, which is its fixed computation time or communications latency, and *height*, which is the fixed difference between the firing number, which counts the number of times a task has fired, at its two ends.

For example, at the producer side, the dotted line from ProducerAcquire to ProducerSend, of weight 448 and height 0, represents computation inside a single iteration. The solid line in the reverse direction, of weight 13 and height 1, is because the producer cannot reuse its single buffer in the current firing until the previous DMA has completed.

Throughput is constrained by the *critical cycle*, which is a cycle with maximum ratio of total weight divided by total height. There are several algorithms to find such a cycle, many based on Karp's Theorem [19], in time $O(|S|^2|T|)$ or so [15], using the terminology of Section 4.

Baseline Algorithm: Our *baseline* algorithm is more general, because it supports variable data rates, computation times, and communication latencies. It finds the bottleneck by analysing wait times in a real execution or simulation.

Figure 6 shows how the stream program and wait times are represented by the algorithm. Subfigure (a) is an example stream graph with three tasks in a triangle. Subfigure (b) is the *wait-for* graph, which has the same three edges per stream as the timed event graph. Following convention for wait-for graphs, the arrows point in the opposite direction, *from* the waiting task. The weight of an edge is the proportion of the total time that the task at the initial vertex, or tail, spent waiting in its communications primitive.

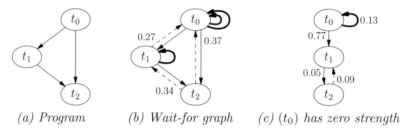

(a) Program   (b) Wait-for graph   (c) (t_0) has zero strength

Fig. 6. Example weighted wait-for graphs

As for the critical cycle algorithm, performance is constrained by dependence cycles in the wait-for graph. We will use two bounds, one local and one global, on the maximum increase in performance from *relaxing* a cycle; i.e. increasing buffering on one of the streams in the cycle that gets full.

Consider the potential benefit from relaxing cycle $C_1 = (t_0\, t_2\, t_1)$. This can only be done by increasing buffering on the stream from t_0 to t_2. Since t_1 waits for 27% of the time, during the ConsumerAcquire primitive in this cycle, we could reduce the execution time of t_1 by *at most* 27%, before the cycle disappears. Since all tasks execute for nearly the same amount of wallclock time, any change in throughput will cause all vertices to have their *total* waiting time, not just on the edges of this cycle, reduced by the same amount. It is therefore likely that the edge in the cycle that disappears first is its weakest edge.

The local bound is the *weight* of cycle C, denoted $w(C)$, which is the minimum weight of its edges. If there is no cycle with non-zero weight, then utilisation is already 100%. This is because every directed *acyclic* graph has a vertex with no outgoing edge, which corresponds to a task that never has to wait.

Figure 6(c) is the motivation for the global bound. The maximum weight cycle is the loop on t_0, of weight 0.13, which we will call C_2. A moment's reflection, however, shows that C_2 cannot really be a bottleneck since neither t_1 nor t_2 ever wait for t_0, even indirectly. If we reduced the time t_0 spent waiting on this loop, it cannot make t_1 or t_2 go any faster. Since throughput would be unchanged, t_0

must spend the same total amount of time waiting, so the waiting time would move from ProducerAcquire to ProducerSend (see Figure 5(b)).

The global bound is the *strength* of the cycle, denoted $s(C)$, which is the lowest value of the maximum flow *through a single path* to the cycle, starting from any other vertex. Since there is no path at all from t_1 to C_2 in Figure 6, the cycle has zero strength: $s(C_2) = 0$. In contrast, the cycle $(t_1\,t_2)$ has strength 0.77, because this is the weight of the only path from the only other vertex, t_0. Increasing the performance of t_1 and t_2 by any means could reduce execution time of the program as a whole by 77%. This cycle is the bottleneck, and it has weight 0.05. The requirement that flow be through a single path makes little difference in practice, but it reduces considerably the algorithmic complexity.

It is possible for the wait-for graph to be disconnected; e.g. when tasks wait for each other only through bus contention. This happens rarely, but it causes all strengths to be zero. Therefore, when all strengths are zero but the utilisation is below some threshold (currently 100%), the strengths are ignored. Since it almost never happens, there is little reason to be more sophisticated.

We first calculate the strength of each vertex by computing the *all-pairs bottleneck paths* [20]. This finds, for every pair of vertices, the value of the maximum flow through a single path from the first vertex to the second. It is solved using a variant of Dijkstra's algorithm, running Dijkstra for each vertex to find the maximum flow paths into it. The strength of that vertex is given by the path with the lowest flow. The total execution time is $O(|S||T| + |T|^2 log|T|)$, using a Fibonacci heap [21,22], with the terminology of Section 4.

The algorithm finds a cycle with the maximum value of the minimum of the local and global bounds. It is straightforward to show that we can take account of both simply by replacing the weight of every edge $e = (a, b)$ by a new weight, $w'(e) = \min(w(e), s(a))$. A maximum weight cycle, according to w', can be found in time $O(|S| \log |S|)$, where S is the set of streams. To find out whether there is a cycle of weight $\geq W$, for some W, just check whether there is any cycle if you ignore all edges of weight $< W$. This can be done in time $O(|S|)$ by attempting to perform a topological sort. To find a maximum weight cycle, first sort the edge weights, and perturb them so that no two are exactly the same. Then use bisection on the sorted edge weights.

The baseline algorithm uses data that is easy to obtain, and is usually quite effective, but it has one limitation. Since each task is represented by a single vertex, it cannot "see" what is happening inside them.

Figure 7(a) shows an example where the baseline algorithm makes a bad decision. The maximum weight cycle is $(t_1\,t_0\,t_2)$, which has weight 0.50. Whether or not this is a bottleneck depends on the internal behaviour of tasks t_1 and t_2. The order of operations per firing of task t_1 is shown in subfigure (b). If we also know that task t_1 *always* waits in step 5, then reducing the waiting time in step 1 will simply result in a longer waiting time in step 5. It can never advance the push in step 6, so the critical cycle cannot be $(t_1\,t_0\,t_2)$.

Token Algorithm: The *token* algorithm addresses this problem by tracking dependencies through tasks. This is somewhat similar to causal chains [23], except

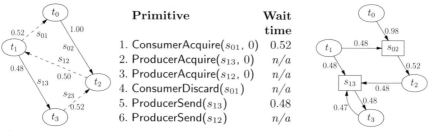

(a) Wait-for graph   (b) Order of primitives in t_1 (c) Indirect wait-for graph

Fig. 7. Example where baseline fails

that the aim is to resolve performance bottlenecks rather than artificial dead-locks. Their algorithm fixes a deadlock after it happens, when all tasks have got stuck, but we cannot expect all tasks in a cycle to ever be waiting simultaneously.

During the simulation, or at runtime in a dynamic scheme, each task t has a *current token*, S_t, which is the stream that most recently made t wait, directly or indirectly, because it got full. It has a *current waiting time*, W_t, which measures how much the task has already had to wait, so that only increases in waiting times are charged to streams. It also has a *waiting vector*, $(V_t)_s$, which gives the total waiting time for each stream in the whole program. Each consumer buffer c has a *current token*, S_c, and *current waiting time*, W_c, which together record the producer's problem at the time the block in that buffer was sent.

When task p blocks for time τ because output stream s is full, it sets $S_p \leftarrow s$ and increases both W_p and $V_p[s]$ by τ. When task p sends a block using buffer c on output stream s, it records a copy of its current state: $S_c \leftarrow S_p$ and $W_c \leftarrow W_p$. When a task q blocks for time τ because input stream s is empty, it also, after the data arrives, reads S_c and W_c, from the consumer buffer c containing the end of the data. It then updates its current token $S_q \leftarrow S_c$ to indicate that it had to wait, indirectly, for whichever stream the producer had to wait for, and calculates the increase in current waiting time $\Delta W_q \leftarrow \min(\tau, W_c - W_q)$, which can be either positive or negative. If it is positive, then $V_q[S_q]$ is increased by ΔW_q. In either case, the current waiting time is then updated using $W_q \leftarrow W_q + \Delta W_q$.

The waiting vectors are used to construct an *indirect wait-for graph*, as shown in Figure 7(c). If $V_t[s] > 0$, there is an edge from task t to stream s with weight $V_t[s]/L$, where L is the total execution time of the run, in the same units. Each stream s also produces an edge from s to its consumer q. The weight of this edge is $s(q)$, the *strength* of q, as defined for the baseline algorithm.

This is effectively viewing each stream as an actor in its own right, which is always blocked waiting for the consumer to discard its data. This is the most convenient place to take account of the strengths, which are still relevant by the same argument as before. The token algorithm finds the maximum weight cycle in the same way as the baseline algorithm.

Figure 8 shows a second example which clarifies the need for the cycle-based algorithm outlined above. In the stream program of Figure 8(a), task t_0 pushes

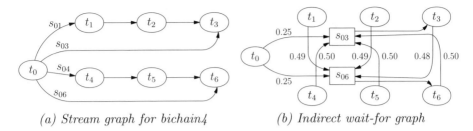

(a) Stream graph for bichain4   *(b) Indirect wait-for graph*

Fig. 8. Token algorithm: bichain4 example

the outputs in the cyclic order (s_{01} s_{03} s_{04} s_{06}), waiting only in ProducerSend for streams s_{03} and s_{06} due to their longer latency.

When it pushes on stream s_{04} of the right branch, the most recent wait was due to stream s_{03} being full, so it sends the token for s_{03}. Similarly, it sends the token for stream s_{06} to stream s_{01} of the left branch. The indirect wait-for graph is shown in Figure 8(b), with cycle (t_3 s_{06} t_6 s_{03}) going through both streams.

5.2   Buffer Size Update Algorithms

The cycle detection algorithm returns a set of edges in the wait-for graph that cause a bottleneck cycle by becoming full. Relaxing the cycle involves increasing memory on one or more of these edges. The purpose of the buffer size update algorithm is to determine *which* edges to enlarge, and by *how many* buffers.

Our simplest algorithm is *miserly*, meaning that it starts at the minimum number of buffers, mentioned in Section 4, and each iteration increases the allocation of a single buffer by one. The other algorithms speculatively assign spare memory, and only take it away if it is needed elsewhere. For all these algorithms, each stream s *demands* some number d_s of buffers, as for the miserly algorithm, and *requests* another r_s to be granted out of unused memory, if there is any. When there is not enough memory to grant all requests within some memory, we used the following algorithm. The total request in bytes is $R = \sum r_s b_c(s)$, where $b_c(s)$ is the size in bytes of a single consumer buffer for stream s. If M bytes are left after granting all demands, so $R > M$, then each stream is initially granted $\lfloor r_j M/R \rfloor$ extra buffers, then possibly one more, if it fits.

In our first alternative, *double*, each edge requests an extra buffer if it is currently allocated only one. In our second alternative, *exponential*, the request is for some multiple, $f - 1$, of the number of buffers demanded. We still use a greedy update algorithm, so that when the number of buffers is increased, the edge demands, on the next iteration, one more buffer than it was given in total last time. We used $f = 2$, so an edge will demand $2^k - 1$ buffers, and request an equal number, for $k = 1, 2, \cdots$, until it is given fewer buffers than it wants.

The third alternative, *level*, uses the *top level*, the length of the longest path from a source node, and *bottom level*, the length of the longest path to a sink node. The algorithm the same as *exponential*, except that the request is the maximum of a) $f - 1$ times the number of buffers demanded, b) twice the difference in top level, and c) twice the difference in bottom level. This tries to give a high initial allocation to streams that cross a high latency.

6   Evaluation

We used the StreamIt 2.1.1 benchmarks [24], random graphs, and sixteen examples, including *chain8, producer-consumer, bad-baseline,* and *bichain4.* For the StreamIt benchmarks, we used the program graph, work estimates and communications rates generated by the StreamIt compiler, and used our algorithm [25] to produce partitions for an IBM QS20 blade, which has two Cell BEs.

Buffer size update: The first three rows of Figure 9 compare the buffer update algorithms from Section 5.2. These plots also contain results for Basten and Hoogerbrugge (B&H) [23] and modified StreamRoller [3], which will be discussed in Section 7. The left column shows as a function of the iteration number, the utilisation, which is proportional to throughput, as remarked at the end of Section 2. The right column shows the tradeoff between latency and utilisation. Any points that cannot be Pareto optimal, because they are beaten on both utilisation and latency by some point to the top-left, have been removed.

The first row is for random stochastic graphs with 32 tasks and 50 streams. The graphs are connected and acyclic, but otherwise unstructured. The computation time of each task is normally distributed with a random mean and variance (clamped above zero). Notice that B&H has poor performance and, since it increases buffering where it isn't necessary, high latency.

We found the upper bound on utilisation using an exhaustive search over all allocations of the buffers on the processor, p, whose memory bound caused the level algorithm to terminate. All other queues on other processors were set to their maximum possible size, assuming that all other queues in the same memory had their minimum size. Since this tends to allow a task near the beginning of the stream graph to work flat out filling downstream buffers, the steady state utilisation would be known only after many firings. Instead, we took the utilisation of the task on p, and scaled by the ratio of the long-term processing times of the most heavily loaded processor and of p.

The second row shows the StreamIt 2.1.1 benchmarks, with an unroll factor of 100. The third row shows the *stochastic* StreamIt benchmarks, which have normally-distributed computation times, and are intended to show how the algorithms fare for realistic program graphs.

The left column shows that the level algorithm always provides the fastest convergence. The modified StreamRoller algorithm is similar to the first iteration of the level algorithm, and B&H is considerably worse. The level heuristic initial allocation is within 15% of the upper bound on optimal performance, and is increased to within 3% of optimal after four iterations.

Cycle detection: We evaluate the cycle detection algorithms only, using greedy buffer update without memory constraints. When task execution times and communications rates are constant, and bus contention is negligible, the critical cycle algorithm of Section 5.1 is optimal. The last row of Figure 9 shows the utilisation

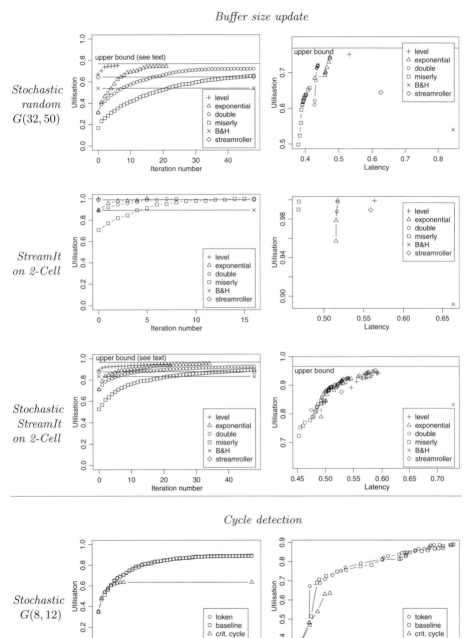

Fig. 9. Comparison of the buffer size update and cycle detection algorithms

and latency for an average of six random graphs with stochastic computation times. The poor performance of the critical cycle algorithm (about 60% utilisation), is because it is unable to detect cycles that arise from execution time variability. The baseline and token algorithms achieve similar performance, although the token algorithm achieves slightly lower latency.

We also evaluated the cycle detection algorithms when there is high bus utilisation, but for space reasons did not include the graph. The critical cycle algorithm cannot model increased communication latency due to contention [26, §E.5]. For a benchmark with a single producer task connected to two consumers, and bus usage close to 100%, the critical cycle algorithm achieves about 70% utilisation. The baseline and token algorithms measure waiting times directly, and consistently achieve 100% utilisation.

7   Related Work

Basten and Hoogerbrugge (B&H) [23] is the only other work that also targets unstructured graphs with variable multiplicities and computation times. Their algorithm sets each FIFO buffer size to be proportional to the amount of data streaming through it. This gives a relative size for each buffer, but it is not motivated by the underlying problems discussed in Section 2, and has poor performance in Figure 9. We interpreted B&H to mean double buffering on the producer side, with all the remaining memory allocated to consumer buffers, rounding the number of buffers *up* to an integer. If rounding up causes the buffer allocation to not fit, we reduced the target memory use until it did fit. The *chain8* example in Figure 1 shows the problem with this heuristic. If all data rates are the same and there is enough memory on t_n for ten buffers, Basten and Hoogerbrugge allocates five buffers to each stream for 70% utilisation, while our heuristic allocates eight to (t_1, t_n) and two to (t_{n-1}, t_n) for 100% utilisation.

The SDF tool [27] uses an exhaustive search to find all Pareto-optimal buffer allocations for an SDF graph. It requires exponentially many steps, and only supports constant computation times and data rates. For an n-way split or join where each stream needs b buffers, their algorithm requires n^b steps, while our level algorithm requires $O(n \log_2 b)$ steps to find a single solution.

StreamRoller [3] performs buffer allocation as part of software pipelining, but it is restricted to graphs with fixed multiplicities and computation times. The algorithm is similar to the first iteration of the *level* algorithm, in that the number of buffers allocated to a stream is always one plus the difference in pipeline stage. The *chain8* example in Section 2 shows that this is conservative, even when there is no variability. Hence the StreamRoller algorithm can require more memory than necessary; if there is insufficient memory, it fails.

Due to the unrolling factor we used, StreamRoller failed on at least one benchmark for all of the graphs in Figure 9. This is true even for the StreamIt benchmarks, for which our algorithm achieves 100% utilisation on at least one processor. We modified StreamRoller to use our arbitration scheme described in Subsection 5.2, and obtained the results shown in Figure 9. Even with this modification, however, our iterative algorithm has about 13% higher performance for the stochastic random graphs and stochastic StreamIt benchmarks.

The SPIR compiler [4] extends StreamRoller to find a partition and software pipeline subject to memory and latency constraints. Unlike our approach, computation times and communication rates are constant. As for StreamRoller, the number of buffers allocated to a stream is one plus the difference in pipeline stage. Since the problem cannot be solved exactly using ILP, it is a heuristic which uses two passes of the commercial CPLEX ILP solver. Our algorithm could be used to improve the buffer allocation of a partition produced by SPIR.

8   Conclusions

In this paper, we presented a feedback-directed algorithm to allocate memory for communications buffers in a statically-allocated stream program. The algorithm achieves close to optimal performance, even when StreamRoller fails due to insufficient memory. It achieves significantly higher performance and lower latency than the previous fully general algorithm, by Basten and Hoogerbrugge.

Acknowledgements

The researchers at BSC-UPC were supported by the Spanish Ministry of Science and Innovation (contract no. TIN2007-60625), the European Commission in the context of the ACOTES project (contract no. IST-34869) and the HiPEAC Network of Excellence (contract no. FP7/ICT 217068). We would also like to acknowledge our partners in the ACOTES project for the insightful discussions on the topics presented in this paper.

References

1. Olukotun, K., Hammond, L.: The future of microprocessors. Queue 3(7), 26–29 (2005)
2. Pham, D., Behnen, E., Bolliger, M., Hofstee, H.: et al.: The design methodology and implementation of a first-generation Cell processor: a multi-core SoC. In: Custom Integrated Circuits Conference 2005, pp. 45–49 (2005)
3. Kudlur, M., Mahlke, S.: Orchestrating the execution of stream programs on multicore platforms. In: Proceedings of the 2008 ACM SIGPLAN conference on Programming language design and implementation, pp. 114–124 (2008)
4. Choi, Y., Lin, Y., Chong, N., Mahlke, S., Mudge, T.: Stream Compilation for Real-Time Embedded Multicore Systems. In: Proceedings of the 2009 International Symposium on Code Generation and Optimization, vol. 00, pp. 210–220 (2009)
5. IST-034869, A.: Advanced Compiler Technologies for Embedded Streaming, http://www.hitech-projects.com/euprojects/ACOTES/
6. ACOTES: IST ACOTES Project Deliverable D2.2 Report on Streaming Programming Model and Abstract Streaming Machine Description Final Version (2008)

7. Becchi, M., Crowley, P.: Dynamic thread assignment on heterogeneous multiprocessor architectures. In: Proceedings of the 3rd conference on Computing frontiers, pp. 29–40. ACM, New York (2006)
8. Hofstee, H.P.: Power efficient processor architecture and the cell processor, pp. 258–262. IEEE Computer Society, Los Alamitos (2005)
9. Parks, T.: Bounded scheduling of process networks. PhD thesis, University of California (1995)
10. Buck, J.: Scheduling dynamic dataflow graphs with bounded memory using the token flow model. PhD thesis, University of California (1993)
11. Geilen, M., Basten, T.: Requirements on the execution of Kahn process networks. LNCS, pp. 319–334. Springer, Heidelberg (2003)
12. van der Wolf, P., de Kock, E., Henriksson, T., Kruijtzer, W., Essink, G.: Design and programming of embedded multiprocessors: an interface-centric approach. In: Proceedings of the 2nd international conference on Hardware/software codesign and system synthesis, pp. 206–217 (2004)
13. Carpenter, P.M., Ramirez, A., Ayguade, E.: The Abstract Streaming Machine: Compile-Time Performance Modelling of Stream Programs on Heterogeneous Multiprocessors. In: SAMOS Workshop 2009, pp. 12–23. Springer, Heidelberg (2009)
14. Ito, K., Parhi, K.: Determining the minimum iteration period of an algorithm. The Journal of VLSI Signal Processing 11(3), 229–244 (1995)
15. Dasdan, A., Gupta, R.: Faster maximum and minimum mean cycle algorithms for system-performance analysis. IEEE Transactions on Computer-Aided Design of Integrated Circuits and Systems 17(10), 889–899 (1998)
16. Govindarajan, R., Gao, G.: A novel framework for multi-rate scheduling in DSP applications. In: International Conference on Application-Specific Array Processors, pp. 77–88 (1993)
17. Lee, E., Messerschmitt, D.: Synchronous data flow. Proceedings of the IEEE 75(9), 1235–1245 (1987)
18. Lee, E.A.: A coupled hardware and software architecture for programmable digital signal processors (synchronous data flow). PhD thesis (1986)
19. Karp, R.: A characterization of the minimum cycle mean in a digraph. Discrete Mathematics 23(3), 309–311 (1978)
20. Pollack, M.: The maximum capacity through a network. Operations Research, 733–736 (1960)
21. Fredman, M., Tarjan, R.: Fibonacci heaps and their uses in improved network optimization algorithms. Journal of the ACM (J. ACM) 34(3), 596–615 (1987)
22. Vassilevska, V., Williams, R., Yuster, R.: All-pairs bottleneck paths for general graphs in truly sub-cubic time. In: Proceedings of the thirty-ninth annual ACM symposium on Theory of computing, pp. 585–589. ACM, New York (2007)
23. Basten, T., Hoogerbrugge, J.: Efficient execution of process networks. Communicating Process Architectures (2001)
24. Gordon, M., Thies, W., Amarasinghe, S.: Exploiting coarse-grained task, data, and pipeline parallelism in stream programs. ASPLOS, 151–162 (2006)
25. Carpenter, P.M., Ramirez, A., Ayguade, E.: Mapping Stream Programs onto Heterogeneous Multiprocessor Systems. In: CASES 2009, October 11-16 (2009)
26. Hennessy, J.L., Patterson, D.A.: Computer Architecture: A Quantitative Approach, 4th edn. Morgan Kaufmann, San Francisco (2007)
27. Stuijk, S., Geilen, M., Basten, T.: Exploring trade-offs in buffer requirements and throughput constraints for synchronous dataflow graphs. In: Proceedings of the 43rd annual conference on Design automation, pp. 899–904 (2006)

Automatically Tuning Sparse Matrix-Vector Multiplication for GPU Architectures

Alexander Monakov[1], Anton Lokhmotov[2], and Arutyun Avetisyan[1],[*]

[1] Institute for System Programming of RAS,
25 Solzhenitsyna street, Moscow, 109004, Russian Federation
{amonakov,arut}@ispras.ru
[2] Department of Computing, Imperial College London,
180 Queen's Gate, London, SW7 2AZ, United Kingdom
anton@doc.ic.ac.uk

Abstract. Graphics processors are increasingly used in scientific applications due to their high computational power, which comes from hardware with multiple-level parallelism and memory hierarchy. Sparse matrix computations frequently arise in scientific applications, for example, when solving PDEs on unstructured grids. However, traditional sparse matrix algorithms are difficult to efficiently parallelize for GPUs due to irregular patterns of memory references. In this paper we present a new storage format for sparse matrices that better employs locality, has low memory footprint and enables automatic specialization for various matrices and future devices via parameter tuning. Experimental evaluation demonstrates significant speedups compared to previously published results.

1 Introduction

Sparse linear algebra is an important class of algorithmic methods on sparse matrices, included by researchers from Berkeley into their set of *motifs* (formerly known as dwarfs) [1]. In many applications, dimensions of sparse matrices exceed tens of thousands rows and columns. However, the fraction of non-zero elements is small relative to the total number of elements, typically in the order of tens of non-zero elements or fewer per row. Therefore, sparse matrices require specialized storage formats with space requirements proportional to the number of non-zero elements, and consequently specialised algorithms.

An example of a problem that requires operations with sparse matrices is solving a partial differential equation using one of the finite elements methods. It includes solving a system of linear equations $Ax = b$, where non-zero elements of A are arranged in a regular or an irregular pattern depending on whether a structured or unstructured mesh is used for discretising the original problem.

Solving $Ax = b$ for sparse A is usually done via iterative methods, in which case the most time-consuming step is computing the matrix-vector product $y =$

* We acknowledge financial support by the Royal Society and the Russian Foundation for Basic Research (grant 08-07-91850-KO_a).

Y.N. Patt et al. (Eds.): HiPEAC 2010, LNCS 5952, pp. 111–125, 2010.
© Springer-Verlag Berlin Heidelberg 2010

$y + At$ for some t. In the conjugate gradient method, for example, other steps operate on vectors and are relatively easy to implement efficiently.

In this paper we discuss implementing the sparse matrix-vector product on NVIDIA GPUs with no specific assumptions about the structure of A. If values or locations of non-zero elements can be efficiently computed (e.g. when A is derived from discretization on a regular mesh, its non-zero elements occupy several diagonals), a specialized implementation will likely demonstrate better performance. Optimizing for symmetric sparse matrices A or computing $y = y + At$ for multiple t simultaneously is also out of the scope of this article.

We present a new storage format and show that our tuned implementation achieves better performance than other implementations we are aware of. Our implementation can be automatically tuned for other devices in the future.

2   Background

2.1   Sparse Matrix-Vector Multiplication

We implement sparse matrix-vector multiplication (SpMV), that is $y = y + Ax$,[1] where A is a $N \times M$ sparse matrix, x and y are dense M-element and N-element vectors, respectively.

SpMV performance largely depends on the memory bandwidth: for every matrix element A_{ij} only two floating-point operations are performed (a multiplication by input vector element x_j and accumulation to output vector element y_i). Since the memory bandwidth of GPUs exceeds that of CPUs by nearly an order of magnitude,[2] using GPUs for SpMV is particularly attractive.

When performing SpMV, memory bandwidth is used for:

1. Reading elements of A, specifically:
    (a) Reading non-zero elements of A;
    (b) Reading explicitly stored zero elements of A, if required by the storage format;
2. Reading coordinates of stored elements;
3. Servicing cache misses on accesses to vector x (if it is allocated in read-only cached texture memory, as in our implementation);
4. Reading and writing elements of vector y.

Bandwidth consumption by items 1a and 4 is not affected by the matrix storage format. In our previous work [6] we have presented an approach to optimize SpMV by using blocked storage format, which allows a reduction in space required for storing coordinates (item 2) and explicitly encode locality in references to x (potentially improving item 3) at the cost of storing additional zero elements (item 1b).

---

[1] Matrix multiplication is fused with vector addition to provide the form usually required by applications.

[2] For example. the theoretical peak bandwidth of NVIDIA GeForce GTX 285 is 159 Gbytes/s, and peak bandwidth of an Intel Core i7 system with DDR3 memory operating at 1066MHz in triple-channel mode on Intel X58 chipset is 25.6 Gbytes/s.

$$\begin{pmatrix} a & 0 & b & 0 \\ 0 & c & 0 & d \\ 0 & e & 0 & 0 \\ 0 & 0 & 0 & f \end{pmatrix}$$

row	0	0	1	1	2	3
column	0	2	1	3	1	3
value	a	b	c	d	e	f

```
for (i = 0; i < NZ; i++)
    y[row[i]] += x[column[i]] * value[i];
```

Matrix   Representation   SpMV pseudocode

Fig. 1. An example of the COO format. NZ is the number of non-zero elements.

In this paper we present a new non-blocked storage format and SpMV implementation, which also has space overhead due to explicitly stored zero elements, but can be tuned to achieve higher performance than other implementations.

2.2   Sparse Matrix Storage Formats

In this section, we briefly describe commonly used formats for storing sparse matrices and motivate our desire of a specialized storage format for implementing SpMV on a GPU.

Coordinate (COO) Format. For each non-zero element, both its column and row indices are explicitly stored (Fig. 1). Elements may either be stored in any order, or elements from the same row may be required to be packed together. This format is well suited with respect to storage space for very sparse matrices with many empty rows, since the storage size is strictly proportional to number of non-zero elements (i.e. it does not have any overhead due to empty rows).

Implementing SpMV on a GPU with this storage formats requires doing atomic updates to y vector from parallel threads, which leads to very low performance. With the additional restriction that elements from the same row are grouped together, a more elaborate implementation is possible [3], which allows a reduction in the number of updates to y.

Compressed Sparse Row (CSR) Format. Non-zero elements are sorted by the row index and stored in array value (ordering of elements within a row is not specified). For each element, only its column index is explicitly stored in array column (Fig. 2). Additionally, vector row_start stores indices in value of the first element in each row. Vector row_start has size $N + 1$; the additional element at the end stores the total number of non-zero elements to allow uniform access to all rows.

Implementing SpMV on a GPU with this format is inefficient, since distributing work across multiple threads leads to various problems. Assigning one thread per row leads to an inefficient memory access pattern to the column and value arrays (due to the lack of coalescing, see Section 2.3), and allocating multiple threads per row to ensure coalescing leads to many idle threads when the average number of non-zero elements per row is fewer than the number of assigned threads.

$$\begin{pmatrix} a\ 0\ b\ 0 \\ 0\ c\ 0\ d \\ 0\ e\ 0\ 0 \\ 0\ 0\ 0\ f \end{pmatrix}$$

row_start	0	2	4 5 6
column	0 2 1	3 1 3	
value	$a\ b\ c$	$d\ e\ f$	

```
for (r = 0; r < N; r++)
  for (i = row_start[r];
       i < row_start[r+1];
       i++)
    y[r] += x[column[i]] * value[i];
```

Matrix   Representation   SpMV pseudocode

Fig. 2. An example of the CSR format

ELLPACK/ITPACK Format. This format is used in the ELLPACK and ITPACK software packages to accelerate SpMV for vector processors [5]. Let K be the maximal number of non-zero elements in one row of the matrix. Then, for each row, exactly K elements are stored (extra zero elements are included for rows that contain less that K non-zero elements). As in the CSR, elements are sorted by row index and only column indices are explicitly stored (Fig. 3).

Note that `column` and `value` arrays in the example are stored in column-major order so that accesses are contiguous with respect to the outer loop. This allows memory access coalescing for concurrent CUDA threads, each executing one iteration of the outer loop.

When the number of non-zero elements per row is uneven, overhead from extra zero elements decreases performance. In extreme cases (e.g., a few rows with thousands of non-zero elements in an otherwise very sparse matrix) this overhead becomes larger than useful payload, making the format inapplicable.

Bell and Garland [3] propose a hybrid storage format based on ELLPACK and COO to address this issue. They choose K for ELLPACK format based on row fill histogram and store extra elements from rows with more that K non-zero elements in COO format so that overall performance is maximized (relative performance of SpMV implementations for COO and ELLPACK formats is evaluated in advance). This allows to use fast ELLPACK storage format for most of the matrix and use COO storage for any remaining non-zero elements, avoiding high overhead in pure ELLPACK format.

value: column:

$$\begin{pmatrix} a\ 0\ b\ 0 \\ 0\ c\ 0\ d \\ 0\ e\ 0\ 0 \\ 0\ 0\ 0\ f \end{pmatrix} \quad \begin{pmatrix} a\ b \\ c\ d \\ e\ 0 \\ f\ 0 \end{pmatrix} \quad \begin{pmatrix} 0\ 2 \\ 1\ 3 \\ 1\ 0 \\ 3\ 0 \end{pmatrix}$$

```
for (r = 0; r < N; r++)
  for (i = 0; i < K; i++)
    y[r] += x[column[i][r]] * value[i][r];
```

Matrix   Representation   SpMV pseudocode

Fig. 3. An example of ELLPACK format

2.3   The CUDA Programming Model

The CUDA programming model closely follows the organization of NVIDIA graphics hardware [7]. Computations are launched as multiple parallel threads executing the same function, called a kernel. The threads are grouped into blocks. Threads within a block have access to common shared memory and may synchronize using a barrier synchronization instruction.

Physically, a block of threads is executed on a GPU "core" called a multiprocessor. NVIDIA GT200 GPUs include up to 30 such multiprocessors. Each multiprocessor contains eight single-precision ALUs, one double-precision ALU and one instruction issue unit. Threads of a block are executed in 32-thread SIMD groups called *warps*. The instruction issue unit can switch between active warps with no overhead, which allows hiding execution latency (most importantly, memory access latency) when sufficient active warps are available on the multiprocessor.

The GT200 allows for up to 32 active warps (and hence up to 1024 active threads) per multiprocessor. The ratio of active warps to the maximum supported by the multiprocessor is called *occupancy*. Maximizing the occupancy is important when optimizing memory-intensive tasks, as it allows improvement of memory latency hiding by switching between active warps.

Each multiprocessor contains a 16-KiB storage area, which serves as shared memory for thread blocks running on this multiprocessor. For example, allocating 5 KiB for each block does not allow for more than 3 active blocks per multiprocessor. The register file is another partitioned resource, as there is no register save/restore on warp switching. Therefore, the amount of shared memory per block and the number of registers allocated per thread both affect the possible amount of active warps.

Off-chip GDDR memory is logically partitioned into the global, texture and constant memory spaces. Only global memory can be updated from the CUDA kernel. Texture and constant memory are read-only, but, unlike global memory, are cached. Constant memory differs from texture memory in maximum size (64 KiB, texture memory size is unlimited) and preferred access pattern (constant memory is optimized for the case when all threads from the warp read the same location).

Memory requests are serviced for halves of a warp at a time. To achieve the highest memory throughput, a memory access pattern must follow *coalescing rules*: accessed addresses must fit into a 64 or 128-byte window, and the window itself must be aligned on 64 or 128 byte boundary, respectively.

3   Sliced ELLPACK

We propose a new storage format, sliced ELLPACK, to improve SpMV performance on GPU architectures. This format is parameterized by slice size S: the input matrix is partitioned into strips of S adjacent rows,[3] and each strip is

---

[3] If the number of rows is not divisible by S, empty rows are added, and vector y must be appropriately padded. Since S is usually small compared to the number of rows, this has a negligible effect on performance.

value: column:

$$\begin{pmatrix} a\ 0\ b\ 0 \\ 0\ c\ 0\ d \\ 0\ e\ 0\ 0 \\ 0\ 0\ 0\ f \end{pmatrix} \qquad \begin{pmatrix} a\ b \\ c\ d \end{pmatrix} \begin{pmatrix} 0\ 2 \\ 1\ 3 \end{pmatrix} \qquad \begin{pmatrix} e \\ f \end{pmatrix} \begin{pmatrix} 1 \\ 3 \end{pmatrix}$$

slice_start 0		4	6
column 0 1 2 3 1 3			
value $a\ c\ b\ d\ e\ f$			

Matrix   Strips in ELLPACK format   Representation

Fig. 4. An example of the sliced ELLPACK format for $S = 2$

```
for (s = 0; s < N; s += S)
  for (r = s; r < s + S; r++)
    for (i = slice_start[s/S] + r - s;
         i < slice_start[s/S + 1];
         i += S)
      y[r] += x[column[i]] * value[i];
```

Fig. 5. SpMV pseudocode for the sliced ELLPACK

stored in the ELLPACK format. However, K, the number of non-zero elements stored per row in the ELLPACK format, may be different for each strip. Additionally, array `slice_start` holds indices of the first element in each strip (and the total number of non-zero elements at the end, as shown in Fig. 4). Thus the number of non-zero elements per row (including explicitly stored zero elements) in strip i can be calculated as

$$K_i = \frac{\texttt{slice\_start}_{i+1} - \texttt{slice\_start}_i}{S}$$

For $S = 1$ no extra zero elements need to be stored, so this approach results in the same representation as CSR. When incrementing S, the number of explicitly stored zero elements increases, reaching the maximum for $S = N$ (the number of rows), when this approach gives the same representation as ELLPACK. This allows choosing S sufficiently small to retain the storage space efficiency of the CSR format, yet large enough so that computations within each strip can be efficiently mapped onto GPU hardware.

3.1   Implementation of SpMV Using Sliced ELLPACK

To implement SpMV in CUDA using sliced ELLPACK format, we organize the computations as follows. We assign one CUDA thread block to each S rows of the matrix, thus launching a one-dimensional grid of $\frac{N}{S}$ CUDA blocks. We assign T CUDA threads to each block, with the restriction that S divides T. In this work, we only consider $T = 2^t$, $6 \le t \le 9$, as blocks of other sizes do not run efficiently on current CUDA devices and $T = 512$ is the maximum number of threads per block. It follows that $S = 2^s$, $0 \leq s \leq t \leq 9$. Let $\tau = \frac{T}{S}$ be the number of threads assigned to each row.

If $\tau = 1$, one thread is assigned to each row. If $\tau > 1$, we assign τ threads with indices $r + kS$, $k \in \{0, 1, \ldots, \tau - 1\}$, to row r, $r \in \{0, 1, \ldots, S - 1\}$, with each thread operating on elements with stride τ. In other words, we have τ thread groups with S threads per group. Every group operates on some columns from the ELLPACK representation of the current strip, with the columns distributed to the thread groups in the round-robin fashion.

When $\tau > 1$, each thread computes a partial update to vector y. After that, full updates are computed via parallel reduction over τ elements in shared memory in $\log_2 \tau$ steps (which, in turn, are performed in parallel for S threads in each group). This step requires storing $\frac{\tau S}{2} = \frac{T}{2}$ floating-point elements in shared memory. It follows that the shared memory requirement of our implementation is two or four bytes per thread (depending on whether single or double precision format is used). Therefore, the shared memory requirement does not limit occupancy in our implementation (as explained in Section 2.3, with no more than 1024 threads and 16 KiB shared memory per multiprocessor, requiring less than 16 bytes of shared memory per thread on average does not limit occupancy).

We use texture memory to optimize accesses to `slice_start` (each thread of the block reads the same pair of elements during the kernel startup) and to cache accesses to vector x.

This approach has the following benefits:

1. Matrices with variations in the number of non-zero elements per row do not suffer from overhead as badly as in the ELLPACK. In addition, having a single kernel (unlike in the hybrid ELLPACK/COO implementation in [3]) helps achieve better performance.
2. The ability to allocate a variable number of threads per row helps to adapt to different matrices. It is possible both to allocate one thread per row in very sparse matrices and to allocate multiple threads per row for matrices with a small number of rows.
3. Configurations with multiple threads per row likely benefit from higher locality in vector x references and lower pressure on the TLB.[4]

3.2   Matrix Reordering for Avoiding Storage Overhead

Our experiments show that the following simple reordering heuristic can greatly improve the performance of our SpMV implementation (provided that the problem being solved, in turn, allows reordering of the matrix without the need to reorder x and y before and after each SpMV operation).

Even though storage overhead in the sliced ELLPACK format is confined only to slices with imbalance in the number of non-zero elements per row, this still can cause noticeable performance degradation. This issue can be mitigated by

---

[4] The TLB existence is not documented by NVIDIA, but Volkov and Demmel [9] show how to derive TLB parameters using a pointer-chasing benchmark.

reordering the rows so that rows with equal numbers of non-zero elements are brought together, forming strips with zero overhead.

It is important to note that reordering rows may result in reduced SpMV performance. Sparse matrices usually have spatial locality: adjacent rows likely have more close non-zero elements than unrelated rows. Shuffling rows reduces this locality, increasing the number of cache misses on accesses to vector x. Thus, reordering is a matter of trade-off.

Since matrix reordering has to be performed at runtime after the matrix has been constructed, the reordering algorithm should have low computational complexity. In our experiments, we have used the following simple heuristic, which is linear in the number of rows.

Suppose we have a set of B buckets, numbered from 0 to $B-1$, for collecting rows. Rows are scanned from top to bottom, and a row with z non-zero elements is added to bucket number z (if $z \geq B$, such row is considered "overly long" and added to the last bucket). If adding a row creates a bucket with exactly S rows, rows from that bucket are output into the new reordered matrix, thus forming a strip with exactly z elements in each row if $z < B - 1$, and the bucket is emptied (and can be filled again as the scan progresses). After the scan is complete, remaining rows from non-empty buckets are appended to the reordered matrix in arbitrary order.

3.3   Variable-Height Slices

Consider a skewed sparse matrix where a low fraction of rows has an order of magnitude more non-zero elements than the average number. Our SpMV implementation, when applied to such matrix, would suffer from *work imbalance:* thread blocks that process slices with longest rows take a long time to complete compared to most of the other thread blocks. This may cause low GPU utilization, when only a few long-running thread blocks are left.

To mitigate this effect, we have implemented the following variation to the proposed sliced ELLPACK format. The height of each slice S_i may be different, with the restriction that S_i divides T (the number of threads per block). To indicate the height of each slice, we store an additional array `slice_pos` that stores the cumulative height of slices: `slice_pos[i]` $= \Sigma_{j=0}^{i-1} S_j$.[5] The kernel is also modified to account for a variable number of rows per slice.

Since this format requires additional space for storing `slice_pos` array and the corresponding SpMV implementation uses some memory bandwidth for reading it, it is not useful for matrices with low variation in the number of non-zero elements per row.

Conversion of the input matrix to variable-height sliced ELLPACK format is parameterized by ω, the approximate number of non-zero elements per thread. We use an approach similar to the reordering algorithm described above, with $B = \omega T$ being the number of buckets for collecting rows. As soon as any bucket

---

[5] For efficiency, in our implementation this array is interleaved with `slice_start` and both are accessed via texture memory.

for rows of z elements contains k rows, where k divides T and $kz \geq \omega T$, rows from that bucket are used to produce a new slice with height k.

4   Experimental Results

To evaluate our implementation, we have used a matrix test suite referenced in [3] and [11] to facilitate comparison with previous work. We have gathered baseline performance data using the hybrid ELLPACK/COO algorithm, as the overall best algorithm described in [3]. The baseline performance data was collected on a GTX 280 card, using CUDA toolkit version 2.3 for compilation. Our implementation was timed on G200-based GTX 280, GTX 260 and Tesla C1060 cards to demonstrate the effect of tuning.

Table 1 briefly characterizes matrices used for evaluation along with performance of our baseline implementation in single and double precision.

Performance in GFLOPS is calculated as $\frac{2 \times \text{NZ}}{T}$, where NZ is the number of non-zero elements and T is the time required for one multiplication by vector (not including the time to copy data to device and back). Our experiments show that the variation of time required for one SpMV kernel launch does not exceed 0.1%. Therefore, we time the second from two consecutive kernel launches (the first is used to exclude one-time overheads from uploading the kernel to the GPU).

4.1   Performance Evaluation

To evaluate our implementation, we have performed a search over a wide range of configurations, where parameters assumed all power-of-two values in the specified

Table 1. Matrix data and reference performance results on GeForce GTX 280

Matrix characteristics			Nonzeros per row		Baseline, GFLOPS	
Name	Rows	Columns	Average	Maximum	32-bit	64-bit
cant	62451	62451	64.16	78	16.56	9.99
consph	83334	83334	72.12	81	21.09	11.96
cop20k_A	121192	121192	21.65	81	8.32	5.08
dense2	2000	2000	2000.00	2000	3.92	3.33
mac_econ	206500	206500	6.16	44	7.78	5.04
mc2depi	525825	525825	3.99	4	19.12	10.72
pdb1HYS	36417	36417	119.31	204	13.28	9.74
pwtk	217918	217918	53.38	180	21.48	13.82
qcd5_4	49152	49152	39.00	39	21.48	12.66
rail4284	4284	1092610	2633.00	56181	2.54	2.04
rma10	46835	46835	50.68	145	11.16	6.91
scircuit	170998	170998	5.60	353	6.81	4.39
shipsec1	140874	140874	55.46	102	18.22	11.44
webbase-1M	1000005	1000005	3.10	4700	6.50	5.10

Table 2. Performance results of the best configurations on GTX 280

Name	Single precision			Double precision		
	Speedup (%)	GFLOPS	Bandwidth	Speedup (%)	GFLOPS	Bandwidth
cant	49.42	24.74	113.08	45.89	14.57	99.32
consph	34.65	28.40	115.18	36.15	16.28	98.55
cop20k_A	56.34	13.01	54.58	86.00	9.45	56.78
dense2	621.28	28.27	114.00	433.35	17.76	106.57
mac_econ	30.31	10.14	48.51	55.56	7.86	57.47
mc2depi	4.75	20.03	98.01	14.28	12.25	98.07
pdb1HYS	92.43	25.56	102.32	52.47	14.85	89.16
pwtk	32.77	28.52	116.66	25.33	17.32	103.98
qcd5_4	19.51	25.67	102.73	22.11	15.46	92.78
rail4284	183.31	7.20	28.86	169.52	5.50	33.02
rma10	84.81	20.62	82.69	95.99	13.54	81.38
scircuit	25.85	8.70	41.23	48.65	6.81	50.73
shipsec1	56.58	28.53	114.21	52.22	17.41	104.56
webbase-1M	46.09	9.50	50.48	37.85	7.19	61.81

ranges. We have tested thread block sizes (T) in the range from 64 to 512. For the sliced ELLPACK format we have tested slice sizes (S) in the range from 8 to 512, and reordering parameter (B) in the range from 1 to 4096. For the variable-height sliced ELLPACK format we have tested work per thread parameter (ω) in the range from 1 to 512.

Table 2 shows performance of the best configurations. Speedups are calculated relative to the baseline implementation [3]. Bandwidth is listed in Gbytes/s and is calculated only for data that has no reuse during kernel execution (`value`, `column`, `slice_start` and `y` arrays). Since vector x elements are fetched via texture caches, their contribution to the total bandwidth is hard to quantify. Therefore, memory bandwidth in Table 2 is the lower bound of the total memory transfer speed achieved during kernel execution. For single precision, the bandwidth is roughly four times larger than the GFLOPS value, since the kernel fetches 8 bytes (one integer from `column` and one float from `value` array) for each two floating-point operations. Likewise, the bandwidth for the double-precision computations is roughly six times larger than the GFLOPS value.

The results clearly show that the performance is limited by the memory bandwidth. For half of the test matrices our implementation approaches the peak memory bandwidth of GTX 280 (which is roughly 120 Gbytes/s on sequential memory reading/writing) on non-cached data alone, which also means that fraction of cache hits on accesses to vector x on those tests is high. On five of the matrices non-cached memory bandwidth does not exceed 60 GBytes/s. This indicates that there is less locality in references to vector x, which causes more cache misses and small scattered reads, which are inefficient on GPUs.

The exceptionally high speedup achieved for the `dense2` matrix is explained by the fact that the baseline implementation launches only 2000 threads (by the number of rows in the matrix), which is not enough to optimally utilize the GPU.

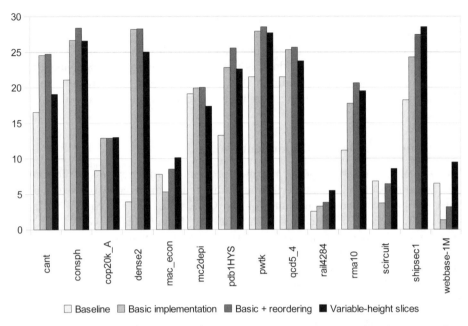

Fig. 6. Performance (in GFLOPS) of different implementations (single precision)

Figure 6 shows the single-precision performance of the baseline SpMV implementation, our basic algorithm and two refined variants: with matrix reordering and with variable-height slices on GTX 280.

Figure 7 shows single-precision performance of all configurations tested for the consph matrix. Different performance values (on the y axis) for a fixed slice

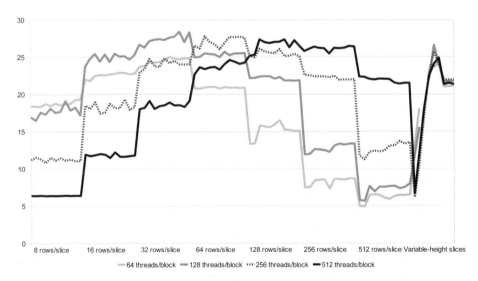

Fig. 7. Performance (in GFLOPS) of different configurations on the consph matrix

size (on the x axis) correspond to different values of the reordering parameter B. In this example, the best performing thread block size is roughly four times the slice size: e.g. for 256 threads per block the optimal slice size is 64. This suggests that the optimal workload is four threads per row or 18 elements per thread on average. Correspondingly, the variable-height slices variant reaches the maximum at 16 elements per thread. Similar behaviour is observed on other test matrices.

4.2   Tuning Is Device-Dependent

Table 3 demonstrates the performance improvement from device-specific tuning. The value in each cell is the performance difference, in percent, between SpMV with the best configuration found for the GTX 280 card and SpMV with the best configuration for the corresponding device (Tesla C1060 or GTX 260). The speedup on the last five matrices from the test suite is insignificant, hence they are not listed. Surprisingly, even for these three cards based on the same architecture, the performance difference exceeds 10% in two cases. Therefore, we believe that automatic tuning is a useful technique of improving SpMV performance.

Table 3. Speedup from device-specific tuning (in %)

	Tesla C1060		GTX 260	
Name	32-bit	64-bit	32-bit	64-bit
cant	9.74	14.21	0.93	2.87
consph	2.27	7.44	3.02	1.55
cop20k_A	3.52	0.44	3.96	0.68
dense2	0.00	1.92	0.29	1.76
mac_econ	1.53	0.81	4.85	2.64
mc2depi	17.55	1.53	0.76	5.08
pdb1HYS	3.31	3.32	1.67	1.38
pwtk	3.42	1.53	5.32	0.81
qcd5_4	6.12	4.83	1.16	1.87

4.3   Space Requirements

Table 4 shows the comparison of space required for storing the matrix in our format to the CSR format and the hybrid format from the baseline implementation. Since space requirements of our implementation depend on slice size and reordering, the table presents results from configurations with best performance on GTX 280 in single precision.

"Explicit zeros" column shows relative amount of explicitly stored zero elements in percent. "To CSR" column shows the difference in space required for storing the whole matrix relative to the CSR format. We see that space requirements of our format are within 2% of the CSR size in most cases. There is a regression on the cant matrix due to large amount of explicitly stored zero elements. Four tests with low average numbers of non-zero elements per row are

Table 4. Comparison of required storage space in single precision (in %)

Name	Our implementation			Distribution in baseline	
	Explicit zeros	To CSR	To baseline	In ELLPACK	In COO
cant	13.56	12.70	-3.24	116.90	0.32
consph	0.01	-0.65	-10.95	112.34	0.00
cop20k_A	0.05	-2.13	-11.70	87.53	17.25
dense2	0.80	0.78	0.00	100.80	0.00
mac_econ	0.05	-7.29	-29.34	113.53	18.88
mc2depi	0.16	-10.90	0.10	100.15	0.00
pdb1HYS	0.09	-0.32	-17.82	115.77	4.03
pwtk	2.25	1.32	0.27	101.15	0.56
qcd5_4	0.00	-1.23	0.04	100.00	0.00
rail4284	0.23	0.22	-38.79	81.88	54.59
rma10	0.21	-0.75	-26.60	108.54	18.67
scircuit	0.66	-7.54	-17.34	89.17	21.78
shipsec1	0.05	-0.83	-7.05	97.38	6.85
webbase-1M	0.03	-13.69	-15.14	64.40	35.79

significantly improved in terms of storage size due to reduction in space required for storing row boundaries: the CSR format stores one integer per row, while our format stores one or two integers per slice, depending on whether fixed-height or variable-height slices are used.

"To baseline" column shows the difference in storage space relative to the baseline format (hybrid ELLPACK/COO, with the number of rows padded to the next multiple of 32). Columns 5 and 6 show the percentage of non-zero elements stored in the ELLPACK and COO parts of the hybrid format. When calculating the ratio of non-zero elements in the ELLPACK part, explicitly stored zeros are included. Therefore, the sum of ELLPACK and COO ratios may exceed 100%. Since our format reduces overhead both from explicitly stored zeros in the ELLPACK format and from row coordinates stored for each element in the COO format, we see a significant reduction in storage size for most matrices. Required space is approximately the same for the matrices with low variation in the number of non-zero elements per row.

5   Related Work

Optimization of SpMV for CPUs has been extensively studied (e.g. see Vuduc's dissertation [10], which includes descriptions of many storage formats and provides experimental data on CPUs). Many researchers note how SpMV implementations usually extract only several percent of CPU's peak performance and note the importance of blocking to reduce pressure on memory subsystem and to explicitly express data reuse.

Williams et al. [11] present evaluation of optimized SpMV implementations on multi-core x86 processors, STI Cell and Sun Niagara 2. Following [3], we use their test suite to evaluate performance of our approach.

Operations on dense matrices on GPUs have been thoroughly analyzed, which is partially due to more regular nature of the problem. Volkov and Demmel [9] present an experimental study of GPU memory subsystem and an efficient implementation of dense matrix-matrix multiplication. The implementation is shown to be nearly optimal under the constraints of hardware implementation.

Several SpMV implementations for GPUs have been described, including [2,3,4,6,8]. Bell and Garland [3] investigate the performance of several non-blocked methods. They propose using a hybrid approach to sparse matrix storage, which results in efficient SpMV implementation for most of the test matrices from [11]. Vázquez et al. [8] improve Bell and Garland's results by 15% on average by augmenting ELLPACK format with explicit count of non-zero elements. SpMV implementations in [2,6] use blocked storage format, which requires costly conversion and makes them not applicable for matrices where sufficiently filled blocks cannot be identified. Buatois et al [4] were one of the first to report implementing SpMV in CUDA; however, they did not achieve high performance due to inefficient usage of GPU memory subsystem.

6   Future Work

We plan to develop this approach into a stand-alone SpMV library with separated off-line (device-specific) and on-line (run-time, matrix-specific) tuning stages. We will look into integration with Fluidity, a mature fluid simulation application. Prediction of good configuration based on matrix characteristics will be important for applications with frequently changing sparsity patterns.

Acknowledgments

We thank Alastair Donaldson, Andrey Belevantsev, Alan Mycroft and Paul Kelly for their helpful discussions and comments. We also thank the anonymous reviewers for their comments that helped to improve this paper.

References

1. Asanovic, K., Bodik, R., Catanzaro, B.C., Gebis, J.J., Husbands, P., Keutzer, K., Patterson, D.A., Plishker, W.L., Shalf, J., Williams, S.W., Yelick, K.A.: The landscape of parallel computing research: A view from Berkeley. Technical Report UCB/EECS-2006-183, EECS Department, University of California, Berkeley (December 2006)
2. Baskaran, M.M., Bordawekar, R.: Optimizing sparse matrix-vector multiplication on GPUs. Technical report, IBM TJ Watson Research Center (2009)
3. Bell, N., Garland, M.: Efficient sparse matrix-vector multiplication on CUDA. NVIDIA Technical Report NVR-2008-004 (2008)
4. Buatois, L., Caumon, G., Lévy, B.: Concurrent number cruncher: An efficient sparse linear solver on the GPU. In: Perrott, R., Chapman, B.M., Subhlok, J., de Mello, R.F., Yang, L.T. (eds.) HPCC 2007. LNCS, vol. 4782, pp. 358–371. Springer, Heidelberg (2007)

5. Kincaid, D.R., Oppe, T.C., Young, D.M.: ITPACKV 2D User's Guide
6. Monakov, A., Avetisyan, A.: Implementing blocked sparse matrix-vector multiplication on NVIDIA GPUs. In: SAMOS, pp. 289–297 (2009)
7. NVIDIA Corporation. NVIDIA CUDA Programming Guide 2.2 (2009)
8. Vázquez, F., Garzón, E.M., Martnez, J.A., Fernández, J.J.: The sparse matrix vector product on GPUs. Technical report, University of Almeria (2009)
9. Volkov, V., Demmel, J.W.: Benchmarking GPUs to tune dense linear algebra. In: SC 2008: Proceedings of the 2008 ACM/IEEE conference on Supercomputing, pp. 1–11. IEEE Press, Los Alamitos (2008)
10. Vuduc, R.W.: Automatic performance tuning of sparse matrix kernels, PhD thesis, University of California, Berkeley (2003); Chair-Demmel, J.W.
11. Williams, S., Oliker, L., Vuduc, R.W., Shalf, J., Yelick, K.A., Demmel, J.: Optimization of sparse matrix-vector multiplication on emerging multicore platforms. In: SC, p. 38 (2007)

Virtual Ways: Efficient Coherence for Architecturally Visible Storage in Automatic Instruction Set Extensions

Theo Kluter[1,5], Samuel Burri[2], Philip Brisk[4],
Edoardo Charbon[2,3], and Paolo Ienne[1]

[1] Ecole Polytechnique Fédérale de Lausanne (EPFL), School of Computer and
Communication Sciences, CH-1015 Lausanne, Switzerland
paolo.ienne@epfl.ch
[2] Ecole Polytechnique Fédérale de Lausanne (EPFL), School of Engineering,
CH-1015 Lausanne, Switzerland
samuel.burri@epfl.ch
[3] Delft University of Technology, Circuits and Systems Group,
NL-2600 AA Delft, The Netherlands
edoardo.charbon@epfl.ch
[4] University of California, Riverside, Department of Computer Science and
Engineering, Riverside, CA 92521, USA
philip@cs.ucr.edu
[5] Bern University of Applied Sciences, EKT, Microlab, Quellgasse 21,
CH-2501 Biel/Bienne, Switzerland
theo.kluter@bfh.ch

Abstract. Customizable processors augmented with application-specific *Instruction Set Extensions (ISEs)* have begun to gain traction in recent years. The most effective ISEs include *Architecturally Visible Storage (AVS)*, compiler-controlled memories accessible exclusively to the ISEs. Unfortunately, the usage of AVS memories creates a coherence problem with the data cache. A multiprocessor coherence protocol can solve the problem, however, this is an expensive solution when applied in a uniprocessor context. Instead, we can solve the problem by modifying the cache controller so that the AVS memories function as extra ways of the cache with respect to coherence, but are *not* generally accessible as extra ways for use under normal software execution. This solution, which we call *Virtual Ways* is less costly than a hardware coherence protocol, and eliminate coherence messages from the system bus, which improves energy consumption. Moreover, eliminating these messages makes Virtual Ways significantly more robust to performance degradation when there is a significant disparity in clock frequency between the processor and main memory.

Keywords: Application-Specific Processors, Memory Coherence, Instruction Set Extensions, Virtual Ways.

1 Introduction

Extensible processors are a cost-effective platform that can help embedded system designers meet their targets for performance and energy efficiency. These

Y.N. Patt et al. (Eds.): HiPEAC 2010, LNCS 5952, pp. 126–140, 2010.

processors are augmented with application-specific custom *instruction set extensions (ISEs)* that improve performance and energy efficiency for critical loops in embedded applications. ISEs can be identified automatically [11,4], and a system designer must only verify the ISEs and their interface to the processor, as the processor itself has been pre-verified by the vendor. Although extensible processors cannot compete with *application-specific integrated circuits (ASICs)* in terms of performance and energy efficiency, they offer an economic advantage through a simplified design and verification process and a reduced time-to-market.

To increase performance, ISEs have been augmented with *Architecturally Visible Storage (AVS)*, which can be registers or compiler-controlled memories [3]. AVS memories are distinct from the cache hierarchy, and *Directed Memory Access (DMA)* transfers move data between main memory and the AVS, bypassing the caches, which creates a coherence problem. Kluter et al. [9] solved the coherence problem using a snoopy hardware coherence protocol, which was designed for use in multiprocessor systems. This solution has two drawbacks: area overhead, and performance degradation due to coherence messages on the system bus competing with off-chip memory accesses.

Virtual Ways, presented here, is a scheme by which the cache controller is modified to ensure coherence between the data cache and the AVS memory. Under this scheme, the data cache and AVS memory share a common interface, and prefetch instructions are used in lieu of DMA transfers. A relaxed form of inclusion between the data cache and AVS memory provides coherence: the data in the AVS memory is always a subset of the data in the cache, but writes in the AVS memory are not automatically written through to the cache, but writes to the AVS memory (cache) and not written through to the cache (AVS memory). The cache controller, therefore, evolves into a low-cost hardware coherence protocol for this specific case.

Virtual Ways and Speculative DMA are compared using a standard cell design flow to estimate the area overhead of the memory subsystem. For JPEG compression, in which the AVS memory is a 64-entry register file containing 8-bit registers, and 8 read and 8 write ports, the area overhead of Speculative DMA was 1.29x, due to the cost of the coherence protocol, including the AVS memory, while the area overhead of Virtual Ways was 1.09x, due mostly to the AVS memory and a slightly larger data cache state machine.

Virtual Ways and Speculative DMA are compared using an FPGA-based soft processor emulation system to measure task latency and memory system energy consumption. The experiments include a detailed case study of JPEG compression, and an evaluation of four EEMBC consumer V2 benchmarks: CJPEGV2 (compression), MPEG encoding and decoding, and AES. The most significant result is that the speedups achieved by Speculative DMA degrade significantly as the frequency of the processor increases while the frequency of off-chip memory remains constant, whereas, Virtual Ways does not suffer from any noticeable performance degradation. For CJPEGV2 and MPEG encoding and decoding, Virtual Ways achieved a higher speedup and reduced energy consumption compared to Speculative DMA, while the results for both metrics were equal for AES, due to the fact that all data structures in the AVS memories are read-only.

We performed a detailed analysis and case study of an internally-modified version of JPEG compression that only compresses one color component; we call this version "JPEG" for simplicity. The analysis of JPEG includes a kernel-by-kernel breakdown of the task latency and energy consumption of the two techniques, and include a design space exploration in which the size and associativity of the instruction and data caches are varied. In the former study, Virtual Ways achieves a significant energy reduction in the Quantisation kernel, while achieving comparable task latencies across all kernels. In the latter study, Virtual Ways reduces task latency and energy consumption, compared to Speculative DMA, for each configuration. Looking across configurations, Virtual Ways generally achieves the best results; however, a handful of the best performing configurations of Speculative DMA do achieve better task latency and/or energy consumption than the worst performing configurations of Speculative DMA; the overall trend, however, favors Virtual Ways.

The remainder of the paper is organized as follows: Section 2 details related work in the domain. Section 3 introduces Virtual Ways and describes their implementation in an extensible processor featuring AVS-enhanced ISEs. Section 4 describes an FPGA-based soft processor emulation system that we use for our performance evaluation, and Section 5 presents an in-depth case study using JPEG compression, followed by a more general study using EEMBC consumer V2 benchmarks. Section 6 concludes the paper.

2   Related Work

In early work on ISEs, the processor's register file was the I/O interface [4,11]. A typical register file has two read ports and one write port, which limit the size of each ISE and the attainable speedup. Multi-cycle ISEs [1,10,12,14,15] overlap computation with I/O operations; however, the I/O interface remained a bottleneck. Several microarchitectural modifications have successfully improved input bandwidth, including *shadow registers* [5], register file clustering [7], and utilizing the pipeline forwarding logic [6]. Although generally effective, these techniques do not improve output bandwidth, and data is transferred to the ISE logic on the granularity of scalar variables; they do not support bulk transfers of arrays.

Biswas et al. [2] introduced *architecturally visible storage (AVS)*, which was limited to small ROMs that hold constant values, and state registers. In a subsequent work, they augmented their ISEs with small compiler-controlled memories that hold arrays. DMA transfers move data into and out of the AVS memories bypassing the cache [3]. This solution is similar to *scratchpad memories* [13], which are also placed under compiler control. Scratchpad memories have been proposed as an *alternative* to caches for embedded systems, because eliminating the tag array reduces per-access energy consumption, and deterministic hit/miss behavior improves predictability of worst-case execution time.

AVS memories, in contrast, co-exist with caches, rather than replacing them. As observed by Kluter et al. [9], this leads to a coherence problem, as the DMA transfers between main memory and AVS memories bypass the cache hierarchy, and no mechanism exists to ensure coherence between the AVS memory and the data cache. They corrected the problem using a hardware coherence protocol; however, the area overhead of the DMA controller and the coherence protocol were significant. Additionally, coherence messages transmitted on the bus consume energy, and may increase the latency of accesses to off-chip memory.

Under this scheme, the compiler inserts *Speculative DMA* transfer instructions to move data from main memory into the AVS memory before an ISE that accesses the latter may execute. Each line of the AVS memory is augmented with *valid* and *dirty* bits, similar in principle to a cache, but without the tag arrays. These bits are required to integrate the AVS memory into the hardware coherence protocol; additionally, the valid bits facilitate the *speculative* aspect of DMA, by suppressing transfers when data in the AVS memory is up-to-date.

The data cache and AVS memory snoop bus transactions. A write to data in the AVS (cache) invalidates a copy of the data that may exist in the cache (AVS). If the processor reads invalid data from the cache, the coherence protocol retrieves the valid copy from the AVS memory. Speculative DMA transfers from main memory into the AVS memory request the write-back o a dirty copy of the data that may exist in the cache. When a DMA transfer overwrites valid and dirty data in the AVS memory, the coherence protocol ensures that the valid data is written back to main memory. When a DMA transfer overwrites valid and dirty data in the AVS memory, the coherence protocol ensures that the valid data is written back to main memory, eliminating the need for explicit DMA transfer instructions to remove data from the AVS memory.

Virtual Ways, presented here, is a lower-cost solution to the coherence problem. Unlike Speculative DMA, Virtual Ways uses a relaxed form of inclusion, in which the AVS memory always contains a subset of the data in the cache; however, ISE writes to the AVS memory employ a write-back policy that only updates the copy in the data cache when the processor, later, tries to read the data from the cache. Speculative DMA, in contrast, does not enforce inclusion.

Under Virtual Ways, data is loaded into the AVS memory using prefetch instructions, which eliminates the DMA engine. There is no hardware coherence protocol, which eliminates both the hardware overhead (i.e., duplicated tags) and the performance and energy overhead due to snooping and coherence traffic on the system bus. This improves both system performance and energy consumption.

Way Stealing is another solution to the coherence problem for AVS-enhanced ISEs [8]. The data cache is modified so that each way can be accessed as a compiler controlled memory, and all of the ways can be read or written in parallel. Each way, however, is a single-ported memory, which can limit the attainable speedup. For JPEG compression, for example, our ideal AVS memory is a 64-entry register file with 8 read and 8 write ports; the large number of read and write ports are feasible for such a small structure, but are not generally scalable

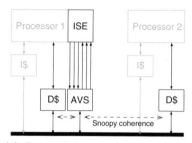
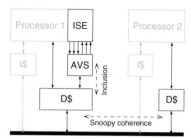

(a) State-of-the-art Automatic Instruction Set Extension algorithms provide high bandwidth to the ISE logic by adding Architecturally Visible Storage; however, they require extensive hardware added to a standard processor pipeline to guarantee memory coherence [3,9].

(b) Virtual Ways, the contribution of this work, puts the AVS on top of the data cache and extends the cache controller state machine to enforce coherence. This approach removes the separate bus interface of the AVS and the need for a coherence protocol in single processor systems.

Fig. 1. The difference between providing coherence in Speculative-DMA and Virtual Ways. In Speculative DMA the AVS is placed at the same level as the L1-caches. In Virtual Ways, on the other hand, the AVS is placed above the L1-caches and coherence is provided by inclusion.

for a larger number of entries. Under Way Stealing, the read and write operations to each stolen way must be serialized due to th small number of ports, which limits the maximum attainable speedup.

3 Virtual Ways

Historically, a single cache based processor system allows for a maximum of two copies of a given data structure in the system. One copy is always in main memory and one can be in the cache. In an n-way set associative cache, the location of a datum within the cache is indicated by the tag arrays and the associated status bits. The cache state-machine keeps track of the datum by updating the tag and state arrays accordingly. Any memory element in the system that is not covered by the tag and state arrays of the cache may exhibit coherence problems. This is precisely what occurs when AVS is introduced to an extensible processor without some form of coherence. The most recent copy of a particular datum may reside in the AVS, rather than the cache. Main memory, therefore, is liable to load an invalid copy of the same datum into the cache, unless it first updates the value from the AVS.

This is the classic problem of cache coherence; the fact that the AVS is not actually a cache does not, in principle, alter the problem; however, it does offer the possibility of a novel lightweight solution that is considerably less costly than a full-blown coherence protocol, which in the past has been used for multiprocessor systems. Our solution, which we call *Virtual Ways*, is to treat the AVS as

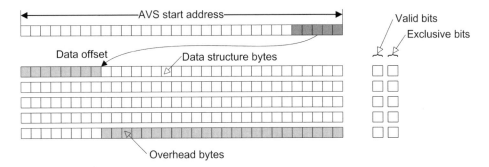

Fig. 2. The AVS is segmented in chunks the size of a cache line and the state is maintained for each segment separately. The tag consists of the start address and end address (length) of the AVS. For optimal performance care must be taken to avoid false sharing between neighboring data structures.

an additional way of the cache with respect to coherence. ISEs still access the AVS memory like a scratchpad under control of the compiler. The tag associated with the AVS memory, which is only used to ensure coherence, is implemented inside the cache. This way, ISE accesses to the AVS memory bypass the tag, which saves energy on each lookup. The cache controller is aware of the status of the data residing in the AVS due to its tag, and takes appropriate actions to ensure coherence. Virtual Ways can ensure coherence between an L1 cache and an AVS memory in a uniprocessor system.

For easier integration into the cache some adaptations are needed in comparison to scratchpad memories. The memory for the data structure held in the AVS memory is padded to a multiple of the size of a cache line. As the data structure to be loaded in the AVS is not necessarily aligned on a cache line boundary, the AVS must hold one additional cache line in order to accommodate all possible alignments. For optimal performance, an AVS-aware compiler could align data structures to avoid false sharing. For example, suppose that one data structure ends near the beginning of a cache line, and another data structure starts somewhere later on the same line. A write to a location in either data structure that resides on the cache line will invalidate the entire line, including a portion of the other data structure. This could, in principle, create unnecessary data transfers between the cache memories and the AVS.

Figure 2 illustrates the memory structure used to implement an AVS as a Virtual Way. Two bits per segment are required: one bit determines whether the segment is valid, and the second bit determines whether the copy in the AVS is exclusive. One set of tags for the AVS indicates the starting and ending addresses of the data structure stored in the AVS. This set of tags is used to determine if a CPU access issued to the cache is within the region contained within the AVS. The set of tags and the state bits permit the cache controller to determine where the most recent copy of the requested datum resides.

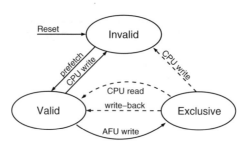

Fig. 3. Transition digram for each segment of the AVS; each segment can be in one of three states Invalid, Valid, or Exclusive. Associated ISEs execute while all segments are either valid or exclusive. ISE writes to an AVS segment cause it to become exclusive. An exclusive segment must be written back to the cache when the segment transitions into another state.

An ISE enhanced with an AVS can only execute when all segments are valid, as all accesses to the AVS must hit. We do not impose any restrictions on the ISE's access patterns within the AVS, beyond the requirement that the data reside in the AVS before the ISE begins to execute. Specialized prefetch instructions are used to load data into the AVS and update the tag before the ISE can execute. Similar to caches, data eviction from the AVS is achieved via lazy write back; however, an AVS-flush instruction is also available. If the data is accessed through a normal software instruction, the cache controller, which maintains coherence, will copy the data into the cache, and invalidate the data in the AVS if it is overwritten. In our experiments, we did not use the AVS-flush operation. Our expectation is that the AVS flush operation would only be used to facilitate context switching; our evaluation platform is application-specific, so we do not employ multiple processes and context switching does not occur.

3.1 AVS Segment States

Each segment of the AVS can be in one of three states. These are:

1. *Invalid State*: the initial state of the AVS, in which no segment contains valid data. This occurs when the processor is first powered up, or if the AVS contains a copy of a data structure that is not the most recent, i.e., a separate copy, either in the cache or main memory, has been modified, while the copy residing in the AVS memory has not been updated.
2. *Valid State*: a segment of the AVS contains the most recent copy of a data structure. Valid copies of the same line also exist in the cache.
3. *Exclusive State*: a segment of the AVS contains the most recent copy of a data structure. The copy in the cache, if any, is dead.

Figure 3 depicts the state machine for one segment of an AVS. Dashed arrows indicate the transitions where the data must be written back to the cache.

3.2   Prefetching Operation

Here, we describe the basic actions of the prefetch instruction, which must complete before an ISE can access the AVS. Here, we define an AVS region to be a set of m segments, each of which is equal to the size of a cache line. There are two general cases to consider:

1. *AVS Region Match*: This occurs if the address of the requested data matches a segment contained within the AVS. If the state of the segment is valid or exclusive, then the most recent copy of the data already exists in the AVS; the data must be loaded into the AVS only if the state is invalid. If a valid copy of the data exists in another way of the cache, then it can be loaded directly into the AVS, bypassing the bus; otherwise, the data is loaded from main memory and is written to the cache and AVS concurrently. See Figure 4 (e) for a prefetch operation that reloads only one segment.
2. *AVS Region Mismatch*: This occurs if the address of the requested data does not match a segment contained within the AVS. If one of the segments contained within the AVS is currently exclusive, then it must be written back to the cache/main memory so that the most recent copy of the data is not lost. Afterwards, all segments are marked invalid and the start and stop tags are updated for the new data structure. The load operation then proceeds as described above, with a region match and the AVS segments in an invalid state. See Figure 4 (f) for the case where the AVS is written back before it is loaded with a new data structure.

The region matching behavior enforces an inclusive, write-through policy. *Inclusion* is maintained, because the lines in the AVS are a subset of the lines in the cache. This is a relaxed form of inclusion, however, because ISE writes that modify an AVS segment do not modify the corresponding line in the cache. The policy is *write through*, in the sense that prefetch instructions write "through" the cache directly to the AVS.

3.3   Maintaining Coherence After the ISE Executes

We assume that the data has been prefetched into the AVS, as described in the preceding section. When an ISE executes, it may modify the data structure in the AVS. If the data is modified, then at least one line is left in the exclusive state. After the ISE executes, control returns to the CPU. The data in the AVS will either be written back upon request, or as dictated by coherence requirements. The correct action to take by a software load or store instruction depends on the state of the segment.

1. *Invalid State*: An invalid segment can be ignored; the data at the requested address resides in the cache or main memory.
2. *Valid State*: Here, the AVS contains valid data that was not modified by the ISE. A valid copy of the data may also exist in the cache. For a read access, either valid copy of the data can be returned. Writes are somewhat more

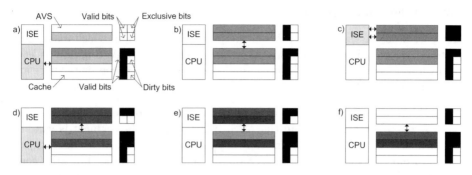

Fig. 4. This figure shows some lines of the cache and the corresponding segments in the AVS together with associated state bits during a typical AVS scenario. The AVS starts up in invalid state (a) and is then preloaded with a data structure (b) and transitions to valid state. Execution of the ISE will modify the data structure turning on (some of) its exclusive bits (c). On a CPU access the data is copied back to the cache and, on a write access, invalidated in the AVS (d). A prefetch instruction for the same structure will restore it to the AVS (e). A prefetch instruction for another structure will write back all exclusive lines and load the requested structure (f).

complex, as coherence must be maintained between the cache and the AVS. One possibility is to employ a write-through policy that updates the data in both the AVS and the cache; a second alternative is to update the data in the cache and invalidate the data in the AVS. We have opted for the latter option, because a pipelined write-through could potentially cause a memory consistence problem between the data cache and the AVS. A memory consistence problem occurs when a read of data does not return the latest value written to it. This situation can occur with a pipelined write-through. Applying a write-through without pipelining would drastically impact the processor's critical path.

3. *Exclusive State*: In this case, only the AVS contains the most recent copy of the data, and this copy must be written back to the cache before the access can complete; the corresponding line in the cache is marked as dirty, and the AVS segment reverts to the valid state, as the data in the AVS is no longer exclusive. Figure 4 (d) depicts the case of a CPU write access when the corresponding AVS segment is in exclusive state.

3.4   Multiple AVS Memories

The preceding discussion assumes that there is one AVS memory. In principle, an ISE may access multiple data structures, and writes to both may benefit from parallel execution. In this case, we would want to instantiate multiple AVS memories: one per data structure. To facilitate this change, we require an additional tag and state bits for each AVS that must be checked to maintain coherence.

The compiler can avoid inter-AVS transfers by guaranteeing that memory regions loaded in distinct AVS memories will never overlap. In the most general case, pointer analysis is undecidable. As described by Biswas et al. [3], only data structures that have been disambiguated can be moved into an AVS memory. Although this approach is conservative, it is necessary to ensure correctness when compiling languages such as $C/C++$ that permit arbitrary pointer arithmetic.

4   Experimental Setup

Our experimental platform is an internally-developed FPGA-based soft processor that implements the OpenRISC instruction set. We modified the data cache implementation to account for Speculative DMA [9] and Virtual Ways. Our multi-processor platform allows us to emulate from one to seven OpenRISC processors. The platform has software-configurable 16 kB instruction caches and software-configurable 16 kB data caches with a choice of MSI-states, MESI-states, or disabled hardware coherence protocol. Our implementation of Speculative DMA uses the MESI-states protocol in our experiments. Our implementation of Virtual Ways eliminates the DMA controller, as data is brought into the AVS memory through the data cache interface. The only other hardware modification was to augment the cache state machine as described in the preceding section.

Mimosys Clarity, a compiler that uses the algorithm proposed by Biswas [3], identified the ISEs and generated the VHDL implementations of the ISE logic. We modified the AVS memory to support Speculative DMA through a DMA interface and Virtual Ways through the data cache interface; the appropriate interface is selected via software control. A system deployed in the real world would support one option or the other, but not both.

Our goal is to demonstrate that Virtual Ways offers a comparable speedup to Speculative DMA, but at a significantly reduced hardware and energy cost. We took the EEMBC consumer V2 testbench suite and performed an ISE identification on the unmodified source code by taking the first dataset of each algorithm as test case. It has to be noted at this point that Mimosys Clarity does not implement the opportunistic Speculative DMA as proposed by Kluter *et al.* [9]. All the C-code has been cross-compiled using a gcc 3.4.4 toolchain based on "newlib" for the OpenRISC.

5   Experimental Results

To perform a comparison between the different methods, we performed a design space exploration of all algorithms on a non-ISE enhanced processor. We varied the size and associativity of both the instruction and data caches. The configuration with the best energy-performance product for a given algorithm and dataset is chosen as reference for comparison. We performed a similar design space exploration for the processor augmented with larger AVS-enhanced ISEs, using both Speculative DMA and Virtual Ways to ensure coherence.

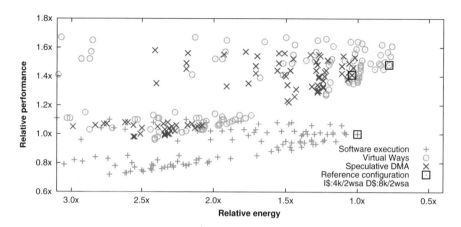

Fig. 5. Design space exploration of the CJPEGV2 dataset 1 compression algorithm for the different architectural versions.

The result of the design space exploration for the CJPEGV2 testbench using the first data set is plotted in Figure 5. Both Speculative DMA and Virtual Ways achieved greater speedups than the original code across all cache configurations. Many, but not all, configurations achieved greater reductions in energy when Speculative DMA or Virtual Ways were used. Except for the reference cache configuration, the figure does not indicate which Speculative DMA and Virtual Way data points correspond to the same configuration; the general trend, however, appears to be that Virtual Ways achieve marginal better performance with a noticeable reduction in energy compared to Speculative DMA.

Figure 6 shows the energy and performance plots of the EEMBC consumer version 2 benchmark suite. For all benchmarks Virtual Ways outperforms the state-of-the-art while consuming significantly less energy. There are two observations to be made: (1) for the AES algorithm both Speculative DMA and Virtual Ways perform equally with an identical energy footprint. The reason lies in the detection of two AVS memories that contain read-only data structures; therefore, both methods do not have to infer coherence traffic, and (2) for the MPEG2_ENC both methods provide better performance at a significant energy cost when compared to the baseline. The increase in energy lies in the access pattern of the detected AVS. In the MPEG2_ENC benchmark a temporary buffer of the size of 8×8 16-bit integers is used to perform a 64-point *Discrete Cosine Transform (DCT)*. The DCT is selected as potential ISE, and the buffer is placed in an AVS. Due to the algorithm the buffer is moved forth and back between the AVS and the data cache consuming significant energy. In case of execution on a non-ISE enhanced processor the buffer is never evicted from the data-cache due to the *Least Recently Used (LRU)* replacement policy. To explain why the other algorithms do not suffer similarly, we compare the data points corresponding to the reference cache configuration of the CJPEGV2 algorithm using dataset 1 in greater detail.

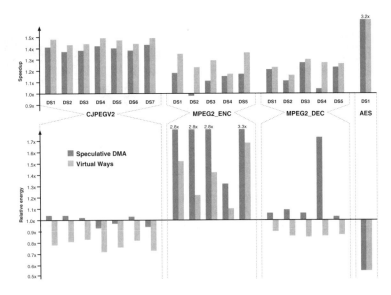

Fig. 6. Performance and energy results for four EEMBC benchmarks. Each of the algorithms, except the AES, contains five to seven different datasets (DSx). The baseline is the cache configuration that provides the best energy-performance product when running on a non-ISE enhanced processor. Overall, Virtual Ways provides similar to more performance with significant reduced energy consumption when compared to Speculative DMA.

Figure 7 shows the performance and energy breakdown for the four different kernels of the CJPEGV2 algorithm for the reference cache configuration. Similarly to the MPEG2_ENC benchmark the DCT kernel is the only kernel containing a custom instruction with an AVS. One would expect to observe two different scenarios: (1) upon entering the DCT kernel, the data has to be copied to the AVS, before the custom instruction can start processing the data, and (2) after leaving the DCT kernel the data has to gradually move back to the data cache for the processor to be able to process it in the quantization kernel.

Looking into the copying of the data structure into the AVS, Figure 7 shows no distinct differences between Speculative DMA and Virtual Ways in terms of performance or energy consumption, contrary our observation for the MPEG2_ENC benchmark. The reason for this lies in the calculation pattern of the color space conversion. The color space conversion processes a "band" of 1024 pixels, 8 rows at a time. As this "band" corresponds to a memory size of 24 kB, it cannot fit in the data cache entirely, and therefore will evict parts of the processed data. By the time the DCT kernel starts processing, the data required in the AVS is no longer present in the data cache; therefore, no coherence problem exists and both Speculative DMA and Virtual Ways need to prefetch the data from main memory. As this process affects both methods, both architectures perform equally and consume about the same amount of energy in this particular case.

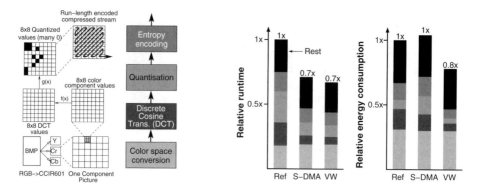

Fig. 7. Left: Schematic diagram of the kernels of the CJPEGV2 compression algorithm. Right: Performance and energy consumption broken down into the different kernels as shown on the left for the baseline (Ref), Speculative DMA (S-DMA), and Virtual Ways (VW).

Figure 7 shows distinct differences for the data eviction process from the AVS. Where for Speculative DMA the energy consumption in the quantization kernel is high ($4.4\times$ the energy consumed by the non-ISE enhanced architecture), Virtual Ways expends a comparable amount of energy as the software implementation. The reason for this is that the data structure in the AVS has been modified by an ISE in the DCT kernel and is then directly used in the quantization kernel. In this case, a coherence problem exists between the AVS and the data cache. In Speculative DMA the coherence protocol will move the data structure back from the AVS to both the data cache and main memory, which includes expensive bus transfers; this consumes a significant amount of energy. In contrast, Virtual Ways simply copies the data directly from the AVS segments to the cache. This eliminates the need for bus transfers and writes to main memory.

The bus dependency of the Speculative DMA coherence mechanism is an uncertainty. Due to the well known *memory wall problem* the processor normally runs at higher clock frequencies than the external memory. For all of the preceding experiments, we assumed memory and processor frequencies of 100 MHz, which is a favorable situation for Speculative DMA. Increasing the processor clock frequency can influence the operation of Speculative DMA in the benchmark, as shown in Figure 8(a); Figure 8(a) also shows that the performance of Virtual Ways is less dependent on the difference between processor and memory frequencies.

To compare the area of Virtual Ways and Speculative DMA, we implemented both data caches, including AVS memories, in a 90 nm standard-cell technology, along with a baseline cache without an AVS; we did not synthesize instruction caches, the processor, or the ISE computational logic. The results are depicted in Figure 8(b), which shows that Virtual Ways increases the area of the baseline cache by 9%, while Speculative DMA increases the area by 29%.

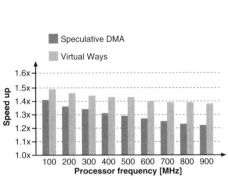

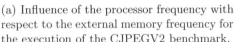

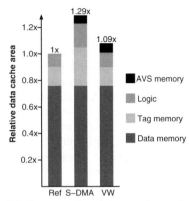

(a) Influence of the processor frequency with respect to the external memory frequency for the execution of the CJPEGV2 benchmark.

(b) Area overhead comparison of a standard data cache (Ref), a Speculative DMA enhanced data cache (S-DMA), and a Virtual Ways enhanced data cache (VW).

Fig. 8. Frequency robustness and Area of Virtual Ways compared to Speculative DMA

6 Conclusion

Prior work has established that AVS-enhanced ISEs provide a performance improvement over ISEs that do not employ AVS; however, the inclusion of AVS in a processor with caches creates a memory coherence problem. This paper has introduced Virtual Ways as a low-cost alternative to using a coherence protocol to maintain this coherence in a single-processor system. Our results show that a cache enhanced with Virtual Ways consumes less area and energy than Speculative DMA; additionally, Virtual Ways was shown to be less sensitive than Speculative DMA to differences in clock frequencies between the processor and main memory. For these reasons, we believe that Virtual Ways is a much more attractive solution than Speculative DMA for customizable processors used in cost and energy-constrained embedded systems.

References

1. Atasu, K., Mencer, O., Luk, W., Özturan, C., Dünda, G.: Fast custom instruction identification by convex subgraph enumeration. In: Proceedings of the 19th International Conference on Application-specific Systems, Architectures and Processors, Leuven, Belgium, July 2008, pp. 1–6 (2008)
2. Biswas, P., Choudhary, V., Atasu, K., Pozzi, L., Ienne, P., Dutt, N.: Introduction of local memory elements in instruction set extensions. In: Proceedings of the 41st Design Automation Conference, San Diego, Calif., June 2004, pp. 729–734 (2004)
3. Biswas, P., Dutt, N., Pozzi, L., Ienne, P.: Introduction of architecturally visible storage in instruction set extensions. IEEE Transactions on Computer-Aided Design of Integrated Circuits and Systems CAD-26(3), 435–446 (March 2007)

4. Clark, N., Zhong, H., Mahlke, S.: Processor acceleration through automated instruction set customisation. In: Proceedings of the 36th Annual International Symposium on Microarchitecture, San Diego, Calif., December 2003, pp. 129–140 (2003)
5. Cong, J., Han, G., Zhang, Z.: Architecture and compiler optimizations for data bandwidth improvement in configurable embedded processors. IEEE Transactions on Very Large Scale Integration (VLSI) Systems 14(9), 986–997 (2006)
6. Jayaseelan, R., Liu, H., Mitra, T.: Exploiting forwarding to improve data bandwidth of instruction-set extensions. In: Proceedings of the 43rd Design Automation Conference, San Francisco, Calif., July 2006, pp. 43–48 (2006)
7. Karuri, K., Chattopadhyay, A., Hohenauer, M., Leupers, R., Ascheid, G., Meyr, H.: Increasing data-bandwidth to instruction-set extensions through register clustering. In: Proceedings of the International Conference on Computer Aided Design, San Jose, Calif., November 2007, pp. 166–171 (2007)
8. Kluter, T., Brisk, P., Charbon, E., Ienne, P.: Way stealing: Cache-assisted automatic instruction set extensions. In: Proceedings of the 46th Design Automation Conference, San Francisco, Calif., July 2009, pp. 31 36 (2009)
9. Kluter, T., Brisk, P., Ienne, P., Charbon, E.: Speculative DMA for Architecturally Visible Storage in Instruction Set Extensions. In: Proceedings of the International Conference on Hardware/Software Codesign and System Synthesis, Atlanta, Ga., October 2008, pp. 243–248 (2008)
10. Pothineni, N., Kumar, A., Paul, K.: Application specific datapath extension with distributed I/O functional units. In: Proceedings of the 20th International Conference on VLSI Design, Bangalore, India (January 2007)
11. Pozzi, L., Atasu, K., Ienne, P.: Exact and approximate algorithms for the extension of embedded processor instruction sets. IEEE Transactions on Computer-Aided Design of Integrated Circuits and Systems CAD-25(7), 1209–1229 (2006)
12. Pozzi, L., Ienne, P.: Exploiting pipelining to relax register-file port constraints of instruction-set extensions. In: Proceedings of the International Conference on Compilers, Architectures, and Synthesis for Embedded Systems, San Francisco, Calif., September 2005, pp. 2–10 (2005)
13. Steinke, S., Wehmeyer, L., Lee, B.-S., Marwedel, P.: Assigning program and data objects to scratchpad for energy reduction. In: Proceedings of the Design, Automation and Test in Europe Conference and Exhibition, Paris (March 2002)
14. Verma, A.K., Brisk, P., Ienne, P.: Rethinking custom ISE identification: A new processor-agnostic method. In: Proceedings of the International Conference on Compilers, Architectures, and Synthesis for Embedded Systems, Salzburg, September 2007, pp. 125–134 (2007)
15. Verma, A.K., Brisk, P., Ienne, P.: Fast, quasi-optimal, and pipelined instruction-set extensions. In: Proceedings of the Asia and South Pacific Design Automation Conference, Seoul, Korea, January 2008, pp. 334–339 (2008)

Accelerating XML Query Matching through Custom Stack Generation on FPGAs

Roger Moussalli, Mariam Salloum, Walid Najjar, and Vassilis Tsotras

Department of Computer Science and Engineering
University of California, Riverside
CA 92521, USA
{rmous,msalloum,najjar,tsotras}@cs.ucr.edu
http://www.cs.ucr.edu

Abstract. Publish-subscribe systems present the state of the art in information dissemination to multiple users. Such systems have evolved from simple topic-based to the current XML-enabled systems. Here, users pose complex queries (expressed in XPath) on the structure and content of the streaming documents. The parts of the documents that match the user queries are then returned to the users. This paper proposes a novel hardware architecture that would exploit the parallelism found in XPath filtering systems. Using an incoming XML stream, parsing and matching with thousands of user profiles are performed simultaneously on a single FPGA, thus yielding up to three orders of magnitude higher throughput when compared to conventional approaches bound by the sequential aspect of software computing. By converting XPath expressions into custom stacks, our architecture is the first providing full support for all structural XPath constructs, including parent-child and ancestor descendant relations, whilst allowing wildcarding and recursion.

Keywords: FPGA, XML, Query, XPath, Compilation.

1   Introduction

Increased demand for timely and accurate event-notification systems has lead to the wide adoption of Publish/Subscribe Systems(or simply pub-sub). A pub-sub is an asynchronous event-based dissemination system which consists of three components: *publishers*, who feed a stream of messages into the system, *subscribers*, who post their interests (also called *profiles*), and an infrastructure for matching subscriber interests with published messages and delivering *matched messages* to the interested subscriber. Pub-sub systems have enabled notification services for users interested in receiving news updates, stock prices, weather updates, etc; examples include google.news.com, pipes.yahoo.com, and www.ticketmaster.com. Pub-sub systems have greatly evolved over time, adding further challenges and opportunities in their design and implementation. Earlier pub-subs involved simple topic-based communication. That is, subscribers could subscribe to a predefined collection of topics (e.g., news, weather, etc.). The

Y.N. Patt et al. (Eds.): HiPEAC 2010, LNCS 5952, pp. 141–155, 2010.

second generation consists of predicate-based systems which employ the Event-Condition-Action paradigm to perform profile matching and selective dissemination of information. Profiles are usually described as conjunctions of (attribute, value) pairs. For example, a profile could be: (concert, Police) AND (city, Los Angeles), for a user interested in being notified of Los Angeles concerts of the Police rock band. The wide adoption of the eXtensible Markup Language (XML) as the standard format for data exchange has led to the third generation, namely XML-enabled pub-sub systems. Here messages are encoded as XML documents and profiles are expressed using XML query languages, such as XPath [19]. Such systems take advantage of the powerful querying that XML query languages offer: profiles can now describe requests not only on the message values but also on the structure of the messages [1].

The wide adoption of XML is due to its self-describing and extensible nature; document content is tagged to provide a detailed description of its organization. An XML document has a hierarchical (tree) structure that consists of a root element and sub-elements. In addition, elements (or tags) can appear multiple times inside the same enclosing element (also referred as *recursion*). In the XPath query language queries are composed of a sequence of location steps. Each location step consists of an axis and an element. An axis specifies the hierarchical relationship between the document nodes. We focus on the two most common axes, namely, parent-child ('/') and ancestor-descendant ('//'). The parent-child axis specifies that two elements should appear at adjacent levels in the XML document tree. Likewise, the ancestor-descendant axis specifies that two elements can be separated by any number of levels in the XML tree. Wildcard characters ('*') are elements of XPath queries, providing a level of freedom by allowing any tag of the XML tree to replace them.

XML-filtering becomes a challenging problem when considering that it should support thousands of subscriptions, high volume of input streams, and should perform complex structural matching in a timely manner. Many software approaches have been presented to solve the XML filtering problem [1,6,7,9]. These memory-bound approaches, however, suffer from the Von Neumann bottleneck and are unable to handle large volume of input streams. On the other hand, Field Programmable Gate Arryas (FPGAs) have been shown to be particularly suited for the stream processing of large amounts of data and do not suffer from the memory bottleneck faced by software implementations [15], [8]. Recently, in [14] we presented a proof-of-concept approach for the use of FPGAs on XML filtering. This approach, however, does not account for recursive elements in XML documents, neither for wildcards in the XPath profile expressions; both features are important constructs for XML documents and the XPath query language.

In this paper we present a novel implementation of XPath queries on FPGA that does support expressions with '/', '//', '*' and recursive elements in the XML documents. We present various alternatives and optimizations of this implementations and report on their respective costs benefits and trade-offs in terms of clock speed and area occupancy on the FPGA. We compare the achieved

---

[1] In the rest we use the terms "profile" and "query" interchangeably.

throughput to two popular software implementations: the LazyDFA [7] and FiST [9]. The results show up to three orders of magnitude of increasing throughput, with the geometric mean of the acceleration reported being 59x.

The rest of the paper is organized as follows: Section 2 presents related work while Section 3 provides in depth description of the proposed architectures targeted for XPath query matching. Section 4 presents an experimental evaluation of the FPGA based hardware approach compared to the state of the art software counterparts. Finally conclusions and open problems for further research appear in Section 5.

2   Related Work

The popularity of XML as a de facto standard for information exchange has triggered several research efforts to build scalable and efficient XML filtering systems. Several approaches have been proposed to solve the XML filtering problem. An early work, XFilter [1], proposed building a Finite State Machine (FSM) for each user profile, such that each element in the XPath expression becomes a state in the FSM. Each profile axis defines the transition between states, where the final state is the accept state for that FSM. The FSM states are executed as XML tag events are generated. An *open(tag)* event drives the FSM to the next state, while a *close(tag)* event drives the FSM back to the previous state. YFilter [6] built upon the work of XFilter, proposed a Non-Deterministic Finite Automata (NFA) representation of query path expressions which combines all queries (profiles) into a single machine. This approach yields better results since it exploits the commonality among path expressions. Green et.al. [7] proposed a lazy Deterministic Finite Automata. [9] proposed a sequence-based approach where both the XML document and query are transformed into Prufer sequences and subsequence matching is performed to determine if the query has a match in the document.

Nevertheless, the approaches discussed above are entirely software-based solutions abiding by the standard Von Neumann organization. One naive solution would be implementing the software-based FSM approaches on FPGAs. Such an approach however, is not efficient because the software approaches must dynamically allocate memory during XML filtering: consider the LazyDFA approach [7], which constructs the DFA in a lazy fashion during XML filtering. This approach cannot be implemented on the FPGA because the number of DFA states is not known in advance. In addition, recursion in XML streams requires dynamic initiation of multiple NFA processing engines during filtering which is not possible on FPGAs.

There are several approaches that use specialized parallel architectures for XML processing [10], [12]. In particular, [10] aimed to accelerate XML parsing using the Cell Broadband Engine multi-processor which consists of 8 independent processors (SPEs) that implement the FSM of the Zurich XML Accelerator (ZuXA) engine. This approach achieves parallelism by parsing (eight) XML documents in parallel at a time. In addition to be only suitable for XML parsing, this solution is a combination of hardware-software approach. Similarly, the work in [12] addresses ways to load-balance parallel threads for low-level XML processing (e.g., XML parsing).

Previous work that have used FPGAs for processing XML documents have mainly dealt with the problem of XML parsing. In particular, [13] proposes the ZuXA engine to parse XML documents. This engine employs state machines for efficient parsing based on set of rules. The paper however does not provide any discussion how this engine can be adapted to evaluate XPath query expressions over the XML input.

The works in [11] propose the use of a mixed hardware/software architecture to solve simple XPath queries having only parent-child axis. A finite state machine implemented in FPGAs is facilitated to parse the XML document and to provide partial evaluation of XPath predicates. The results are then reported to the software part for further processing. Similarly to the ZuXA engine, this architecture is limitted to support simple XPath expressions with the parent-child axis.

Our previous work [14] was the first to propose a pure-hardware solution to the XML filtering problem. Improvements of more than one order of magnitude were reported when compared to software. However, this method is unable to handle recursion in XML documents or wildcards '*' in XPath profiles; such issues as well as various optimizations are handled by the novel architecture we present in this paper.

3   XPath Matching Hardware Architecture

Using an XML stream as input, we present a full-hardware XPath matching system on FPGAs; this section describes the details of the proposed approach. We start by providing an overview of our SAX Parser implementation, built upon a tag decoder, leading to a resource-optimized XML event notifier and overall architecture. The intuition behind mapping XPaths into stacks is then described, while contrasting with the shortcomings of previous approaches. We then propose some area saving optimizations through the reduction of the average width of required stacks. These optimizations would potentially imply a decrease in the operational frequency of the overall system on FPGA, a limitation which we prove to overcome using fan-out trees. Finally, we present the incentive behind the clustering of XPath matching engines, and the underlying technique used to report matches.

3.1   SAX Parser and Tag Decoder Implementation

The (*Simple API for XML*) (SAX) Parser [17], is an event-driven XML parser, ideal for streaming applications. Unlike other parsers (such as DOM [5]), where the entire XML document need be stored in memory before processing can start, SAX Parsers would generate *open(tag)* and *close(tag)* events on the fly, with all XPath query matching engines updating states accordingly. As a result, matching ends when the XML stream is complete.

With FPGAs being limited in hardware resources, a tag decoder is a desirable feature operating in conjunction with the SAX Parser. Since all query matching engines would need comparisons against respective tags, all engines executing in a parallel fashion, many redundant comparisons would take place across several engines, thus unnecessarily wasting resources. Decoders solve this issue by centralizing comparisons, and mapping decoded tags into single bit lines. All remaining comparisons are then translated into simple *AND* gates, hence, allowing the FPGA resources to be used for more useful computations. Our tag decoder is inspired from character decoding, the latter becoming conventional in pattern matching on FPGAs [16], [14], and which was shown to offer up to 83% of area savings in [14].

Fig. 3 shows how a tag decoder would operate in parallel with a SAX Parser in order to generate *open* and *close* tag events, with a tag being a single bit line out of the possible n decoded ones. Note that only one of those bit lines is high at a given point in time. Furthermore, the tag decoder is configured at compile time to recognize the n unique tags that would appear in the stream of XML documents.

3.2 Matching XPaths Using Path Specific Stacks

Due to the occurrence of parent-child relations, a stack is an essential feature of XML filtering systems, where an *open(tag)* is translated into a *push* event, and conversely, a *close(tag)* would be translated onto a *pop* event. For instance, matching the XPath *a/b* would take place when the *open(b)* event arises, with '*a*' being the top of stack. There is no bound to the number of children '*a*' could have within the XML document, any of those coming about prior to '*b*'. Thus, it would not be sufficient to check for the latest tag opened, but instead, the latest tag opened that still has not been closed.

A single global stack is needed to support the matching of parent-child relations for all XPath profiles. On the other hand, when using conventional state machine approaches, matching ancestor-descendant relations of the form *c//d* can be translated into a 3-state FSM, as we described in [14].

However, such methods fail to support recursion, a key aspect of XML documents, where certain tags are allowed to appear as their own children and/or descendants. Instead of using one global stack and one state machine per XPath user profile, we propose mapping each XPath into a customized stack, namely a *Path Specific Stack* (PSS). The PSS depth would be that of the XML document; furthermore the PSS width is equivalent to the depth of the XPath profile, where each tag of the query expression is mapped to a unique column, with regard to the order in which they appear in the XPath. A '1' would be stored in a column when matching for the tag mapped to it is true. This occurs with an *open(tag)* event for that tag being generated from the SAX Parser, with all previous tags having matched earlier. The storing of a '1' in the right-most column indicates a successful match for the entire XPath expression. The width of the stack, the surrounding logic alongside the tag decoded bit lines routed to it for matching purposes are all specific to each XPath query.

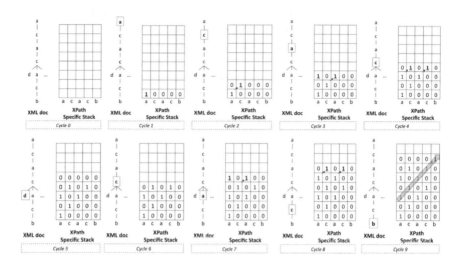

Fig. 1. Overview of the matching of XPath $a/c/a/c/b$. Each cycle refers to an *open(tag)* or *close(tag)* event, relative to the highlighted tag.

Fig. 1 shows a cycle by cycle overview of all the steps required for the matching of the XPath $a/c/a/c/b$, where, for simplification purposes, a cycle refers to a SAX Parser event. Cycle 0 reflects on the initial state of the system prior to any streaming taking place: the XML document to be streamed is drawn on the left hand side, whereas a PSS of width five is shown to the right. Each column is labeled with the corresponding tag of the $a/c/a/c/b$ expression.

When the *open(a)* event takes place in cycle 1, the first column of the PSS would store a '1'. Consequently, with an *open(c)* event occurring in cycle 2, a '1' is stored in the second column, allowing the previous partial match stored in column 0 of the previous Top Of PSS (TOPSS) to propagate diagonally. In other words, an *open(c)* event alone is not enough to validate the matching of tag 'c'. The fourth column in that same cycle demonstrates this behavior, for no matching was reported, due to no diagonally propagating '1'.

Support for recursion is depicted in cycle 3, where both the first and third columns indicate a match for tag 'a' simultaneously, thus, allowing two possible matches of the same XPath to be in progress concurrently: one having started at cycle 1, the other at cycle 3. The state maching approach described in [14] would not take the new possible matches into consideration, since an FSM cannot reside in two states simultaneously. Moreover, each XPath query expression is mapped into a single state machine; therefore, multiple possible matches require multiple state machines, an issue which we solve using Path Specific Stacks.

With an *open(c)* event on cycle 4, both previous partial possible matches propagate diagonally. The occurrence of tags irrelevant to the XPath query has no negative effect on the matching process. For instance, with 'd' pushed onto the stack on cycle 5, no partial matches are propagated. Moreover, roll-back to the previous state took place on cycle 6 with the *close(d)* event taking place, thus popping the TOPSS.

A third partial possible match spawns off on state 7 (first column), while the first partial match that awaited an *open(b)* event had to stop propagation for the moment being, and can only resume matching until the currently pushed '*a*' is popped.

Propagation of partial matches resumes in cycle 8. Ultimately, a match has been found in cycle 9, thanks to the partial matching starting propagation from cycle 3. A match can be seen as a diagonal of 1's, ending in the fifth column.

Since our proposed architecture is not based on state machines as in [14], we offer support specific to our system for ancestor-descendant relations, as explained in Section 3.4.

3.3   Applied Optimizations for PSS Reduced Resource Utilization

As described in Section 3.2, PSS's have a width equivalent to the depth of the XPath profile mapped to it. With FPGAs being limited in resources, we propose some area reduction optimizations to be applied to the PSS. In this section, we focus on optimizing the PSS mapping of the same XPath profile used as a base example in Section 3.2.

One key observation reflected in Fig. 1 is that at most, two columns can be written to with regard to the occurrence of a single event. In other words, tag '*a*' maps to no more of two of the possible five stack columns, specifically columns one and three. Similarly, tag '*c*' maps to columns two and four, whereas tag '*b*' solely maps to column 5.

We base our optimizations on the introduction of a global stack. The decoded representation of tags would be pushed or popped onto this stack, in the case of *open(tag)* and *close(tag)* events respectively. Each of the global stack and Path

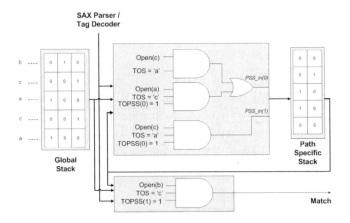

Fig. 2. Optimized hardware mapping for the matching of XPath $a/c/a/c/b$. Stack contents reflect on a *macthed* state of the expression.

Specific Stacks are pushed to and popped from concurrently. We refer to the top of the global stack as TOS. Fig. 2 shows the optimized mapping of the XPath expression $a/c/a/c/b$.

One intuitive optimization is not to map the final tag of the XPath expression to the PSS, rather to the match output signal, indicating whether or not a match of the query has occurred.

Moreover, with the help of the global stack, the first tag in an XPath need not be mapped to the PSS. Checking for the second tag consists of *AND*-ing the first label's decoded bit of the TOS, with the tag decoder output bit corresponding to the second tag; the top most *AND* gate in Fig. 2 connects the first bit of the TOS and the bit corresponding to tag 'c' from the tag decoder output, in order to match a/c, the two initial tags of the XPath studied.

One more general optimization that aims to reduce the PSS width is to map multiple occurrence of different tags to the same column. The rule is to map one occurrence of a given tag from the XPath query onto the column following the mapping of the *last* occurrence of that *same* tag. By doing so, we fold the diagonal previously noted in Fig. 1, into the minimal number of columns; with the exception of the first and last tag in an XPath query expression, the needed PSS width is defined as the greatest number of repetitions accross all tags. Considering the expression $a/c/a/c/b$, tag 'c' has the highest number of occurrences, being equal to two. Note that tag 'a' has only one occurrence to be considered for PSS mapping, since the first tag in an XPath would not be mapped, as explained earlier. Since tag 'c' has the most repetitions, namely two, the required PSS would have a width of two; the first initial of 'c' and the second occurrence of 'a' would map to the first PSS column, whereas the second occurrence of 'c' is mapped onto the second column.

When propagating a '1', the global stack is essential in order to distinguish between multiple tags mapped to the same column. For instance, in the previous example, a '1' in the first column of the TOPSS accompanied by a decoded 'c' in the TOS, would refer to the second tag in the XPath expression. On the other hand, a '1' in the first column of the TOPSS accompanied by a decoded 'a' in the TOS states that the partial match has reached the third tag in the XPath expression.

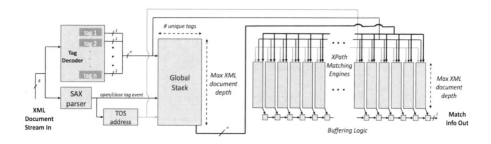

Fig. 3. High-Level system overview

The need of the global stack is reflected by some penalty on the logic surrounding the PSS. Looking at Fig. 2, it can be seen that, with the exception of the top-most *AND* gate, all remaining gates require an extra input, taking into account one bit from the TOS. Moreover, since two tags map to the same column, a 2-input *OR* gate was inserted prior to the first column of the PSS. Nonetheless, the reduction in required PSS width is noticeable; the overall area savings would be used to place structures relevant to achieving high throughput, as explained in Section 3.5.

3.4   Supporting Wildcards and Ancestor-Descendant Relationships

Wildcards, represented as '*' within XPath query expressions, imply that any tag from the XML document can be used as a valid replacement. In our architecture, this would mean that any decoded tag would help propagate the diagonal '1'. In other words, no global stack output is needed at the input of the corresponding *AND* gate. In the case of the unoptimized PSS, wildcards are translated into the output of the previous column directly routed into the input of the wildcard column, thus no extra logic is required. However, each wildcard should be mapped to a column of its own, since the tag used to replace a wildcard at a given point could be similar to any other tag from the XPath query. Therefore, wildcards exhibit a negative impact on the total occupied area.

Likewise, ancestor-descendant relations also have negative impact on resource utilization. Tags followed by ancestor-descendant relations should be mapped onto exclusive columns. The reasoning is that one column would reflect that tag being an ancestor, having appeared earlier in the document. In order to do so, the input of the PSS column consists of the regular matching logic propagating the previous '1', *OR*-ed with the output of the column itself. Note that PSS entries are updated solely upon push events. Thus, once the ancestor column stores a '1', all later pushed entries of that column would reflect the match, until the initial '1' is popped.

The optimization introduced in Section 3.3 regarding the first tag of an XPath expression, does not hold when that tag is followed by an ancestor-descendant relation, unless that tag is a wildcard; in that case, the second tag's propagating input is the *stack_not_empty* signal generated from the global stack.

3.5   System Architecture

We propose a scalable architecture appropriate for the simultaneous matching of thousands of XPath profiles.

Addressing Inner and Outer Fan-Outs via Clustering. One observation is that all stacks on chip would be updating concurrently; hence, all of the stacks' addresses would be generated from a common structure, which in turn requires push and pop notifications from the SAX Parser. Figure 3 illustrates this matter, where the TOS address is routed to the global stack and all remaining Path Specific Stacks (in the case of unoptimized PSS's, there is no need of a global stack). This approach however creates a fan-out issue, where the address signal, the global stack output and the tag decoder output are replicated as many times as there are XPath profile matching engines (see Fig. 3), thus, affecting the allowed operational frequency.

A solution to this problem would be clustering, where the global stack, the SAX parser and the tag decoder would be replicated for clusters of PSS's, thus reducing the fan-out. This in turn raises the issue of the fan-out on the input stream, which would have to be replicated to feed into all clusters.

We refer to the fan-out within clusters as the *inner-fanout*; moreover, as the name indicates, the *outer-fanout* is caused by the out-of-cluster replication of the input stream.

One attempt to reduce the outer-fanout is the insertion of a binary fan-out tree on the input stream. Each node in that tree is a 9-bit buffer, capable of storing the input stream and an input valid bit. With each leaf of that tree feeding a single cluster, the outer fan-out would be eliminated, at the cost of many on-chip resources. Section 4.1 provides a thorough design space exploration on the allowed inner-fanout vs. tree size compromise. A reduced fan-out tree is introduced, which occupies less resources than a full tree, while keeping outer fan-out within reasonable bounds.

Reporting Matches. With thousands of matching engines co-existing on chip, reporting matches becomes a more complicated issue, where mapping each match signal exclusively to an FPGA pin is not an option. Our previous approach [14] suggested the use of priority encoders, where upon the event of a match, the unique encoded ID of the expression is returned. However, such an approach fails to acknowledge multiple matches occurring concurrently. XPaths $a//b$ and $c/a/d/b$ are such examples.

For the application of interest (filtering), the number of matches of each profile is of no interest, rather whether or not there was at least one match. Thus, we enhance our matching logic with one bit buffers relative to each PSS (Fig. 3); these buffers are connected serially. Upon the completion of the input stream, all of these results would be streamed out in a pipelined fashion, with a single bit port required. There would be N cycles of overhead required for this mechanism to complete streaming out, with N being the number of profiles. Nonetheless, this overhead is minimal when compared to the size of the documents streamed through the FPGA. In the case of clustering, we provide the option of having one match output signal per cluster. This would help reduce the overhead of sending the information out of the FPGA.

4   Experimental Results

We proceed with a design space exploration, where the effects of inner and outer fan-out, resource utilization and throughput are studied. We present four hardware systems, namely:

- No Optimization No Tree (**NONT**), where the PSS optimizations described in 3.3 are not applied.

- With Optimization No Tree (**WONT**), where the PSS optimizations for area reduction are applied, but the outer fan-out issue is not addressed.
- With Optimization With Tree (**WOWT**), where we apply both PSS optimizations and a binary fan-out tree having as many leaf nodes as there are clusters. This system cancels outer fan-out by using part of the optimized resources.
- With Optimization With reduced Tree (**WOWrT**); this is an architecture similar to WOWT, however the fan-out tree is reduced, having fewer leaf nodes than the number of clusters. While this approach would not eliminate outer fan-out, we expect that it would scale much better with almost no penalty on performance.

Our target platform is the Xilinx Virtex 5 LX330 [18] FPGA. With the proposed architecture heavily relying on memory structures, we make use of on-chip Block RAMs (BRAMs) [3]. These are highly configurable hard-wired memory blocks embedded in most Xilinx FPGAs. However, since the number of BRAMs is far fewer than that of all (global and path specific) required stacks, we only map global stacks to BRAMs. XPath queries on the other hand would be implemented using Distributed Memories (DMEMs) [4], memory structures built from slice LUTs. We provide a thorough resource utilization and performance study on the underlying tradeoffs of all of the four aforementioned hardware systems.

The reported performance is measured in throughput (MB/s), i.e., the average amount of data that can be processed over one second. All hardware systems assume a single character of 8 bits per cycle from the input stream's end. We compare the performance of our hardware systems against both of the LazyDFA [7] and FiST [9] software approaches.

We used a highly recursive XML Document Type Definition (DTD; which defines the allowed XML document structure) to generate XML documents and XPath queries for our experiments. The XML document datasets were generated by the ToXGENE XML Generator [2], setting the number of unique tags to 32, each consisting of two bytes. We generated documents of sizes of 5 and 50 MB, with a maximum XML document depth of 16. The same XML DTD was used to generate the set of user profiles using the XPath generator package provided by [6]. The maximum depth of a user profile was fixed at 6 and the probability of '*' and '//' occurrences was set to 10 percent. We varied the number of user profile datasets from 128 to 8192 queries.

All software experiments were ran on a quad core 2.33GHz Intel Xeon machine with 2GB of RAM, running Linux Red Hat 2.6.

4.1   Design Space Exploration

In order to evaluate the tradeoffs of excessive vs. sparse clustering, we ran a series of experiments, fixing the number of XPath queries at 2048, while varying the number of queries per cluster, up to 256 clusters (eight queries per cluster). We could not provide results beyond that point due to the limitation in the number of available BRAMs. We first compare NONT, WONT and WOWT.

The larger number of queries in each cluster, the higher the inner fan-out, thus the lower the outer fan-out, and vice versa. As expected, Fig. 4 shows that with the absence of clustering, inner fan-out is dominant and the operational frequency is much lower than achievable for all of three systems studied. Clustering proves to be beneficial up to a certain point, where the balance between outer and inner fan-out allows operational frequencies around the best achievable of 200 MHz. This behavior occurs around 128 queries per cluster. Beyond that point, where outer fan-out becomes dominant, both of NONT and WONT's performance deteriorates. On the other hand, WOWT would exhibit a rather constant superior performance at around 200 MHz. This is due to the full binary fan-out tree introduced as an effort to eliminate the effects of outer fan-out (at the expense of a higher area utilization). This penalty is tolerable and benefiting while the tree is kept small, up to 128 queries per cluster (where the tree has 16 leaf nodes and the WOWT area still is smaller than NONT's). Beyond that point, the tree grows too large, displaying up to 200% increased resource utilization.

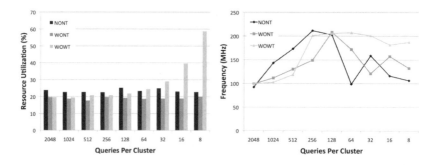

Fig. 4. Design space exploration with regards to the inner vs. outer fan-out compromise across three systems at 2048 queries

We then explore the scalability of the proposed architectures with the number of XPath queries ranging from 128 to 8192 (Fig. 5) and 200 MHz being our target operational frequency. We fix the number of queries per cluster at 128 (being the point where the best performance was realized at 2048 queries). However, we now evaluate the WOWrT setup, where the fan-out tree has a fixed 16 leaf nodes, the most adequate tree size from the previously shown exploration. Such an approach would not eliminate outer fan-out, but would keep the area utilization minimal, while almost no performance deterioration is noticed. For this approach only, we fix the number of queries per cluster to a more conservative 64. The intuition is that with outer fan-out reduced thanks to the tree, inner fan-out should be kept minimal with the help of extra clustering. Furthermore, since the target operational frequency of 200 MHz was achieved with no tree at 2048 queries, we only evaluate WOWrT for systems having at least 4098 queries (knowing that no tree is needed otherwise).

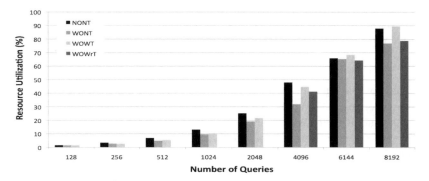

Fig. 5. Resource utilization comparison across all four proposed systems. NONT, WONT and WOWT results shown for 128 queries per cluster. WOWrT makes use of a 16 leaf-tree at 64 queries per cluster.

As shown in Fig. 5, all approaches scale surprisingly well, almost doubling the resource utilization while doubling the number of XPath queries.

PSS optimizations offer an average 20% of area savings. For the most part, WOWrT seems to scale as well as WONT, whereas WOWT suffers from the full binary fan-out tree.

Figure 6 presents the throughput for all approaches: as expected, a throughput superior to 200 MB/s is achieved up to 2048 queries across all systems. Beyond that point, a fan-out tree is needed, thus illustrating the benefits of WOWT and WOWrT, the latter being more consistent, having a smaller fixed size tree. Otherwise, a decrease in throughput is revealed across the remaining systems.

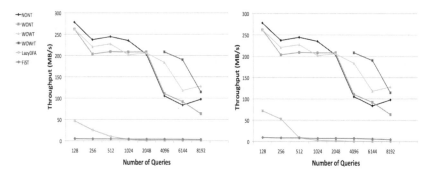

Fig. 6. Hardware vs. software performance with an increasing number of queries for streams of 5 MB (left) and 50 MB (right)

4.2   Performance Evaluation

In order to evaluate the performance of our proposed hardware architectures, we provide a comparison against two state of the art software approaches, namely

LazyDFA abd FiST (see Fig. 6). We report the throughput as the number of XPath queries increases from 128 to 8192, for two sets of XML streams of sizes 5 and 50 MB respectively.

Hardware throughput, being the operational frequency of the system, is independent of the input stream. On the other hand, the negative effects from the sequential computing aspect of the software approaches, is noted as the number of queries increases. Moreover, we show to overcome the Von Neumann memory bottleneck as hardware systems exhibit a speedup of up to three orders of magnitude, with a geometric mean of 59x. LazyDFA performs much better with the number of queries kept small; that approach does not scale too well, where FiST would outperform it beyond 2048 queries.

5   Conclusions and Future Work

In this paper, we presented a novel FPGA based hardware architecture to address the XML filtering problem. Using custom stack generation, our architecture is the first providing full support for all structural XPath constructs, including parent-child and ancestor descendant relations, whilst allowing wildcarding and recursion. Hardware architectures do not suffer from the memory bottleneck problem (better known as the Von Neumann bottleneck), since they are highly suitable for stream processing; they would also not suffer from the limitations of sequential processing, as the proposed architecture would support thousands of matching engines operating in a parallel fashion.

We were able to show that through moderate clustering and proper fan-out reduction, an average throughput of 200 MB/s can be maintained for up to 8192 matching engines, thus yielding up to three orders of magnitude accelerated throughput when compared to state of the art software approaches for various stream sizes. The reported geometric average of the acceleration is 59x.

As part of our future work, we would be looking into enhancing our Path Specific Stacks to support twig matching; here, user profiles are more complicated as they resemble trees. One common approach used by software systems is to split the twig into multiple XPaths. However, we are interested in holistic twig matching, where each engine would detect a twig without splitting it into multiple paths. The resulting system would be fully implementable on hardware, as no false positives are generated to reconstruct the twigs using any accompanying software.

References

1. Altinel, M., Franklin, M.J.: Efficient Filtering of XML Documents for Selective Dissemination of Information. In: Proceedings of the 35th Int'l Conference on Very Large Data Bases (VLDB), pp. 53–64 (2000)
2. Barbosa, D., Mendelzon, A., Keenleyside, J., Lyons, K.: ToXgene: a template-based data generator for XML. In: Proceedings of ACM Management of Data (SIGMOD), p. 616 (2002)

3. Block RAM v1.00a,
   `http://www.xilinx.com/support/documentation/ip_documentation/`
   `bram_block.pdf`
4. Distributed Memory Generator v4.1,
   `http://www.xilinx.com/support/documentation/ip_documentation/`
   `dist_mem_gen_ds322.pdf`
5. W3.org on DOM, `http://www.w3.org/DOM`
6. Diao, Y., Altinel, M., Franklin, M.J., Zhang, H., Fischer, P.: Path sharing and predicate evaluation for high-performance XML filtering. ACM Trans. on Database Systems (TODS) 28, 467–516 (2003)
7. Green, T.J., Gupta, A., Miklau, G., Onizuka, M., Suciu, D.: Processing XML streams with deterministic automata and stream indexes. ACM Trans. on Database Systems (TODS), 752–788 (2004)
8. Guo, Z., Najjar, W., Vahid, F., Vissers, K.: A quantitative analysis of the speedup factors of fpgas over processors. In: Proc. of the 12th ACM/SIGDA Int'l Symp. on Field programmable gate arrays (FPGA), pp. 162–170 (2004)
9. Kwon, J., Rao, P., Moon, B., Lee, S.: FiST: scalable XML document filtering by sequencing twig patterns. In: Proceedings of the 31st international conference on Very Large Databases (VLDB), pp. 217–228 (2005)
10. Letz, S., Zedler, M., Thierer, T., Schutz, M., Roth, J., Seiffert, R.: XML offload and acceleration with Cell broadband engine. XTech.: Building Web 2.0 (2006)
11. Linderman, R.W., Lin, C.S., Linderman, M.H.: FPGA acceleration of information management services. In: High Performance Embedded Computing, HPEC (2004)
12. Lu, W., Gannon, D.: ParaXML: A Parallel XML Processing Model on Multicore CPUs, Techincal Report (2008)
13. Lunteren, J.V., Engbersen, T., Bostian, J., Carey, B., Larsson, C.: XML accelerator engine. In: 1st Int. Workshop on High Performance XML Processing (2004)
14. Mitra, A., Vieira, M.R., Bakalov, P., Najjar, W., Tsotras, J.T.: Boosting XML Filtering with a Scalable FPGA-based Architecture. In: 4th Biennial Conference on Innovative Data Systems Research, Asilomar (2009)
15. Muller, R., Teubner, J., Alonso, G.: Streams on Wires – A Query Compiler for FPGAs. In: Proceedings of the 35th Int'l Conference on Very Large Data Bases, VLDB (2009)
16. Clark, C.R., Schimmel, D.E.: Efficient Reconfigurable Logic Circuits for Matching Complex Network Intrusion Detection Patterns. In: 13th international conference on Field Programmable Logic and Applications, pp. 956–959. Springer, Lisbon (2003)
17. SAX home page, `http://www.saxproject.org`
18. XILINX DELIVERS 65nm VIRTEX-5 LX330,
   `http://www.xilinx.com/prs_rls/2006/silicon_vir/061301x330delivery.htm`
19. XML Path Language (XPath) Version 1.0, W3C Recommendation (1999),
   `http://www.w3.org/TR/xpath`

An Application-Aware Load Balancing Strategy for Network Processors

Rainer Ohlendorf, Michael Meitinger, Thomas Wild, and Andreas Herkersdorf

Technische Universität München, Institute for Integrated Systems,
Arcisstrasse 21, 80290 Munich, Germany
Rainer.Ohlendorf@tum.de

Abstract. This paper presents and compares different load balancing strategies in multi-core network processor (NP) chips. In our FlexPath NP system, packets are differentiated according to application-dependent processing requirements and optimized processing paths are provisioned for these applications. We derive a novel load balancing mechanism (S&H) by combining two schemes for stateful and stateless network applications in order to achieve better overall system throughput and reduced packet latencies. We show that appropriate QoS for the different regarded application types can be achieved under varying NP load conditions, while maintaining an almost uniform utilization of the available processing resources. Even though the investigations are focused on the FlexPath NP architecture, the concepts can also be applied to other architectures, where the incoming load has to be distributed among several parallel entities within an NP.

Keywords: Communication Systems, Computer Networks, Load Balancing, Network Processors, Multi-Processor System-on-Chip.

1 Introduction

The trend to implement Internet access and edge nodes with increasing intelligence, moving away from the traditional best effort model of IP packet delivery, has led to network processor (NP) architectures with many processing cores and a requirement to inspect and classify incoming traffic flows towards different service classes. The FlexPath NP is one architecture proposal that eases the deployment of such a service differentiation on an NP's architectural level. In this paper, we focus on the load balancing problem for NPs with parallel processing resources. Starting from state-of-the-art hashing-based load assignment schemes, we investigate how to increase the system performance in an NP that processes an application mix. Our main focus is to meet the Quality-of-Service (QoS) requirements for the network traffic and improve processing resource utilization for both stateful and stateless networking applications.

Section 2 presents an overview of existing load balancing schemes for network processors, and an introduction to the FlexPath NP architecture. Section 3 explains the concept and implementation of the proposed load balancing strategies that improve the

Y.N. Patt et al. (Eds.): HiPEAC 2010, LNCS 5952, pp. 156–170, 2010.

system performance for stateful and stateless networking applications. A simulation model in SystemC (section 4) is used to evaluate and compare the performance of prior art and our new load assignment strategies. Experimental results based on real Internet traffic are presented in section 5. Section 6 concludes the paper.

2 Prior Art

2.1 Load Balancing Schemes in Network Processors

In [1] Dittmann introduces a hashing-based load balancing system for parallel network processors. For each incoming packet a hash-value is computed out of certain flow-identifying header fields (typically the IP five-tuple consisting of source and destination addresses, protocol number, and L4 port numbers). A load balancing table maintains a list of such hash values, their associated processor, and a timestamp, when the last packet of the hash value had entered the system. If the incoming packet's flow has not expired, the packet is forwarded towards the processing engine (PE) queue specified in the table. If the time stamp for the hash value of the incoming packet is older than a pre-defined timeout value, the entry is updated to route the packet towards the least loaded PE queue. Two exceptions from this basic scheme are presented: An existing flow entry may be re-mapped to another PE before the timeout, if the corresponding PE queue is overloaded, in order to avoid unnecessary packet loss. Second, if a single flow entry would exceed the processing capabilities of a single PE, its packets may be distributed over several PEs, which is called packet spraying. It is important to realize that packets may be re-ordered, when a re-mapping takes place during a flow bundle's lifetime, and - of course - when packets of an excessive flow bundle get sprayed. Packet reordering has been identified to cause problems with the congestion avoidance of TCP, and should be avoided as far as possible [5].

This simple, hashing-based scheme is modified by Kencl in [2] to feature an adaptive control loop in combination with a robust highest-random weight (HRW) hashing, called AHH (Adaptive HRW Hashing). The adaptive control loop assures that the weights for the HRW hashing are modified, such that the assignment of flow bundles to the PEs is more evenly balanced for biased hash bundles found in real Internet traffic. Packet reordering may occur, when the weight adaptation triggers a re-balancing of flow bundles from one PE to another.

Internet traffic usually consists of many flows with low activity and only a few flows with high activity (aggressive flows)[6]. In contrast to AHH, the Adaptive Burst Shifter (ABS) [3] shifts only the aggressive flows in an unbalanced situation, whereas the non-aggressive flows are mapped by hashing. Since the shift of few aggressive flows already has an appreciable effect on PE load, the number of hash flow shifts can be reduced and thus also packet reordering. ABS uses a Flow Classifier to identify the aggressive flows, whereas a Load Adapter remaps the aggressive flows to the least loaded PE, when needed.

Finally, in [4] Shi and Kencl propose to combine their previously developed AHH and ABS schemes, such that the burst shifting is applied after assigning flows according to the AHH method. In this way, the Burst Shifter helps to move loads directly away from most-loaded PEs towards the least-loaded PE, even before the AHH hashing weight adaptation might react. In addition, the algorithm insures that flows may only be re-mapped at the beginning of a burst, i.e. when no other packet of the same flow is already in the system. The combined scheme (referred to as HABS in the following) results in the best performance of the prior art schemes with respect to the number of active flow re-mappings and packet reordering rates. However, the burst shifting algorithm requires maintenance of a lot of state information, which makes the algorithm somewhat complex for implementation in a high-speed NP system.

2.2 FlexPath NP Architecture

Our FlexPath NP concept, which has already been presented in [7], consists of a cluster of PEs (e.g. PowerPC 405 cores or hardware accelerators like crypto cores) and some architecture-specific hardware units as shown in Figure 1.

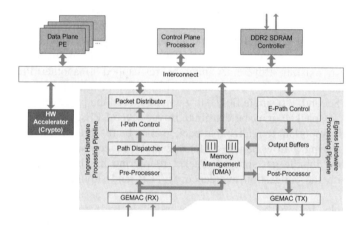

Fig. 1. FlexPath NP Architecture

The basic idea of the FlexPath NP is to support different processing paths that are optimized for various networking applications. In a FlexPath NP some functions, which might traditionally be implemented in software on one of the processors, is moved to hardware situated near the networking interfaces. This hardware is implemented as a data path pipeline running at full aggregated line speed. It relieves the PEs from often recurring tasks and also facilitates real time traffic differentiation and load assignment towards the PEs. When a packet is received from a link, its header is inspected by the Pre-Processor and a classification for several application types takes place in the Path Dispatcher [8]. The Packet Distributor consists of a set of FIFOs for traffic differentiation before the processor cluster and the Multi-Processor Interrupt Controller. After processing, the packets are sent to the Egress Path Control [9], which insures correct packet sequence for packets that belong to the same flow. This is achieved by analyzing flow-specific sequence numbers issued by the Ingress

Path Control and queuing out-of-order packets before forwarding them towards the output buffers of the NP. Thus, our architecture provides an effective means to reduce the packet reordering observed in parallel forwarding architectures. Finally, the packets are sent towards the egress interfaces of the NP. As we have already shown the architectural concept and implementation results in previous publications, we will focus on the load balancing problem in the following.

3 Application-Aware Load Balancing for FlexPath NP

We are looking for load balancing strategies that optimize the NP performance with respect to QoS requirements and maximize PE utilization. As we have laid out in 2.2, our FlexPath NP environment provides the Path Control unit to solve the problem of packet reordering in parallel PE network processor units (NPUs). Therefore, we do not consider this problem to the extent that schemes from the prior art do. We approach the problem from a different point of view: What would be the optimum load balancing strategies with respect to overall system utilization, minimum packet loss rates and processing latencies? As we differentiate the networking applications in the ingress pipeline of our NPU, we apply a combination of several load balancing strategies; one for each application type. We will focus on stateless and stateful networking applications and derive optimized load assignment schemes for these two classes. For the remainder of this paper, we will use QoS-aware IP forwarding and IPsec encryption as two representative examples for stateless and stateful network processing applications.

IP forwarding operates only on the header fields of the current packet to determine the packet's destination and thus does not require maintenance of a flow-specific state. In addition, it is still possible to differentiate various QoS priorities according to the DSCP field in the IP header, if we assume to be within a DiffServ cloud [10], where packets with a marked priority should be forwarded on a higher priority level in both the PEs and the output queues.

In contrast, when processing IPsec traffic [11], a flow-specific state has to be maintained. The state information consists of the connection parameters, sequence numbers and cryptographic keys. In order to guarantee processing state consistency, it is necessary to protect the state information by a semaphore locking mechanism, if it needs to be accessed from several PEs that work on the same flow in parallel. Such concurrent accesses may however deteriorate the performance significantly due to blocking accesses.

3.1 Support for Stateless Processing Applications

For stateless IP forwarding traffic, referred to as best effort (BE) and DiffServ high priority (QoS) in the following, we propose to use a slightly modified form of packet spraying [1]. The idea behind this is that the packets will experience optimum processing, as we can exploit a pooling gain from distributing them over a multitude of PEs. In contrast to the packet spraying mechanism as defined in [1], we do not maintain a single queue per processor, into which the packets are sprayed. The spraying is performed out of a single queue per traffic class (e.g. QoS priority level) by means of the Interrupt Controller. We assign the BE and QoS packets to two different queues in the Packet Distributor, who will in turn notify all PEs by interrupt that a packet is waiting to be processed (see also Figure 2). The interrupt priorities for the processors are configured in such a way that the QoS queue will be worked off before the BE queue. While a PE is working on a packet, it will mask all interrupts such that only idling PEs will react to a new packet arrival. As a consequence of the statistical assignment of packets we can expect a well balanced distribution of the load among all active PEs, and each packet at the head of the queue will experience the shortest possible wait time until it gets serviced. The modified spraying technique avoids head-of-line blocking effects associated with queues dedicated for individual PEs and also minimizes packet reordering probabilities, as packets only experience varying processing latencies, but not different queuing delays. However, we do not guarantee packets from the same flow to be processed by the same PE. The higher packet reordering rate in comparison to hash-based load assignment schemes is eliminated by our Path Control unit before the packets reach the NP output buffers.

3.2 Support for Stateful Processing Applications

Due to the consistency and performance implications of shared state information, we do not apply packet spraying for the class of stateful traffic. Stateful flows are processed on a single PE with a local copy of the processing state. In case that the aggregate of flows assigned to a single PE exceeds the overall processing capacity, re-balancings have to be performed along with a (possibly costly) state information migration among the involved PEs. The class of adaptive hashing-based schemes (AHH and HABS) referenced in the prior art section would serve as potential candidates for balancing this type of traffic.

While analyzing the details of the AHH and HABS schemes, we realized that the evaluation of the highest random weight is quite computationally intensive and that flows from an overloaded PE are not necessarily assigned to the least-loaded PE. The implementation effort becomes even higher for HABS, which complements AHH with a burst shifter unit that requires additional maintenance of flow state information.

In order to minimize the effort spent for load balancing, while maintaining a close to optimal PE resource utilization, we propose a new simple, adaptive, hashing-based scheme, called HLU. The following sections describe the load assignment process of HLU that has to be performed within the Control Plane processor of the NP. The resulting flow to PE assignment is then configured into the Path Dispatcher rule base, which makes the real-time path decision for each incoming packet.

At system startup, we need to make an assignment for all possible flows (distinguished by a hash value computed from the Internet five-tuple, called FlowID in the following) to the individual PEs in the processor cluster. A FIFO-type list is maintained in the Control Plane that stores the assigned FlowIDs for each PE. From these FIFOs, the hash table used within the Path Dispatcher [8] can be easily derived. Initially, we fill these FlowID FIFOs with an equal amount of flows. As we know from previous publications (especially [2]), this initial assignment may not be optimal due to a bias in the hash value distribution of real Internet traffic.

During system runtime, we measure the load of the individual PEs and adapt the load assignment by re-balancing flows from the highest-loaded PE towards the least-loaded PE when an unbalanced situation is observed. In contrast to some schemes presented in the prior art, we do not rely on queue lengths as a measurement for PE load; instead we measure the load of the PEs directly. This may be achieved by inserting only two instructions into the processing software that inform a set of hardware counters of beginning and end of the processing routine. When provisioning two counters per PE, we are easily able to determine the individual shares that stateful and stateless flows have generated on the respective PE.

By removing FlowIDs from the front of the overloaded PEs' FIFO and appending it to the end of the least-loaded PEs' FIFO, we insure that flows that have been re-balanced stick with the new assignment as long as possible. This behavior is in contrast to AHH, where load variations may lead to oscillations of flow assignments due to the nature of the HRW algorithm. The assignment persistence is beneficial in the context of stateful networking applications, where re-balancings not only pose the risk of packet reordering, but also come at the cost of migrating processing context from one PE to another. Code Listing 1 describes the adaptation routine of HLU, which is executed periodically (T_{adapt}) within the Control Plane processor.

The current load figures resulting from the HLU-assigned traffic (i.e. no spraying) are gathered for each PE $\rho(i,t)$ and are low pass filtered according to the following iterative formula:

$$\rho_{low\_pass}(i,t) = .05 \times \rho(i,t) + .95 \times \rho_{low\_pass}(i,t - T_{adapt}) .$$

From these individual PE loads, maximum, minimum and average utilization figures are computed as follows:

$$\rho_{max} = \max_i(\rho_{low\_pass}(i,t)), \quad \rho_{min} = \min_i(\rho_{low\_pass}(i,t))$$

$$\rho_{avg} = \frac{\sum_i \rho_{low\_pass}(i,t)}{i}$$

An adaptation is triggered, when the utilization of the highest-loaded PE ρ_{max} exceeds an adaptation threshold AT_1 and the imbalance between the highest and least-loaded PE exceeds an adaptation threshold AT_2. If ρ_{max} is excessively exceeding the average load, flows are moved towards the least-loaded PE. The number of flows moved depends on the amount of overload ($\rho_{max} - \rho_{avg}$) and number of flow bundles currently assigned to the highest-loaded PE (FIFO[max].size()). The term is multiplied with a low-pass factor of s_{over} to factor in the risk of moving an aggressive flow. Analogous to this, flows are assigned towards an excessively under-utilized PE with a slower low-pass factor of s_{under}. The low pass factors help to evenly balance the loads over several adaptation periods, and wildly oscillating load assignments caused by aggressive flows are avoided. The algorithm's parameters have been determined by a set of simulations with realistic Internet backbone traffic and yield optimal results for the considered traffic with the following values:

AT_1=40%, AT_2=15%, s_{over}=0.125, s_{under}=0.0625, T_{adapt}=50ms.

```
if(rho_max > AT_1)
            if(rho_min < rho_avg-AT_2 or rho_max > rho_avg+AT_2)
            if(rho_max-rho_avg > rho_avg-rho_min)
                flows=s_over*(rho_max-rho_avg)*FIFO[max].size();
            else
                flows=s_under*(rho_avg-rho_min)*FIFO[max].size();
            while(flows>0) {
                FIFO[min].push_back(FIFO[max].pop_front());
                flows--;
            }
```

Code Listing 1: HLU Adaptation Routine

If HLU shall be applied for traffic with different statistical properties as observed in the traces we used in this paper, an adaptation of the parameters may be necessary. This adaptation may also be accomplished during system runtime by implementing a learning algorithm in the control plane of the NP. However, a detailed discussion is beyond the scope of the work presented in this paper.

In the following parts of the paper the performance of the proposed load balancing strategies is shown. In scenarios with a mix of stateful and stateless networking applications, S&H refers to the combination of spraying and HLU for the respective application classes.

4 Simulation Model

For evaluating the different strategies we have developed a SystemC [12] model of the NP system as depicted in Figure 2.

Packet classification and hash table lookup (as required both for AHH and HLU) are performed by the Path Dispatcher. For FlexPath NP, we demonstrate S&H, where QoS and BE forwarding traffic is separated into two queues with different interrupt priorities for spraying. IPSec traffic is assigned to dedicated queues that are associated to a single PE each using the HLU algorithm. For the reference simulations, the Path Dispatcher only performs the AHH hash lookup used in HABS. The Burst Shifter model is only included in the reference simulations. It remaps the flows in overload situations based on the queue fill levels (indicating a PE's load situation) and the current flow table entries. The flow table size is fixed to 16 entries in our simulations. The Packet Distributor contains 16 queues for dedicated assignment, as well as one spraying queue for QoS and one for BE traffic – with QoS having the highest and the BE queue having the lowest priority. The queue size is initially set to 32 packet descriptors for all queues. A packet is lost, when it is assigned to a full queue. Each queue informs the Multi-Processor Interrupt Controller, whenever a packet is waiting for processing.

It is important to realize that the queues in the packet distributor should not be seen as input buffers of a switch architecture, which are generally known to have inferior throughput performance. Our FlexPath architecture can rather be seen as a concatenation of two output buffer switch architectures. At first, incoming packets from all input links are stored in the central packet memory. In parallel to the DMA function, the packets are classified by the Path Dispatcher and packet descriptors are assigned to the corresponding queue in the packet distributor in front of the processor complex. The queues can be seen as output buffers of the Path Dispatcher unit, which is guaranteed to provide line speed performance on the aggregate of incoming links. If the processor complex is dimensioned for worst case traffic, the queues in the packet distributor will be emptied instantly. However, we also consider average case dimensioning, where temporary overloads may occur. In this situation we guarantee by provisioning application-specific queues that high priority flows cannot be blocked by lower priority flows, thus avoiding head-of-line blocking effects. Output port contention is finally resolved by the output buffers behind the processor complex.

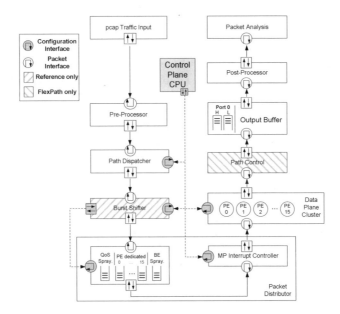

Fig. 2. FlexPath NP and Reference Architectures as SystemC Model

The processing latencies in the data plane cluster are derived from a real PPC 405 packet processing software implementation on our Virtex-4 FPGA FlexPath NP demonstrator system (see [7], and Figure 1) and have been measured as 10 μs for IPv4 forwarding and

$$t_{proc, IPSec} = 310 \mu s + \frac{packet \; length}{64 \, Byte} \cdot 112 \mu s$$

for IPSec processing (encryption) for packets processed by a single CPU in the system. In order to cover processing jitter effects, like shared resource conflicts (e.g. bus or memory), 20% of the packets get a factor of 1.5 and another 10% a factor of 2 processing time penalty in the subsequent system simulations. It is important to mention that the processing performance of the PPC cores in the demonstrator system (simple C programming, 200 MHz clock frequency) is not competitive with commercial NP cores processing multi-Gigabit/s links. However, we prefer to base our simulations on measured values obtained from our implementation instead of estimated software performance. Anyway, the effectiveness of the investigated load assignment schemes is independent of the individual PE's maximum forwarding rate.

In contrast to the original AHH implementation, which assumes uniform processing latencies for all packets, we are using the real PE loads as input to the AHH algorithm. Kencl calculated the PE load by multiplying the packet rate with the processing latency per packet, leading to a theoretical PE load that may exceed 100% in overload situations. Since in a heterogeneous application-mix the processing latency cannot be predicted we have to use the real PE loads.

We employ real backbone traffic traces from CAIDA in this publication (see Table 1). The first set of traces is generated from the Anonymized OC-48 Traces dataset [13], which consists of five-minute traces taken in 2002. The link is only about 30% utilized, so we have multiplexed the first packets of traces recorded at 15 minute intervals into a single file. This increases the load but preserves the original time differences between packets of the original flows. The multiplexed trace is limited to one minute duration and 3.2 Gbit/s, as this is the limit for our NP data path modules (32 bit @ 100 MHz on our FPGA demonstrator). This trace is referred to as OC-48_mux in the following. The second trace set is obtained from the Anonymized 2008 Trace set [14]. We use multiplexed and rate-limited traces from the ChicagoA trace as OC-192_mux. The trace taken on the ChicagoB link is highly utilized with bursts exceeding 9 Gbit/s for periods of a few seconds and intermediate idle times. We have slowed down the trace by a factor of four and limited bursts to 3.2 Gbit/s (OC-192_quarter). Comparing the traces from 2002 and 2008, we see that both IPSec and QoS-marked traffic shares have increased significantly - still BE traffic accounts for more than 90% of the packets seen on a high-speed link.

Although our NP scenario encompasses networking applications usually applied at the network edge, we had to resort to using backbone traffic traces as edge or access traces are not made publicly available for privacy and security concerns. We consider our results to be still valid because backbone traffic is essentially a multiplex of edge traffic streams, thus the protocol distribution and flow characteristics are preserved.

Table 1. Key Figures of Used Internet Traces

Trace Name	Packets	Data Rate	IPSec	QoS	BE
OC-48_mux	22,086,716	1.955Gb/s	0.07%	4.14%	95.79%
OC-192_mux	41,223,895	2.819Gb/s	0.40%	4.04%	95.56%
OC-192_quarter	26,473,646	1.320 Gb/s	0.63%	7.39%	91.98%

5 Experiments

5.1 Best-Effort Forwarding Scenario

As the load balancing techniques from the prior art are designed for a homogeneous processing scenario, we start our investigations with best effort forwarding. This provides the opportunity to compare HLU and spraying individually to the schemes from the prior art. The Path Dispatcher only performs the various load assignments without classifying the traffic into the QoS, IPSec and BE classes. The PEs apply only the forwarding latency. The benefits of our proposed combination of spraying and HLU for stateful processing will be investigated in detail in section 5.2. All simulations in sections 5.1 and 5.2 are performed with the OC-48_mux trace.

In Figure 3 we show the minimum and maximum averaged PE loads of the NP system using the different presented load balancing techniques in isolation. We investigate the load balancing behavior with an increasing number of PEs in the data plane cluster. For packet spraying all PEs are evenly sharing the load. The difference of individual PE loads from the cluster average is by design limited to $AT_2=15\%$ in HLU – we see that it is in practice even less than this threshold. In stark contrast are the characteristics of the HABS algorithm, which may be explained by the fact that both AHH and ABS parts are designed to eliminate overloads, but don't further optimize on the balancing in underload situations, e.g. when the average PE load drops below 60% for more than 8 PEs in the cluster.

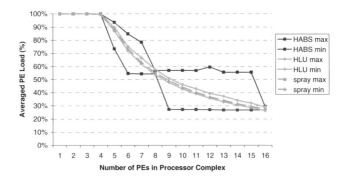

Fig. 3. Minimum and Maximum CPU Loads Observed with Different Load Balancing Strategies

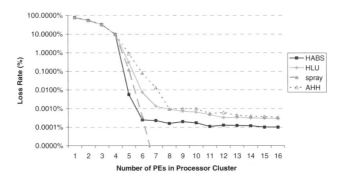

Fig. 4. System Packet Loss Rates for Different Load Balancing Strategies

Figure 4 shows the resulting packet loss rates of the NP system. It is important to realize that less than five PEs are inadequate for processing the incoming traffic, i.e. the NP is in overload with very high packet loss rates. As the overall PE load declines between 5 and 6 PEs, the packet loss rate is reduced to less than 10^{-5}. With more than 7 PEs, the provided processing power is greater than necessary to cope with the load, thus the packet loss rate directly corresponds to the effectiveness of the load balancing algorithm. We can see that the loss rate is the worst with AHH and HLU, HABS is about half an order of magnitude better, and spraying performs best with lossless operation. This result may be explained by the fact that AHH and HLU with their fixed assignment of certain flows to PEs are not so good at dealing with short-lived bursts in the traffic. These short bursts lead to temporary overflows in the Packet Distributor buffers. The ABS algorithm performs better by rebalancing such bursts in between two consecutive adaptation cycles. Packet spraying exhibits the best performance, because there is no aggregation of burst packets in front of a single PE. We also see that the performance of HLU roughly matches the performance of AHH beyond 8 PEs, as both schemes rely on a pure dedicated assignment with the same adaptation interval.

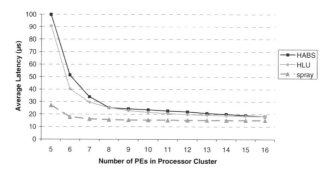

Fig. 5. Average Packet Latency for Different Load Balancing Strategies

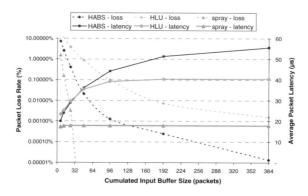

Fig. 6. Packet Loss Rate and Average Latency for Different Input Buffer Sizes (6 PEs)

For the remainder of this paper, we exclude the NP overload scenarios and focus on the range between 5 and 16 PEs. Figure 5 compares the average packet latencies achievable with each load balancing scheme. The stated latency figures are measured from receive interface to transmit interface and thus include pre-processing delay, PE processing delay and possible re-sequencing delays. For packet spraying, the packet latency is reduced very effectively, until it reaches a minimum floor which is defined by the processing time without any queuing delays. As PEs have the more evenly balanced load in contrast to HABS, the latency achieved with HLU is also slightly better than that of HABS, because shorter average queue lengths can be assumed.

Packet loss rates and latencies are not only dependent on the number of provisioned PEs, but are heavily dependent on dimensioning the queues in the system. As we can see in Figure 6, the packet loss rate may be reduced by provisioning larger packet descriptor queues in the Packet Distributor. In turn, the average packet latency is increasing, because packets from short bursts now remain sitting in the queue, while they were lost before. In general, we can see that when architecting an NP system we can trade off additional PEs with an increased input buffer size. However, the increased latency might have a negative effect on interactive applications like voice-over-IP or Internet video. While packet spraying operates losslessly and with constant latency beyond 48 packets, the other schemes require significantly larger buffers to reduce losses.

5.2 FlexPath Scenario with QoS Forwarding and IPSec

In the following part we show the performance of combining spraying and HLU (S&H) with the differentiated processing approach in FlexPath NP. The Path Dispatcher is now configured to assign QoS and BE packets directly to the two queues that spray the traffic over all PEs. Only packets identified as IPSec are assigned to dedicated PEs using the HLU algorithm. As schemes from the prior art do not consider such a heterogeneous processing approach, we use HABS to balance the load, irrespective of the actual packet processing requirements. However, in both cases the PEs will determine whether to apply the forwarding or IPSec latency. Therefore, the processing requirements are the same for the reference simulations and the proposed S&H assignment scheme.

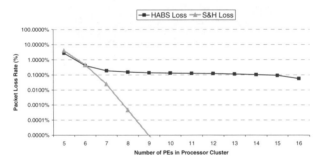

Fig. 7. Packet Loss Rate of S&H vs. HABS

The results in Figure 7 show a consistent behavior with respect to the individual characteristics described in section 5.1. As the vast majority of the traffic belongs to the BE class (see Table 1), we see the same kind of "waterfall" packet loss rate for the traffic in FlexPath (spraying dominates). However, as IPSec processing takes roughly a factor of 1,000 longer than plain forwarding, the lossless case for BE forwarding is achieved only beyond 9 provisioned processors, in contrast to 7 PEs as in the plain BE forwarding scenario (Figure 4).

Figure 8 shows the average packet latencies, differentiated by their respective networking application. By giving priority to the QoS packets in FlexPath, we are able to forward them with almost minimum latency, even while the buffers for BE are in overload and packets are lost. The latency figures for BE and QoS converge towards the minimum from 9 PEs onwards. In contrast, the latency for the forwarding packets is about a factor of three to four larger in the reference simulation (HABS), as the packets occasionally get stuck in the queue behind IPSec packets (head-of-line blocking effect).

In Figure 9 we show the shares of sprayed and dedicated loads for PE0 from the 12 PE scenario. The combination of packet spraying and dedicated assignment allows some load "breathing". While a burst of IPSec packets consumes a larger share of the

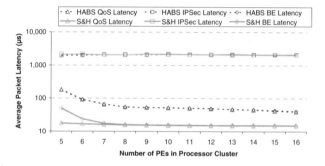

Fig. 8. Packet Latency of S&H vs. HABS

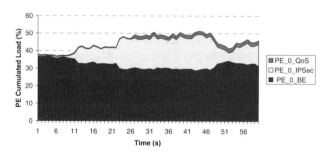

Fig. 9. Different Traffic Classes' Load Share (S&H)

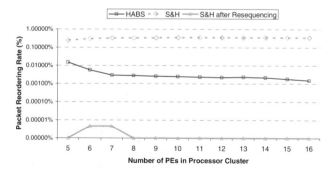

Fig. 10. Packet Reordering with HABS and S&H

PE's resources, sprayed traffic is superseded (and processed by other PEs, which carry less IPSec traffic at the same moment). The supersession is not explicitly triggered by the control plane CPU, thus it happens instantaneously and packets from the spraying queues don't get stuck waiting for the IPSec packet to finish.

Figure 10 summarizes the packet reordering rates observed with the reference and proposed techniques. While spraying most of the incoming traffic initially increases the packet reordering rate to 0.35%, it can be fully eliminated by the Path Control unit except for the 6 and 7 PE scenarios, where we observe a single out-of-order packet. In contrast, HABS achieves a packet reordering rate of 2×10^{-5} on average.

5.3 Results for Different Traces

We have performed the same simulations as presented in section 5.2 for the two other traces. The general behavior of our load balancing strategy in comparison to the schemes from the prior art remains unchanged. The key performance figures obtained for all three sets of simulations are summarized in Table 2 below. We quote figures for the minimum number of PEs necessary to achieve lossless operation for the two sprayed traffic classes with S&H. In both S&H and HABS, packets with dedicated assignment may be lost due to temporary bursts exceeding the buffer capacity.

Table 2. NP Performance Characteristics for S&H and HABS

Trace	# of PEs		Packet loss	QoS latency	IPSec latency	BE latency
OC-48_mux	10	S&H	0.0000%	15,177 ns	2,131,125 ns	15,378 ns
		HABS	0.1311%	51,600 ns	2,044,273 ns	52,624 ns
OC-192_mux	16	S&H	0.0002%	15,926 ns	3,122,052 ns	16,139 ns
		HABS	0.2865%	66,928 ns	1,586,312 ns	69,614 ns
OC-192_quarter	15	S&H	0.0010%	15,266 ns	3,896,399 ns	15,058 ns
		HABS	0.4792%	159,945 ns	2,124,968 ns	157,635 ns

6 Conclusion

In this paper, we have investigated the performance of various load balancing schemes used in a multi-processor NP chip. Based on a survey of NP load balancing schemes from the prior art, we propose to apply a combination of packet spraying and a simple hashing-based flow assignment (S&H) for different application types on the same NP. We have shown that our proposed scheme outperforms the schemes from the prior art with respect to packet loss rates, latencies, processor utilization and packet reordering. For packet spraying, which we propose to use for stateless networking applications, we can exploit a pooling gain effect and achieve an evenly balanced processor utilization. This even load distribution helps reduce packet loss and queuing latencies. In addition, we have shown how we can effectively implement QoS differentiation in the NP to give certain traffic flows priority over others.

As we have seen in the in-depth analysis in section 5.2, our scheme works best if a large share of the traffic belongs to the stateless traffic class, which can be distributed by packet spraying. This assumption is valid as we can see from an analysis of current traffic traces (see Table 1). Even when we assume that the share of stateful applications further increases, the stateless forwarding applications will remain dominant for the foreseeable future. When the share of sprayed traffic decreases, the behavior of the entire system is approaching the characteristics of the individual schemes as discussed in section 5.1. With 100% of dedicated traffic assignment, we can still achieve the same performance as with any of the schemes known from the prior art.

We would like to thank the German Research Foundation (DFG) for supporting the FlexPath NP project within the SPP1148 priority program and CAIDA for providing the Internet traffic traces. CAIDA is supported by the National Science Foundation, the US Department for Homeland Security and CAIDA members.

References

[1] Dittmann, G., Herkersdorf, A.: Network Processor Load Balancing for High-Speed Links. In: SPECTS 2002, San Diego, CA, USA, July 2002, pp. 727–735 (2002)

[2] Kencl, L.: Load Sharing for Multiprocessor Network Nodes, Dissertation, EPFL, Lausanne, Switzerland (March 2003)

[3] Shi, W., MacGregor, M., Gburzynski, P.: Load Balancing for Parallel Forwarding. IEEE Transactions on Networking 13(4), 790–801 (2005)

[4] Shi, W., Kencl, L.: Sequence-Preserving Adaptive Load Balancers. In: ANCS 2006, San Jose, CA, USA (December 2006)

[5] Govind, S., Govindarajan, R., Kuri, J.: Packet Reordering in Network Processors. In: IPDPS 2007, Long Beach, CA, USA (March 2007)

[6] Brownlee, N., Claffy, K.C.: Understanding Internet Traffic Streams: Dragonflies and Tortoises. IEEE Communications Magazine (October 2002)

[7] Meitinger, M., Ohlendorf, R., Wild, T., Herkersdorf, A.: FlexPath NP - A Network Processor Architecture with Flexible Processing Paths. In: SoC 2008, Tampere, Finland (November 2008)

[8] Ohlendorf, R., Meitinger, M., Wild, T., Herkersdorf, A.: A Processing Path Dispatcher in Network Processor MPSoCs. IEEE Transactions on VLSI Systems 16(10), 1335–1345 (2008)

[9] Meitinger, M., Ohlendorf, R., Wild, T., Herkersdorf, A.: A Hardware Packet Resequencer Unit for Network Processors. In: Brinkschulte, U., Ungerer, T., Hochberger, C., Spallek, R.G. (eds.) ARCS 2008. LNCS, vol. 4934, pp. 85–97. Springer, Heidelberg (2008)

[10] An Architecture for Differentiated Services, IETF RFC 2475 (December 1998), http://tools.ietf.org/html/rfc2475

[11] Security Architecture for the Internet Protocol, IETF RFC 4301 (December 2005), http://tools.ietf.org/html/rfc4301

[12] SystemC Homepage, http://www.systemc.org

[13] Shannon, C., Aben, E., Claffy, K.C., Andersen, D., Brownlee, N.: The CAIDA OC48 Traces Dataset, http://www.caida.org/data/passive/passive_oc48_dataset.xml; files used: 20020814-090000-1-anon.pcap, 20020814-091500-1-anon.pcap, 20020814-093000-1-anon.pcap, 20020814-094500-1-anon.pcap

[14] Shannon, C., Aben, E., Claffy, K.C., Andersen, D.: The CAIDA Anonymized 2008 Internet Traces, http://www.caida.org/data/passive/passive_2008_dataset.xml, files used: eq-chic.dirA.20080717-130000.UTC.anon.pcap, eq-chic.dirA.20080717-130500.UTC.anon.pcap, eq-chic.dirA.20080717-131000.UTC.anon.pcap, eq-chic.dirA.20080717-131500.UTC.anon.pcap, eq-chic.dirB.20080717-132000.UTC.anon.pcap

Memory-Aware Application Mapping on Coarse-Grained Reconfigurable Arrays*

Yongjoo Kim[1], Jongeun Lee[2],**, Aviral Shrivastava[3], Jonghee Yoon[1],
and Yunheung Paek[1]

[1] School of EECS, Seoul National University, Seoul, Korea
[2] School of ECE, Ulsan National Institute of Science and Technology, Ulsan, Korea
Tel.: +82-52-217-2116
jlee@unist.ac.kr
[3] Compiler Microarchitecture Lab, Arizona State University, USA

Abstract. Coarse-Grained Reconfigurable Arrays (CGRAs) are a very promising platform, providing both, up to 10-100 MOps/mW of power efficiency and are software programmable. However, this cardinal promise of CGRAs critically hinges on the effectiveness of application mapping onto CGRA platforms. While previous solutions have greatly improved the computation speed, they have largely ignored the impact of the local memory architecture on the achievable power and performance. This paper motivates the need for memory-aware application mapping for CGRAs, and proposes an effective solution for application mapping that considers the effects of various memory architecture parameters including the number of banks, local memory size, and the communication bandwidth between the local memory and the external main memory. Our proposed solution achieves 62% reduction in the energy-delay product, which factors into about 47% and 28% reduction in the energy consumption and runtime, respectively, as compared to memory-unaware mapping for realistic local memory architectures. We also show that our scheme scales across a range of applications, and memory parameters.

1 Introduction

Coarse-Grained Reconfigurable Arrays, or CGRAs, are a very promising platform, providing up to 10 to 100 MOps/mW of power efficiency [1] while still retaining software programmability. CGRAs are essentially an array of processing elements (PEs), like ALUs and multipliers, interconnected with a mesh-like network. PEs can operate on

---

* This work was supported by the Korea Science and Engineering Foundation(KOSEF) NRL Program grant funded by the Korea government(MEST) (No. 2009-0083190), the Engineering Research Center of Excellence Program of Korea Ministry of Education, Science and Technology(MEST)/ Korea Science and Engineering Foundation(KOSEF) (R11-2008-007-01001-0), Seoul R&BD Program(10560), the Korea Research Foundation Grant funded by the Korean Government(MOEHRD) (KRF-2007-357-D00225), 2009 Research Fund of the UNIST (Ulsan National Institute of Science and Technology), and grants from Raytheon, Stardust foundation, and NSF (grant no. 0916652).
** Corresponding author.

Y.N. Patt et al. (Eds.): HiPEAC 2010, LNCS 5952, pp. 171–185, 2010.
© Springer-Verlag Berlin Heidelberg 2010

the result of their neighboring PEs connected through the interconnection network. In addition, each PE has a small number of local registers to store constants and temporary values. Array variables are typically stored in the local memory, also called frame buffer, which is an on-chip SRAM memory with a very high bandwidth toward the PE array. The word-wide datapaths, area-efficient routing, and word-level programmability make them especially suited for multimedia and compute-intensive applications, whereas FPGAs can be more appropriate for complex logic and bit manipulation. Several CGRAs such as MorphoSys [2], RSPA [3], and ADRES [4], have been proposed and implemented, and a comprehensive summary of many of them can be found in [5].

One of the biggest challenges for CGRAs is application mapping, or compilation. Compilation for CGRAs has traditionally focused on two issues: i) placing *operations* (such as arithmetic/logic, multiplication, and load/store) of a loop kernel onto the PE array, and ii) guaranteeing the data flow, or *communication*, between operations using the existing interconnection resources. The third dimension, which has been typically ignored in previous CGRA compilation techniques [6, 7, 8, 9, 10, 11, 12, 13, 14, 15], is where to place *data*, typically array variables, in the local memory. We refer to operation placement and array placement as *computation mapping* and *data mapping*, respectively. Data mapping is not an issue if the local memory has uniform memory access (UMA) architecture—for instance, if the local memory consists of a single large bank. Then any PE can access any local memory address with equal timing, and thus it does not matter where to place an array. However, if the local memory has nonuniform memory access (NUMA) architecture—for instance, if it consists of multiple banks and each bank is connected to only one row of PEs—where to place array variables among multiple banks can affect computation mapping and greatly impact the quality of the overall mapping. Since the local memory of a CGRA is accessed by many PEs each cycle, typically more than a dozen ports exist between the local memory and PEs. Implementing UMA architecture with such a large number of ports is very expensive, either by single-bank multi-port memory [9, 13] or through hardware arbitration [16]. Thus a compiler technique that can effectively manage the complexity of NUMA architecture for CGRA mapping is highly desirable.

Computation mapping and data mapping are two very closely related problems, so solving them sequentially does not give the optimal solution. If array placement is fixed first, and operations are placed later, the computation mapping problem will involve far more constraints than without array placement, that it may be unsolvable or generate poorer solutions than without array placement. Besides, it is not clear how to fix array placement first without doing at least part of computation mapping. On the other hand, if computation mapping is done first, it automatically determines data mapping, which can lead to other problems. First, the same array may be placed in multiple banks (*duplicate array*) if the array is reused in multiple references in the loop (i.e., by multiple loads with different indexes). This can lower the effective size of the local memory and can significantly degrade the performance especially if the local memory is not very large. Second, bank utilization can be unbalanced to a large degree, which can lower the performance if the unbalance in the bank utilization causes extra buffering in the local memory. Third, in recurrent loops, dependent memory operations must be able to

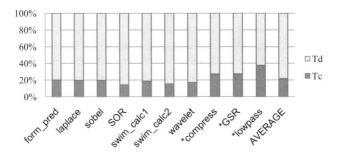

Fig. 1. Many multimedia kernels are memory-bound on RSPA. Td$= t_d/(t_c + t_d)$ and Tc$= t_c/(t_c + t_d)$. Asterisk (*) indicates recurrent loop, where II and t_c can be increased due to data dependence.

access the same array from the same bank. This could be taken care of by constraining dependent memory operations to be mapped to the same rows, for instance, but other constraints (e.g., port contention, memory size restriction) may also be necessary. In general, to guarantee the correctness and optimality of mapping for memory-bound loops on NUMA CGRAs, we must consider not only computation mapping but also data mapping. In this paper we propose a compilation technique, which is aware of the local memory architecture and can find near-optimal mapping considering both array variables and computation operations in memory-bound loops.

After motivating in Section 2 the need for considering the memory architecture and data placement during mapping, we explain our target architecture and application mapping in general in Section 3, and discuss the related work in Section 4. In Section 5 we present our memory-aware heuristic that can be applied to any modular scheduling algorithm such as [9, 13]. Our proposal introduces new costs such as data reuse opportunity cost and bank balancing cost to steer the mapping process to be more aware of the architectural peculiarities. Our experimental results indicate that not only is our proposed heuristic able to achieve near-optimal results as compared to single-bank memory mapping, it can also achieve 62% reduction in the energy-delay product as compared to memory-unaware mapping for multi-bank memory, which factors to 47% and 28% reductions in the energy consumption and runtime, respectively. We also demonstrate that our scheme scales across a range of applications, and memory parameters.

2   Why Consider Data Placement?

If the local memory is large enough, duplicate arrays and unbalanced bank utilization may not be a problem—simply duplicate arrays as many times as needed if each memory bank is unlimited. However, we find that it is not the case in many CGRAs such as MorphoSys and RSPA, and in fact, for larger arrays and loops the entire arrays cannot fit in the local memory and multiple buffer switchings are necessary even during a single loop execution. To minimize slowdown due to buffer switching, those architectures often provide hardware double buffering [2], such that computation (on the PE array) and data transfer (between the local memory and the system memory) can work on different hardware buffers, overlapping computation and data transfer, and buffer switching can be done instantly, typically in a few cycles. Even with such hardware support, for memory-bound applications it is hard to avoid data transfer becoming the performance bottleneck, since memory bandwidth is not as scalable as increasing the number of PEs on a CGRA.

Figure 1 plots the ratio between t_c and t_d of important loop kernels from MiBench and SPEC benchmark, using the EMS algorithm [13] on the RSPA architecture [3]. The terms t_c and t_d are the computation time and the data transfer time for a tile of a loop, where tile is defined by buffer switching. Then the total execution time of a tile is determined by $\max(t_c, t_d)$. The graph shows that all these loop kernels are indeed memory-bound, i.e., $t_d > t_c$, with the average $t_c/(t_c + t_d)$ being just 22%. Even if we double the memory bandwidth (of between the local memory and the system memory) from 2 bytes per cycle to 4 bytes per cycle, most of the loops still remain memory-bound, with the average $t_c/(t_c + t_d)$ increasing to just 37%. Thus it is important to optimize the data part of the mapping, not just the computation part of it, and even sacrificing computation mapping to some degree in order to gain in data mapping, or in other words balancing t_c and t_d, could lead to enhancement in the overall performance.

3   Background: Architecture and Application Mapping

3.1   CGRA Architecture

CGRA is essentially an array of processing elements (PEs), connected through a mesh-like network (see Figure 2(b)). Each PE can execute an arithmetic or logic operation, multiplication, or load/store. PEs can load or store data from the on-chip local memory, but they can also operate on the output of a neighboring PE connected through the interconnect network. Many resource-constrained CGRA designs have some PEs dedicated for some specific functionality. For example, in each row, typically a few PEs are reserved for multiplication in addition to ALU operations, and a few can perform loading and storing from/to the local memory. The functionality of a PE, i.e., the choice

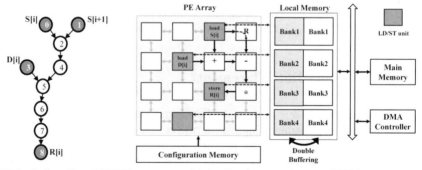

(a) DFG of a loop from MPEG2   (b) Application mapping onto CGRA

Fig. 2. CGRA architecture and application mapping

of source operands, destination of the result, and the operation it performs is specified in the *configuration*, which is generated as a result of compiling the application on to the CGRA.

A CGRA processor is used as a coprocessor to a main processor. The main processor manages CGRA execution, such as loading of CGRA configurations and initiating CGRA execution, through memory-mapped I/O. Once the CGRA starts execution, the main processor can perform other tasks. Interrupts can be used to notify the completion of CGRA execution. The local memory of a CGRA is managed by the CGRA through DMA. Hardware double buffering allows for full overlap between computation and data transfer on the CGRA, as well as quick switches between buffers; this becomes very critical for large loops, which may require multiple buffer switches during the execution of a single loop.

3.2 Application Mapping

CGRAs are typically used to accelerate the innermost loops of applications, thereby saving runtime and energy. The innermost loop of a perfectly nested loop can be represented as a data flow graph, in which the nodes represent micro-operations (arithmetic and logic operations, multiplication, and load/store), and the edges represent the data dependency between the operations. A loop kernel from MPEG2 is illustrated in Figure 2(a), where dark nodes represent memory operations. While not for this loop, the data dependency can be in general loop-carried. The task of mapping an application onto a CGRA traditionally comprises of mapping the nodes of the data flow graph onto the PE array of the CGRA, and to map the edges onto the connections between the PEs. Since the mesh-like interconnection can be restrictive for application mapping, most CGRAs allow PEs to be used for routing of data (*routing PE*). In the routing mode, the PE does not perform any operation, but just transfer one of the inputs to its output. This flexibility can be exploited by allowing the edges in the data flow graph to be mapped onto paths (composed alternatively of interconnection and a free PE, starting and ending in an interconnection) in the CGRA. Pipelining is explicit in the CGRA, in the sense that the result of computation inside one PE can be used by the neighboring PEs in the next cycle. For effective application mapping, the compiler must software-pipeline the loop before mapping it onto the the PEs for effective mapping. Thus in addition to the problem of expressing the application in terms of the functionality of PEs, a CGRA compiler must explicitly perform resource allocation, pipelining, and routing of data dependencies on the CGRA. It is for these reasons that the problem of application mapping on CGRA is challenging.

4 Related Work

Earlier research on CGRAs was mostly about architecture design [5], but with the recognition that application mapping is the bottleneck, recent work increasingly focuses on application mapping techniques.

4.1 Architecture

Data transfer architectures between local memory and PEs can be classified into implicit load-store and explicit load-store architecture. Implicit load-store CGRA architectures, e.g., MorphoSys [2], do not have explicit load and store instructions. Data has to be pre-arranged in the local memory, organized like a queue, and the topmost element is broadcast to the CGRA every cycle. On the other hand, in explicit load-store CGRAs, e.g., ADRES [4], PEs can explicitly compute the address of the memory location that they intend to access, and read/write to that location. While the implicit load-store architectures are potentially much more power efficient, they are more challenging to program, and also incur penalties relating to the efforts required to arrange the data in a very specific order in the local store.

Local memory can be designed as single-bank or multi-bank. Single-bank memory makes programming much easier; however, it is very difficult to provide all the necessary ports for the PE array with just one bank. One solution is to use multi-port SRAM cells, which are however extremely expensive in terms of area, power, and speed [17]. With multi-bank memory, it is the responsibility of the programmer/compiler to make sure the data that a PE accesses is present in a bank that it has access to. Alternatively, one can use hardware arbitration to make every bank accessible to any PE [16], which makes the local memory design more complicated with higher power, area, and possibly cycle time compared to multi-bank memory without hardware arbitration. Our work provides a software solution rather than a hardware solution to the problem of managing multi-bank memory.

Hardware double buffering, e.g., MorphoSys [2] and RSPA [3], can speed up the data transfer between the system memory and the CGRA local memory, while some architectures, e.g., ADRES [16], opt for a single large buffer. Double buffering becomes more useful if the local memory size is smaller, or the loops and arrays of the applications are larger. We assume explicit load-store, multi-bank, and double-buffered local memory in this work.

4.2 Compilation

Most previous work on application mapping for CGRA [6, 7, 8, 9, 10, 11, 12, 13, 14, 15] does not explicitly consider the local memory architecture or data placement. They assume that all the required data is already present in the local memory, and every load-store PE can access that data whenever they need to. Even with such a simplification, the application mapping problem for CGRA is shown to be very hard [11], having to deal with operation placement on a 2D array considering the communication between them (*spatial mapping*) [12], as well as possibly changing configurations every cycle (*temporal mapping*) [8, 13].

One exception to this is [18], which assumes a hierarchical memory architecture, where the PEs are connected to a L0 local memory, which connects to the external main memory through an L1 local memory. Since both these local memories are scratchpads, and therefore statically scheduled, their main interest is in improving the reuse between the L0 and L1 local memories. An early work [19] on CGRA presents a methodology to evaluate memory architectures for CGRA mapping; however, it lacks a detailed mapping algorithm. [20] also considers memory architecture for mapping, and is therefore most closely related to our work. However, their mapping assumes multi-bank memory with arbitration logic and single buffering, and therefore is not applicable to our target architecture while we explore the impact of partitioned, or multi-banked, memory architecture and also explore the impact of limited memory bandwidth on the mapping.

5   Our Approach

The real challenge of considering data placement during CGRA mapping is in how to minimize *both* t_c and t_d together within a single framework or algorithm. Simply minimizing t_d is trivial; for instance, fixing the placement of all the arrays beforehand will do, but it may increase t_c excessively. Considering t_d only is what has been typically done in previous approaches, which may fail to minimize the overall t, or the maximum of t_c and t_d. Moreover, data mapping should be emphasized only if the application is memory-bound, which adds to the complexity of our problem. Thus, our CGRA mapping problem considering both computation and data mapping is more complicated than the traditional CGRA mapping problem considering computation only, which is already NP-hard [11]. Hence we propose a heuristic in this paper. We will also demonstrate through our experiments that our heuristic can achieve near-optimal results for many loops.

Our heuristic considers: i) minimizing duplicate arrays (or maximizing data reuse), ii) balancing bank utilization, and iii) balancing t_c and t_d. A unique feature of our heuristic is that it merely defines some cost functions for those memory-related considerations, rather than prescribing a whole new algorithm, so that our heuristic can be easily integrated with other existing memory-unaware mapping algorithms. While our technique is generally applicable to any modular scheduling algorithm considering one operation at a time such as [8, 13], for the sake of the discussion we use the EMS algorithm in this paper as it is one of the best known.

5.1   Balancing Computation and Data Transfer

To balance optimization effort for computation and data parts we first perform *performance bottleneck analysis*. *Performance bottleneck analysis* determines whether it is computation or data transfer that limits the overall performance. We define the data-transfer-to-computation time ratio (DCR) as $DCR = t_d/t_c$. For this we generate an initial, memory-unaware mapping and compute t_c and t_d. t_c is equal to the II multiplied by the tile size, and t_d includes both, the time to bring the data needed for the iteration, and also the time to writeback the data that needs to be committed back to the memory, after each tile. A loop is memory-bound if $DCR > 1$, and roughly represents the optimization opportunity for our memory-aware mapping.

5.2   Maximizing Data Reuse

Temporal reuse of data, or the use of the same data or array elements in different iterations of a loop, is frequently found in many loop kernels. Temporal as well as spatial reuse is automatically exploited by data caches for general purpose processors; however, for CGRAs everything must be explicitly controlled by compilers. Traditional compilation flows for CGRA, which are memory unaware, do not treat specially arrays with reuse. As a result, two load operations, even if they read from the same array, will typically be mapped to different rows. Note that this is not an issue of functional correctness, but of performance in NUMA CGRAs, since duplicating the arrays in multiple banks solves the correctness problem. An alternative approach is to realize reuse by mapping to the same row all the load operations accessing the same array, which we call *reuse through the local memory*.[2]

Reuse through the local memory has the benefit of lowering the local memory pressure, but at the cost of constraining the computation mapping. Therefore whether and how much reuse to realize should be decided carefully for optimal results. To guide the decision we introduce *data reuse opportunity cost* (DROC). DROC is defined for an operation and a PE, and measures the goodness of a reuse opportunity which will be forfeited if the operation is mapped to the PE. Intuitively, if two load operations have a reuse relation (i.e., they load from the same array), placing them on the same row has merit, which is forfeited if they are placed to PEs on different rows. This reuse opportunity is what DROC tries to quantify.

Data Reuse Analysis: Data reuse analysis finds the amount of potential data reuse between every pair of memory operations. Our data reuse analysis first creates a Data Reuse Graph (DRG) from the data flow graph of a loop. DRG is an undirected graph, where nodes correspond to memory operations and edge weights approximate the amount of reuse between two memory operations. Edges with zero weight are omitted. If two memory operations access different arrays, then the edge weight is zero. Otherwise, the edge weight is estimated to be $TS - rd$, where TS is the tile size, and rd the reuse distance in iterations. Although the eventual tile size for the mapping can only be determined after the loop has been mapped, and it depends on the amount of reuse realized, even an approximate value will do. This is because, all we want by these weights is that the memory operations that share more data should have greater chances to be mapped to the same row. We approximate $TS \approx MS/D_i$, where MS is the size of the local memory, and D_i is the average amount of data that needs to be transferred between the local memory and the external main memory for one iteration of our initial memory-unaware mapping ($D_T = T \cdot D_i$). MS/D_i would have been the tile size for the initial memory-unaware mapping on a single-bank memory architecture. The bigger challenge is to estimate rd, and in general, it can be extremely hard to analyze, especially in the presence of pointers and aliases. Fortunately in many cases reuse takes a very obvious form which can be found even by a very simple analysis. When the access functions (or index expressions) of two references to the same array have an affine form with the same coefficient, rd can be approximated to the difference in the constants divided by the coefficient.[3]

---

[2] When there is data reuse between two memory operations, the reuse can be realized by routing the data through either the register file (assuming it is rotating) , through routing PEs, or through the memory. Routing data either through the register file or through routing PEs can be wasteful since the involved PEs cannot perform any other operation. In addition, the number of wasted PEs to route data using these schemes is proportional to II, and therefore can be rather large. Therefore, we realize all the data reuse through the local memory.

[3] Only if the coefficient divides the difference; otherwise, there is no reuse between the two references.

Once the DRG is constructed, computing DROC is easy. Given scheduling context information such as what operations have been already scheduled and which operation is about to be scheduled, we first find the set of edges, called *frontier edge set*. For operation u, which is about to be scheduled, the frontier edge set of u includes every edge that connects u and another memory operation, v, in the DRG, and can be found very easily. Then for each edge e in the frontier edge set, we compute its reuse opportunity as $ro_e = w_e \cdot DCR/s_u$, where w_e is the nonzero weight of edge e in the DRG, DCR is the data-transfer-to-computation time ratio of the loop, and s_u is the size of the frontier edge set, or the number of edges in it. (Dividing by the number of edges is necessary to prevent DROC from increasing disproportionately compared to other costs that may exist.) Finally, the reuse opportunity of each edge e induces DROC of the same amount, for all the load-store PEs other than the PE to which v is mapped. DROC induced by all reuse opportunities are added up if the frontier edge set is larger than one. DROC is zero if the frontier edge set is empty.

Example: Consider mapping the DFG shown in Figure 3(b) (dark nodes are memory load operations) onto the 2x2 CGRA shown in Figure 3(a) (dark PEs are load-store PEs). The DRG for the DFG is shown in Figure 3(c). Figure 3(d)–(g) illustrate the mapping results in a tabular format, where the vertical direction represents time in cycles. Suppose that we are about to schedule the edge connecting operations 7 and 8 after having scheduled operations 0 through 6 as shown in Figure 3(d). Operation 7 is a load operation $B[i + 1]$, and operation 8 is an arithmetic operation.

The EMS algorithm works as follows: first the routing costs for each open PE slot where the memory operation can be scheduled are updated as in Figure 3(d). Routing cost is calculated by multiplying the unit routing cost (which is assumed to be 10) by the number of routing PEs needed to map the edge. In this example, if we schedule operation 7 in time slot 1 of PE3, at least two routing operations are needed to map operation 8. Thus, routing cost in the time slot 1 of PE3 is 20. Considering these costs, operation 7 will be mapped onto the time slot 3 of PE1, which has the minimum cost. The final solution generated by EMS is shown in Figure 3(e). However, this mapping requires array B to be duplicated in two banks.

DROC helps avoid duplicating reused arrays. In the same example the DROC cost induced by the reuse relation between operations 1 and 7 is 30, assuming that the DCR parameter is 3. This DROC cost is added to all the load-store PEs except for PE3, which forces operation 7 to be scheduled onto the time slot 2 of PE3, as shown in Figure 3(g). Though this new mapping results in the use of an extra PE as a routing PE, it increases the utilization of array B, which may reduce the overall execution time.

5.3   Balancing Bank Utilization

The next important issue in application mapping onto a NUMA CGRA is that, if the scheduler is not careful, it can skew the distribution of the data in the memory banks. For example, the solution can result in mapping all the data to just one bank, and not utilizing the other banks. This can happen, if the application mapping is unaware of the banked memory architecture, but also if we apply our data reuse optimization too aggressively and map all the arrays to the same bank. Such a mapping can reduce the performance, since it decreases the effective local memory size, results in smaller tiling

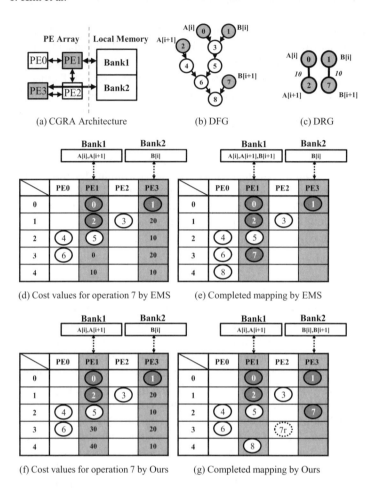

Fig. 3. Data reuse example. Mapping operation 7 to PE3 allows the reuse of array B between operations 1 and 7. Assuming: Base Routing Cost = 10, DCR = 3.

factor for the loop, and may cause very frequent buffer switching for hardware buffering. One desirable shape of the data placement is uniform distribution of the data among the banks. This can be rather easily solved by adding an additional cost to the PEs to which load/store operations have been mapped, called *bank balancing cost*. We define the bank balancing cost for a PE p, as $BBC(p) = b \cdot m(p)$, where b is a design parameter called the base balancing cost, and $m(p)$ is the number of memory operations already mapped onto PE p.

Figure 4 illustrates our compilation flow. The two analyses, performance bottleneck analysis and data reuse analysis, are performed before time-consuming modulo scheduling. Memory-aware modulo scheduling refers to the EMS algorithm extended by adding DROC and BBC to the existing cost function, which does not significantly increase the complexity of the mapping algorithm. The partial shutdown exploration is explained in Section 6.3.

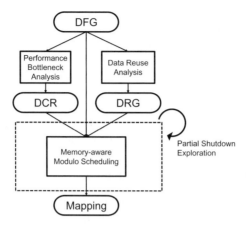

Fig. 4. Application mapping flow. Note: DFG (Data Flow Graph), DCR (Data-transfer-to-Computation time ratio), and DRG (Data Reuse Graph).

6 Experiments

6.1 Setup

We demonstrate the effectiveness of our memory-aware compilation heuristic on a set of important kernels from the MiBench benchmark suite [21], multimedia benchmarks, and SPEC 2000. Our target architecture is a 4x4 architecture, as illustrated in Figure 2(b), with load-store units alternating in the two middle columns. The 4x4 configuration is the basic unit in many CGRA architectures including ADRES (4x4 tiles), MorphoSys (4x4 quadrants), and also frequently used to evaluate various mapping algorithms (e.g., [9, 12, 13]). For the PE array, we assume that a PE is connected to its four neighbors and four diagonal ones. The local memory architecture has 4 banks, each connected to each row (i.e., to the load-store unit of the corresponding row). The detail of the local memory architecture is modeled after the RSPA architecture [3]. The local memory is double buffered in hardware and the buffers can be switched in one cycle. The size of each buffer is 768 bytes, or 384 16-bit words, and is connected to the system memory through a high-performance 16-bit pipelined bus. The system memory operates at half the frequency of the processor, thus the memory bandwidth is 16 bits per 2 cycles.

In the literature mapping algorithms are often compared in terms of II, which is valid, since CGRA processors are under a complete compile-time control; it is like a VLIW processor without pipeline stall. However II captures the quality of the computation mapping only, and cannot capture the possible delay due to the memory bottleneck. We therefore use the CGRA runtime, which is computed by adding up tile execution times, where tile execution time is the maximum of computation II multiplied by the tile size and the memory access time for the tile. We assume that an array shared by two references such as $A[i]$ and $A[i+5]$ requires $T+5$ elements per tile instead of just T, where T is the tile size. If an array is duplicated in multiple banks with different offsets, we assume that the array is loaded twice from the system memory, which is the most straightforward way to load them; otherwise, the DMA would have to be smart enough to copy a part of the array from one bank to another, and manage the remaining part.

For the energy model of the CGRA, we consider both the dynamic power and the leakage power of PEs and memory banks. The dynamic power model of a PE is derived from RSPA, considering three operating states: ALU (including load/store), multiplication, and routing. The dynamic power model of a memory bank is given by CACTI 5.1 [17]. The leakage power is assumed to be 20% of the dynamic power of an ALU operation for a PE, and of a read operation for a memory bank.

6.2 Efficiency of Our Memory-Aware Mapping

Though our memory-aware mapping may reduce the total execution time of a loop (i.e., $\max(t_c, t_d)$), the computation time (t_c) will be minimized in the case of traditional memory-unaware mappings such as EMS. The minimum computation time could be realized if single-bank memory were used, although it seems likely to have other negative effects such as increased cycle time, power, and area, and may cancel out the benefit. Thus we compare three cases: *Ideal* (single-bank + EMS), *EMS* (multi-bank + EMS), and *MA* (multi-bank + our memory-aware extension of EMS). For a realistic multi-bank local memory, the *Ideal* single-bank performance only serves as the upper limit that a realistic multi-bank mapping could achieve. We compare the three cases in terms of cycle count. In the case of *Ideal*, the possible cycle time increase is not taken into account, nor is the memory bandwidth restriction (hence the name). In the case of *EMS*, the array placement is determined in a straightforward manner after computation mapping is done.

Figure 5 compares the runtime of the three cases (in cycle count), normalized to that of *EMS*. Comparing *Ideal* and *EMS* indicates that for memory-bound loops, the cost of not considering array placement early in the compilation flow is quite high. By sequentially mapping computations and arrays, the runtime can increase by more than 40% on average compared to the Ideal case for memory-bound loops. On the other

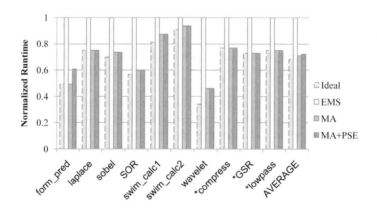

Fig. 5. Runtime comparison

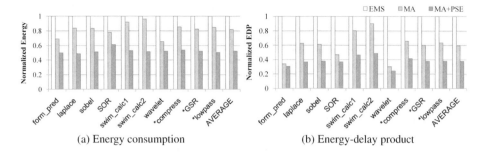

(a) Energy consumption   (b) Energy-delay product

Fig. 6. Energy efficiency comparison

hand, if data mapping is considered proactively along with computation mapping as in our heuristic, the runtime increase can be very effectively suppressed. Compared to the *EMS*, our heuristic can reduce the runtime by as much as 30% on average for memory-bound loops. This strongly motivates the use of less expensive multi-bank memories for CGRAs rather than the more expensive and more power-dissipating single-bank memories.

Reduced runtime by our heuristic also translates into reduced energy consumption on the CGRA. Figure 6(a) compares the energy consumption by the base EMS vs. our heuristic. While our heuristic can sometimes generate less efficient computation mappings compared to the base EMS, for instance, by using more routing PEs, our heuristic can effectively reduce the leakage energy by reducing the runtime, which leads to significant energy reduction by our heuristic. Accordingly, the EDP, or the energy-delay product, is also reduced significantly by our heuristic, as indicated by Figure 6(b).

6.3   Partial Shutdown Exploration

For a memory-bound loop, the performance is often limited by the memory bandwidth rather than by computation, which will be increasingly the case as the number of PEs increases. For such a case we can dramatically reduce the energy consumption of CGRA by shutting down some of the rows of PEs and the memory banks, effectively balancing computation and memory access. While this kind of optimization could be applied with any mapping algorithm, it becomes more interesting with our memory-aware mapping heuristic, as both our heuristic and partial shutdown try to exploit the same opportunity existing in memory-bound loops; one by reducing the memory access load, the other by reducing the computation rate.

We explore all the partial shutdown combinations on the PE rows and the memory banks, to find the best configuration that gives the minimum EDP. The design space is not large, with only 16 configurations to explore as there are 4 rows and 4 banks. The results are summarized in Figures 5 and 6 (the last bars). The results suggest that the partial shutdown optimization can considerably reduce the energy consumption and the EDP, by more than 35% on average, even after our memory-aware heuristic is applied. Compared to previous memory-unaware technique without partial shutdown optimization, our technique can achieve 62% reduction in the energy-delay product, which factors into

Table 1. Best configurations by partial shutdown exploration (r=#rows, m=#banks)

Mem BW	form_pred	laplace	sobel	SOR	swim_calc1	swim_calc2	wavelet	*compress	*GSR	*lowpass
1w/2cyc	2r1m	2r1m	3r2m	2r1m	3r1m	3r1m	2r1m	1r1m	1r1m	2r2m
1w/1cyc	2r2m	3r2m	4r4m	2r2m	4r2m	3r2m	3r2m	2r2m	2r2m	2r2m

about 47% reduction in the energy consumption and 28% reduction in the runtime. For this exploration we also vary the memory bandwidth. The runtime and energy reduction shows a similar trend (not shown), but interestingly the best configurations (shown in Table 1) tend to be larger as the memory bandwidth is increased.

Our partial shutdown exploration gives further justification for the multi-bank memory architecture, as it is more amenable to partial shutdown than the single-bank memory architecture. And it also reinforces the importance of developing memory-aware mapping techniques for multi-bank or NUMA memory architectures, such as ours.

7   Conclusion

The promise of Coarse-Grained Reconfigurable Arrays (CGRAs) providing very high power efficiency while being software programmable, critically hinges on the effectiveness of application mapping. While previous solutions have focused on improving the computation speed of the PE array, we motivate the need for considering the local memory architecture and data placement to achieve higher performance and energy efficiency for memory-bound loops on CGRAs. We propose an effective heuristic that can be easily integrated with existing modular scheduling based algorithms, and which considers various memory architecture parameters including the number of banks, local memory size, and the communication bandwidth between the local memory and the system memory. Our experimental results on memory-bound loops from MiBench, multimedia, and SPEC benchmarks demonstrate that not only is our proposed heuristic able to achieve near-optimal results as compared to single-bank memory mapping, it can also achieve 62% reduction in the energy-delay product as compared to memory-unaware mapping for multi-bank memory, which factors into 47% and 28% reductions in the energy consumption and runtime, respectively. Further, our extensive experiments show that our scheme scales across a range of applications, and memory parameters.

References

1. Bormans, J.: Reconfigurable array processor satisfies multi-core platforms. Chip Design Magazine (2006)
2. Singh, H., Lee, M.-H., Lu, G., Bagherzadeh, N., Kurdahi, F., Filho, E.: Morphosys: An integrated reconfigurable system for data-parallel and computation-intensive applications. IEEE Trans. Comput. 49(5), 465–481 (2000)
3. Kim, Y., Kiemb, M., Park, C., Jung, J., Choi, K.: Resource sharing and pipelining in coarse-grained reconfigurable architecture for domain-specific optimization. In: DATE 2005, Washington, DC, USA, pp. 12–17. IEEE Computer Society, Los Alamitos (2005)

4. Mei, B., Vernalde, S., Verkest, D., Lauwereins, R.: Design methodology for a tightly coupled vliw/reconfigurable matrix architecture: A case study. In: DATE 2004, p. 21224 (2004)
5. Hartenstein, R.: A decade of reconfigurable computing: a visionary retrospective. In: DATE 2001, Piscataway, NJ, USA, pp. 642–649. IEEE Press, Los Alamitos (2001)
6. Lee, J., Choi, K., Dutt, N.: Compilation approach for coarse-grained reconfigurable architectures. IEEE D&T 20, 26–33 (2003)
7. Lee, J., Choi, K., Dutt, N.: An algorithm for mapping loops onto coarse-grained reconfigurable architectures. ACM SIGPLAN Notices 38(7), 183–188 (2003)
8. Mei, B., Vernalde, S., Verkest, D., De Man, H., Lauwereins, R.: Dresc: a retargetable compiler for coarse-grained reconfigurable architectures, December 2002, pp. 166–173 (2002)
9. Park, H., Fan, K., Kudlur, M., Mahlke, S.: Modulo graph embedding: mapping applications onto coarse-grained reconfigurable architectures. In: CASES 2006, pp. 136–146. ACM, New York (2006)
10. Hatanaka, A., Bagherzadeh, N.: A modulo scheduling algorithm for a coarse-grain reconfigurable array template. In: IPDPS 2007, March 2007, pp. 1–8 (2007)
11. Ahn, M., Yoon, J., Paek, Y., Kim, Y., Kiemb, M., Choi, K.: A spatial mapping algorithm for heterogeneous coarse-grained reconfigurable architectures. In: DATE 2006, 3001 Leuven, Belgium, pp. 363–368. European Design and Automation Association (2006)
12. Yoon, J., Shrivastava, A., Park, S., Ahn, M., Jeyapaul, R., Paek, Y.: Spkm: a novel graph drawing based algorithm for application mapping onto coarse-grained reconfigurable architectures. In: ASP-DAC 2008, pp. 776–782 (2008)
13. Park, H., Fan, K., Mahlke, S., Oh, T., Kim, H., Kim, H.: Edge-centric modulo scheduling for coarse-grained reconfigurable architectures. In: PACT 2008, pp. 166–176. ACM, New York (2008)
14. Venkataramani, G., Najjar, W., Kurdahi, F., Bagherzadeh, N., Bohm, W.: A compiler framework for mapping applications to a coarse-grained reconfigurable computer architecture. In: CASES 2001, pp. 116–125. ACM Press, New York (2001)
15. Lee, W., Barua, R., Frank, M., Srikrishna, D., Babb, J., Sarkar, V., Amarasinghe, S.: Space-time scheduling of instruction-level parallelism on a raw machine. In: ASPLOS-VIII, pp. 46–57 (1998)
16. Bougard, B., De Sutter, B., Verkest, D., Van der Perre, L., Lauwereins, R.: A coarse-grained array accelerator for software-defined radio baseband processing. IEEE Micro 28(4), 41–50 (2008)
17. Thoziyoor, S., Muralimanohar, N., Ahn, J., Jouppi, N.: Cacti 5.1. Technical report (2008)
18. Dimitroulakos, G., Galanis, M., Goutis, C.: Alleviating the data memory bandwidth bottleneck in coarse-grained reconfigurable arrays. In: ASAP 2005, Washington, DC, USA, pp. 161–168. IEEE Computer Society, Los Alamitos (2005)
19. Lee, J., Choi, K., Dutt, N.: Evaluating memory architectures for media applications on coarse-grained reconfigurable architectures. In: Proc. ASAP, pp. 172–182. IEEE, Los Alamitos (2003)
20. Dimitroulakos, G., Georgiopoulos, S., Galanis, M., Goutis, C.: Resource aware mapping on coarse grained reconfigurable arrays. Microprocess. Microsyst. 33(2), 91–105 (2009)
21. Guthaus, M., Ringenberg, J.S., Ernst, D., Austin, T.M., Mudge, T., Brown, R.B.: Mibench: A free, commercially representative embedded benchmark suite. In: IWWC, pp. 3–14 (2001)

Maestro: Orchestrating Lifetime Reliability in Chip Multiprocessors

Shuguang Feng, Shantanu Gupta, Amin Ansari, and Scott Mahlke

Advanced Computer Architecture Laboratory
University of Michigan, Ann Arbor, MI 48109
{shoe,shangupt,ansary,mahlke}@umich.edu

Abstract. As CMOS feature sizes venture deep into the nanometer regime, wearout mechanisms including negative-bias temperature instability and time-dependent dielectric breakdown can severely reduce processor operating lifetimes and performance. This paper presents an introspective reliability management system, Maestro, to tackle reliability challenges in future chip multiprocessors (CMPs) head-on. Unlike traditional approaches, Maestro relies on low-level sensors to monitor the CMP as it ages (introspection). Leveraging this real-time assessment of CMP health, runtime heuristics identify wearout-centric job assignments (management). By exploiting the complementary effects of the natural heterogeneity (due to process variation and wearout) that exists in CMPs and the diversity found in system workloads, Maestro composes job schedules that intelligently control the aging process. Monte Carlo experiments show that Maestro significantly enhances lifetime reliability through intelligent wear-leveling, increasing the expected service life of a population of 16-core CMPs by as much as 38% compared to a naive, round-robin scheduler. Furthermore, in the presence of process variation, Maestro's wearout-centric scheduling outperformed both performance counter and temperature sensor based schedulers, achieving an order of magnitude more improvement in lifetime throughput – the amount of useful work done by a system prior to failure.

1   Introduction

In recent years, computer architects have accepted the fact that transistors become less reliable with each new technology generation [4]. As technology scaling leads to higher device counts, power densities and operating temperatures will continue to rise at an alarming pace. With an exponential dependence on temperature, faults due to failure mechanisms like negative-bias temperature instability (NBTI) and time-dependent dielectric breakdown (TDDB) will result in ever-shrinking device lifetimes. Furthermore, as process variation (random + systematic) and wearout gain more prominence in future technology nodes, fundamental design assumptions will become increasingly less accurate. For example, the characteristics of a core on one part of a chip multiprocessor (CMP) may, due to manufacturing defects, only loosely resemble an *identically designed* core on a different part of the CMP [23,26]. Even the behavior of the same core can be expected to change over time as a result of age-dependent degradation [18,25].

In light of this uncertain landscape, researchers have begun investigating dynamic thermal and reliability management (DTM and DRM). Such techniques hope to sustain

Y.N. Patt et al. (Eds.): HiPEAC 2010, LNCS 5952, pp. 186–200, 2010.

current performance improvement trends deep into the nanometer regime, while maintaining the levels of reliability and life-expectancy that consumers have come to expect, by hiding a processor's inherent susceptibility to failures and hotspots. Some recent proposals rely on a combination of thread scheduling and dynamic voltage and frequency scaling (DVFS) to recover performance lost to process variation [23,26]. Others implement intelligent thermal management policies that can extend processor lifetimes and alleviate hotspots by minimizing and bounding the overall thermal stress experienced by a core [7,9,16,17]. There have also been efforts to design sophisticated circuits that tolerate faults and adaptive pipelines with flexible timing constraints [10,24]. Although many DTM schemes actively manipulate job-to-core assignments to avoid thermal emergencies, most existing DRM approaches only *react* to faults, tolerating them as they develop.

In contrast, Maestro takes a proactive approach to reliability. To the first order, Maestro performs fine-grained, module-level wear-leveling for many-core CMPs. Although analogous to wear-leveling in flash devices, the challenge of achieving successful wear-leveling transparently in CMPs is considerably more difficult. Left unchecked, wearout causes all structures within a core to age and eventually fail. However, due to process variation, not all cores (or structures) will be created equal. Every core will invariably possess some microarchitectural structures that are more "damaged" (more susceptible to wearout) than others [23,24]. Performing post-mortems on failed cores (in simulations) often reveals that a single microarchitectural module, which varies from core to core, breaks down long before the rest. Maestro extends the life of these "weak" structures, their corresponding cores, and ultimately the CMP by ensuring uniform aging with scheduling-driven wear-leveling across all levels of the hierarchy.

Maestro dynamically formulates wearout-centric schedules, where jobs are assigned to cores such that cores do not execute workloads that apply excessive stress to their weakest modules (i.e., a floating-point intensive thread is not bound to a core with a weakened floating-point adder). This accomplishes *local wear-leveling* at the core level, avoiding failures induced by a single weak structure. When two cores both have a strong affinity for the same job, a heuristic, which enforces *global wear-leveling* at the CMP level determines which core is given priority. Typically, unless there is a substantial negative impact on local wear-leveling, deference is given to the weaker of the two cores. This ensures that, when necessary, stronger cores are allowed to execute less desirable jobs in order to postpone failures in weaker cores (details in Section 3.2).

By leveraging the natural, module-level diversity in application thermal footprints (Section 2.1), Maestro has finer-grained control over the aging process than a standard core-level DVFS approach, without any of the attendant hardware/design overheads. Given the complex nature of wearout degradation, Maestro departs from the conventional reliance on static analysis to project optimized schedules. Instead, the condition of the underlying CMP hardware is continuously monitored, allowing Maestro to dynamically refine and adapt scheduling algorithms as the system ages. Architectures like those envisioned in [22], with low-level circuit sensors, can readily supply this real-time "health" monitoring.

Maestro offers two key benefits for future CMP systems. First, the fine-grained, local wear-leveling prevents unnecessary core failures, maximizing the life of *individual* cores. Longer lasting cores translates to more work that can be done over the life of the system. Second, it improves the ability of the system to sustain heavy workloads despite the effects of aging. Enforcing global wear-leveling maximizes the *number* of functional cores (throughout its useful life), which in turn maximizes the computational horsepower available to meet peak demands. With higher degrees of process variation on the horizon, premature core failures will make it increasingly more difficult to design and qualify future CMPs. However, by harnessing the potential of Maestro, proactive management will enable semiconductor manufacturers to provide chips with longer life-times as well as ensure that system performance targets are consistently met throughout that lifetime. The central contributions of this paper include:

- An evaluation of workload variability and its impact on reliability/wearout.
- An introspective system, Maestro, that utilizes low-level sensor feedback and application-driven wear-leveling to proactively manage lifetime reliability.
- The design and evaluation of two reliability-centric job scheduling algorithms.

2   Scheduling for Damaged Cores and Dynamic Workloads

Scheduling, in the context of this paper, refers to the process of assigning jobs to cores in a CMP, and is conceptually decoupled from the operating system (OS) scheduler. The schedulers proposed by microarchitects in the past typically resided in a virtualization layer (i.e., system firmware) that sits between the OS and the underlying hardware. At each scheduling interval, the OS supplies a set of jobs, J, to this virtualization layer, and it is the task of the low-level scheduler to bind the jobs to cores. Prior works have investigated techniques that leverage intelligent job scheduling to manage on-core temperatures or cope with process variation. However, none have studied the impact that wearout-centric scheduling alone can have on the evolution of aging within a core.

Embracing process variation and workload diversity, Maestro can enhance lifetime reliability without the extensive hardware support for adaptive body biasing (ABB) and adaptive supply voltage (ASV) required by other approaches [25]. The remainder of this paper targets TDDB and NBTI, which are expected to be the two leading causes of wearout-related failures in future technologies, but can be easily extended to address any progressive failure mechanisms that may emerge. Since both TDDB and NBTI are highly dependent on temperature, it is important to understand the thermal footprints of typical applications in order to appreciate the potential for reliability-centric scheduling. Section 2.1 examines the module-level thermal diversity seen across a set of SPEC2000 applications and Section 2.2 presents preliminary results quantifying the impact of this variation on processor lifetimes.

2.1   Workload Variation

Figure 1 shows the range of temperatures experienced by different structures within an Alpha21364-like processor [1] across a set of 8 SPECINT (*bzip2, gcc, gzip, mcf, perlbmk, twolf, vortex, vpr*) and 9 SPECFP benchmarks (*ammp, applu, apsi, art, equake, galgel, lucas, sixtrack, swim, wupwise*). All temperatures are normalized to the peak temperature, T_{max}, seen across all modules and benchmarks, which corresponds to the

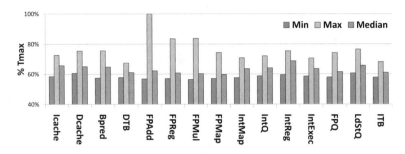

Fig. 1. Variation of module temperatures across SPEC2000 workloads. All temperatures are normalized to T_{max}, the peak temperature seen across all benchmarks and modules (83°C).

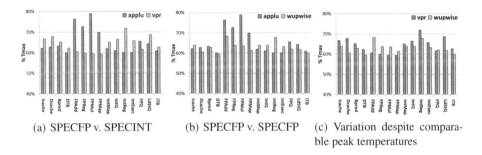

(a) SPECFP v. SPECINT   (b) SPECFP v. SPECFP   (c) Variation despite comparable peak temperatures

Fig. 2. Head-to-head comparisons of applu (SPECFP), vpr (SPECINT), and wupwise (SPECFP). No one benchmark in (a), (b), or (c) strictly dominates the other (with respect to temperature) across all modules.

temperature of the FPAdd module when running *lucas* (83°C). Notice the significant variation in temperature within nearly every module. Apart from the more than 40% variation seen in FPAdd (a 37°C swing), other structures (whose utilizations are not as strongly correlated with the execution of floating-point and integer benchmarks) also exhibit significant temperature shifts, 10-15% for Bpred and IntReg. These large temperature ranges suggest that scheduling alone can be a powerful tool for manipulating aging rates.

Figure 2 selects a few representative applications and examines them in greater detail. Figures 2(a) and 2(b) highlight how the traditional view of "hot" and "cold" applications is perhaps too simplistic. Without accounting for the module-level variation in temperatures, one could incorrectly assume that *applu* is more taxing, from a reliability perspective, than *vpr* or *wupwise* simply because it exhibits a higher peak operating temperature (FPMul). However, this would neglect the fact that for many structures, like IntReg, temperatures for *applu* are actually much lower than the other two applications. For completeness, Figure 2(c) is included to show that variations in module temperatures exist even between applications with comparable peak temperatures. All things considered, deciding where on the CMP to schedule a particular application, to achieve the least reliability impact, requires additional information about the strength of individual structures within every core. Although the magnitude of the temperature differences may not seem impressive at first, with peak deltas in module temperatures around 10-20% in Figure 2(a), these modest variations in temperature can have dramatic impacts on a processor's mean time to failure (MTTF).

2.2 Implications for Mean Time to Failure

From Figure 2, one could expect a core consistently running *applu* to fail because of a fault in the FPMul unit due to its high operating temperatures. However, in the presence of process variation other structures within the core could have been manufactured with more defects (or tighter timing margins), and therefore even more susceptible to failure despite not ever realizing the same peak temperatures as FPMul. In this environment, a reliability-centric job scheduler must take into consideration the extent of damage present within a core in addition to the per-module thermal footprint of running applications. Figure 3 presents the expected lifetime of a core running *applu* or *vpr* as a function of the module identified as the weakest structure. The lifetimes are projected based on well-known MTTF equations for NBTI and TDDB [15,21]. The values are normalized to the best achievable MTTF, which in this comparison is attained if FPMap is the weakest module in the core and the core is running *vpr*. The optimal job to schedule on a particular core to maximize its lifetime is dependent not just on the application mix currently available, but also on the strengths of individual structures within that core. Scheduling *applu* on a core with a weak IntReg can nearly triple its operating lifetime compared to naively forcing it to run *vpr*. Similarly, scheduling *vpr* instead of *applu* on a core with a weak FPAdd improves its projected lifetime by more than 4x.

To further highlight the need to address process and workload variation, a quick examination of the processors simulated in Section 4.1 reveals that 35% of core failures are the result of failing structures that never experience peak on-chip temperatures. Furthermore, 22% of core failures are caused by modules that do not rank among the top three most thermally active. By accounting for the impact of process variation and module-level thermal variation of applications, Maestro can prevent premature core failures and reap the opportunity left on the table by previous schedulers.

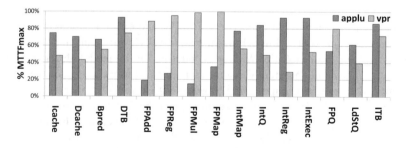

Fig. 3. Projected core lifetime based on execution of *applu* and *vpr* as a function of the module identified as the weakest structure. Values are normalized to the best achievable MTTF.

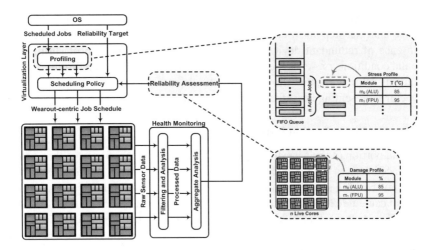

Fig. 4. A high-level block diagram of the Maestro introspective reliability management system. Dynamic monitoring of sensor feedback and detailed characterization of workload behavior enables Maestro to improve lifetime system reliability with wearout-centric scheduling.

3   Maestro

Figure 4 presents a block diagram of Maestro, which consists of two main components: 1) a health monitoring system (introspection) and 2) a virtualization layer that implements wearout-centric job scheduling (management). Although this paper targets reliability-centric scheduling, a broader vision of introspective reliability management could use online sensor feedback to guide a range of solutions from traditional DVFS to more radical approaches like system-level reconfiguration [14].

3.1   Health Monitoring

Tracking the evolution of wearout damage within a CMP (i.e., health monitoring) is essential to forming intelligent reliability-centric schedules. Maestro assumes that the underlying CMP is provisioned with circuit-level sensors like those described in [22]. Recognizing that the two mechanisms addressed in this work, NBTI and TDDB, both impact physical device parameters as they evolve has led researchers to actively develop circuit-level sensors that can track these changes. NBTI is known to shift threshold voltage (V_t) leading to slower devices and increased subthreshold/standby leakage current (I_{ddq}), while TDDB increases gate currents (I_{gs} and I_{gd}). Both result in statistically measurable degradation in timing paths at the microarchitectural-level [3,6].

A runtime system collects raw data streams from the array of circuit-level sensors and applies statistical filtering and trend analysis (similar to what is described in [3]) to convert these streams into descriptions of system characteristics including, delay profiles, leakage currents, and operating temperatures. These individual channels of information are then processed to generate a comprehensive microarchitectural-level reliability assessment of the CMP. This is shown in Figure 4 as a vector of per-module damage values (relative to the maximum damage sustainable prior to failure). Introducing the additional analysis step allows the health monitoring system to account for things like the presence of redundant devices within a structure, the influence of shifting environmental conditions on sensor readings, and the interaction between different wearout mechanisms. Ultimately, this allows the low-level sensor feedback to be abstracted with each vector representing the effective damage profile for a particular core.

3.2 Maestro Virtualization Layer

The second portion of the Maestro framework resides in system firmware that serves as the interface between the OS and the underlying hardware. The OS provides the virtualization layer with a set of jobs that need to run on the CMP and other meta-data (optional) that can guide Maestro in refining its scheduling policies (Section 3.2.3). Online profiling of system workloads identifies application-specific thermal footprints, shown in Figure 4 as a vector of per-module temperatures for each application. This thermal footprint can either be generated by brief exploratory execution of jobs on the available cores, similar to what is done in [26], or projected by correlating thermal behavior with program phases (leveraging the existing body of work on runtime phase monitoring and prediction). Given the prevalence of on-chip temperature sensors [13], Maestro assumes low-overhead exploration is performed during each scheduling interval. Coupled with the real-time health assessments, this detailed module-level application characterization enables Maestro to create wearout-centric job schedules that intelligently manage CMP aging.

As previously defined, scheduling in this paper will refer to the act of mapping threads to cores and is initiated by two main events, 1) the OS issues new jobs for Maestro to execute (pushes into a FIFO queue) or 2) the damage profile of the underlying CMP has changed sufficiently (taking on the order of days/weeks) to warrant thread migration. The two reliability-centric scheduling policies evaluated in this work illustrate two approaches to lifetime reliability. The greedy policy (Section 3.2.2) takes the position that all core failures are unacceptable and aggressively preserves even the weakest cores. The adaptive policy (Section 3.2.3) champions a more unconventional philosophy that claims individual core failures are tolerable provided the lifetime reliability of the CMP system is maximized.

Both wearout-centric policies, and the naive baseline scheduler, are presented below along with corresponding pseudocode. Unless otherwise indicated, the following definitions are common to all policies: m, a microarchitectural module (i.e., FPMul, IntReg, etc.); $LiveCores$, the set of functional cores in the CMP, $\{c_0, c_1, ..., c_N\}$; $JobQueue$, the set of **all** pending, uncompleted jobs issued from the OS; $ActiveJobs$, the set of the N oldest, uncompleted, jobs, $\{j_0, j_1, ..., j_N\}$; $Dmg(m)$, the entry in the CMP damage profile for module m; $Temp(j, m)$, the entry for module m in the temperature footprint for job j.

3.2.1 Naive Scheduler

A standard round-robin scheduler is used as the baseline policy. The least-recently-used (LRU) core in the set of $LiveCores$ is assigned the oldest job from the set of $ActiveJobs$. This process is repeated until all jobs in $ActiveJobs$ have been scheduled.

Algorithm 1. Greedy wearout-centric scheduler

Step 1:
    foreach $c \in LiveCores$ **do**
        find c_{dmg} , the damage present in core c , **where**
            $c_{dmg} \longleftarrow Dmg(m') \mid m' \in c \wedge Dmg(m') \geq Dmg(m), \forall m \in c$
    end
    sort $LiveCores$ based on c_{dmg}
end
Step 2:
    until $ActiveJobs$ is empty
        $c_w \longleftarrow$ weakest core in $LiveCores$ based on c_{dmg}
        $m_w \longleftarrow m' \mid m' \in c_w \wedge Dmg(m') \geq Dmg(m), \forall m \in c_w$
        foreach $j \in ActiveJobs$ **do**
            find $cost_{j,c_w}$, the cost of executing job j on core c_w , **where**
                $cost_{j,c_w} \longleftarrow Temp(j, m_w)$
        end
        $j_{opt} \longleftarrow j' \mid j' \in ActiveJobs \wedge cost_{j',c_w} \leq cost_{j,c_w}, \forall j \in ActiveJobs$
        Assign job j_{opt} to core c_w
        Remove c_w from $LiveCores$ and j_{opt} from $ActiveJobs$
    end
end

This policy maintains high-level load balancing by distributing jobs uniformly across the cores. However, without accounting for core damage profiles or application thermal footprints, the resulting schedule is effectively a random mapping (from a reliability perspective).

3.2.2 Greedy Scheduler

This policy attempts to minimize the number of premature core failures by greedily favoring the weakest cores (Algorithm 1). Cores are sorted based upon their damage profiles and priority is given to the cores whose weakest modules possess the most damage (Step 1 of Algorithm 1). These "weak" cores are greedily assigned jobs with the most favorable thermal footprints with respect to their damage profiles (Step 2 of Algorithm 1), minimizing their effective thermal stress. This *local wear-leveling* reduces the probability that these weak cores will fail due to a *single* damaged structure. Scheduling the weak cores first maximizes the probability of finding jobs with favorable thermal footprints with respect to each weak core since there is a larger application mix to choose from. However, this also forces the stronger cores to execute the remaining, potentially less desirable, jobs. In practice, this means that the stronger cores in the CMP actually sacrifice a portion of their lifetime to lighten the burden on their weaker counterparts (*global wear-leveling*).

3.2.3 Adaptive Scheduler

The adaptive scheduler recognizes that many CMP systems are often underutilized, provisioned with more cores than they typically have jobs to run (see Section 4.3). The scheduler exploits this fact by allowing a few weak cores to be sacrificed in

---

Algorithm 2. Adaptive wearout-centric scheduler

---

let $GA(J, C)$ be the optimal schedule generated by the GA for jobs J and cores C

Step 1:

> **foreach** $c \in LiveCores$ **do**
>
> > **find** c_{dmg} , the damage present in core c , **where**
> > $c_{dmg} \longleftarrow \sum_{m_i}^{c} \alpha_i Dmg(m_i)$ and α_i is a scaling factor biased toward modules with more damage
>
> **end**
> **sort** $LiveCores$ in increasing order of c_{dmg}
> $PrimaryCores \longleftarrow$ first n cores **where** n is set by the user through the OS
> $SecondaryCores \longleftarrow$ remaining $N - n$ cores

end

Step 2:

> **let** $S_{primary}$, be the set of job-to-core assignments, $(j, c), \forall c \in PrimaryCores$
> $S_{primary} \longleftarrow GA(ActiveJobs, PrimaryCores)$
> Assign jobs for $PrimaryCores$ according to $S_{primary}$
> Remove assigned jobs from $ActiveJobs$

end

Step 3:

> **let** $S_{secondary}$, be the set of job-to-core assignments, $(j, c), \forall c \in SecondaryCores$
> $S_{secondary} \longleftarrow GA(ActiveJobs, SecondaryCores)$
> Assign jobs for $SecondaryCores$ according to $S_{secondary}$

end

---

order to preserve the remaining stronger cores (Algorithm 2). Although being complicit in core failures may seem non-intuitive, in systems that are underutilized, the greedy scheduler can lead to CMPs that are overprovisioned early in the CMP's life ($LiveCores >> JobQueue$) while not assuring enough available throughput ($LiveCores < JobQueue$) later on. This insight forms the basis of the adaptive policy.

Promoting a survival-of-the-fittest environment, this policy maximizes the functional life of the strongest subset of cores ($PrimaryCores$ in Step 1 of Algorithm 2), those with the least amount of initial damage and the potential to have the longest lifetimes. By assigning jobs to the $PrimaryCores$ first, Maestro ensures that they execute applications with the most appropriate thermal footprints (Step 2 of Algorithm 2). The remaining jobs are assigned amongst the $SecondaryCores$ (Step 3 of Algorithm 2). This can lead to some weak cores failing sooner than under a greedy policy. Note, however, in Step 3 of Algorithm 2, the scheduler is still looking amongst the remaining jobs for the one with the best thermal footprint given a core's damage profile. This *local wear-leveling*, common to both the greedy and adaptive policies, ensures that the weaker cores even under the adaptive policy survive longer than they would under the naive policy. Ultimately, over the lifetime of the CMP, if $PrimaryCores \geq JobQueue$ consistently, while avoiding periods when $PrimaryCores >> JobQueue$ or $PrimaryCores < JobQueue$, then Maestro has maximized the total amount of computation performed by the system. The proper size of $PrimaryCores$, n, is exposed to the OS so that the behavior of the scheduler can be customized to the needs of the end user.

Finally, note in Step 2 and Step 3 of Algorithm 2, the scheduler uses an optimization scheme based on a genetic algorithm (GA) to identify the least-cost schedules for both the $PrimaryCores$ and $SecondaryCores$. This allows the adaptive scheduler to consider the effect scheduling a job has on all structures within a core (unlike the greedy scheduler which only looks at the weakest structure) for more effective *local wear-leveling*. The optimization used in this work is derived from [8], a standard solution of the generalized assignment problem. The cost function used by the GA is recalculated at each scheduling interval, based on the CMP damage profile and application thermal footprints, according to Equation 1, where $Cost(S)$ is the cost of schedule S and $Cost(j, c)$ is the cost of scheduling job j on core c[1].

$$Cost(S) = \sum_{j,c}^{S} Cost(j,c) = \sum_{j,c}^{S} \left(\sum_{m}^{c} Dmg(m) \cdot Temp(j,m) \right) \qquad (1)$$

4   Evaluation and Analysis

This section evaluates Maestro's reliability-centric scheduling policies using lifetime reliability simulations. A variety of system parameters including CMP size and system utilization are varied to investigate their impact on Maestro's performance. The effectiveness of each wearout-centric policy is measured in terms of *lifetime throughput* (LT), the number of cycles spent executing active jobs (real applications not idle threads), summed across all cores, throughout the entire lifetime of the CMP. LT improvement metrics are the result of comparisons with the naive, round-robin scheduler presented in Section 3.2.1.

Monte Carlo experiments are conducted using a simulation setup similar to the framework in [12]. The standard toolchain of SimAlpha, Wattch [5], and Hotspot [20] is used to simulate the thermal characteristics of workloads and Varius [19] is used to model the impact of process variation. An *adaptive* simulation scheme is employed that interleaves detailed and accelerated simulation phases, dramatically reducing simulation runtimes and minimizing error (addressed in greater detail by [11]). Results presented in this section, unless otherwise indicated, are for a 16-core CMP with processors modeled after the DEC Alpha 21264/21364 [1].

4.1   Lifetime Throughput Enhancement

Figure 5 shows the normalized LT improvement as a function of the scheduling policy, CMP size, and failure threshold. In the context of this paper, failure threshold is defined as the number of cores that must fail before a chip is considered unusable. This is the point at which the risks/costs associated with maintaining a system with only a fraction of its original computational capacity justifies replacing the chip. The CMP is considered dead even though functional cores still remain. The results shown in Figure 5

---

[1] The runtime overhead of the GA is negligible for long-running scientific and server workloads. However, for shorter-running applications the GA optimization can be replaced by a greedy version without severely impacting the effectiveness of the adaptive scheduler.

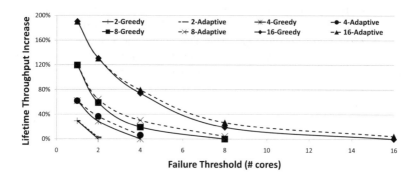

Fig. 5. Performance of wearout-centric scheduling policies verses CMP size and failure threshold

are conducted for 2 to 16-core systems, and failure thresholds ranging from 1 core to all cores. The value of the failure threshold is passed to the adaptive policy so that it can optimize for the appropriate number of cores. Results are shown for CMP utilizations of 100%, providing a lower-bound on the benefits of the adaptive policy (Section 4.3 examines the impact of CMP utilization).

As expected, both the greedy and adaptive policies perform well across all CMP sizes and the majority of failure thresholds. As the size of the CMP grows, Maestro has more cores to work with, increasing the chances of finding complementary job-to-core mappings. This results in more effective schedules for both wearout-centric policies improving their performance. Yet even with the lack of scheduling alternatives in a 2-core system, both policies can still achieve a respectable 30% improvement.

A strong dependence on failure threshold is also evident. By aggressively minimizing premature core failures, the greedy scheduler achieves large gains for small failure thresholds. However, as the failure threshold nears the size of the CMP, the LT improvement attenuates. This is expected since under the greedy policy, stronger cores sacrifice a portion of their lifetime in order to preserve their weaker counterparts. The cost of this sacrifice is most apparent when the failure threshold allows all the cores to fail. In these systems, the increased contribution toward LT by the weak cores is offset by the loss in LT resulting from the strong cores failing earlier. Notice also that the adaptive scheduler outperforms greedy by the largest margins when the failure threshold is roughly half the size of the CMP. In these situations, the adaptive scheduler has the maximum freedom to sacrifice *SecondaryCores* to preserve *PrimaryCores* (Section 3.2.3). At either extreme for failure threshold, it performs similarly to greedy.

Lastly, it is important to note that, although the benefits of wearout-centric scheduling are less impressive for these extreme values of failure threshold, the scenarios when a user could actually afford to wait for all the cores within a system to fail are also quite remote. For the remainder of the paper, all the experiments shown are for a 16-core CMP with a failure threshold of 8 cores and 100% system utilization unless otherwise indicated.

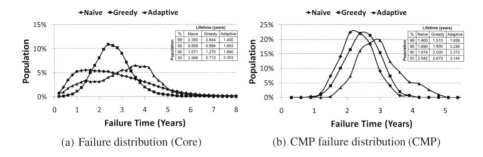

Fig. 6. Failure distributions for individual cores and the 16-core CMP with a failure threshold of 8 cores and 100% utilization. Trendlines are added (between markers) to improve readability.

4.2 Failure Distributions

Figure 6 presents the failure distributions for the individual cores, as well as the CMPs that correspond to the results in Figure 5. Figure 6(a) illustrates the effectiveness of the wearout-centric policies at distributing the workload stress appropriately. The distribution for the baseline naive policy reveals a bias towards early premature core failures. The greedy scheduler, exploiting effective wear-leveling, produced a tighter distribution, lacking in both premature failures as well as cores that significantly outlasted their peers. Lastly, the adaptive policy also delivers on its promises by preserving a subset of cores for a longer period of time than either the naive or greedy schedulers.

Figure 6(b) tells a similar story, but with chip-level failures. As with the individual core distributions, both wearout-centric policies are able to increase the mean failure time of the CMP population. Note that because the failure time of a CMP is limited by the weakest set of its constituent cores, the distributions in Figure 6(b) are considerably tighter than those in Figure 6(a). The corresponding tables of expected lifetimes embedded within the plots present the data slightly differently. From a product yield/warranty perspective, intelligent wearout-centric scheduling can be thought of as an additional means of ensuring that cores meet their expected reliability qualified lifetimes. For example, the table in Figure 6(b) shows that the adaptive scheduler enabled 99% of the chips to survive beyond 1.9 years, compared to just 1.4 years with the naive baseline, a 38% improvement. Granted, job assignment alone cannot make *guarantees* on lifetime, but it can complement existing more aggressive techniques like thermal throttling.

4.3 Sensitivity to System Utilization

The utilization of computer systems can be highly variable, both within the same domain (e.g., variability inside data centers) and across domains. One might expect computationally intensive scientific codes (e.g., physics simulations, oil exploration, etc.) to consistently utilize the hardware. On the other hand, since designers build web servers to accommodate peak loads (periodic by season, day, and hour), they are often over-provisioned for the common case. Some reports claim average utilization as low as 20% of peak [2].

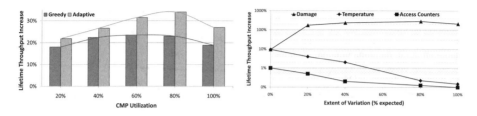

Fig. 7. Impact of CMP utilization on reliability enhancement

Fig. 8. Performance of wearout-centric scheduling with different sensors

Figure 7 plots the performance of Maestro's wearout-centric schedulers as a function of system utilization. The results are shown for nominal utilizations ranging from 20% (light duty mail server or embedded system) to 100% (scientific cluster)[2]. Note that initially as average utilization drops, improvement in lifetime throughput actually increases. A system that is slightly underutilized can be more aggressively load balanced since some cores are allowed to remain idle. However, as utilization continues to drop these gains are eventually lost, until finally improvements are actually worse than at full utilization. In these highly over-provisioned systems, the efforts of wearout-centric scheduling to prevent premature failures are *partially* wasted because so few cores are actually necessary to sustain demand. Nevertheless, in the long run, the periodic spikes in utilization do accumulate, and thanks to the longer overall core lifetimes (lower utilization means less overall stress that translates to longer lifetimes), the greedy and adaptive schedulers still manage to exhibit improvements.

4.4 Sensor Selection

Lastly, Figure 8 presents a comparison between the low-level damage sensors advocated in this work and more conventional hardware like temperature sensors and performance counters. Given that Maestro is targeting an environment with significant amounts of process variation, it is not surprising that employing temperature and activity readings as proxies for wearout/manufacturing induced damage is inadequate. They are unable to account for the extent to which non-uniform, pre-existing damage within the CMP responds to the same thermal stimuli. In the absence of variation, a scheduler relying on only temperature might effectively enhance lifetime reliability by evenly distributing the thermal stress across the CMP. However, without any knowledge of CMP damage profiles, as process variation is swept from one extreme (no variation) to the other (100% expected variation at 32nm), thermal load balancing alone is insufficient and Figure 8 shows a dramatic plunge in the effectiveness of these temperature based schemes. Similarly, the performance counter approach performed poorly across the spectrum of variation.

---

[2] Although the mean utilization per simulation run is fixed, the instantaneous utilization experienced by the CMP is allowed to vary over time, sometimes peaking at 100% even for a system nominally at 20% load. Furthermore, the average *effective* utilization is also changing as cores on the CMP begin to fail.

5   Conclusion

As large CMP systems grow in popularity and technology scaling continues to exacerbate lifetime reliability challenges, the research community must develop innovative ways for systems to dynamically adapt. Although issues like process variation are the source of design and validation nightmares, this inherent heterogeneity in future systems is also a source of potential opportunity. Maestro recognizes that although emerging reliability obstacles cannot be ignored, with the appropriate monitoring and intelligent management, they can be overcome. By exploiting low-level sensor feedback, Maestro was able to demonstrate the effectiveness of wearout-centric scheduling at preventing premature core failures, improving expected CMP lifetimes by as much as 38%. Formulating wearout-centric schedules that achieved both local and global wear-leveling, Maestro enhanced the lifetime throughput of a 16-core CMP by as much as 180%. Future work that leverages sensor feedback to improve upon other traditional reliability management mechanisms (e.g., DVFS) could demonstrate still more potential.

Acknowledgements

We thank the anonymous referees for their valuable comments and suggestions. We also owe thanks to Jason Blome and Prabhakar Kudva for their feedback on initial drafts of this work. This research was supported by National Science Foundation grants CPA-0916689 and CCF-0347411, ARM Limited, and the Gigascale Systems Research Center, one of five research centers funded under the Focus Center Research Program, a Semiconductor Research Corporation program.

References

1. Alpha. 21364 family (2001), http://www.alphaprocessors.com/21364.htm
2. Andrzejak, A., Arlitt, M., Rolia, J.: Bounding the resource savings of utility computing models. HP Laboratories (December 2002),
   http://www.hpl.hp.com/techreports/2002/HPL-2002-339.html
3. Blome, J., Feng, S., Gupta, S., Mahlke, S.: Self-calibrating online wearout detection. In: Proc. of the 40th Annual International Symposium on Microarchitecture, pp. 109–120 (2007)
4. Borkar, S.: Designing reliable systems from unreliable components: The challenges of transistor variability and degradation. IEEE Micro 25(6), 10–16 (2005)
5. Brooks, D., Tiwari, V., Martonosi, M.: A framework for architectural-level power analysis and optimizations. In: Proc. of the 27th Annual International Symposium on Computer Architecture, June 2000, pp. 83–94 (2000)
6. Cabe, A., Qi, Z., Wooters, S., Blalock, T., Stan, M.: Small embeddable nbti sensors (sens) for tracking on-chip performance decay, Washington, DC, USA. IEEE Computer Society, Los Alamitos (2009)
7. Choi, J., Cher, C., Franke, H., Haman, H., Wedger, A., Bose, P.: Thermal-aware task scheduling at the system software level. In: Proc. of the 2007 International Symposium on Low Power Electronics and Design, August 2007, pp. 213–218 (2007)
8. Chu, P.C., Beasley, J.E.: A genetic algorithm for the generalised assignment problem 24(1), 17–23 (1997)
9. Donald, J., Martonosi, M.: Techniques for multicore thermal management: Classification and new exploration. In: Proc. of the 33rd Annual International Symposium on Computer Architecture (June 2006)

10. Ernst, D., Das, S., Lee, S., Blaauw, D., Austin, T., Mudge, T., Kim, N.S., Flautner, K.: Razor: Circuit-level correction of timing errors for low-power operation. In: Proc. of the 37th Annual International Symposium on Microarchitecture, pp. 10–20 (2004)

11. Feng, S., Gupta, S., Ansari, A., Mahlke, S.: Maestro: Orchestrating lifetime reliability in chip multiprocessors. Technical Report CSE-TR-557-09, University of Michigan, Ann Arbor (November 2009),
    http://cccp.eecs.umich.edu/papers/CSE-TR-557-09.pdf

12. Feng, S., Gupta, S., Mahlke, S.: Olay: Combat the signs of aging with intropsective reliability management. In: Proc. of the Workshop on Architectural Reliability (June 2008)

13. Friedrich, J., et al.: Desing of the power6 microprocessor. In: Proc. of ISSCC (February 2007)

14. Gupta, S., Feng, S., Ansari, A., Blome, J., Mahlke, S.: The stagenet fabric for constructing resilient multicore systems. In: Proc. of the 41st Annual International Symposium on Microarchitecture, pp. 141–151 (2008)

15. Li, X., Huang, B., Qin, J., Zhang, X., Talmor, M., Gur, Z., Bernstein, J.B.: Deep submicron cmos integrated circuit reliability simulation with spice. In: Proc. of the 2005 International Symposium on Quality of Electronic Design, March 2005, pp. 382–389 (2005)

16. Lu, Z., Lach, J., Stan, M.R., Skadron, K.: Improved thermal management with reliability banking. IEEE Micro 25(6), 40–49 (2005)

17. Powell, M., Gomaa, M., Vijaykumar, T.: Heat-and-run: Leveraging smt and cmp to manage power density through the operating system. In: 12th International Conference on Architectural Support for Programming Languages and Operating Systems, October 2004, pp. 260–270 (2004)

18. Roberts, D., Dreslinski, R., Karl, E., Mudge, T., Sylvester, D., Blaauw, D.: When homogeneous becomes heterogeneous: Wearout aware task scheduling for streaming applications. In: Proc. of the Workshop on Operationg System Support for Heterogeneous Multicore Architectures (September 2007)

19. Sarangi, S., Greskamp, B., Teodorescu, R., Nakano, J., Tiwari, A., Torrellas, J.: Varius: A model of process variation and resulting timing errors for microarchitects. IEEE Transactions on Semiconductor Manufacturing, 3–13 (February 2008)

20. Skadron, K., Stan, M.R., Sankaranarayanan, K., Huang, W., Velusamy, S., Tarjan, D.: Temperature-aware microarchitecture: Modeling and implementation. ACM Transactions on Architecture and Code Optimization 1(1), 94–125 (2004)

21. Srinivasan, J., Adve, S.V., Bose, P., Rivers, J.A.: The case for lifetime reliability-aware microprocessors. In: Proc. of the 31st Annual International Symposium on Computer Architecture, June 2004, pp. 276–287 (2004)

22. Sylvester, D., Blaauw, D., Karl, E.: Elastic: An adaptive self-healing architecture for unpredictable silicon. IEEE Journal of Design and Test 23(6), 484–490 (2006)

23. Teodorescu, R., Torrellas, J.: Variation-aware application scheduling and power management for chip multiprocessors. In: Proc. of the 35th Annual International Symposium on Computer Architecture, June 2008, pp. 363–374 (2008)

24. Tiwari, A., Sarangi, S., Torrellas, J.: Recycle: Pipeline adaptation to tolerate process variation. In: Proc. of the 34th Annual International Symposium on Computer Architecture, June 2007, pp. 323–334 (2007)

25. Tiwari, A., Torrellas, J.: Facelift: Hiding and slowing down aging in multicores. In: Proc. of the 41st Annual International Symposium on Microarchitecture, December 2008, pp. 129–140 (2008)

26. Winter, J., Albonesi, D.: Scheduling algorithms for unpredictably heterogeneous cmp architectures. In: Proc. of the 2008 International Conference on Dependable Systems and Networks (June 2008) (to appear)

Combining Locality Analysis with Online Proactive Job Co-scheduling in Chip Multiprocessors

Yunlian Jiang, Kai Tian, and Xipeng Shen

Computer Science Department,
The College of William and Mary, Williamsburg, VA, USA 23187
{jiang,ktain,xshen}@cs.wm.edu

Abstract. The shared-cache contention on Chip Multiprocessors causes performance degradation to applications and hurts system fairness. Many previously proposed solutions schedule programs according to runtime sampled cache performance to reduce cache contention. The strong dependence on runtime sampling inherently limits the scalability and effectiveness of those techniques. This work explores the combination of program locality analysis with job co-scheduling. The rationale is that program locality analysis typically offers a large-scope view of various facets of an application including data access patterns and cache requirement. That knowledge complements the local behaviors sampled by runtime systems. The combination offers the key to overcoming the limitations of prior co-scheduling techniques.

Specifically, this work develops a lightweight locality model that enables efficient, proactive prediction of the performance of co-running processes, offering the potential for an integration in online scheduling systems. Compared to existing multicore scheduling systems, the technique reduces performance degradation by 34% (7% performance improvement) and unfairness by 47%. Its proactivity makes it resilient to the scalability issues that constraints the applicability of previous techniques.

1   Introduction

With the advent of Chip Multiprocessor (CMP) and Simultaneous Multithreading (SMT), on-chip cache sharing becomes common on various computing systems, including embedded architectures, desktop computers, clusters in data centers, and so on. The sharing shortens inter-thread latency and allows flexible cache usage. However, it also brings cache contention among co-running jobs, causing programs different degrees of performance degradation, hence impairing system fairness and overall performance [3,6,7,8,9,11,19,29]. The problem is especially important for embedded systems due to the more limited cache on them [20].

In operating systems (OS) research, the recent attempts in alleviating cache contention mainly focus on reactive process scheduling[1] [2, 4, 6, 7, 8, 18, 25]. These techniques typically sample job executions periodically. During the sampling, they track hardware performance counters to estimate the cache requirement of each process and

---

[1] In this work, we concentrate on the schedule of *independent* jobs.

Y.N. Patt et al. (Eds.): HiPEAC 2010, LNCS 5952, pp. 201–215, 2010.
© Springer-Verlag Berlin Heidelberg 2010

derive a better schedule. (For a system containing multiple CMP chips, a better schedule usually means a different assignment of jobs to processors or a different allocation of CPU timeslices to processes.)

Although these techniques work well under certain conditions, the strong reliance on runtime sampling imposes some limitations on their effectiveness and applicability. The main obstacle is that the sampled behavior only reflects the behavior of a process during a *certain time period* when it co-runs with a *certain subset* of processes. Whereas, good scheduling need recognize the inherent cache requirement of a process and its influence on and from all possible co-runners. As a result, most prior techniques require both periodic re-sampling and frequent reshuffles of processes among different co-run groups [8, 25].

These requirements not only cause more sampling overhead (cache performance is often inferior during sampling periods) but also limit the applicability of previous scheduling techniques. For instance, cache-fair scheduling needs the sampling of 10 different co-runs (i.e., runs with different co-runners) per process in every sampling phase, and requires the system to contain a mix of *cache-fair* and *best-effort* processes [8]; symbiotic scheduling [4,25], which samples program performance under various schedules and estimates the best schedule, is difficult to be applied to large problems—the number of possible schedules increases exponentially with the numbers of jobs and processors (e.g., there are 2 million ways to co-schedule 16 jobs on 8 dual-cores).

This work attempts to free prior techniques from those constraints by integrating the knowledge of programming systems[2]. Our exploration combines program behavior analysis with operating systems' control of underlying resources. The motivation for the combination is that *program characteristics determine the cache requirement of a program, and it is programming systems that have the best knowledge of those characteristics.*

To be beneficial, the combination must meet two requirements. First, it needs a lightweight locality model to efficiently predict the cache requirement and co-run performance of programs. Based on reuse distance analysis, this work develops a lightweight co-run locality model—a unified sensitivity and competitiveness model—to enable fast prediction of the influence that a process may impose on and receive from its co-runners. The model is cross-input predictive. The second requirement is that the system scheduler must effectively integrate the locality model into runtime scheduling. This work presents the design of cache-contention aware proactive scheduling (CAPS), which assigns processes to processors according to the predicted cache-contention sensitivities. In our experiments, CAPS reduces performance degradation by 33.9% (7% performance improvement) and unfairness by 47.5%.

This work is not the first one to combine program-level locality analysis with thread or process scheduling. In time-sharing environment, there have been some studies [31, 28] in exploiting footprint size of programs to help schedule threads to minimize the influence on cache imposed by context switches. In traditional SMP (Symmetric Multiprocessing) systems, there have been some work [18] transforming programs to minimize cache false sharing. But none of those studies have tackled systems with

---

[2] Programming systems is an expanded term for compilers, referring to both static and dynamic systems for program behavior analysis.

shared cache. To the best of our knowledge, this work is the first offering a lightweight formulation of program-level data locality applicable for runtime CMP co-scheduling.

In the rest of this paper, we describe the background on co-run locality prediction in Section 2, present a lightweight locality model for scheduling in Section 3, explain the design of CAPS in Section 4, report results in Section 5, compare with previous co-scheduling in Section 6, and summarize the paper in Section 7.

2   Background on Co-run Locality

Co-run locality analysis enables the prediction of the performance of co-running programs, laying the foundation for contention-aware proactive scheduling. This section first introduces concurrent reuse distance, a concept closely related to shared-cache performance, and then describes a theorem establishing the basis for the cache-contention sensitivity model to be presented in the next section.

In the following discussion, we assume that the architecture is an SMP machine with multiple CMP chips, the cores on a chip share an on-chip L2 cache, and each core has a dedicated L1 cache. Since our focus is on cache sharing, by default, the memory references in the discussion do not include the references that are L1 cache hits.

2.1   Reuse Distance

Underlying the co-run locality model is the concept of **reuse distance** or LRU stack distance, defined as the number of *distinct* data items accessed between the current and the previous reference to the same data item [16, 5]. Treating a cache block as a single data item leads to cache-block reuse distance. Researchers have used cache-block reuse distance histograms, also called *reuse signatures* [36], to predict the performance of dedicated caches. Figure 1 illustrates the prediction: Every memory reference on the right side of the cache-size line is considered a cache miss because too many other data have entered the cache between two references to the same data item. The estimation is precise for fully-associative cache, but also applicable for set-associative cache [15, 35].

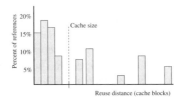

Fig. 1. An example of cache-block reuse signature

We use **concurrent reuse distance** to refer to the extension of reuse distance on shared caches. It is defined as the number of distinct data items that are referenced by *all* cache sharers (i.e., processes sharing a cache) between the current and the previous access to the same data item. For clarity, we use *standalone reuse distance* for the traditional concept of reuse distance. The histograms are named as *concurrent reuse* *signatures* and *standalone reuse signatures* respectively. Using concurrent reuse signatures, we can predict shared-cache misses in the manner similar to the prediction of dedicated-cache misses.

2.2   Derivation of Concurrent Reuse Signatures

Concurrent reuse signatures, although good for corun-locality prediction, is hard to measure. The main reason is that direct measurement requires detailed memory monitoring, which both disturbs the order of memory references conducted by cache sharers, and slows down program executions by hundreds of times.

Fortunately, concurrent reuse signatures can be derived from the corresponding standalone reuse signatures through a statistical model [22, 23]. Furthermore, prior work has shown that standalone reuse signatures of a program can be accurately predicted across the program's inputs [5]. These make concurrent reuse signature cross-input predictable: The concurrent reuse signatures of new executions of a group of co-running programs can be derived from the executions of those programs on some training inputs. Cross-input predictability is vital to the use in contention-aware scheduling because of the strong dependence of cache contention on program inputs.

The cost of the statistical model increases quadratically in the length of an execution [22], infeasible to be used in runtime scheduling. We use **distinct data blocks per cycle (DPC)** to simplify the process. The DPC of a process in a given interval is the average number of distinct data blocks (typically in the size of a cache line) accessed by the process in a CPU cycle through the interval. Roughly speaking, DPC is the average footprint in a cycle. It reflects the aggressiveness of a process in competing for cache resource. As an example, suppose a program accesses the following data blocks in 100 cycles: b1 b1 b3 b5 b3 b1 b4 b2. The corresponding DPC is $5/100 = 0.05$ (footprint is 5). Correspondingly, the DPC of a set of processes, P, is defined as the number of distinct data blocks that are accessed in a CPU cycle by all the processes in P, that is, $DPC(P) = \sum_{q \in P} DPC(q)$.

To ease explanation, we define the *reuse interval* of a reference as the interval between this and the previous reference to the same data item. The following theorem more precisely characterizes the connection between DPC and cache contention.

Theorem 1. *Suppose, process p shares a fully-associative cache of size L with a set of processes P ($p \notin P$). (No shared data among processes.) Consider a cache hit by p that has standalone reuse distance of d ($d < L$). Let σ and σ' be the average DPC of p and P during the reuse interval of the reference. Then, if and only if $\frac{d}{L-d} < \frac{\sigma}{\sigma'}$, the reference remains a cache hit in the presence of cache competition from P.*

The proof of this theorem is straightforward if it is noticed that the concurrent reuse distance of the reference is $(d + \sigma'd/\sigma)$.

This theorem suggests that along with standalone reuse signatures, knowing the DPC of every reuse interval is enough to compute the miss rate of a co-run. It is however too costly to get DPCs in such detail. We use the averaged value of the DPCs of all reuse intervals of a program to obtain a suitable tradeoff between the accuracy and efficiency of locality prediction. Although the theorem assumes fully-associative caches, its application produces good estimation for set associative caches as well [22].

3   Cache-Contention Sensitivity and Competitiveness

Theorem 1 provides a way to estimate concurrent reuse signatures and thus co-run performance. It is lightweight enough for offline analysis and batch job scheduling [22], but not for runtime uses: It takes more than 2,000 μs to predict the performance of 32 jobs co-running on dual-core processors. This work simplifies it to a competitiveness-sensitivity model. *Competitiveness* and *sensitivity* respectively characterize the statistical expectation of the influence that a process may impose on and receive from random co-runners. This model is important for making runtime proactive scheduling scalable. As we will see in Section 5, CAPS capitalizes on the model to make sensitive processes co-run with uncompetitive ones to achieve better performance.

3.1   Sensitivity

The definition of cache-contention sensitivity is as follows:

$$Sensitivity = \frac{\overline{CPI_{co}} - CPI_{si}}{CPI_{si}} \tag{1}$$

where, CPI_{si} is the cycles per instruction (CPI) of a process's single run, and $\overline{CPI_{co}}$ is the statistical expectation of the CPI of that process when it co-runs with random processes.

The estimation of CPI_{si} is straightforward: As explained in Section 2.1, we can predict the cache miss rate of a process's single run from its standalone reuse signatures; the corresponding CPI (given the cache miss rate) can be estimated using existing techniques (e.g. [26]).

To estimate $\overline{CPI_{co}}$ in the same way, we have to obtain the statistical expectation of the cache miss rates of the process's co-runs. The number of co-run misses equals the sum of single-run misses and the extra misses caused by co-run contention. Since single-run misses are obtainable as mentioned in the previous paragraph, the problem becomes the computation of the statistical expectation of the number of extra misses. The following corollary of Theorem 1 offers the solution.

Corollary 1. *Let $F()$ be the cumulative distribution function of the DPCs of all programs, and L be the shared cache size. Suppose a process p has H memory references whose standalone reuse distances, d_i, are smaller than L (i=1, 2, $\cdots$, H). Let σ_i represent the DPC of the corresponding reuse interval. When process p co-runs with some randomly-picked programs that share no data with p, the expectation of the cache miss rate of the H memory references is*

$$\delta = 1 - \frac{1}{H} \sum_{i=1}^{H} F(\sigma_i(L - d_i)/d_i). \tag{2}$$

Proof. Let σ' represent the average DPC of the co-runners of p in the reuse interval corresponding to σ_i. Theorem 1 tells us that if and only if $\sigma' < \sigma_i(L - d_i)/d_i$, reference i remains a hit. Since the probability for that condition to happen is $F(\sigma_i(L - d_i)/d_i)$, the expectation of the number of cache hits among the H references is $\sum_{i=1}^{H} F(\sigma_i(L - d_i)/d_i)$. The conclusion follows.

With this corollary, we can compute the sensitivity of a process from its DPC and standalone reuse signature. Since references are grouped in bars in reuse signatures, the computation uses a bar as a unit; H thus equals the number of bars whose reuse distances are smaller than L. For computing the $F()$ items efficiently, we build a lookup table for F by using 3.9 billion data reuses from a dozen randomly chosen SPEC CPU2000 programs (included in Figure 2). The table contains 200 items corresponding to 200 evenly-spaced points between 0 and 0.237.

3.2   Competitiveness

We initially intended to use a process's average DPC as competitiveness. But our experiments reveal the strong correlation between the influence a process imposes on and receives from its co-runners. This observation leads to a unified competitiveness and sensitivity model.

Figure 2 plots the performance degradation of all the 66 pair-wise co-runs of a dozen SPEC CPU2000 programs (*train* runs) on an Intel Xeon 5150 processor (specified in Section 5). In the graph, points on solid curves show the program's own degradation and points on broken curves show the degradation of its co-runner. For legibility, each program's data are sorted in ascending order of self degradation and then connected into curves. The two curves corresponding to every program show similar trends. The correlation coefficient between all the self and co-runner degradations is 0.75. (As an extra evidence, the coefficient is 0.73 for the 13 SPEC programs shown in Figure 3.)

The intuition behind the strong correlation is that, a program that is sensitive to cache contention tends to fetch data from a large portion of the shared cache frequently. Hence, it tends to impose strong influence on its co-runners, that is, it tends to be competitive. As an exception, stream programs are competitive but insensitive. Although they access cache intensively, those programs have few data reuses and thus rely on no

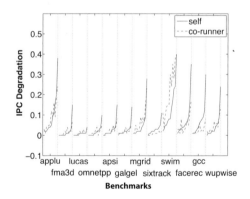

Fig. 2. Each program has 11 pair-wise co-runs, respectively with each of the other 11 programs. The points on the solid curve show the degradations of this program in those co-runs; the points on the broken curve are of its co-runners. (The points are connected for legibility.) The similarity between the two kinds of curves shows the strong correlations between the degradations of a program and those of its co-runners.

cache for performance. Fortunately in offline training, it is easy to detect stream programs thanks to their distinctive data access patterns. The scheduling process, CAPS, treats those programs as competitive programs and pair them with other insensitive programs (detailed next). For other programs, CAPS simply uses sensitivity for competitiveness. This unified model simplifies the design of runtime scheduler.

4   Contention-Aware Proactive Scheduling (CAPS)

The principle of CAPS is to couple sensitive processes with insensitive (thus likely uncompetitive) processes. This section uses Linux as an example to explain how CAPS can be integrated in runtime schedulers.

In default Linux SMP scheduling (e.g., Linux 2.6.23), when a program is launched, one of the CPUs will receive that signal and assign the process to the best available CPU for execution. Each CPU has a scheduler managing the jobs assigned to it.

For CAPS, CPUs are classified evenly into two groups, G_s and G_i, dedicated to sensitive and insensitive processes respectively. For the CPUs sharing a cache, half of them belong to G_s and the others belong to G_i. The scheduler on each CPU maintains a sensitivity threshold h, which is equal to the decayed average of the sensitivities of all the processes that the scheduler has assigned (may or may not to this CPU). Formally, h is computed as follows when the scheduler assigns the nth process:

$$h_n = \alpha h_{n-1} + (1 - \alpha)S_n \tag{3}$$

where, α is a decay factor (0 to 1), and S_n is the sensitivity of the newly launched process. The use of the decay factor makes the scheduler adaptive to workload changes. Similar to other factors in OS, its appropriate value should be determined empirically.

When a program is launched, the CPU that receives the launching signal computes the sensitivity of the process, S_n. It then updates h using equation 3. If $S_n > h$, it schedules the process to a CPU in G_s, otherwise, to a CPU in G_i. The way to select a CPU inside a group is the same as in the default Linux scheme. (Stream programs are assigned to G_s directly.) For processes without locality models, the scheduler falls back to the Linux default scheduling.

Equation 3 attempts to obtain load balance by dynamically adjusting threshold h. If unbalance still occurs due to certain patterns in the sensitivities of subsequent jobs, the existing load balancer in Linux, which is invoked periodically, can rebalance the workload automatically.

We note on two facts. First, the scheduler makes no change to the default management of run-queues and timeslice allocation in Linux. This is essential for maintaining the proper treatment to priorities. Second, although it is possible for different CPUs to get different h values, some degrees of difference is tolerable for CAPS. Furthermore, during rebalance, the rebalancer can obtain the average of all CPUs' h values and update the h values for every CPU accordingly.

The sensitivity of a program is obtained from its predicted reuse signature and DPC, both of which have shown to be cross-input predictable [5, 10]. But predictive models have to be constructed for each program through an offline profiling and learning process. This step, although being automatic, may still seem to be a burden to scheduling. There are two ways to make it transparent to the users of CAPS. First, the learning step can occur during the typical performance tuning or correctness testing stage in the development of a software. The program developers only need to run the program on several of the inputs they have; whereas, the outcome is beneficial: Besides for scheduling, the predictive locality model can also benefit data reorganization [5], cache resizing [24], and cache partition [12]. In this case, the scheduler can use the model for free. The second solution is to make the learning occur implicitly in the real runs of an application through incremental learning techniques. Through multiple runs, online learner learns the relation between memory behavior and program inputs, and builds the predictive model for co-run locality prediction. Detailed studies are out of the scope of this paper.

5   Evaluation

For evaluation, we employ 12 randomly chosen SPEC CPU2000 programs, as shown in Table 1, and a sequential stream program (derived from [17] with each data element covering one cache line) on a Dell PowerEdge 1850 server. The machine is equipped with Intel Xeon 5150 2.66 GHz quad-core processors; every two cores have a 4MB shared L2 cache (64B line, 4-way). Each core has a 32KB dedicated L1 data cache. The information shown in Table 1 are collected on the *ref* runs of the benchmarks on the Xeon machine. We use PIN as the instrumentation tool [14] for locality measurement, and use the PAPI [1] library for hardware performance monitoring. In the collection of co-run behavior, in order to avoid the distraction from program lengths, we follow Tuck and Tullsen's practice [33], wrapping each program to make it run 10 times consecutively, and only collecting the behavior of co-runs—that is, the runs overlapping with another program's run.

Table 1. Performance Ranges of Benchmarks on Intel Xeon 5150

Program	cycles per instruction			L2 misses per mem. acc.(%)		
	single-run	corun-min	corun-max	single-run	corun-min	corun-max
ammp	1.01	1.03	1.31	0.51	0.60	1.6
art	0.93	0.96	1.55	0.0028	0.095	3.8
bzip	0.49	0.49	0.66	0.11	0.18	0.76
crafty	0.72	0.73	0.80	0.00010	0.0028	0.21
equake	1.28	1.38	2.13	3.8	3.9	4.5
gap	0.91	0.91	1.16	1.3	1.5	1.6
gzip	0.72	0.72	0.77	0.078	0.079	0.14
mcf	2.47	2.70	4.84	4.4	5.0	8.6
mesa	0.51	0.52	0.56	0.23	0.26	0.38
parser	1.15	1.18	1.50	0.31	0.44	1.2
twolf	1.06	1.07	1.24	0.0014	0.0015	0.40
vpr	1.06	1.09	1.44	0.0053	0.0067	0.015

The focus of our evaluation is the examination of the effectiveness of the unified sensitivity model in serving as a locality model for shared-cache-aware scheduling. To avoid distractions from the many random factors (e.g., job arriving time, load balance) in online schedulers, we use offline measurement to uncover the full potential.

We compute the sensitivities of the programs from their reuse signatures and DPCs, based on which, we separate the 12 SPEC programs into two equal-size classes shown as the two sequences of *caps-pred* below. For comparison, we report the ideal separation as *caps-real*. We obtain them by first running all possible pairs of the 12 programs, and then taking the average co-run degradation of each program as its real sensitivity. In both separation results, we list the programs in descending order of sensitivity.

caps-pred:

Sensitive:	mcf	art	equake	vpr	parser	bzip
Insensitive:	twolf	ammp	crafty	gap	mesa	gzip

caps-real:

Sensitive:	mcf	equake	art	vpr	bzip	ammp
Insensitive:	parser	gap	crafty	mesa	twolf	gzip

The sequences, although differing in the relative positions of the benchmarks, only mismatch on two programs, *parser* and *ammp*. Two reasons cause the differences: locality prediction errors and the difference between statistical expectation and a particular problem instance. We note that CAPS has good tolerance to ordering difference: As long as programs are put into the right sequences, the order inside a sequence has no effects on CAPS. This property is essential for making the lightweight locality prediction applicable for CAPS.

We compare the performance result of CAPS on predicted sensitivities (denoted as *caps-pred*) with the results of the default Linux scheduler (*default*) and CAPS on real sensitivities (*caps-real*). We measure the performance of a program by **degradation factor**, defined as $(CPI_{co} - CPI_{si})/CPI_{si}$, where, CPI_{co} and CPI_{si} are the respective CPIs of the program's co-run and single run. Following prior work [34], we measure the fairness of a schedule by **unfairness factor**, defined as the coefficient of variation (standard deviation divided by the mean) of the normalized performance (IPC_{co}/IPC_{si}) of all applications.

To prevent randomness from obscuring the comparison, we obtain a program's performance in a schedule by averaging the performance of all the program's co-runs that are allowed by the schedule. The *default* scheduler, for example, allows all 12 possible co-runs per program, whereas *caps-pred* and *caps-real* allow a program to run with only the programs in a different class.

Figure 3 shows the performance of the three schedulers, with sensitive programs (judged by *caps-pred*) on the left and insensitive programs on the right. For sensitive programs, *caps-pred* reduces performance degradation by 4% to 30.2% (15.7% on average); as a tradeoff, insensitive programs have 1.4% to 8.1% more degradation (4.1% on average). In comparison, *caps-real* shows 2.5% less reduction for sensitive programs and 3.3% more for insensitive programs than *caps-pred*. It is important to note that the goal of job co-scheduling is to increase the overall computing efficiency of the system

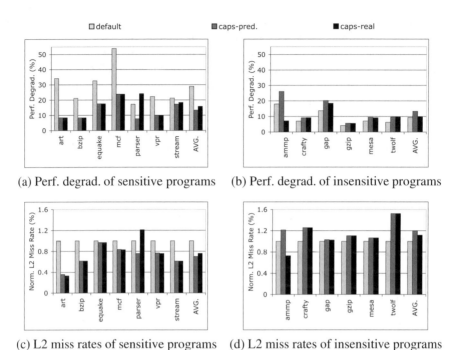

(a) Perf. degrad. of sensitive programs   (b) Perf. degrad. of insensitive programs

(c) L2 miss rates of sensitive programs   (d) L2 miss rates of insensitive programs

Fig. 3. Performance degradation and normalized L2 miss rates by different scheduling

rather than maximize the performance of each individual program. So it is normal that some programs (e.g. *parser*) perform better in *caps-pred* than in *caps-real*.

Table 2 reports the performance, normalized to the default performance, of each program when they run in *caps-real* and *caps-pred*. The sensitive programs show 12% and 14% speedup on average. All of them have speedup over 11% except *parser* and *stream*. In *caps-real*, *parser* has 6% slowdown because it is classified as insensitive programs and co-runs with sensitive programs. The small speedup of *stream* is consistent with our intuition conveyed in Section 3.2—such programs are competitive but insensitive for their special memory access patterns. It is remarkable that the significant speedup for sensitive programs comes with almost no slowdown of insensitive programs. The average slowdown is 1% in *caps-real* and 3% in *caps-pred*. The small slowdown is no surprise given that those program are insensitive to cache sharing. The program *ammp* shows 10% speedup in *caps-real* because the scheduler labels the program as a sensitive program and lets it co-run with insensitive programs.

The intuition behind the effectiveness of CAPS is that it successfully recognizes the programs to which cache contention matters significantly. By giving an favorable schedule to those programs, CAPS accelerates them without hurting the programs that are not sensitive to cache contention.

Table 3 contains the overall performance degradation factors and unfairness factors of the schedules. The two *reduction* columns report the relative reduction ratios of *caps-pred* and *caps-real* compared to *default*. Schedule *caps-pred* reduces degradation

Table 2. Whole-Program Speedup Brought by CAPS

Sensitive Programs			Insensitive Programs		
Programs	caps-real	caps-pred	Programs	caps-real	caps-pred
art	1.24	1.24	ammp	1.10	0.94
bzip	1.12	1.12	crafty	0.98	0.98
equake	1.13	1.13	gap	0.94	0.94
mcf	1.24	1.24	gzip	0.99	0.99
parser	0.94	1.09	mesa	0.98	0.98
vpr	1.11	1.11	twolf	0.97	0.97
stream	1.03	1.02	–	–	–
Average	1.12	1.14	Average	0.99	0.97

factor by 32.6% and unfairness factor by 46.9%, respectively 1.3% and 2.4% less than *caps-real*.

Figure 3 (c) and (d) show the normalized L2 miss rates (L2 misses per memory reference) collected using PAPI library [1]. Although they roughly match the performance results, the L2 miss rates impose different influence on the programs. For example, the 52% more L2 miss rates of *twolf* only cause 3.2% performance difference, while 3.3% less miss rates of *equake* reduce 15% performance degradation. This difference is due to bus-contention differences and the different significance of L2 misses. The L2 miss rates of *twolf* are hundreds of times smaller than those of *equake*. This agrees with the fact that both *caps-pred* and *caps-real* label *twolf* insensitive and *equake* sensitive.

Table 3. Overall Performance Degradation Factors and Unfairness Factors

	Performance Deg. (%)		Unfairness (%)	
	factor	reduction	factor	reduction
default	20.0	–	11.6	–
caps-pred	13.5	32.6	6.2	46.9
caps-real	13.4	33.3	6.0	48.5

These results demonstrate the potential of the locality model in supporting job co-scheduling. The performance of actual on-line schedulers depends on many other factors, such as the job arrival time and order, system load balance and its dynamic adjustment, job priorities, and so forth. Detailed discussion is out of the scope of this paper.

Overhead of CAPS. The major runtime overhead of CAPS consists of the prediction of standalone reuse signatures and the computation of sensitivities, both determined by the granularity of standalone reuse signatures. Since reuse distances smaller than cache size are more critical for CAPS, reuse signatures organize them in linear scale (1K distance per bar), and use log scale for others. Because each bar in a signature corresponds to one linear function, there are $A + log(N/L)$ linear functions to solve in the reuse-signature prediction, where, A is the number of bars in the linear range, N is program data size (the upper bound of reuse distance), and L is cache line width. The computation of sensitivity relies on only reuse distances smaller than cache size, because only those references can be the victims of cache contention. Thus, the time complexity is $O(A)$.

In our experiments, $L = 64$, A is 64 and N is from 32,606 (*crafty*) to 4.1 million (*gap*) with average of 1.0 million. The numbers of linear functions range from 79 to 86 per program. The computation cost of CAPS is negligible.

6   Comparison

Recent years have seen a number of studies on scheduling in CMP. Some concentrate on scheduling threads in a single application. For example, thread clustering [30] tries to recognize patterns of data sharing using hardware performance counters and locates threads accordingly. The technique cannot apply to the problems tackled in this work as no data are shared among jobs. Some studies [13] tackle the scalability and fairness of scheduling on CMP, but without considering interferences on shared cache in the fairness criterion. Some studies [11, 32] conduct theoretical analysis to uncover the complexity of optimal co-scheduling on CMP. They are useful for offline analysis but not for runtime scheduling.

This section concentrates on the studies that schedule independent jobs to reduce the interferences on shared cache. Most of those studies have used simulators (e.g., [6, 8, 21, 25]), whereas, we use a real machine for all the experiments. Furthermore, CAPS has applicability different from previous techniques (elaborated next). We hence concentrate on qualitative comparisons.

First, the applicability of CAPS differs from prior techniques. Unlike techniques based on cache activity vectors or other hardware extensions (e.g., [6, 21, 27]), this work is a pure software solution applicable to existing systems. On the other hand, hardware extensions may reveal fine-grained cache conflicts, complementary to the coarse-grained locality information used in this work.

Previous explorations in scheduling for CMP or SMT rely on either hardware performance counters or offline memory profiling, showing different applicability from CAPS. The cache-fair scheduling [8] from Fedorova et al. is applicable when the processes have various cache-access patterns and have already been labeled either *cache-fair* or *best-effort*. Its main goal is performance isolation, accomplished by controlling CPU timeslice allocation instead of process assignment. Zhang et al. use hardware counters to guide scheduling on SMP machines without shared caches [34]. Snavely et al. have proposed symbiotic scheduling, which is based on sampling of various co-runs [4, 25], suiting the problems having a small number of jobs and processors. Some explorations use offline collected memory information to guide scheduling [3, 6]. They use the same program inputs for training and testing, not applicable to input-sensitive programs.

CAPS overcomes the above constraints, but requires each process of interest to be equipped with a cross-input predictive locality model (whose construction, fortunately, can be transparent to the users of CAPS as discussed in Section 4). The combination of CAPS with runtime sampling-based techniques may be beneficial: The former overcomes scalability issues, and the latter offers on-line adaptivity. In addition, the combination of CAPS with locality phases [24] may add adaptivity to phase shifts as well.

Second, the program behavior models introduced in this work may benefit other techniques as well. Essentially, the models offer an alternative way to estimate cache requirement and co-run performance, which are exactly the major sources of guiding information used by many cache management schemes.

7   Conclusion

This work, based on the concept of concurrent reuse distance, develops a lightweight locality model for shared-cache contention prediction. The model offers the basis for a runtime contention-aware proactive scheduling system. Experiments on a recent CMP machine demonstrate the effectiveness of the technique in alleviating cache contention, improving both system performance and fairness. On the high level, this work shows the potential of combining program behavior analysis by programming systems and global resource management by operating systems. Interactions between these two layers may also help other issues in computing systems.

Acknowledgment

We are grateful to the anonymous reviewers for their helpful suggestions. We thank Avi Mendelson at Microsoft for his help on the preparation of the final version of this paper. This material is based upon work supported by the National Science Foundation under Grant No. 0720499 and 0811791 and IBM CAS Fellowship. Any opinions, findings, and conclusions or recommendations expressed in this material are those of the author(s) and do not necessarily reflect the views of the National Science Foundation or IBM.

References

1. Browne, S., Deane, C., Ho, G., Mucci, P.: PAPI: A portable interface to hardware performance counters. In: Proceedings of Department of Defense HPCMP Users Group Conference (1999)
2. Bulpin, J.R., Pratt, I.A.: Hyper-threading aware process scheduling heuristics. In: 2005 USENIX Annual Technical Conference, pp. 103–106 (2005)
3. Chandra, D., Guo, F., Kim, S., Solihin, Y.: Predicting inter-thread cache contention on a chip multi-processor architecture. In: Proceedings of the International Symposium on High Performance Computer Architecture (HPCA), pp. 340–351 (2005)
4. DeVuyst, M., Kumar, R., Tullsen, D.M.: Exploiting unbalanced thread scheduling for energy and performance on a cmp of smt processors. In: Proceedings of International Parallel and Distribute Processing Symposium, IPDPS (2006)
5. Ding, C., Zhong, Y.: Predicting whole-program locality with reuse distance analysis. In: Proceedings of ACM SIGPLAN Conference on Programming Language Design and Implementation, San Diego, CA, June 2003, pp. 245–257 (2003)

6. El-Moursy, A., Garg, R., Albonesi, D.H., Dwarkadas, S.: Compatible phase co-scheduling on a cmp of multi-threaded processors. In: Proceedings of the International Parallel and Distribute Processing Symposium, IPDPS (2006)
7. Fedorova, A., Seltzer, M., Small, C., Nussbaum, D.: Performance of multithreaded chip multiprocessors and implications for operating system design. In: Proceedings of USENIX Annual Technical Conference (2005)
8. Fedorova, A., Seltzer, M., Smith, M.D.: Improving performance isolation on chip multiprocessors via an operating system scheduler. In: Proceedings of the International Conference on Parallel Architecture and Compilation Techniques (2007)
9. Hsu, L.R., Reinhardt, S.K., Iyer, R., Makineni, S.: Communist, utilitarian, and capitalist cache policies on CMPs: caches as a shared resource. In: Proceedings of the International Conference on Parallel Architecture and Compilation Techniques (2006)
10. Jiang, Y., Shen, X.: Exploration of the influence of program inputs on cmp co-scheduling. In: Luque, E., Margalef, T., Benítez, D. (eds.) Euro-Par 2008. LNCS, vol. 5168, pp. 263–273. Springer, Heidelberg (2008)
11. Jiang, Y., Shen, X., Chen, J., Tripathi, R.: Analysis and approximation of optimal co-scheduling on chip multiprocessors. In: Proceedings of the International Conference on Parallel Architecture and Compilation Techniques (PACT) (October 2008)
12. Kim, S., Chandra, D., Solihin, Y.: Fair cache sharing and partitioning in a chip multiprocessor architecture. In: Proceedings of the International Conference on Parallel Architecture and Compilation Techniques (2004)
13. Li, T., Baumberger, D., Hahn, S.: Efficient and scalable multiprocessor fair scheduling using distributed weighted round-robin. In: Proceedings of ACM Symposium on Principles and Practice of Parallel Programming, pp. 65–74 (2009)
14. Luk, C.-K., et al.: Pin: Building customized program analysis tools with dynamic instrumentation. In: Proceedings of the ACM SIGPLAN conference on Programming language design and implementation, Chicago, Illinois, June 2005, pp. 190–200 (2005)
15. Marin, G., Mellor-Crummey, J.: Cross architecture performance predictions for scientific applications using parameterized models. In: Proceedings of Joint International Conference on Measurement and Modeling of Computer Systems, New York City, June 2004, pp. 2–13 (2004)
16. Mattson, R.L., Gecsei, J., Slutz, D., Traiger, I.L.: Evaluation techniques for storage hierarchies. IBM System Journal 9(2), 78–117 (1970)
17. McCalpin, J.D.: Memory bandwidth and machine balance in current high performance computers. IEEE TCCA Newsletter (1995), http://www.cs.virginia.edu/stream
18. Parekh, S., Eggers, S., Levy, H., Lo, J.: Thread-sensitive scheduling for smt processors. Technical Report 2000-04-02, University of Washington (June 2000)
19. Rafique, N., Lim, W., Thottethodi, M.: Architectural support for operating system-driven cmp cache management. In: Proceedings of the International Conference on Parallel Architecture and Compilation Techniques (2006)
20. Sarkar, S., Tullsen, D.: Compiler techniques for reducing data cache miss rate on a multithreaded architecture. In: Proceedings of The HiPEAC International Conference on High Performance Embedded Architectures and Compilation (2008)
21. Settle, A., Kihm, J.L., Janiszewski, A., Connors, D.A.: Architectural support for enhanced smt job scheduling. In: Proceedings of the International Conference on Parallel Architecture and Compilation Techniques, pp. 63–73 (2004)
22. Shen, X., Jiang, Y., Mao, F.: Caps: Contention-aware proactive scheduling for cmps with shared caches. Technical Report WM-CS-2007-09, Computer Science Department, The College of William and Mary (2007)
23. Shen, X., Shaw, J., Meeker, B., Ding, C.: Locality approximation using time. In: Proceedings of the ACM SIGPLAN Conference on Principles of Programming Languages, POPL (2007)

24. Shen, X., Zhong, Y., Ding, C.: Locality phase prediction. In: Proceedings of the International Conference on Architectural Support for Programming Languages and Operating Systems, Boston, MA, pp. 165–176 (2004)
25. Snavely, A., Tullsen, D.M.: Symbiotic jobscheduling for a simultaneous multithreading processor. In: Proceedings of ASPLOS (2000)
26. Solihin, Y., Lam, V., Torrellas, J.: Scal-tool: Pinpointing and quantifying scalability bottlenecks in dsm multiprocessors. In: Proceedings of the 1999 Conference on Supercomputing (1999)
27. Suh, G., Rudolph, L., Devadas, S.: Dynamic partitioning of shared cache memory. Journal of Supercomputing 28, 7–26 (2004)
28. Suh, G.E., Devadas, S., Rudolph, L.: Analytical cache models with applications to cache partitioning. In: Proceedings of the 15th international conference on Supercomputing (2001)
29. Suh, G.E., Devadas, S., Rudolph, L.: A new memory monitoring scheme for memory-aware scheduling and partitioning. In: Proceedings of the 8th International Symposium on High-Performance Computer Architecture (2002)
30. Tam, D., Azimi, R., Stumm, M.: Thread clustering: sharing-aware scheduling on smp-cmp-smt multiprocessors. SIGOPS Oper. Syst. Rev. 41(3), 47–58 (2007)
31. Thiebaut, D., Stone, H.S.: Footprints in the cache. ACM Transactions on Computer Systems 5(4) (1987)
32. Tian, K., Jiang, Y., Shen, X.: A study on optimally co-scheduling jobs of different lengths on chip multiprocessors. In: Proceedings of ACM Computing Frontiers (2009)
33. Tuck, N., Tullsen, D.M.: Initial observations of the simultaneous multithreading Pentium 4 processor. In: Proceedings of International Conference on Parallel Architectures and Compilation Techniques, New Orleans, Louisiana (September 2003)
34. Zhang, X., Dwarkadas, S., Folkmanis, G., Shen, K.: Processor hardware counter statistics as a first-class system resource. In: Proceedings of the 11th Workshop on Hot Topics in Operating Systems (2007)
35. Zhong, Y., Dropsho, S.G., Shen, X., Studer, A., Ding, C.: Miss rate prediction across program inputs and cache configurations. IEEE Transactions on Computers 56(3), 328–343 (2007)
36. Zhong, Y., Orlovich, M., Shen, X., Ding, C.: Array regrouping and structure splitting using whole-program reference affinity. In: Proceedings of ACM SIGPLAN Conference on Programming Language Design and Implementation, June 2004, pp. 255–266 (2004)

RELOCATE: Register File Local Access Pattern Redistribution Mechanism for Power and Thermal Management in Out-of-Order Embedded Processor

Houman Homayoun[1], Aseem Gupta[2], Alex Veidenbaum[1],
Avesta Sasan (M.A. Makhzan)[3], Fadi Kurdahi[3], and Nikil Dutt[1]

[1] Department of Computer Science, University of California, Irvine, CA, USA
[2] Freescale Semiconductor Inc. Austin, TX 78729, USA
[3] Department of Electrical Engineering and Computer Science, University of California, Irvine, CA 92697-3435, USA
{hhomayou,aseemg,mmakhzan,alex.veidenbaum,kurdahi,dutt}@uci.edu

Abstract. In order to reduce register file's peak temperature in an embedded processor we propose RELOCATE: an architectural solution which redistributes the access pattern to physical registers through a novel register allocation mechanism. RELOCATE regionalizes the register file such that even though accesses within a region are uniformly distributed, the activity levels are spread over the entire register file in a deterministic pattern. It partitions the register file and uses a micro-architectural mechanism to concentrate the accesses to a single or a subset of such partitions through a novel register allocation mechanism. The goal is to keep some partitions unused (idle) and cooling down. The temperature of idle partitions is further reduced by power gating them into destructive sleep mode to reduce their leakage power. The *redistribution mechanism* changes the active region periodically to modulate the activity within the register file and prevent the active region from heating up excessively. Our approach resulted in an average reduction of 8.3°C in the register file's peak temperature for standard benchmarks.

Keywords: Register file, Temperature, Power, Local Activity Redistribution, Out of Order Embedded Processor.

1 Introduction

Continued CMOS process technology scaling has led to designs of much more complex embedded processors with significantly higher computational power. The high level of integration in SoC designs today has, however, led to correspondingly higher power densities (Watt per mm2) which in turn lead to higher operating temperatures. High operating temperatures have many unfavorable consequences: (i) Increased probability of timing violations because of higher signal propagation delay and switching time, (ii) Reduced lifetime because of phenomena such as electromigration, (iii) Lower clock frequencies of designs because of higher device and interconnect delays, (iv) Increased

Y.N. Patt et al. (Eds.): HiPEAC 2010, LNCS 5952, pp. 216–231, 2010.

leakage power due to super-linear relationship with temperature, (v) need for expensive cooling mechanisms, such as fans, and (vi) Overall increase in design effort and cost.

Components within a processor operate at different temperatures as function of their circuit design and activity levels. One of the hottest components is the integer register file. Recent embedded processors such as MIPS-74K or IBM PowerPC 750FX, use a large register file to support out-of-order execution. The register file is accessed every cycle, unless the processor is stalled, for both reads and writes. In addition, multiple instruction issue further increases the number of register file accesses per cycle. Thus in these processors the register file is one of the most active components which also makes it the hottest unit. Numerous academic and industrial papers have pointed out this fact [1,15,19]. For example, Koren et al. [19] show that the register file is hotter by as much as 20°C than any other block in a processor. This peak temperature determines the "design temperature", i.e., the reference temperature, which is used to characterize the performance of the design. Therefore, there is a critical need to reduce the peak operating temperature of the register file.

One general approach to reduce temperature of a given processor unit, including the register file, is to reduce its activity level by activity migration. This approach requires a replicated unit to be available in the system [16]. Once the unit reaches a critical temperature, its activity is migrated to the replicated unit and the hot unit becomes idle, allowing it to cool down.

While activity migration is effective in reducing the temperature of the register file it requires a replicated register file [16], which is expensive and complex (30% area overhead [16]). It can also lead to performance degradation (3~12% [16]), because of migration overhead. For instance, in [16] copying registers from a register file to its replica requires the pipeline to be drained and multiple additional reads and writes to be performed.

This paper introduces the idea of local activity migration to manage register file temperature in embedded out-of-order processors. It proposes a REgister file LOCal Access paTtern rEdistribution mechanism (or, in brief, RELOCATE). RELOCATE redistributes the access to physical registers through a novel register allocation mechanism. By "local" we mean that a replicated register file is not required; instead the register file access activity is "migrated" or redistributed from one part of the register file to another. This is accomplished without a noticeable impact on register usage and has no performance degradation.

RELOCATE uses a register file partitioned into multiple regions. This partitioning allows the RF access activity to be distributed in a non-uniform pattern over the regions. This pattern is such that the regions accessed are spatially and temporally apart allowing the opportunity for other regions to cool-down. The goal is to keep some regions unused and cooling down while other regions are active. This requires a new micro-architecture because in current micro-architectures the accesses are fairly uniformly distributed over the RF.

RELOCATE is based on the observation that only a small subset of physical registers is used (mapped) at any given time during the course of program execution. Therefore there is room for the migration (redistribution) within the RF itself instead of migrating the activity to a replicated unit. The micro-architectural solution to redistribute the physical registers and their access pattern is based on a novel register renaming mechanism. The new register renamer attempts to allocate new registers from a given RF region and thus to concentrate the accesses in this region. The renamer partitions the free list to correspond to regions in the register file. After a partition is used for a period of N clocks, the renamer switches to a new partition. Choosing a large enough N (10K cycles) allows the RF regions to cool down if they can be kept idle (not accessed).

Successful local activity migration keeps some RF regions idle and this lack of activity is the reason why these regions can cool down. However, such idle partitions still dissipate leakage power, slowing down their cooling. Our approach further reduces the temperature by power-gating an idle region. This should be doable since an idle region has no accesses.

The experimental evaluation of the proposed mechanism is performed using an integrated architectural/temperature simulator. The results show that a 64-entry physical register file with 4 partitions performs best and achieves an average peak temperature reduction of 8.3°C and 6.9°C for SPEK2K and MiBench benchmarks respectively. The temperature is reduced without any impact on performance with minimal area and hardware overhead.

2 Background

2.1 On-Chip Thermal Behavior

Today's chips are operating at very high temperatures due to high power densities. Within a processor, regions operate at different temperatures due to their varying activity levels. The temperature of a region in a VLSI chip does not depend only on its own power dissipation. At any given time there are two phenomena, that determine the temperature of a region: *spatial* and *temporal*. Due to thermal diffusion, the temperature of a region also depends on the temperature of neighboring regions. This is the spatial phenomenon. Unlike power dissipation, the temperature of a region cannot change very quickly. It can take up to several milliseconds for a region's temperature to rise or cool down. This temporal phenomenon is characterized by the thermal resistance and thermal capacitance of the material. For any thermal management solution to be effective, it must consider both the spatial and temporal phenomena.

2.2 Conventional Register File Organization

An out-of-order embedded processor uses a larger register file with logical to physical register renaming and a dynamic physical register allocation policy. The same approach has been used in high performance superscalar processors such as Alpha 21264 [5] and MIPS R10000 [6].

The pipeline of an out-of-order embedded processors is capable of fetching, decoding, renaming several instructions per processor clock cycle. The processor can also execute and later commit up to as many instructions in each cycle as the issue width. This type of out-of-order multiple-issue processor accesses the register file very frequently. Up to 2*N reads and N writes can be issued to the register file per clock cycle, where N is processor issue width. Thus the register file is one of the most active components in a processor.

Due to frequent accesses the register file is one of the hottest units in an embedded processor. The physical register file is typically designed as a SRAM structure with as many write and twice as many read ports as the maximum number of instructions the processor can issue in each cycle.

The register renamer in these processors is implemented either as a CAM (IBM POWER4 [22] and Alpha 21264[5]) or a RAM (MIPS R10K[6]). This paper discusses issues assuming a RAM based register renaming mechanism similar to the one used in the MIPS R10K processor [6]. However, the techniques proposed in this work also can be applied to a CAM based renamer.

2.3 Activity Migration

One general approach to reduce the temperature of a given processor block is to modulate (or vary) its activity level. One such method is activity migration, where the heat is spread by moving an activity to another block with the same functionality. This technique requires availability of redundant blocks in the system [16]. Once a block reaches a critical temperature, its activity is migrated and it becomes idle allowing it to cool down and reduce its temperature as shown in Figure 1(a). Notice that both temperature increase and decrease are non-linear functions of time.

Activity migration was used in [16] for different units in a processor. It was shown that to benefit the most from this technique the migration period should be significantly smaller than the time constant of the equivalent thermal RC circuit (shown in Figure 1(a)). While short migration periods can result in larger temperature decrease, they incurred large power/performance overhead, as reported in [16].

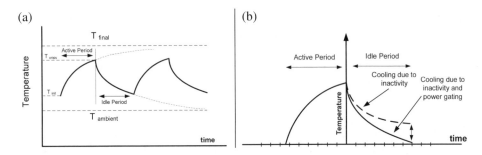

Fig. 1. Thermal benefit of (a) activity migration and (b) combination of activity migration and power gating

2.3.1 AM and Power Gating

Once the activity is migrated completely to a redundant block the base block can be put into a low-power mode to further reduce its temperature. The main reason for this is the reduction in idle leakage power, as described below. The decrease in temperature ΔT is given by:

$$\Delta T = \left(\frac{T_{old}}{R_{th} \times C_{th}} - \frac{P}{C_{th}} \right) \times \Delta t \tag{1}$$

where Δt is the time interval, P is total power dissipation ($P_{total} = P_{dynamic} + P_{leakage}$), T_{old} is the original temperature, and R_{th} and C_{th} are the thermal resistance and capacitance, respectively. From EQ.1 the rate of cooling is faster if P_{total} becomes smaller. This is shown in Figure 1(b) where cooling accelerates due to base block inactivity as well as due to turning off the unused regions. The difference between the two curves (marked d) is the additional temperature reduction on account of leakage power saving.

3   Analysis of Register File Operation

In this section we examine the register file access pattern and register file occupancy. This analysis allows us to propose a solution which reduces register file temperature without any performance degradation and at a minimal cost.

3.1   Register File Occupancy

Figure 2 shows the register file occupancy results for the MiBench and SPEC2K integer benchmarks. We observe that for nearly 60% of the time only half of all register file entries are occupied across the MiBench benchmarks. For SPEC2K only half of all register file entries are occupied for about 80% of the time. For 35% of the time only a quarter of the register file is occupied in MiBench benchmarks. This ratio is 60% for SPEC2K benchmarks. Such low register file occupancy raises the question: *why do we need such a large register file in the first place?* To answer this question, consider Figure 3 which shows the performance degradation as a result of using a smaller register file --with 16, 32, and 48 registers, instead of the original size of 64. We observe significant performance degradation across most SPEC2K and MiBench benchmarks. The performance impact is up to 36% and 19% in SPEC2K and MiBench benchmarks respectively when a register file with half its size (32 entries) is used. An even larger performance impact is observed as we shrink the size of the register file further.

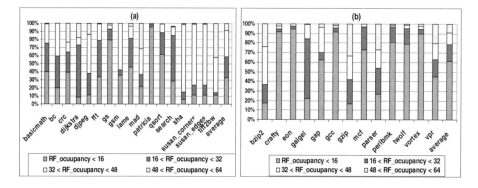

Fig. 2. Register file occupancy results for (a) MiBench and (b) SPEC2K integer benchmarks

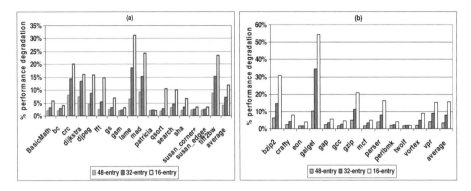

Fig. 3. Performance degradation as a result of using a smaller register file -with 16, 32, and 48 registers for (a) MiBench and (b) SPEC2K integer benchmarks

Thus in spite of low average occupancy, using a smaller register file degrades the performance noticeably. In fact, a smaller register file fills up faster when a long latency operation occurs. For instance, after a load instruction miss in L2 cache it stays on top of the *ROB* and doesn't allow the subsequent instructions to be committed. Therefore the dependent instruction's corresponding physical registers can not be released until the cache miss is serviced. During every cycle the processor fills up the register file with up to 2 physical registers whereas it releases registers at a slower rate. Consequently, the register file occupancy grows until it gets filled completely.

3.2   Register File Access Pattern

In this section we study how accesses to physical registers are distributed. We used coefficient of variation (CV) as a metric to indicate the distribution of accesses to physical registers. The coefficient of variation of accesses to the physical registers is a normalized measure of dispersion of registers access distribution. It is defined as the ratio of the standard deviation (σ) to the mean (μ).

$$CV_{access} = \frac{\sqrt{\frac{1}{N}\sum_{i=1}^{n}(na_i - \overline{na})^2}}{\overline{na}} \qquad (2)$$

where na_i is the number of accesses (read or write) to the physical registers i during a specific period (10K cycles). N is the total number of physical registers.

As shown in Figure 4, most benchmarks have a uniformly distributed access pattern to register file. It was also observed that register file occupancy is low for a large portion of program execution time. *Put together, while only a small number of registers are occupied at any given time, the total accesses are uniformly distributed over the entire physical register file during the course of execution.*

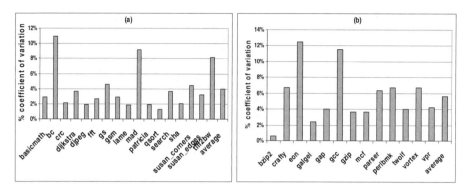

Fig. 4. Coefficient of variation of accesses to physical register file for (a) MiBench and (b) SPEC2K benchmarks

4 RELOCATE: Local Activity Redistribution within a Register File

Activity migration is effective in reducing temperature but it typically requires replicated units. As shown above, only a small subset of physical registers is in use at any given time during program execution. Therefore, instead of migrating the activity of this set of active registers to a replicated register file, one can do it within a single register file (activity redistribution). This paper proposes to partition the (single) register file into multiple regions and to spread the register allocation and therefore their access activity in a deterministic pattern over these regions. Activity of a region will be migrated after a certain amount of time to limit its temperature rise as such idle regions (or partitions) will be cooling off. To further improve the temperature reduction benefit of the proposed activity redistribution, one can power gate the idle regions of the register file.

Let us assume that, on average, 16 registers are being used at any given time. Results in the previous section showed that a small subset of active registers is distributed fairly uniformly over the entire register file during any time interval. The logical view of the baseline register file activity shown in Figure 5(a) represents 16 active registers distributed almost uniformly during a specific timing interval ($4*\tau_c$). This makes it impossible to perform any activity redistribution.

Now let us assume a register file is partitioned into four equal sized regions (partitions) with 16 entries each. Assuming that the 16 active registers are allocated such that they are concentrated in one partition for a certain period (we refer to this as a convergence period or τ_c as shown in Figure 5(b)), other register regions can be kept idle and cooling off. The activity needs to be moved to another partition after τ_c. There are a number of ways to modulate the activity within the register file, e.g., in a round-robin in-order pattern (AP1—AP2 —AP3 —AP4 as shown in Figure 5(b)). The activity is modulated to another region after every convergence period. Note that within a convergence period the activities are uniformly distributed within the active region, similar to the baseline register file. Once the activity is modulated to a new

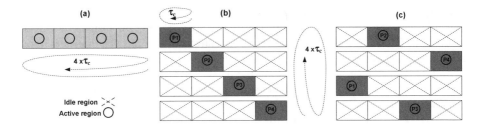

Fig. 5. Examples of register activity distribution (a) baseline, (b) in-order (c) distant patterns

region (active region) all other regions (idle regions) are cooling down. The in-order pattern spaces accesses in time, but there is not enough spatial separation (See Section 2 on Background). An access pattern with spatial as well as temporal separation between active regions would further reduce the temperature. The following redistribution pattern shown in Figure 5(c) can be used to achieve this: AP2 — AP4 — AP1 — AP3 (round-robin distant pattern). When a region becomes active and dissipates power, other regions get an opportunity to cool down. For instance, when AP1 is active, regions AP2 and AP4 are cooling down. AP4 is spatially distant from AP1 while AP2 is temporally distant from AP1.

4.1   The Architectural Mechanism to Support Activity Redistribution

This section introduces an architectural mechanism that attempts to concentrate active physical registers (live registers) in one register file region. This is accomplished through a novel register allocation mechanism that "concentrates" all register allocations during renaming in a given time period (convergence period) in one partition. It partitions the free register list into multiple consecutive partitions and allocates all new physical registers from one partition. Each partition of the free register list corresponds to a certain region in the register file. If there are no more registers in a given partition then the next partition is "activated", even if the time period (convergence period) is not over yet. We refer to the partition(s) currently participating in register renaming as *active partitions* and the rest as *idle partitions*.

The following terms will be used in the rest of the paper:

- Active partition: a register renamer partition which participates in register renaming.
- Idle partition: a register renamer partition which does not participate in renaming.
- Active region: a region of the register file corresponding to a register renamer partition (whether active partition or idle) which has live registers.
- Idle region: a region of the register file corresponding to a register renamer partition (whether active partition or idle) which has no live registers.

The activity concentration and redistribution in the register file occur via two techniques described next.

The concentration mechanism: At any given time registers are allocated from only one partition, referred as the default active partition (DAP), for instance P1 in the example of Figure 6. While our goal is to concentrate all live physical registers in one region, the default partition may run out of free registers before the convergence period is over. Once the free list of the DAP (P1) is empty, the next partition (according to some algorithm) is activated (referred to as additional active partitions or AAP) and is used for register renaming along with the default active partition. In Figure 6 the second and fourth partitions are idle (and power gated) and are activated only when the first and third partitions' free lists are empty, in that order. To facilitate physical register concentration in DAP, if two or more partitions are active and have free registers, allocation is performed in the same order in which partitions were activated. By doing this the default active partition gets the highest priority to allocate physical registers if it has any free registers, thus further concentrating the accesses in the DAP. For instance, if AAPs P2 and P3 were activated in this order, a new register will be allocated from P2.

The redistribution mechanism: The default active partition is changed once every N cycles (we used N=10K) to redistribute the activity within the register file (according to some algorithm). For instance, one can use a round-robin distant pattern algorithm (P2 — P4 — P1 — P3) to maximize the distance between regions. Once a new default partition (NDP) is selected, all active partitions (DAP+AAP) become idle. While these idle partitions do not participate anymore in register renaming, their corresponding regions in the register file are kept active (powered up) until their active list becomes empty. At this time the corresponding physical registers become idle and are power gated as well. Recall that an idle partition does not participate in register renaming. However, it is possible that a physical register belonging to an idle partition may need to be read as a source register of a scheduled instruction. An active region of the RF corresponding to an idle register renaming partition can be powered down provided that all of its physical registers have been released (no live registers left).

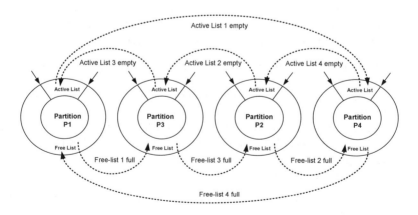

Fig. 6. Partitioned register renaming

We assume a two-cycle delay to wakeup a power gated physical register (the detailed wakeup power/delay overhead will presented later). It should be noted that after this wakeup delay is paid, there is no further effect on the register file access. Thus our technique has no performance penalty in this case. This can be explained as follows: the register renaming occurs in the front end of the microprocessor pipeline whereas the register access occurs in the back end. There is a delay of at least two pipeline stages between renaming and accessing a physical register file. These two cycles allow us to wake up the physical register's region without incurring any performance penalty at the time of access.

The mechanism described above can be implemented by partitioning the circular FIFO free list into multiple smaller size circular FIFOs dynamically adjusting the circular FIFO size. A design proposed in [21] can be used for this, which has no impact on queue performance. A CAM-based renamer [22] can also be similarly partitioned.

5   Experimental Setup

We used the following experimental setup for evaluating this work. We used an extensively modified version of MASE (SimpleScalar 4.0) [13] to model an architecture similar to the MIPS-74K embedded processor [14]. Table 1 describes the processor architecture in detail, which operates at 800 MHz frequency. MiBench and SPEC2K benchmarks were compiled with the O4 flag using the Compaq compiler and executed with reference data sets. The benchmarks were simulated for 1 billion instructions or until completion.

Table 1. Processor Architecture

L1 I-cache	8KB, ,4 way, 2 cycles
L1 D-cache	8KB, 4 way, 2 cycles
L2-cache	128KB, 15 cycles
Fetch, dispatch	2 wide
Register file	64 entry
Memory	50 cycles
Instruction fetch queue	2
Load/store queue	16 entry
Arithmetic units	2 integer
Complex unit	2 INT
Pipeline	12 stages
Processor speed	800 MHz
Issue	Out-of-order

Table 2. RF Design specification

Process	45nm-CMOS 9 metal layers	Register file layout area	0.009mm^2
Operating Modes	Active:R/W Sleep: no data retention	Operating Voltage	0.6V~1.1V
Read Access Cycle	200MHz to 1.1GHz	Access time typical corner (0.9V, 45°)	0.32ns
Active Power (Total) in typical corner (0.9V, 45°)	66mW @ 800MHz	Active Leakage Power typical corner (0.9V, 45°)	15mW
Sleep Leakage Power in typical corner (0.9V, 45°)	2mW	Wakeup Delay	0.42ns
Wakeup Energy per register file row (64bits)	0.42nJ		

To accurately model the register file, an industrial memory compiler was used to generate a dual read and single write port, 64-entry, 64bit single-ended SRAM memory in TSMC 45nm technology. The design including the wordline drivers, the wordline pulse generator circuit, the memory bit-cells and the output drivers is then scaled to model a 4-read, 2-write port SRAM. The register file operates in two modes: an active mode where it can be accessed, and a deep sleep mode where it does not keep the bit-cell data and can not be accessed. Table 2 shows the design specification of this 6-port 64x64 bits SRAM memory. All measurements are done using Spice simulation. The register file access time is 0.32 ns for a typical corner (0.9V and 45°C). The total power in typical corner is 66mw while the active leakage power is 15mw (for the entire register file). The deep sleep data-destructive state leakage is 2mw, almost 86% lower than the active leakage.

The power and delay overhead of transition from low leakage sleep mode to active mode are presented in Table 2. The area overhead for implementing the power gating technique is fairly small, almost 1% of the RF size (using one sleep transistor per register file entry). Total dynamic power of the register file was computed as N*Eaccess/Texec, where N is the total number of accesses (obtained from simulation) and Eaccess is the single-access energy (from Table 2). Leakage power computations are similar, but leakage energy is dissipated on every cycle. If the RF entry is put into sleep mode the sleep leakage power is dissipated, otherwise the active leakage power is dissipated. We used HotSpot [15] to estimate thermal profiles for the register file. We integrated HotSpot into our simulator. The temperature trace is obtained every 10K cycles. Once the temperature is calculated it is reported back to the simulator for the next interval leakage power computation. Since the leakage power is a function of temperature, the power simulator includes a lookup table for leakage power dissipation as a function of temperature in the range from 45°C to 120°C in increments of 5°C.

6 Experimental Results

Figure 7 shows the average register file power reduction over the course of execution of different benchmarks as a result of applying RELOCATE and for different number of RF partitions. We used the experimental setup described in Section 5. We observe that on average there is a reduction of 15% and 25% in the total power of MiBench and SPEC2K benchmarks, respectively. We also observe that many benchmarks, such as patricia (MiBench), eon and vortex (SPEC2K) have a power reduction of about 40%. However, it should be noted that the goal of our work is to reduce the peak temperature of the register file. Usually, the peak temperature is attained as a result of sustained peak power dissipation over a period of time. A workload can have a low overall average power but a very high peak temperature or vice versa due to variation in activity levels. The reduction in the average power does not have a direct correlation with the reduction in the peak temperature of register file. Overall, increasing the number of RF partitions provides more opportunity to capture and cluster unmapped registers to a partition, indicating that the wakeup overhead is amortized for larger number of partitions. There are some benchmarks (highlighted in Figure 7) in which increasing the number of partitions results in smaller power

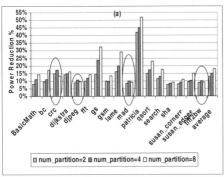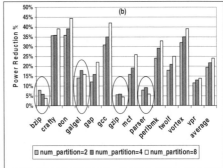

Fig. 7. Register file power reduction for (a) MiBench and (b) SPEC2K integer benchmark

Table 3. Peak temperature reduction for MiBench benchmarks

	base temperature (C°)	temperature reduction for different number of partition (C°)		
		2P	4P	8P
basicMath	94.3	3.6	4.8	5.0
bc	95.4	3.8	4.4	5.2
crc	92.8	5.3	6.0	6.0
dijkstra	98.4	6.3	6.8	6.4
djpeg	96.3	2.8	3.5	2.4
fft	94.5	6.8	7.4	7.6
gs	89.8	6.5	7.4	9.7
gsm	92.3	5.8	6.7	6.9
lame	90.6	6.2	8.5	11.3
mad	93.3	3.8	4.3	2.2
patricia	79.2	11.0	12.4	13.2
qsort	88.3	10.1	11.6	11.9
search	93.8	8.7	9.3	9.1
sha	90.1	5.1	5.4	4.5
susan_corners	92.7	4.7	5.3	5.1
susan_edges	91.9	3.7	5.8	6.3
tiff2bw	98.5	4.5	5.9	4.1
average	92.5	5.6	6.8	6.9

Table 4. Peak temperature reduction for SPEC2K integer benchmarks

	base temperature (C°)	temperature reduction for different number of partition (C°)		
		2P	4P	8P
bzip2	92.7	4.8	3.9	3.1
crafty	83.6	9.5	11	10.4
eon	77.3	10.6	12.4	12.5
galgel	89.4	6.9	7.2	5.8
gap	86.7	4.8	5.9	7.1
gcc	79.8	7.9	9.4	10.1
gzip	95.4	3.2	3.8	3.9
mcf	85.8	6.9	8.7	9.4
parser	97.8	4.3	5.8	4.8
perlbmk	85.8	10.6	12.3	12.6
twolf	86.2	8.8	10.2	10.5
vortex	81.7	11.3	12.5	12.9
vpr	94.6	4.9	5.2	4.4
average	87.4	7.2	8.3	8.2

reduction. In fact in these benchmarks the overall power overhead associated with waking up an idle region is become larger as the number of partition increases. This is in fact due to frequent but ineffective power gating and its overhead as the number of partition increases. Table 3 and Table 4 show the peak temperature reduction result.

We observe that benchmarks from both MiBench and Spec2K show a noticeable reduction in the register file's peak temperature. While increasing the number of partitions in all benchmarks provides more opportunity to capture and cluster unmapped registers, it does not always result in additional temperature reduction. This is especially noticeable in djpeg, mad and tiff2wb (MiBench) and galgel and parser (SPEC2K). In these cases increasing the number of partitions results in larger power density in each partition because RF access activity is concentrated in a smaller partition. While capturing more idle partitions and power gating them *may potentially* result in higher power reduction, larger power density due to smaller partition size results in overall higher temperature. The average reduction in the register file's peak temperature across all the benchmarks is 6.9 °C for MiBench benchmark and 8.2 °C for SPEC2K benchmark. This is very significant in light of the fact that the register file is the hottest block in an embedded processor. The peak temperature of register file determines the design temperature for which the embedded system is designed. Thus the proposed technique can reduce the design temperature by 8°C.

6.1 Additional Benefits of Temperature Reduction

Let us try to quantify the design gains as a result of reduction in the design temperature by 8°C:

(i) The Mean Time To Failure (MTTF) of an electrical interconnect depends on temperature because of electromigration. Depending on the base temperature, a 8°C decrease in the operating temperature can increase the MTTF of an interconnect by up to 2 years.

(ii) A reduction of 8°C in the design temperature means a lower switching delay of transistors. The rated frequency of the design is increased. Based on [20] we estimate that at 45nm technology, a circuit's rated frequency can be increased from 800 MHz to 880 MHz because of the 8°C reduction in peak operating temperature.

(iii) The leakage power has a super linear dependency on temperature. Depending on the process parameters, the leakage power of a cell can be lower by as much as 18% as a result of lowering of temperature by 8°C.

A 8°C reduction also delivers additional power savings since the fan can be run slower by reducing its duty cycle. However, these are difficult to estimate.

7 Related Work

Processor thermal characteristics at the architectural level have been studied extensively in recent years [15].

Several techniques have been proposed to reduce chip temperature. Many of these techniques are reactive in nature in response to a thermal emergency detected by temperature sensors. These techniques either migrate the processor activity [16] or adapt processor resources to reduce temperature [15]. Brooks et al. [3] introduced dynamic thermal management (DTM) in reaction to thermal measurements. They applied techniques such as stalling execution or migrating activity to reduce temperature. Among DTM techniques, clock gating was shown to be effective in reducing temperature across the chip in response to a thermal emergency. This technique has been used in many processors including Intel's Pentium M [25].

Leveraging the redundancy in a processor pipeline, several techniques have been proposed for temperature reduction. In [15] the power density is controlled by balancing the utilization of register file, issue queues, and functional units. Fetch throttling was also shown to be effective in reducing the temperature [15].

Dynamic voltage and frequency scaling in response to thermal emergency has been studied in [15, 24]. Temperature-aware task scheduling has been investigated at both architectural level and operating system levels for multiprocessors [11]. Ku et al. [23] proposed techniques for reducing cache temperature through power density minimization. They introduced a cache block permutation to maximize the distance between blocks with consecutive addresses. Several thermal management techniques for multi-core architectures are explored in [27]. Various core throttling policies were applied at core and processor level for chip thermal management. Heo et al. [16] have introduced a power density minimization through computational activity migration. They applied this technique to many processor blocks including the register file. This technique is effective, but incurs into a large area overhead since it requires replicating processor blocks.

Many recent works have focused mainly on reducing the power density and peak temperature of a processor. They specifically target the register file as it has been shown to be one of the hottest units in a processor [1, 15, 17, 19]. Previous work on the register file's power has mainly attempted to reduce the number of access to the register file, reduce the number of ports [10], or reduce the number of entries [8,9]. The algorithm we proposed in this work can be combined with these algorithms for further power and a potentially larger temperature reduction. Replication or banking register file has been studied in [2, 4, 12, 16,17, 26]. This work does not rely on either register file replication or banking, and as a result no significant area overhead is incurred except for region power down. However the benefit of our proposed approach can be improved in presence of replicated register file. Register assignment algorithm for low-power, low temperature VLIW register files were also introduced in [7]. These algorithms are applied at compiler level to an architecture where no renaming exists.

8   Conclusion

The register file is the most active and the hottest unit in an embedded processor. In this paper we proposed RELOCATE, an architectural solution to reduce the peak temperature of the register file. We analyzed the register file accesses and observed that while only a small number of physical registers are occupied at any given time, the total accesses are uniformly distributed over the entire physical register file during the course of execution. Our solution redistributes the access pattern to physical registers through a novel register allocation mechanism. We regionalize the register file such that even though accesses within a region are uniformly distributed, the activity levels are spread over the entire register file in a deterministic pattern. This allows us to power gate the unused regions of the register file. This resulted in a reduction of an average of 8.3°C in register file's peak temperature for standard benchmarks.

References

1. Mesa-Martinez, F.J., Nayfach-Battilana, J., Renau, J.: Power model validation through thermal measurements. In: International Symposium on Computer Architecture (2007)
2. Homayoun, H., Pasricha, S., Makhzan, M.A., Veidenbaum, A.: Dynamic register file resizing and frequency scaling to improve embedded processor performance and energy-delay efficiency. In: Design Automation Conference (2008)
3. Brooks, D., Martonosi, M.: Dynamic thermal management for high-performance microprocessors. In: High-Performance Computer Architecture (2001)
4. Tseng, J.H., Asanović, K.: Banked Multiported Register Files for High-Frequency Superscalar Microprocessors. In: International Symposium on Computer Architecture (2003)
5. Kessler, R.: The Alpha 21264 Microprocessor. IEEE Micro (March/April 1999)
6. Yeager, K.: The MIPS R10000 Superscalar Microprocessor. IEEE Micro (April 1996)
7. Zhou, X., Yu, C., Petrov, P.: Compiler-driven register re-assignment for register file power-density and temperature reduction. In: Design Automation Conference (2008)
8. Balasubramanian, R., Dwarkadas, S., Albonesi, D.H.: Reducing the complexity of the register file in dynamic superscalar processors. Micro (2001)
9. Borch, E., Tune, E., Manne, S., Emer, J.: Loose loops sink chips. In: HPCA (2002)
10. Park, I., Powell, M.D., Vijaykumar, T.N.: Reducing register ports for higher speed and lower energy. In: International Symposium on Microarchitecture (2002)
11. Murali, S., Mutapcic, A., Atienza, D., Gupta, R., Boyd, S., Benini, L., Micheli, G.D.: Temperature control of high-performance multicore platforms using convex optimization. In: Design, Automation and Test in Europe (2008)
12. Chaparro, P., Magklis, G., Gonzalez, J., Gonzalez, A.: Distributing the Frontend for Temperature Reduction. In: High-Performance Computer Architecture (2005)
13. SimpleScalar4 tutorial, SimpleScalar LLC,
    http://www.simplescalar.com/tutorial.html
14. MIPS Technologies MIPS32® 74K^{TM} Licensable Processor Core,
    http://www.mips.com/media/files/74k/FINAL_BDTI_MIPS_74k.pdf
15. Skadron, K., Stan, M.R., Huang, W., Velusamy, S., Sankaranarayanan, K., Tarjan, D.: Temperature-aware microarchitecture. In: ISCA 2003 (2003)
16. Heo, S., Barr, K., Asanović, K.: Reducing Power Density through Activity Migration. In: International Symposium on Low Power Electronics and Design (2003)
17. Patel, K., Lee, W., Pedram, M.: Active Bank Switching for Temperature Control of the Register File. In: GLSVLSI 2007 (2007)
18. Powell, M., Yang, S., Falsafi, B., Roy, K., Vijaykumar, T.N.: Gated Vdd: A circuit technique to reduce leakage in deep-submicron cache memories. In: International Symposium on Low Power Electronics and Design (2000)
19. Han, Y., Koren, I., Moritz, C.A.: Temperature Aware Floorplanning. In: Workshop on Temperature Aware Computer Systems (June 2005)
20. Kumar, R., Kursun, V.: Impact of temperature fluctuations on circuit characteristics in 180 nm and 65nm CMOS technologies. In: International Symposium on Circuits and Systems 2006 (2006)
21. Dynamically adjustable load-sharing circular queues, US patent 6782461
22. Buti, T.N., McDonald, R.G., Khwaja, Z., Amdedkar, A., Le, H.Q., Burky, W.E., Williams, B.: Organization and implementation of the register-renaming mapper for out-of-order IBM POWER4 processors. IBM Journal of Research and Development (2005)

23. Ku, J.C., Ozdemir, S., Memik, G., Ismail, Y.: Thermal Management of On-Chip Caches Through Power Density Minimization. In: International Symposium on Microarchitecture 2005 (2005)
24. Donald, J., Martonosi, M.: Techniques for multicore thermal management: Classification and new exploration. In: International Symposium on Computer Architecture (2006)
25. Rotem, E., Naveh, A., Moffie, M., Mendelson, A.: Analysis of Thermal Monitor Features of the Intel Pentium M Processor. In: TACS Workshop at ISCA-31 (June 2004)
26. Homayoun, H., Pasricha, S., Makhzan, M.A., Veidenbaum, A.V.: Improving performance and reducing energy-delay with adaptive resource resizing for out-of-order embedded processors. In: Conference on Languages, Compilers and Tools for Embedded Systems (2008)
27. Donald, J., Martonosi, M.: Leveraging simultaneous multithreading for adaptive thermal control. In: Second Workshop on Temperature-Aware Computer Systems (2005)

Performance and Power Aware CMP Thread Allocation Modeling

Yaniv Ben-Itzhak, Israel Cidon, and Avinoam Kolodny

Electrical Engineering Department, Technion, Haifa, Israel
yanivbi@tx.technion.ac.il, {cidon,kolodny}@ee.technion.ac.il

Abstract. We address the problem of performance and power-efficient thread allocation in a CMP. To that end, based on analytical model, we introduce a parameterized performance/power metric that can be adjusted according to a preferred tradeoff between performance and power. We introduce an iterative threshold algorithm (ITA) for allocating threads to cores in the case of a single application with symmetric threads. We extend this to a simple and efficient heuristic for the case of multiple applications. We compare the performance/power metric value of ITA with constrained nonlinear optimization, pattern search algorithm and genetic algorithm. ITA outperforms the best of these methods by 9%, while consuming on average 0.01% and at most 2.5% of the computational effort.

Keywords: thread allocation algorithm, performance power metric, Chip Multi-Processor, CMP, coarse grain multi-threading, many core.

1 Introduction

The inherent scalability limitations of a single processor design combined with the advancement of VLSI technology drove the introduction of chip multi-processors (CMP). CMPs promise higher power efficiency, better performance and lower design complexity. However, CMP architectures introduce new challenges associated with thread level parallelism [1],[2]. Today's CMPs carry parallelism beyond the traditional super-computing markets to notebooks, PDAs and other mobile devices running a mix of applications and involving complex energy saving requirements.

In this paper, we address the problem of efficient allocation of applications and threads to cores in a CMP, taking into account the desired tradeoff between performance and power, unlike works which are limited to performance [5]-[7] or power [8].

Our system includes a number of cores with a shared cache interconnected by a network on chip (NoC) [2] (e.g., Piranha [3] and Nahalal [4]). The CMP executes multiple multi-threaded applications and its cores perform coarse-grain multithreading. For reducing power consumption, unused cores are shut down. Varying conditions and battery levels may dynamically change the preferred balance between performance and power and dictate changing targets for the threads allocation solution.

Y.N. Patt et al. (Eds.): HiPEAC 2010, LNCS 5952, pp. 232–246, 2010.

To maximize the performance threads should be spread over many cores, which in turn increases power consumption. On the other hand, running all threads in a single core minimizes the power (since other cores are shut-down), but greatly impairs the performance. Our algorithm for thread allocation utilizes the CMP resources in a way that maximizes a performance/power metric that can be adjusted according to the preferred balance between performance and power.

Fig. 1 presents a 9-cores CMP example (each core includes a private first-level cache), connected by a NoC to a shared second-level cache. The CMP concurrently executes four multi-threaded applications that need to be allocated to single-pipe coarse-grain multi-threaded cores. Naturally, only a single thread can run at each core at a given time. We assume that such a thread runs until it incurs a miss in its private cache and then waits for the shared cache response. At that time, the core may perform context switching to another ready thread (i.e., a thread that already received its response from the shared cache). It is clear that the shared cache response time has a major effect on the thread performance. The response time is the sum of the shared cache access time and the NoC latency, which depends on the distance between the corresponding core and the shared cache. Therefore, both the number of threads allocated to each core and the location of these cores in respect to the shared cache are important for the system performance.

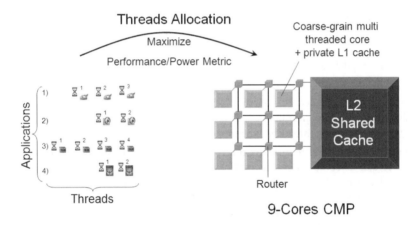

Fig. 1. Example of the thread allocation problem

Our goal is to find a thread allocation that maximizes a given performance/power metric. Our performance model considers both communication delays between the cores and the shared cache, and the core performance dependence on the number of the threads it executes. Our power model considers both active and idle power of the cores. Based on these models, a parameterized performance/power metric is defined, which can be adjusted to the relative importance of performance versus power consumption. We introduce an Iterative Threshold based thread allocation Algorithm (ITA) that maximizes the performance/power metric for the case of a single application with symmetric threads and is extended for the case of multiple applications. ITA achieves better and faster results than standard optimization algorithms.

Previous works have addressed somewhat related problems: [9] proposed thread allocation that maximizes a performance/power metric while considering process variations in the cores. However, their model is restricted to a single thread in each core while our work deals with multi-threaded cores. Furthermore, unlike [9], our work deals with shared memory architecture and considers the cache miss rate. [10] introduced performance and power aware thread allocation for NoC-based CMP, which attempts to optimize a "locality metric" of data accesses. In contrast, our work uses explicit power and performance models, and introduces an adjustable metric for thread allocation according to the relative importance of performance versus power.

The rest of this paper is structured as follows: Section 2 presents the performance and power models and the performance/power metric. Section 3 introduces the *single application problem* and the iterative algorithm for thread allocation and extends the problem into the *multiple applications problem*. Section 4 presents numerical results for both problems and demonstrate the efficiency of the algorithm for the case of multiple applications relative to several standard optimization algorithms. Section 5 concludes the paper.

2   Power and Performance Models

[13] proposed a coarse-grain multi-threaded core model which we extend for our analysis. We define $n^{(c)}$ as the number of threads executed by a multi-threaded core c with a first-level private cache and assume that all threads are independent of each other. We define δ_j as the average number of core cycles between private cache misses for thread j, i.e., $\delta_j = 1/(r_{m,j} \cdot \text{m.r}_j)$, where $r_{m,j}$ is the ratio of memory access instructions out of the total instruction mix and m.r_j is the cache miss rate for thread j. Also, we define $T^{(c)}$ as the cycles of core c required to satisfy such a request from the shared cache. For simplicity, at this point, we assume that $T^{(c)}$ is fixed for all threads. On average, thread j executes instructions for δ_j cycles until it incurs a private cache miss, and then waits for $T^{(c)}$ cycles for the miss request to be satisfied before it can execute more instructions. For simplicity, we assume that context switches happen only at private cache misses and ignore the thread-switching cycles and their associated power.

Generally, as the number of threads allocated over a core increases their miss rates also increase due to the sharing effect. In this paper, for the sake of simplicity, we assume that sharing does not affect the miss rates of the threads. This assumption is reasonable in cases where the entire footprints of the threads are located on the private cache and thus hold for a relatively small number of threads per core. In order to quantify the validity range of this assumption, for each of the benchmarks presented in [16] we simulated a single thread, measured its miss rate versus cache size by *PIN tool* and obtained its footprint size. Our results show that *blackscholes* has footprint of 3kB, *fluidanimate* 7kB and *freqmine* 8kB. Therefore, such benchmarks satisfy our assumption. Future work will address the case where the cache sharing effect cannot be ignored.

Coarse-grain multi-threaded cores utilize cache access time by running other threads. Fig. 2(b) shows that while thread 1 is waiting for its cache response, other $(n^{(c)}\text{-}1)$ threads are executed, and the total idle period decreases compared to Fig. 2(a).

Fig. 2(c) presents the case where thread 1 cannot be executed immediately when its cache response arrives, because the other $(m^{(c)}-1)$ threads didn't finish their execution. This case is denoted as *saturation* of the core.

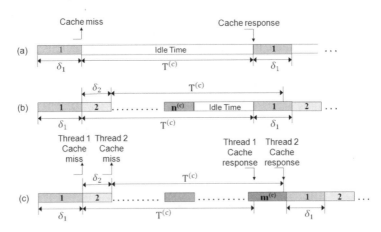

Fig. 2. A single threaded core (a) vs. multi threaded core (b,c). Saturation of the core(c).

[13] assumes that all threads are symmetric (i.e., all threads have the same fixed number of cycles between private cache misses). In this paper, we extended the model for asymmetric threads. Under the assumption that a context switch happens only at private cache misses, when threads with different cache miss rates run in a multi-threaded core, a cache response may arrive while another thread is running and waits for its execution until the core becomes available. Assuming that thread 1 has the largest value δ_1 among all threads, we prove in [17] that the execution order of the threads eventually reach a periodic steady state, in which thread 1 runs first and all the other threads run after it with no gaps (see Fig. 3(a)). In the steady state, if the core is not saturated, then thread 1 runs immediately after its cache response arrives, and any other thread has to wait for its execution although its cache response has already arrived.

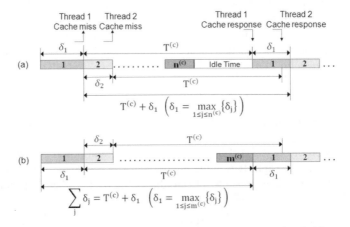

Fig. 3. (a) Steady state and the period time, (b) *saturation threshold* case

We define $\Delta^{(c)} \triangleq \max_{1 \leq j \leq n^{(c)}}\{\delta_j\}$, as the largest value of δ_j among all threads which are executed by core c. Therefore, in the unsaturated steady state, the time between executions of any thread j is $T^{(c)} + \Delta^{(c)}$. Core saturation happens when thread 1 has to wait for execution after its cache response arrives. Therefore, *saturation threshold* is defined as $th_{sat}^{(c)} \triangleq T^{(c)} + \Delta^{(c)}$. Fig. 3(b) presents the *saturation threshold* case. In saturation, the time between executions of thread j is $\sum_j(\delta_j)$, and it exceeds $th_{sat}^{(c)}$.

We define the performance of thread j in core c as the percentage of time the thread is executed and the utilization of core c, $\eta^{(c)}$, as the busy time percentage of the core.

$$\text{Thread}_j \text{Performane}^{(c)} = \begin{cases} \dfrac{\delta_j}{th_{sat}^{(c)}} & ; \sum_k \delta_k \leq th_{sat}^{(c)} \\ \dfrac{\delta_j}{\sum_k \delta_k} & ; \sum_k \delta_k > th_{sat}^{(c)} \end{cases}. \tag{1}$$

$$\eta^{(c)} = \begin{cases} \dfrac{\sum_k \delta_k}{th_{sat}^{(c)}} & ; \sum_k \delta_k \leq th_{sat}^{(c)} \\ 1 & ; \sum_k \delta_k > th_{sat}^{(c)} \end{cases}. \tag{2}$$

The power consumption of core c depends on its utilization, such as:

$$\text{CorePower}^{(c)} = \begin{cases} \eta^{(c)} P_{active} + (1 - \eta^{(c)}) P_{idle} & ; 0 < \eta^{(c)} \leq 1 \\ 0 & ; \eta^{(c)} = 0 \end{cases}. \tag{3}$$

P_{active} is the power consumption of a fully utilized core. In our model we also take into account a possibly lower idle power consumption, P_{idle}, that may results from power saving mechanisms in the processor during the idle time, such as clock gating [14]. We assume that when the core has no active threads (i.e., its utilization equals zero) it is shut down so its power consumption becomes zero. Therefore, the thread allocation algorithm should shut down as many cores as possible and properly utilizing all other cores in order to maximize the performance/power metric.

Our example for a NoC based CMP is depicted in Fig. 1. The system has several cores with different distances from the shared cache. The distance from a core to the shared cache affects the value of $T^{(c)}$, the number of cycles required to obtain a response from the shared cache. Assuming that each hop has a constant latency denoted by τ, we get:

$$T^{(c)} = T_{cache} + h^{(c)}\tau \Rightarrow th_{sat}^{(c)} \triangleq T^{(c)} + \Delta^{(c)} = T_{cache} + h^{(c)}\tau + \Delta^{(c)}. \tag{4}$$

Where, $h^{(c)}$ is the number of NoC hops from core c to the shared cache and T_{cache} is the shared cache latency.

Our definition of the tradeoff between performance and power follows definitions used in logic circuit design. If E is the energy and t is the delay, [11] introduces the $E \cdot t$ and $E \cdot t^2$ metrics, extended by [12] to the metric $E \cdot t^\alpha$, where α becomes larger as the performance becomes more important.

The general performance/power ratio metric is: $\left(\dfrac{\text{Average Performance}^\alpha}{\text{Consumed Power}^\beta}\right)$.

Given a CMP with M cores and N threads, our goal is to find the optimal threads allocations which allocate each thread j to core c such that the performance/power metric is maximized. It can be easily shown that if $\beta > \alpha$, the optimal allocation is to allocate all threads in a single core. Therefore, similar to [12], we use $\beta = 1$ and $\alpha \geq 1$, α is made larger as the performance becomes more significant. Consequently, $PPM \triangleq \left(\frac{\text{Average Performance}^{\alpha}}{\text{Consumed Power}}\right)$. PPM stands for Performance Power Metric.

3 Problems Statements and Allocation Algorithms

3.1 The Single Application Problem

Given: A CMP with M identical cores and a shared-cache, which executes an application with N symmetric threads$(\delta_j = \delta, \forall j)$. $h^{(c)}$ is the hop distance between core c and the shared cache. α – represents the relative importance of performance compared to power consumption (as the performance is more important as a becomes larger)

Find: Optimal thread allocation, $n^{(c)}$ the number of threads are executed by core c.

Which: maximizes $PPM = \left(\frac{\text{Average Performance}^{\alpha}}{\text{Consumed Power}}\right)$.

Subject to: $\sum_{c=1}^{M} n^{(c)} = N, n^{(c)} \geq 0$.

Where: $\alpha \geq 1$

$$\text{Average Performance} = \sum_{c=1}^{M} \left(\frac{n^{(c)} \cdot \text{Thread Performance}^{(c)}}{N}\right).$$

(Thread Performance$^{(c)}$ is defined by equation (6))

$$\text{Consumed Power} = \sum_{c:n^{(c)} \neq 0} \left(\eta^{(c)} \cdot P_{active}\right) + \left(1 - \eta^{(c)}\right) \cdot P_{idle}.$$

($\eta^{(c)}$ is defined by equation (7))

With the assumptions above, the *saturation threshold* of core c, $th_{sat}^{(c)}$, and the performance of each thread j running in core c can be written as:

$$th_{sat}^{(c)} = T_{cache} + h^{(c)}\tau + \delta. \tag{5}$$

$$\text{Thread Performane}^{(c)} = \begin{cases} \frac{\delta}{th_{sat}^{(c)}} & ; n^{(c)} \leq \frac{th_{sat}^{(c)}}{\delta} \\ \frac{\delta}{n^{(c)}\delta} & ; n^{(c)} > \frac{th_{sat}^{(c)}}{\delta} \end{cases}. \tag{6}$$

Where $n^{(c)}$ indicates the number of threads executed by core c.

When $n^{(c)} < \frac{th_{sat}^{(c)}}{\delta}$, the core can execute more threads without performance reduction.

When $n^{(c)} \geq \frac{th_{sat}^{(c)}}{\delta}$, the core is saturated and achieves its maximum total performance.

The core utilization $\eta^{(c)}$ is calculated by:

$$\eta^{(c)} = \begin{cases} \dfrac{n^{(c)}\delta}{th_{sat}^{(c)}} & ; n^{(c)} \leq \dfrac{th_{sat}^{(c)}}{\delta} \\ 1 & ; n^{(c)} > \dfrac{th_{sat}^{(c)}}{\delta} \end{cases} . \tag{7}$$

In the following we develop an efficient algorithm for the *single application problem* termed Iterative Threshold Algorithm (ITA). ITA computes the (discrete) number of threads that are executed by each core.

First, we assume that $n^{(c)}$ is a continuous variable. While this formulation is not realistic, as threads cannot be split, it leads to a good approximation for a large numbers of threads. This continuous version is entitled Continuous ITA (CITA). CITA results should be discretized in order to get the ITA results.

We define a Distance Core Cluster (in short, a cluster) of distance d, noted as Ω_d, to be the group of all cores located d hops from the shared cache $\left(. \text{i.e., } \Omega_d = \{c | h^{(c)} = d\} \right)$. The number of cores in Ω_d is $|\Omega_d|$. The algorithm starts to allocate threads in cores that belong to the closest cluster (i.e., smallest d) and continues to allocate threads to the closest unallocated clusters till the last iteration. In each iteration, the algorithm allocates threads to a core only if its final utilization exceeds a minimum utilization value termed MU.

The need for such a minimum utilization value stems from the following reason: When a core is brought into operation it causes a minimal increase of P_{idle} in the power consumption (see equation (3)) that results in a reduction of the PPM. Therefore, in order to justify this new core operation, an appropriate minimal increase in the performance metric is required. In order to compute MU, we compare the PPM value of two cases. The two cases are either m over-saturated cores or m saturated cores in exactly the *saturation threshold* and the $(m+1)$th core utilization equals MU.

This results in the following equation:

$$\underbrace{\frac{\left(\frac{m}{\text{Amount of Threads}}\right)^{\alpha}}{m \cdot P_{active}}}_{\text{PPM of the first case}} = \underbrace{\frac{\left(\frac{m+\text{MU}}{\text{Amount of Threads}}\right)^{\alpha}}{m \cdot P_{active}+(P_{active}-P_{idle})\cdot \text{MU}+P_{idle}}}_{\text{PPM of the second case}} . \tag{8}$$

$$\Rightarrow \text{MU} = \left(\frac{1}{P_{active}-P_{idle}}\right) \cdot \left[P_{active}\left(\frac{m(m+\text{MU})^{\alpha}}{m^{\alpha}} - m\right) - P_{idle} \right] . \tag{9}$$

Using Taylor series approximation, we get:

$$(m + \text{MU})^{\alpha} \approx m^{\alpha} + \alpha m^{\alpha-1}\text{MU} + O(\text{MU}^2) , \text{ and finally:}$$

$$\text{MU} \approx \frac{P_{idle}}{(\alpha-1)P_{active}+P_{idle}} . \tag{10}$$

Fig. 4 presents the PPM of the two cases in a CMP with two cores (c and c') and symmetric threads. The steep drop in the value of PPM for $th_{sat}^{(c)}/\delta$ threads in the 2nd case is due to the increase of power by P_{idle} (i.e. turning on the second core). When the second core utilization equals MU, the PPM values for the two cases are equal. Therefore, the second core is brought to operation only if its utilization exceeds MU.

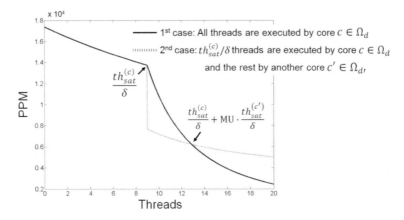

Fig. 4. PPM for the 2 cases using two cores

Generally, MU depends on m, the number of already operating cores, (equation (9)) however the value of MU varies by no more than 8% as m increases. Therefore, the approximated MU of equation (10) is sufficient and offers a fast calculation alternative for decreasing the allocation algorithm overhead. As α increases, the weight of the performance metric increases that in turn decreases the value of MU. This means that the algorithm brings cores into operation at a lower utilization and therefore increases the performance at the expense of increasing the power.

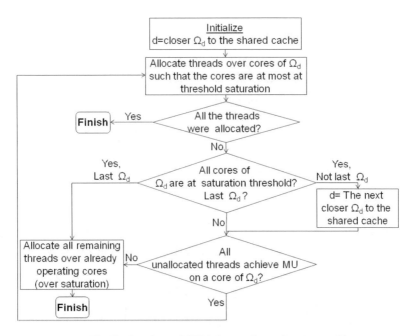

Fig. 5. Flowchart of CITA for *single application problem*

Fig. 5 depicts a flowchart of CITA for the *single application problem*. The concept of CITA is to allocate threads a cluster by cluster, starting from the cluster which is closest to the cache. Within each cluster CITA allocates threads to each core up to the threshold saturation of the cores. Once a core is saturated, another core is assigned only if its utilization would be at least MU. If it does not hold, the remaining threads may be allocated to any of the operating cores .A pseudo code is presented in [17].

3.2 The Multiple Applications Problem

Given: A CMP with M cores and a shared-cache, which execute P multi-threaded applications with N_i $(1 \leq i \leq P)$ symmetric threads in each application, respectively (i.e., the threads of application i have a constant number of cycles between private cache misses, δ_i). The hop distance between core c and the shared cache is $h^{(c)}$. As before, α represents the relative importance of performance compared to power consumption, and α is made larger as the performance becomes more significant.

Find: Optimal allocation of threads to cores, $n_i^{(c)}$ the number of threads of application i are executed by core c.

Which: maximizes PPM $= \left(\dfrac{\text{Average Performance}^\alpha}{\text{Consumed Power}}\right)$.

Subject to: $\sum_{c=1}^{M} n_i^{(c)} = N_i$, $n_i^{(c)} \geq 0$; $1 \leq c \leq M$, $1 \leq i \leq P$.

Where: $\alpha \geq 1$

$$\text{Average Performance} = \frac{\sum_{i=1}^{P}\sum_{c=1}^{M}\left(n_i^{(c)} \cdot \text{Thread}_i\text{Performance}^{(c)}\right)}{\sum_{i=1}^{P} N_i}.$$

(Thread$_i$Performance$^{(c)}$ is defined by equation (12))

$$\text{Consumed Power} = \sum_{c:\sum_{i=1}^{P} n_i^{(c)} \neq 0}\left(\eta^{(c)} \cdot P_{active}\right) + \left(1 - \eta^{(c)}\right) \cdot P_{idle}.$$

($\eta^{(c)}$ is defined by equation (13))

The *saturation threshold*, thread performance and utilization for each core c in this case are:

$$th_{sat}^{(c)} = T_{cache} + h^{(c)}\tau + \max_j\left\{\delta_j | n_j^{(c)} \neq 0\right\}. \tag{11}$$

$$\text{Thread}_i\text{Performane}^{(c)} = \begin{cases} \dfrac{\delta_i}{th_{sat}^{(c)}} & ;\sum_{j=1}^{P}\left(n_j^{(c)}\delta_j\right) \leq th_{sat}^{(c)} \\ \dfrac{\delta_i}{n^{(c)}.\delta} & ;\sum_{j=1}^{P}\left(n_j^{(c)}\delta_j\right) > th_{sat}^{(c)} \end{cases}. \tag{12}$$

$$\eta^{(c)} = \begin{cases} \dfrac{\sum_{j=1}^{P} n_j^{(c)}\delta_j}{th_{sat}^{(c)}} & ;\sum_{j=1}^{P}\left(n_j^{(c)}\delta_j\right) \leq th_{sat}^{(c)} \\ 1 & ;\sum_{j=1}^{P}\left(n_j^{(c)}\delta_j\right) > th_{sat}^{(c)} \end{cases}. \tag{13}$$

As in the single application case, we first use the continuous thread allocation approximation. We calculate the minimum utilization required in order to justify operation of a core, MU, in a similar way as in the *single application problem* (section 3.1).

Unlike CITA for a single application, which is based on the fact that $th_{sat}^{(c)}$ is the same for all cores $c \in \Omega_d$, in the multiple-application problem, $th_{sat}^{(c)}$ depend both on the hop distance to the shared cache and on the application with the lowest cache miss rate allocated in core c $\left(\max_j \{ \delta_j | n_j^{(c)} \neq 0 \}, \text{equation (11)} \right)$. Therefore, unlike the single application case, in each iteration, CITA for the *multiple applications problem* allocates threads in a single core. The solution space of the *multiple application problem* is very large and increases exponentially with M, P and N_i. It can be shown that the optimization problem is not convex.

Fig. 6 depicts a flowchart of CITA for the *multiple applications problem*. CITA concept is to allocate applications according to their cache miss rate such that applications with a high miss rate are allocated to cores which are close to the shared cache. The algorithm allocates threads a core by core, starting from the cores which are closest to the cache. Once a core is saturated, another core is assigned only if its utilization would surpass MU. A pseudo code for this procedure is presented in [17].

The rationale for allocating applications with higher miss rate closer to the shared cache is to maximize the average performance. The higher the miss rate of the threads is, the bigger is the gain in performance caused by allocating them closer to the shared cache (see equations (11)&(12)). Moreover, $th_{sat}^{(c)}$ is affected by the lowest miss rate among all threads which are executed by the core c (see equation (11)). CITA minimizes its value and thus maximizes performance by minimizing the differences of the miss rates of threads which are executed by each core.

In addition, although our model does not consider the power consumption of the NoC, this approach should minimize it as well. Threads with higher miss rate introduce higher loads to the NoC. Therefore, reducing the number of NoC hops between these threads to the shared cache minimizes the NoC power consumption.

3.3 Discretization of CITA Result

As mentioned, CITA produces a continuous $n_i^{(c)}$, which is not a final solution to our thread allocation problem, as threads cannot be split. Therefore we need to convert every allocation vector of application i, $n_i^{(c)}$, to a discrete vector. This process converts the CITA results to the ITA results. We propose an example of a method to convert the CITA results into a discrete allocation (i.e., ITA) by the following iterative discretization method, the method result example denoted by $m_i^{(c)}$.

$$\forall i: \qquad m_i^{(1)} = \text{round}\left(n_i^{(1)} \right).$$

$$m_i^{(c)} = \text{round}\left(\text{round}\left(\sum_{k=1}^{c} n_i^{(k)} \right) - \sum_{k=1}^{c-1} m_i^{(k)} \right); 2 \leq c \leq M. \tag{14}$$

The iterative algorithm above starts from the first core and in every iteration it produces the discrete value of the threads are executed by the next core, it equals to rounded value of the accumulated error between the continuous and the discrete vectors, as described in equation (14). This method is used for histogram specification [15]. Of course, there are other possible methods to convert the CITA results into the ITA results.

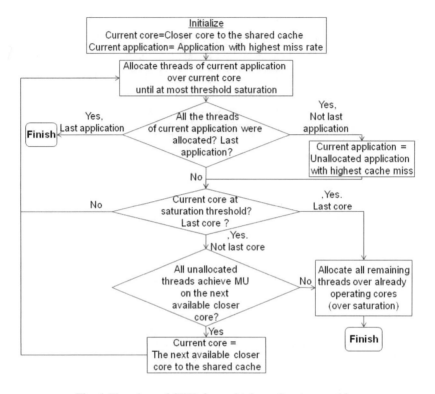

Fig. 6. Flowchart of CITA for *multiple applications problem*

4   Numerical Results

4.1   Single Application Results

Fig. 7 presents several results of CITA and ITA for different numbers of threads in a *single application problem*. The CMP in this example includes three cores with 1, 2 and 3 hop distances to the shared cache, respectively. P_{idle} and P_{active} values were selected to be in the range of PowerPC440 and MIPS power consumption specifications. It can be seen that when there are 6 or 11 threads to allocate (Fig. 7(a,c)), the CITA results do not conform to discrete values and the final results are derived by finding discrete allocations close to the CITA results. In both cases the PPM values of the discrete allocations are within 2-4% from the CITA results. The discretized results for all cases are also the optimal allocation (computed over all possible allocations). In the 9 threads case (Fig. 7(b)) the CITA, ITA and optimal results are identical. In this case although the first two cores are saturated, the third core is shut down since there are not enough

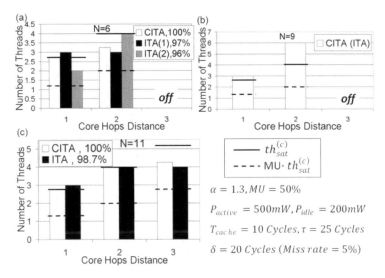

Fig. 7. Single application results example

threads to execute at least $MU \cdot th_{sat}^{(3)}/\delta$ threads by it, while the first two cores execute $th_{sat}^{(1)}/\delta$ and $th_{sat}^{(2)}/\delta$ threads respectively.

4.2 Multiple Applications Results

In order to evaluate our multiple-application solution, we compare CITA results and run-time with several general-purpose optimization algorithms. The optimization algorithms used are: a constrained nonlinear optimization, a pattern search algorithm and a genetic algorithm (all from Matlab library). The optimizations algorithms were executed for the continuous version of the problem and were not discretisized.

Fig. 8 presents the PPM ratio of CITA and the best result of the optimization algorithms, for all cases in the range of 2-8 cores and applications. Each case was simulated for 200 random instances of the problem and in each simulation the CMP and applications parameters were selected according to the distributions included in Fig. 8. On average, CITA outperforms the best optimization algorithms by 9%.

Fig. 8 also presents the average number of cores operating by CITA and by the best among the optimization algorithms for several cases. It can be seen that the PPM ratio is higher as the difference between these values is higher. This occurs as the CMP load becomes lower (i.e., there are more cores and less applications). In these cases, CITA operates significantly fewer cores in comparison to the optimization algorithms.

Fig. 9 demonstrates by an example the efficiency and the low computational overhead of CITA. For a CMP with 8 cores and 4 applications, we calculated the allocation using CITA, a constrained nonlinear optimization, a pattern search algorithm and a genetic algorithm and compared them to a naïve approach which obtains a uniform utilization of the cores. CITA achieves the highest PPM percentage improvement relative to the naïve approach, with the fastest execution time.

Fig. 9(a) presents the allocation results and cores utilizations according to the constrained nonlinear optimization and pattern search algorithm. The genetic algorithm

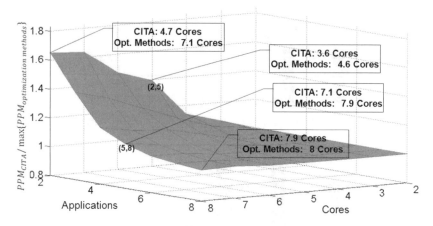

$$T_{cache} \sim U(10,30), \tau \sim U(10,40), h^{(c)} \sim U(1,8), \delta_i \sim U(1,40), N_i \sim U(1,25), \alpha \sim U(1,6)$$
$$P_{active} = 500mW, P_{idle} = 200mW$$

Fig. 8. $PPM_{CITA}/max\{PPM_{optimization\ methods}\}$

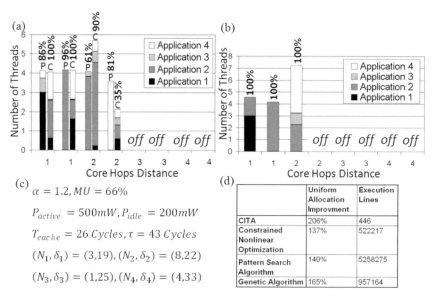

Fig. 9. (a) Legend: C- Constrained nonlinear optimization result, P- Pattern search result

allocation result allocates all applications to execute in the first core. Fig. 9(b) presents the allocation results and cores utilizations according to CITA, where application 1 which has the highest cache miss rate is allocated to the core closest to the shared cache and application 4 which has the lowest cache miss rate is allocated to the remote core. Fig. 9(d) presents the PPM improvement relative to the naïve approach, and the number of execution lines required for the allocation calculation in Matlab workspace. It can be seen that CITA achieves the highest improvement relative to the naïve approach with the lowest lines of execution.

4.3 Discretization Results

ITA results are drived by the discretization of CITA results. We use the discretization method described by equation (14). Fig. 10 presents the PPM ratio between ITA results and CITA results, for all cases in the range of 2-8 cores and 2-8 applications. Each case was simulated for 10,000 random instances of the problem and in each simulation the CMP and applications parameters were selected according to the distributions included in Fig. 8. On average, discretization of CITA results reduces the PPM value by 5%.

Fig. 11(a) and Fig. 11(b) present an example of CITA and constrained nonlinear optimization algorithm result discretization respectively. Fig. 11(d) presents the CITA improvement relative to the optimization algorithms continuous results and also the ITA improvement relative to the optimization algorithms discrete results. The relative improvement doesn`t decrement by much due to the discretization and offers a realistic and efficient thread allocation.

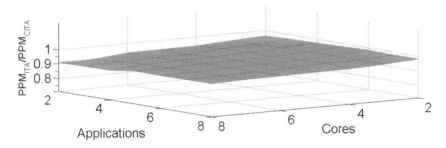

Fig. 10. PPM_{ITA}/PPM_{CITA}

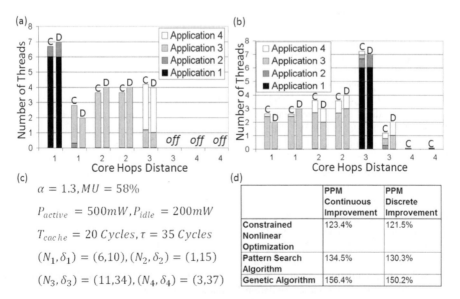

Fig. 11. Example of results discretization. Legend: C-Continuous result, D-Discretization of the continuous result.

5 Conclusions

Assignment of threads to cores in a CMP according to desired performance/power tradeoffs was accomplished by a computationally-efficient algorithm (ITA) which achieves close to optimal results. ITA is guided by the characteristics of the problem, such as core saturation threshold, core idle power, NoC hop delay, and the relative importance of performance versus power.

References

1. Olukotun, K., Hammond, L.: The future of microprocessors. Queue 3, 26–29 (2005)
2. Spracklen, L., Abraham, S.G.: Chip Multithreading: Opportunities and Challenges. In: High-Performance Computer Architecture, pp. 248–252 (2005)
3. Barroso, L.A., Gharachorloo, K., McNamara, R., Nowatzyk, A., Qadeer, S., Sano, B., Smith, S., Stets, R., Verghese, B.: Piranha: a scalable architecture based on single-chip Multiprocessing. ACM SIGARCH Computer Architecture News, 282–293 (2000)
4. Guz, Z., Keidar, I., Kolodny, A., Weiser, U.: Nahalal: Memory Organization for Chip Multiprocessors. IEEE Computer Architecture Letters 6(1) (2007)
5. McCann, C., Vaswani, R., Zahojan, J.: A dynamic processor allocation policy for multi programmed shared memory multiprocessors. ACM Transactions on Computer Systems (1993)
6. Fedorova, A., Seltzer, M., Small, C., Nussbaum, D.: Performance of multithreaded chip multiprocessors and implications for operating system design. In: USENIX 2005 Annual Technical Conference, pp. 395–398 (2005)
7. Kim, S., Chandra, D., Solihin, Y.: Fair Cache Sharing and Partitioning in a Chip Multiprocessor Architecture. In: 13th International Conference on Parallel Architecture and Compilation Techniques, pp. 111–122 (2004)
8. Yang, C., Chen, J., Kuo, T.: An Approximation Algorithm for Energy-Efficient Scheduling on A Chip Multiprocessor. IEEE Computer Society, 468–473 (2005)
9. Ding, Y., Kandemir, M., Irwin, M.J., Raghavan, P.: Adapting Application Mapping to Systematic Within-Die Process Variations on Chip Multiprocessors. LNCS, vol. 5409, pp. 231–247. Springer, Heidelberg (2009)
10. Chen, G., Li, F., Son, S.W., Kandemir, M.: Application mapping for chip Multiprocessors. In: Proceedings of the 45th Annual Design Automation Conference, pp. 620–625 (2008)
11. Burd, T., Brodersen, R.W.: Energy efficient CMOS microprocessor design. In: 28th Hawaii International Conference on System Sciences, pp. 288–297 (1995)
12. Penzes, P.I., Martin, A.J.: Energy-delay efficiency of VLSI computations. In: Proceedings of the 12th ACM Great Lakes Symposium on VLSI, pp. 104–111 (2002)
13. Agarwal, A.: Performance tradeoffs in multithreaded processors. IEEE Transactions on Parallel and Distributed Systems 3(5), 525–539 (1992)
14. Benini, L., Bogliolo, A., De Micheli, G.: A survey of design techniques for system- level dynamic power management, pp. 231–248. Kluwer Academic Publishers, Dordrecht (2002)
15. Gonzalez, C.R., Woods, R.E.: Digital image processing, 3rd edn., pp. 128–138 (2008)
16. Bienia, C., Kumar, S., Singh, J.P., Li, K.: The PARSEC benchmark suite: characterization and architectural implications. In: Proceedings of the 17th international Conference on Parallel Architectures and Compilation Techniques, pp. 72–81 (2008)
17. Ben-Itzhak, Y., Cidon, I., Kolodny, A.: Performance and Power Aware CMP Thread Allocation Modeling. Technical Report, CCIT #735 (2009)

Multi-level Hardware Prefetching Using Low Complexity Delta Correlating Prediction Tables with Partial Matching*

Marius Grannaes, Magnus Jahre, and Lasse Natvig

Norwegian University of Science and Technology

Abstract. This paper presents a low complexity table-based approach to delta correlation prefetching. Our approach uses a table indexed by the load address which stores the latest deltas observed. By storing deltas rather than full miss addresses, considerable space is saved while making pattern matching easier. The delta-history can predict repeating patterns with long periods by using delta correlation. In addition, we propose L1 hoisting which is a technique for moving data from the L2 to the L1 using the same underlying table structure and partial matching which reduces the spatial resolution in the delta stream to expose more patterns.

We evaluate our prefetching technique using the simulator framework used in the Data Prefetching Championship. This allows us to use the original code submitted to the contest to fairly evaluate several alternate prefetching techniques. Our prefetcher technique increases performance by 87% on average (6.6X max) on SPEC2006.

1   Introduction

In 2004, Gracia Perez et al. [1] published a paper that evaluated several prefetching techniques in a common framework. They found that several techniques were not as good as the original authors claimed. This discrepancy was due to researchers using different simulator infrastructure and benchmarks as well as the difficulty in implementing other techniques due to a lack of documentation. In this work, we avoid these problems by using the simulation infrastructure and original code from the first Data Prefetching Championship (DPC-1). This competition was similar to the earlier JILP Championship Branch Prediction Competition (CBP). In order to ensure a fair comparison of prefetcher performance, the organizers published a common simulator framework. Each prefetcher could use a maximum of 4KB of storage, but there was no limit on prefetcher complexity. Each contestant submitted their code to the competition for evaluation. This code was later published. This allows us to do a fair comparison with the top three DPC entries using their submitted code.

Our submission, Delta Correlating Prediction Tables (DCPT), used a table indexed by the PC of the load [2]. Each table entry stores a large amount of

---

* This work was supported by the Norwegian Metacenter for Computational Science (Notur).

Y.N. Patt et al. (Eds.): HiPEAC 2010, LNCS 5952, pp. 247–261, 2010.

history per load instruction in the form of deltas. By storing deltas rather than full miss addresses, we save a significant amount of memory and make pattern matching easier. Pattern matching is done by using Delta Correlation, originally proposed by Nesbit et al. [3]. This technique is very effective at detecting patterns with periods shorter than the amount of history stored.

In this paper, we improve DCPT by proposing DCPT-P which incorporates many of the lessons learned during DPC-1. We introduce the concept of L1 hoisting, which is a highly accurate and timely method for moving data into the L1 cache. L1 hoisting does not require complex additions to the L1 cache which could interfere with the critical path of the processor. The key idea in L1 hoisting is to first issue prefetches to the L2 cache with a high prefetch distance, thus ensuring timeliness in the L2 cache. To further increase performance, we predict when the prefetched data will soon be used and hoist it to the L1 cache.

Second, we introduce partial matching which is a technique to enhance delta correlation in hard to predict cases such as pointer chasing. Partial matching reduces the spatial resolution in the delta stream to reveal more possibilities for prefetching. Thus, this technique increases coverage at the price of reduced accuracy, for an overall increase in performance.

2   Previous Work

Because of the large gap between the latency of the processor and main memory, prefetching has a large potential for increasing processor performance. Therefore, it has been an active research topic for several decades. The simplest prefetcher is sequential (next line) prefetching, which simply fetches the next line whenever a cache line is accessed, thus exploiting spatial locality [4]. Its improvement, tagged sequential prefetching, uses an extra bit per cache line to indicate that this cache line was prefetched. When the processor subsequently hits in the cache on a cache block with this bit set, it fetches the next block.

Reference prediction tables use a table to store the recent history of a single load [5]. Each table entry is indexed by the address of the load and contains the last miss address as well as the delta (the difference between the address of the latest consecutive misses) as well as a state [6]. Then, on the next miss, the delta between the first miss address and the current is computed and stored in the table and the entry enters the training state. Finally, on the third miss, a new delta is computed. If that delta matches the one found in the table, the entry enters the prefetching state and prefetches are issued by using the computed delta.

The use of a Global History Buffer (GHB) was proposed by Nesbit et al. [3]. A GHB is essentially a FIFO containing the last misses observed by the memory system. Each entry in the GHB is linked to the previous entry of its class by a pointer. Because of the versatility of the GHB, a class can be defined in multiple ways such as belonging to the same memory region (C/DC) or originating from the same load (PC/DC) [7]. In PC/DC the entries in the GHB belong to the same class if they originate from the same load instruction.

By traversing the linked list, a miss history can be obtained for that load. This operation can be expensive in terms of energy and latency as the GHB structure is read multiple times to generate the miss history. In PC/DC, the deltas between consecutive misses are computed and stored in a delta table. This operation is repeated every time a L2 miss occurs. After the history of deltas are computed, delta correlation begins. Delta correlation means searching for the most recent pair of deltas in the delta history. If a corresponding pair is found in the delta history, the deltas after the match is used to predict future deltas.

During the first Data Prefetching Championship (DPC-1) several novel prefetcher designs were presented. Second place was awarded to GHB-LDB (Global History Buffer - Local Delta Buffer) which was proposed by Dimitrov et al. [8]. GHB-LDB improves upon the PC/DC prefetcher by also including global correlation (as opposed to the local correlation directed by the PC of the load) and most common stride prefetching. Furthermore, their prefetcher issues prefetches directly into the L1 cache.

Third place was awarded to Ramos et al. [9] for their multi-level prefetcher based on the PC/DC concept. Their PDFCM (Prefetching based on a Differential Finite Context Machine) prefetcher uses a hash-based approach with two tables. The History Table is indexed by the PC which contains a hashed representation of the recent history of that entry. This hash points to an entry in the Delta Table which contains the predicted delta. By computing new hashes based on the predicted deltas, an arbitrary prefetch degree and distance can be used.

Finally, the winner was the AMPM (Access Map Pattern Matching) prefetcher proposed by Ishii et al. [10]. Their prefetcher divides memory into hot zones similar to Czones [7]. Each hot zone is tracked by using a 2-bit vector for each cache line in that zone. This vector is then analyzed to see if there are any constant stride patterns in that zone. If there are any patterns, the predicted pattern is prefetched.

3   Delta Correlating Prediction Tables

3.1   Overview

The core of our prefetching heuristic is a table indexed by the PC of the load. Each entry has the format shown in Figure 1. In addition to the PC tag, each entry holds the last miss address, the address of the last prefetch that was issued in addition to a circular buffer containing the last n deltas. The circular buffer is managed by the *delta pointer*. This field points to the most recently added delta.

This organization has a number of advantages. Each entry holds a comparatively large history which can be used to predict any repeating pattern as long as the period is shorter than $n-2$. In addition, entries do not compete for space, thus ensuring that the amount of history per entry is monotonically increasing, which reduces the risk that prefetches are issued for the same line. Finally, by storing deltas, rather than full miss addresses it is possible to save considerably memory space.

Fig. 1. Format of a single DCPT-P entry

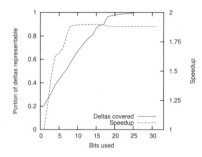

Fig. 2. Impact of increasing the numbers of bits used to represent a delta

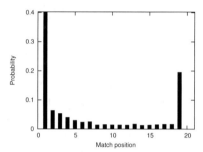

Fig. 3. Position in the circular buffer where a match is found

In Figure 2, we show the portion of deltas we observed that can be represented as a function of the number of bits used to represent each delta in the table. By far, the most common delta is one which is to be expected as this represents the common sequential pattern. As the number of bits per delta increases, the portion of the deltas we can represent increases monotonically.

Figure 2 also plots the performance impact of increasing the number of bits used to represent a single delta. Interestingly, the speedup has a much steeper slope than the coverage. Performance rises sharply as one increases the number of bits up to 12, and then trails off. Although more bits increases the information content, performance degrades because of false matches (high delta values are often generated by pointer chasing codes). Thus, performance can be improved and the memory footprint reduced by limiting the number of bits used.

3.2 DCPT-P Implementation

A basic implementation of the DCPT-P pipeline is shown in Figure 4. When there is an access to the L2 cache the same request enters the pipeline. The first step is to look up the PC of the load in the table. If a corresponding entry is not found, an old entry is replaced using a LRU replacement policy. This new entry is initialized with the miss address and the rest of the entry is initialized to zero.

If a corresponding entry is found, we first compute the delta between the current access and the value stored in *last address*. If the delta is not zero, then the delta is stored in the circular buffer and the *delta pointer* and *last address* is updated. In our experiments, the L2 cache uses 128 byte cache blocks. To conserve space we mask out the lower six bits (64). Thus, a delta of two represents an increment of a single cache block. As shown by Hur et al. [11],

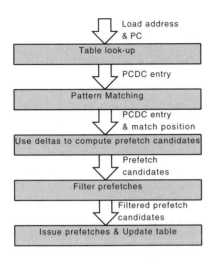

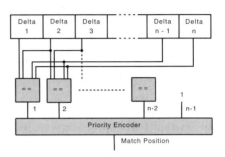

Fig. 4. DCPT-P Pipeline

Fig. 5. Pattern matching implementation

many streams are short (2-4 cache lines). By using deltas that are smaller than a cache block we enable DCPT-P to start prefetching without waiting for too many misses to the L2. If we cannot represent a delta with the available bits, we store a zero instead (not valid). Finally, the entry is passed on to the pattern matching step.

The pattern matching logic is similar to the logic used in PC/DC [3]. In essence, we search for the first occurrence of the last pair of deltas in the circular stream. In Figure 3, we show the distribution of match locations in a 20 entry circular delta buffer. There are two peaks. The first peak is at the first possible position (the last two deltas in the circular buffer matches the first two deltas). This position represents constant strides or repeating patterns (for example 1-2-1-2-1-2). However, a match in the first possible position does not necessarily mean that the other stored deltas are redundant. Consider a blocking implementation of a matrix multiply. In this situation, the access pattern would be a series of sequential accesses followed by a large stride when the blocking algorithm moves to the next row, which in turn would be followed by a series of sequential accesses. By storing multiple deltas in this manner, this behaviour can be effectively captured by DCPT-P. The last peak (at 19) represent situations where the pattern is not found. This data point is included to illustrate the amount of times no pattern is found. Our implementation of the pattern matching step uses several comparators working in parallel in combination with a priority encoder as shown in Figure 5.

The next step is to generate prefetch candidates. The first prefetch candidate is generated by adding the first delta after the match to the current miss address. The second prefetch candidate is generated by adding the second delta after the match to the previous miss address. This is done for all deltas after the match. Thus, by increasing the number of deltas per table entry the prefetch distance is also increased.

Table 1. Example delta stream

Address:	10	11	20	21	30
Deltas:		*1*	*9*	**1**	**9**

As an example, consider the stream shown in Table 1. In this example, time increases to the right (i.e. the most recent address observed is 30). The last pair of deltas is thus (1,9) (Marked with **boldface**). We search for this pair of deltas and find the same pair of deltas in the beginning of the stream (Marked with *italics*). The next delta after this match is 1. We then add 1 to the last *last address* (30) and obtain 31. This is our first prefetch candidate. The next delta is 9. In a similar manner we add 9 to the previous prefetch candidate and obtain 40. We repeat this procedure for all the deltas in the circular buffer.

This approach generates several redundant prefetches so prefetch filtering is needed. The most important mechanism is the *last prefetch* field in each entry. This entry keeps the address of the last prefetch issued by that entry. If a candidate is made that matches the *last prefetch* field during prefetch candidate generation, all previous prefetch candidates are dropped. In the steady state, this ensures that only a single prefetch is issued.

We use a 32 entry pending prefetch buffer to store the prefetches that have been issued. This table serves a dual purpose; first it is checked prior to issuing a prefetch request, thus eliminating redundant prefetches. Second, by only allowing 32 outstanding prefetch requests we limit the amount of bandwidth used by the prefetcher and the probability of severe bandwidth contention.

3.3   L1 Hoisting

Although the greatest latency is from the last level cache to the main memory, there is a significant performance potential to prefetching into the L1 cache. However, due to its limited capacity, cache pollution becomes a significant problem. To avoid this, highly accurate and timely prefetches are needed. In addition, because the L1 cache is on the critical path it becomes much more difficult to construct large and complex prefetch heuristics that interact with the L1 access stream without degrading overall performance.

To overcome this problem we propose L1 hoisting. L1 hoisting is a natural addition to DCPT-P. DCPT-P is highly accurate, but issuing prefetches directly into the L1 cache brings the data in too early and displaces data that is currently needed, which in turn reduces overall performance. Our solution is prefetch hoisting. The first prefetch candidate that is generated is treated as a candidate for prefetch hoisting as well. This candidate is predicted to be the next required by the processor. In the steady state, this candidate has already been prefetched into the L2 by an earlier miss by the same load. Thus, we check if this block is present in the L2. If it is present, then the block is moved (hoisted) into the L1. Even though prefetch distance is low (only one block) it is enough to be timely, because the latency from the L1 cache to L2 cache is much lower than the latency from L1 to main memory.

```
1  for (i = x.size(); i-- > 0; ++xi) {
2      svec = const_cast<SVector*>(& A[*xi]);
3      elem = &(svec->element(0));
4      last = elem + svec->size();
5      y = vl[*xi];
6      for (; elem < last; ++elem)
7          v[elem->idx] += y * elem->val;
8  }
```

Listing 1.1. Loop from 450.Soplex

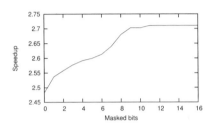

Fig. 6. Speedup of Sphinx as a function of LSB masked in partial matching

3.4   Partial Matching

DCPT captures most regular repeating patterns. However, many programs exhibit more complex and irregular patterns. Consider the code from soplex shown in Listing 1.1. Although the load in line 7 might seem hard to predict there is some structure to the addresses issued. One pattern of deltas we observed was *-2, -1, 4, -2, -3, -3, -1, 3*. In this case, there are no repeating pair of deltas, but most deltas are small. Because the observed deltas are so small, using previous deltas to issue new prefetches might be beneficial. Another pattern we observed was *9, 9, 9, 9, 9, -54, 73, 9, 9, 9.* In this case, a regular pattern is interrupted by an abrupt jump. Simply prefetching using the most common delta (9) would be preferable.

In this work, we propose a general approach to exposing such patterns called partial matching. If a pattern is not found using the exact match, we try partial matching. In essence, we reduce the spatial resolution by masking out the least significant bits and try to find a match using only the MSB's of the delta. This allows us to issue prefetches in both of the cases above.

In Figure 6, we show the speedup of the benchmark sphinx as a function of the number of LSB masked. Increasing the number of masked bits increases the number of prefetches issued. In the case of Sphinx, many of these prefetches are hits, but in other benchmarks increasing the number of masked bits increases the probability of cache pollution and wasted bandwidth.

4   Methodology

Gracia Perez et al. [1] showed that the choice of simulator and benchmarks as well as the implementation of other data cache mechanisms can severely bias the results when evaluating prefetcher performance. Therefore, to evaluate our prefetcher proposal we have used the Data Prefetching Championship (DPC-1) simulator framework [12] as well as the code submitted by the contestants to the competition.

The simulator framework is based on the CMP$im simulator [13]. This framework models a simple 15 stage, 4 wide out-of-order core with a 128-entry instruction window. The core can issue a maximum of two loads and a single store each cycle. The framework models a two level cache hierarchy, consisting of a 32KB, 8-way L1 cache with 64B cache lines. The L2 is a 2MB 16-way set-associative cache with 128 Byte cache lines and a LRU replacement policy. The second level cache has a 20 cycle latency, while main memory has a 200-cycle latency. Each cache is coupled with a queue for storing outstanding requests to the next level in the hierarchy. These queues issues requests in FIFO order and does not prioritize demand requests over prefetch requests [12]. The queue to main memory issues one request per 10 clock cycles, while the queue to the L2 issues 1 per clock cycle. This simulator setup was referred to as configuration 2 in DPC-1.

For our experiments we have generated traces for the SPEC2006 [14] benchmark suite. Each benchmark was fast forwarded by 40 billion instructions and then executed for 100 million instructions. The benchmarks were compiled with the Intel C Compiler version 10.0.

To evaluate the performance of our prefetching heuristic we have selected 5 state-of-the-art prefetchers. In the study by Gracia Perez et al. [1] mentioned earlier, Reference Prediction Tables [5] and PC/DC using a GHB [3] were found to give the highest performance. Therefore, we have implemented these two approaches with the same 4KB limitation. In addition, we have selected the top three performers from DPC-1. The contestants' prefetching code was made public after the competition so we have used their code without modification. The top performers were AMPM [10], PDFCM (Maxperf) [9] and GHB-LDB [8].

To keep within the same 4KB limit imposed on the other prefetcher implementations we have used a 95 entry table with 20 12-bit deltas. On the pattern matching pass with partial matching we mask the low 8 bits of the delta. The pending prefetch buffer can hold a maximum of 32 requests.

5   Results

We begin our evaluation by comparing the performance of our prefetcher to the top three DPC-1 prefetchers, Reference Prediction Tables and PC/DC with the SPEC2006 benchmark suite. The results are shown in Figure 7 and 8. In all of the results presented in this paper, speedup refers to a speedup compared to a baseline where no prefetching is performed. Because there is a wide range of speedups (up to 6.6X) we have opted to use two graphs to increase readability.

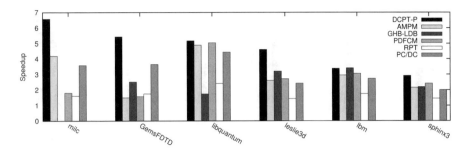

Fig. 7. 2 MB L2 cache. Benchmarks with large speedups.

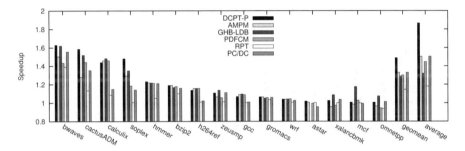

Fig. 8. 2 MB L2 cache. Benchmarks with small speedups.

In addition, we do not show the benchmarks dealII, gobmk, tonto, perlbench, sjeng, gamess, namd, povray. In all of these benchmarks, the performance impact of prefetching was less than 5% for all the prefetchers. In cases where the simulation did not terminate within 48 hours we show an speedup of 0, rather than tampering with the original code.

Overall, DCPT-P shows good performance across all benchmarks. DCPT-P is the best performing prefetcher on 11 of the 21 benchmarks shown. The good performance of both soplex and sphinx3 is due to partial matching. Leslie3d and milc benefits greatly from the L1 hoisting technique. Also, it is worth noting that GHB-LDB performs very well on xalncbmk, mcf and omentpp. This is due to the global (intra-PC) analysis done by this type of prefetcher. However, GHB-LDB performs worse than it's predecessor, PC/DC, on GemsFDTD and libquantum. Although both GHB-LDB and PDFCM both extends PC/DC, their performance is on average almost equal. Although AMPM prefetching is not the best prefetcher for any single benchmark, it nevertheless achieves signifcant speedups across the entire benchmark suite. On average, DCPT-P provides an arithmetic mean speedup of 87%. AMPM, GHB-LDB and PDFCM has speedups of 50%, 32% and 44% respectively.

In Figure 9 and 10 we reduce the L2 capacity to 512KB. This is the same configuration as config 3 in DPC-1. Overall, we observe the same general trends. The most significant changes from reducing the size of the L2 can be observed

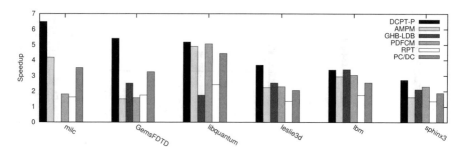

Fig. 9. 512KB L2 cache. Benchmarks with large speedups.

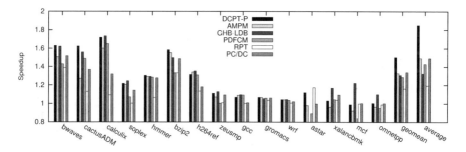

Fig. 10. 512KB L2 cache. Benchmarks with small speedups.

on leslie3d, calculix, bzip2 and h264ref. In this configuration PDFCM causes performance degradation on astar and omnetpp. Surprisingly, RPT prefetching is the best prefetcher on astar. On this benchmark, most of the other prefetchers has very high miss rates, especially when prefetching into the L1 cache. Thus, the more conservative prefetcher performs well. Additionally, the benefits of GHB-LDB on mcf, omnetpp and xalncbmk increases.

Figure 11 and 12 provides insight into the relative performance benefits of the three techniques proposed in this work. Undoubtedly, the basic DCPT design is responsible for most of the performance gain. This is because it is responsible for bridging the last level cache to main memory gap and thus has the most potential. Both Partial matching and L1 hoisting contribute to the overall performance. Interestingly, the effects of the two does not seem to be cumulative, but rather synergistic. For instance, on libquantum, switching off partial matching reduces performance somewhat. Switching off L1 hoisting reduces performance even more, but there is no difference between this configuration and switching both L1 hoisting and partial matching off. On both omnetpp and astar we see that partial matching actually causes a performance degradation. This effect is due to the much lower accuracy of partial matching, which in turn causes bandwidth saturation.

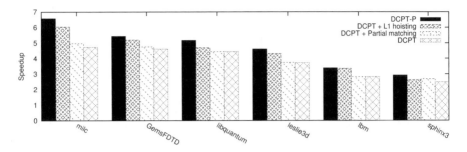

Fig. 11. Breakdown of performance contribution of DCPT-P. Benchmarks with large speedups.

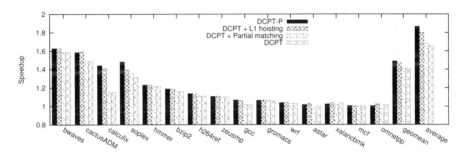

Fig. 12. Breakdown of performance contribution of DCPT-P. Benchmarks with small speedups.

5.1   Area and Performance Trade-Offs

So far, we have focused our attention on performance. However, it is possible to optimize for area as well. The largest structure in DCPT-P is the table holding the entries. In this section, we explore the area and performance trade-off of changing some of the key table parameters. In Figure 13, we show the performance impact of increasing the number of deltas in each entry. The speedups are reported relative to the same case with no prefetching. Although the unlimited bandwidth case has higher absolute performance, the relative speedup of prefetching is lower. Increasing the number of deltas has three distinct effects. Firstly, it increases the probability of a match, thus the number of prefetches increases. Secondly, it increases the effective prefetch distance. Finally, it increases power and area as the number of comparators has to be increased. Although DCPT-P is highly accurate, a large prefetch distance can cause problems, because blocks are fetched too soon. This poses a problem because the blocks may be either evicted before they are used and/or displace other data that is currently needed. This effect can be seen by examining the difference between the 2MB and 512K cases in Figure 13. In the 512K case, performance starts to drop after about 18 deltas, and declines faster than in the 2MB case. Additionally, the

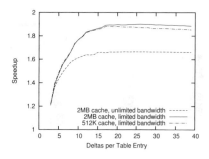

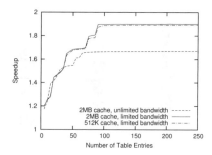

Fig. 13. Average speedup as a function of the number of deltas in each entry

Fig. 14. Average speedup as a function of the number of table entries

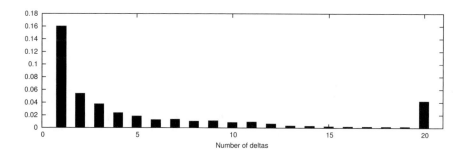

Fig. 15. Distribution of the number of deltas registered in a table entry upon replacement

knee in the graph in the bandwidth unlimited case is shifted to the left compared to the bandwidth limited cases. This suggests that a higher prefetching distance can mask some transient bandwidth contention as well.

In Figure 14, we show the average speedup as a function of the number of entries in the DCPT-P table. Performance increases as the number of entries is increased. After roughly 100 entries there is no performance gain in increasing the size of the table.

6   Discussion

In the design of DCPT-P we have omitted several interesting design ideas, either because they provide little performance benefit or that they will increase the overall complexity of the design and obscure the more central mechanisms in DCPT-P. In this section, we will discuss some of these design options.

In Figure 15, we show the distribution of the number of deltas that has been registered in a entry when it is replaced. DCPT-P requires at least three deltas before it can begin prefetching. As such, the wast majority of table entries are never used for actual prefetching. Thus, much of the table space is wasted on inactive table entries. A possible solution is to use two tables. The first table is a smaller version of the DCPT table, that can hold up to two deltas. If the entry produces more deltas, then that table entry is promoted into the larger table. A second approach is to modify the simple LRU replacement policy in the table to give increased weight to entries with more deltas.

We observed that several of the patterns are simple repeating patterns with a short period. It is possible to capture much of the benefit of DCPT-P by using fewer deltas and analyze the delta pattern to see if it repeats. If it does, then the pattern can be extrapolated. In addition to decreasing the storage requirements by requiring fewer deltas, this approach also gives the possibility of varying the prefetch distance dynamically [15,16].

The pattern matching step is at the core of the DCPT-P heuristic. It is possible to implement this step in a variety of ways depending on the performance and area requirements. Our implementation uses several comparators to examine every possible match location in parallel. To reduce the number of comparators, it is possible to split this step into multiple stages. Consequently, pattern matching can be performed in an iterative fashion by reusing the comparators. As previously shown in Figure 3, the probability of finding a match in the beginning of the delta stream is high. This is because of the prevalence of repeating patterns with short periods. Thus, the probability of finding a match during the first few iterations is high, reducing the average latency.

Another possibility is to limit the search to a subset of the deltas, thus reducing the number of comparators or iterations needed. We investigated limiting the number of deltas searched for a match. As expected, reducing the probability of finding a match decreases overall performance because patterns with long periods are not detected.

Partial matching increases coverage at the cost of decreased prefetcher accuracy. In our implementation we treat prefetches generated by full and partial matching equally. In a more bandwidth-constrained environment it might be beneficial to not treat them equally and only issue prefetches generated by partial matching if there is ample off-chip bandwidth available [17].

Finally, we looked at allowing partial matching to issue multiple prefetches per delta. Because partial matching reduces spatial resolution, the deltas after the match also have reduced resolution. It is possible to compensate for this reduced resolution by issuing multiple prefetches covering the range of possible LSBs. However, because partial matching reduces overall accuracy, we found that issuing multiple prefetches quickly saturated off-chip bandwidth which resulted in reduced performance.

The simulation framework we have opted to use has some limitations. For instance, the look-up time of the predictor is not accounted for. Furthermore, a very simple DRAM model is used, the 4KB storage limit is somewhat arbitrary and techniques which can deal with large off-chip meta-data has been developed [18]. Overall, we chose to use this framework so that a fair comparison with previously proposed prefetchers could be conducted.

7   Conclusion

In this paper, we have presented a novel low-complexity prefetching heuristic called DCPT-P. DCPT-P uses a table indexed by the PC of the load. Each table entry stores a large amount of history per load instruction in the form of deltas. By storing deltas rather than full miss addresses, we save a significant amount of memory and make pattern matching easier. Pattern matching is done by using Delta Correlation, originally proposed by Nesbit et al. [3]. This technique is very effective at detecting patterns with periods shorter than the amount of history stored.

We also introduce the concept of L1 hoisting. L1 hoisting is a technique that combines with DCPT-P to issue highly accurate and timely prefetches into the L1 cache. To deal with several real-world problems with prefetching, we have introduced a mechanism called partial matching which reveals previously hidden patterns by reducing spatial resolution.

Our technique builds upon and expands several ideas presented during the first data prefetching championship (DPC-1). We have examined the top performers extensively and extracted key properties of these prefetchers and improved upon their ideas and synthesised them into a low complexity, storage efficent and high performance prefetcher. By using the code submitted to the DPC-1 contest we can be confident that the comparison with other prefetching techniques is accurate. On average, DCPT-P provides an arithmetic mean speedup of 87% on the SPEC2006 benchmark suite.

References

1. Perez, D.G., Mouchard, G., Temam, O.: Microlib: A case for the quantitative comparison of micro-architecture mechanisms. In: MICRO 37: Proceedings of the 37th annual IEEE/ACM International Symposium on Microarchitecture, Washington, DC, USA, pp. 43–54. IEEE Computer Society, Los Alamitos (2004)
2. Grannaes, M., Jahre, M., Natvig, L.: Storage efficient hardware prefetching using delta correlating prediction tables. In: Data Prefetching Championships (2009)
3. Nesbit, K.J., Smith, J.E.: Data cache prefetching using a global history buffer. In: International Symposium on High-Performance Computer Architecture, p. 96 (2004)
4. Smith, A.J.: Cache memories. ACM Comput. Surv. 14(3), 473–530 (1982)
5. Chen, T.F., Baer, J.L.: Effective hardware-based data prefetching for high-performance processors. IEEE Transactions on Computers 44, 609–623 (1995)
6. Dahlgren, F., Stenstrom, P.: Evaluation of hardware-based stride and sequential prefetching in shared-memory multiprocessors. IEEE Transactions on Parallel and Distributed Systems 7(4), 385–398 (1996)
7. Nesbit, K.J., Dhodapkar, A.S., Smith, J.E.: AC/DC: An adaptive data cache prefetcher. In: Proceedings of the 13th International Conference on Parallel Architecture and Compilation Techniques, pp. 135–145 (2004)
8. Dimitrov, M., Zhou, H.: Combining local and global history for high performance data prefetching. In: Data Prefetching Championship-1 (2009)

9. Ramos, L.M., Briz, J.L., Ibáñez, P.E., Viñals, V.: Multi-level adaptive prefetching based on performance gradient tracking. In: Data Prefetching Championship-1 (2009)
10. Ishii, Y., Inaba, M., Hiraki, K.: Access map pattern matching prefetch: Optimization friendly method. In: Data Prefetching Championship-1 (2009)
11. Hur, I., Lin, C.: Feedback mechanisms for improving probabilistic memory prefetching. In: HPCA 2009: Proceedings of the 15th International Symposium on High-Performance Computer Architecture, pp. 443–454 (2009)
12. DPC-1: Data prefetching championship rules,
    `http://www.jilp.org/dpc/framework.html`
13. Jaleel, A., Cohn, R.S., Luk, C.K., Jacob, B.: CMP$im: A pin-based on-the-fly multi-core cache simulator. In: MoBS (2008)
14. SPEC: Spec 2006 benchmark suites (2006), `http://www.spec.org`
15. Srinath, S., Mutlu, O., Kim, H., Patt, Y.N.: Feedback directed prefetching: Improving the performance and bandwidth-efficiency of hardware prefetchers. Technical report, University of Texas at Austin, TR-HPS-2006-006 (May 2006)
16. Grannaes, M., Natvig, L.: Dynamic parameter tuning for hardware prefetching using shadow tagging. In: CMP-MSI: 2nd Workshop on Chip Multiprocessor Memory Systems and Interconnects (2008)
17. Grannaes, M., Jahre, M., Natvig, L.: Low-cost open-page prefetch scheduling in chip multiprocessors. In: IEEE International Conference on Computer Design, ICCD (2008)
18. Wenisch, T., Ferdman, M., Ailamaki, A., Falsafi, B., Moshovos, A.: Practical off-chip meta-data for temporal memory streaming. In: High Performance Computer Architecture, HPCA (2009)

Scalable Shared-Cache Management by Containing Thrashing Workloads

Yuejian Xie and Gabriel H. Loh

Georgia Institute of Technology
College of Computing
{corvarx,loh}@cc.gatech.edu

Abstract. Multi-core processors with shared last-level caches are vulnerable to performance inefficiencies and fairness issues when the cache is not carefully managed between the multiple cores. Cache partitioning is an effective method for isolating poorly-interacting threads from each other, but designing a mechanism with simple logic and low area overhead will be important for incorporating such schemes in future embedded multi-core processors. In this work, we identify that major performance problems only arise when one or more "thrashing" applications exist. We propose a simple yet effective *Thrasher Caging* (TC) cache management scheme that specifically targets these thrashing applications.

1 Introduction

Modern multi-core processors often employ a large last-level cache (LLC) shared between all of the cores. In particular, a core with a high LLC access rate can quickly cause cachelines used by other cores to be evicted, which can have a negative impact on the performance of other cores, overall system throughput, quality-of-service and fairness. As a result, many researchers have proposed a variety of techniques to manage the LLC to provide better performance and fairness [2,3,4,9,10,12,18,19,21,22,23,25].

As multi-core processors move into the embedded domain, effective management of shared resources will still be important. In this work, we demonstrate that the performance benefits of explicit cache partitioning can indeed be achieved with simpler mechanisms that are more amenable to implementation in future multi-core embedded platforms. In particular, we observe that most performance-degrading cache contention scenarios are caused by the presence of one or more threads exhibiting *thrashing* behaviors characterized by a large number of overall accesses resulting in a large number of cache misses. By simply keeping these few disruptive threads under control, we can achieve the benefits of more complex cache partitioning schemes with significantly simpler hardware.

1.1 Review of Related Work

There have been many recent efforts to develop hardware techniques to manage the shared last-level cache (LLC) between multiple competing cores [2,3,4,8,

Y.N. Patt et al. (Eds.): HiPEAC 2010, LNCS 5952, pp. 262–276, 2010.

$9, 10, 12, 18, 19, 21, 22, 23, 25$]. In this section, we focus primarily on one recent proposal called *Utility-based Cache Partitioning* (UCP) [18].

The UCP mechanism consists of two primary components. The first is the *Utility Monitor* (UMON) that observes cache access patterns for each core and determines how much additional benefit or *utility* could be gained by assigning that core more ways in the cache. In principle, UCP augments the cache's tag array with *shadow tags* that track what the contents of the cache would be if one core had sole access to the entire LLC, as illustrated in Figure 1(a). Each core also maintains a set of w counters (for a w-way cache) that are updated as follows. Each time a core has a hit in way i in the core's *shadow tags*, then the ith counter gets incremented. That is, the ith counter records the number of cache hits that would have occurred if the core had the entire cache to itself and the cacheline that provided the hit was currently the ith-most recently used line (assuming an LRU replacement policy). These counters are also called *marginal gain counters* [23] since they record the number of additional hits that could be achieved for each additional way allocated to the core. Finally, UCP uses the counters to find a partitioning of the cache that minimizes the total number of misses. In the example in Figure 1(b), we have considered all possible partitionings where each core receives at least one way of the cache, and in this case an allocation of five lines to core-0 and three lines to core-1 minimizes the overall number of misses. As the number of cores increases, UCP is faced with a combinatorial explosion in the number of possible partitionings, as illustrated in Figure 1(c) for $N=4$ cores.

To implement the shadow tags, UCP requires that the tag array for the cache be replicated for each core. That is, for an N-core system, the cache requires its original tag array plus N additional copies. The shadow tag overhead also increases directly proportionally to the number of cores and the number of ways in the LLC. To help cut down on the cost of these shadow tag arrays, Qureshi and Patt made use of *Dynamic Set Sampling* (DSS) [17] as shown in Figure 1(d). In this scenario, only some fraction α of the sets of the cache are tracked in the shadow tags.

There are two primary scaling parameters that impact the overhead and complexity of the UCP approach. The first is that more cores requires more sets of shadow tags, thereby increasing storage overhead. The second parameter is the set-associativity of the cache. If the set associativity of the cache is doubled, then the UMON overhead also doubles. The complexity of the partitioning logic also increases with these parameters. To find the optimal partitioning for N cores and w ways, there are $O(w^N)$ possible partitionings that must be considered if the optimal solution is to be found. Approximations such as incrementally increasing or decreasing allocations are not always effective because in some situations multiple ways must be added before any significant gains be can observed. To address this problem, Qureshi and Patt proposed the *Lookahead* approximation algorithm that performs close to optimal, and has a reduced running time of $O(w^2 N)$ operations. It is important to note that UCP only attempts to repartition the cache once every few million cycles, and so the latency of making the

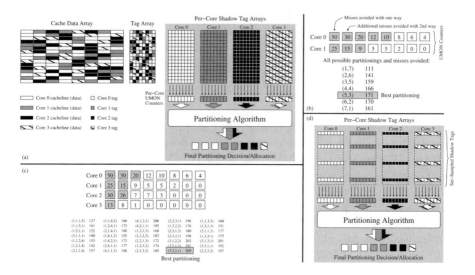

Fig. 1. (a) Data and tag arrays for an eight-way set-associative cache, along with the structures for implementing Utility-based Cache Partitioning (UCP). (b) Example UMON marginal gain counter values for two cores with an enumeration of the utilities for all possible partitionings, and (c) the same but for four cores. (d) Modification to the UCP overhead when Dynamic Set Sampling is employed.

partitioning decision is not crucial. The number of required operations provides a measure of the complexity of implementing the partitioning algorithm in hardware. If nothing else, the verification effort for the partitioning algorithm would be extremely challenging.

Another limitation of cache partitioning approaches is that strict partitioning can lead to underutilization of cache capacity (i.e., if a core receives a larger allocation than it needs). Other works have taken advantage of this in different ways [19, 25]; the approach proposed in this paper also leverages non-strict allocation.

The discussion in this section does not try to claim that UCP is impractical; there are simply some costs and overheads associated with UCP that increase with the number of cores and the set-associativity of the LLC. Chip designers may decide that the performance benefits outweigh the overheads. In this work, however, we propose a partitioning scheme that delivers the performance benefits of traditional cache partitioning with much simpler hardware. There are a variety of other previous cache management proposals, many of which we feel are orthogonal to this work.

2   When Does Partitioning Help?

Several past studies have presented a variety of approaches to classify programs' cache behaviors in a multi-core context [2, 12, 15, 18]. In this section, we provide a simple classification for separating programs into cache-thrashing or non-thrashing applications. Our classification is not meant to be exhaustive and cover all possible memory access patterns, but we focus on simply determining when partitioning helps compared to when a conventional sharing-oblivious policy like LRU works about as well.

We observe the behavior of a program over an interval of T cycles. During this time, we track the total number of $Accesses$ to the LLC, what the total number of $Misses_{solo}$ would be if the core had the entire cache to itself, and $MissRate_{solo} = \frac{Misses_{solo}}{Accesses}$. The $Misses_{solo}$ metric is tracked by the per-core shadow tags just like in UCP. Based on these metrics, we apply the following simple rule:

If $((Accesses \geq \theta_{acc})$ AND $((MissRate_{solo} > \theta_{MR})$ OR $(Misses_{solo} > \theta_{miss})))$
        Classification := **Thrasher**

Else
        Classification := **Non-Thrasher**

For our initial experiments, we used T=1 million cycles, θ_{acc}=4000, θ_{miss}=1000, and θ_{MR}=0.1; we have experimented with some other thresholds but the overall trends are consistent. The intuition for this classification rule is that if a program does not access the cache very much at all (low $Accesses$), then it does not have a way to greatly impact the cache contents of any other cores. If the $MissRate_{solo}$ is too high, then that means that the lines that are being cached exhibit relatively low locality, and therefore are likely to provide low utility as well. If the raw number of $Misses_{solo}$ is high, then even though many of the cached lines may provide a lot of hits for the core, the large miss count indicates a large working set which will tend to cause the eviction of other cores' cache lines. Note that we re-evaluate the classification every T cycles, and so some benchmarks may exhibit thrashing behaviors during some phases, but not for others. Our classification rule is admittedly ad hoc, but it is sufficient for our purpose of classifying when cache partitioning will be useful.

2.1 Simulation Methodology

For our simulations, we used the SimpleScalar toolset for the x86 ISA [13]. Table 1 lists the simulated processor configuration. Hardware prefetchers are used for all levels of the cache hierarchy. For dual-core workloads, we simulate a 4MB, 16-way cache, whereas for quad-core workloads, we use a 8MB, 32-way cache. While a 32-way cache may be aggressive, especially in the embedded domain, part of the goal of this work is to demonstrate that our simple techniques scale with increasing cache complexity.

We use a variety of benchmarks from SPEC2000 and SPEC2006 from both the integer and floating point suites, PhysicsBench [26], MediaBench [5, 11], MineBench [16], MiBench [6] and BioPerf [1]. For SPEC, We use reference inputs. Table 2 lists the applications and their baseline statistics. Most applications with very low DL1 miss rates were not considered for workload creation because they have practically no impact on sharing/contention in the LLC.

Table 1. Baseline 4-wide processor configuration. All caches use 64-byte lines.

Parameter	Value	Parameter	Value
ROB Size	96 entries	RS Size	32 entries
LDQ/STQ Size	32/20 entries	IL1/DL1	32KB/8-way/3-cyc
Shared L2 (dual-core)	4MB/16-way/9-cyc	Shared L2 (quad-core)	8MB/32-way/9-cyc
Function Units	3 IALU, 1 IMul, 1 FAdd, 1 Div, 1 FMul, 1 Load, 1 STA, 1 STD		
Main Memory	SDRAM, 800MHz bus (DDR), 6-6-6, 3.2GHz CPU speed		

Table 2. Benchmark classification. APKI stands for accesses per thousand instructions. Codes: F0 (SpecFP'00), F6 (SpecFP'06), I0 (SpecInt'00), I6 (SpecInt'06), MI (MiBench), MD (MediaBench), MN (MineBench), PB (PhysicsBench), BI (BioPerf). Benchmarks N6-N18 spend <0.5% of the time thrashing.

	Benchmark Name	Base IPC	4M/1M Slowdown	APKI	% Time Thrashing		Benchmark Name	Base IPC	4M/1M Slowdown	APKI
T0	F6-milc	0.28	0.4%	60.9	100.0%	N6	MD-g721-enc	1.23	0.0%	0.0
T1	F6-lbm	0.23	0.0%	14.1	100.0%	N7	I6-h264ref	1.07	16.7%	10.0
T2	F6-soplex	0.26	5.5%	87.5	99.4%	N8	I6-astar	1.08	8.2%	6.7
T3	F0-equake	0.32	45.8%	129.2	98.6%	N9	I6-bzip2.3	0.99	0.9%	1.5
T4	F6-sphinx3	0.40	3.1%	69.8	96.2%	N10	F0-art	0.47	75.0%	129.3
T5	I6-gcc	0.60	0.6%	30.0	92.8%	N11	PB-continuous	0.82	45.9%	13.6
T6	I6-libquantum	0.28	0.0%	149.5	63.2%	N12	I0-eon	1.20	0.0%	2.6
N0	MN-semphy	1.06	5.4%	1.3	37.5%	N13	MD-jpeg.d	1.34	0.7%	0.6
N1	I6-perl	1.04	14.8%	10.0	19.9%	N14	MI-rijndael	1.74	0.0%	0.6
N2	I6-bzip2.1	1.08	35.7%	11.6	5.6%	N15	BI-predator	1.24	0.0%	0.0
N3	I6-bzip2.2	1.00	24.3%	11.7	1.2%	N16	MN-bayes	1.11	0.0%	0.0
N4	I6-sjeng	0.92	0.4%	2.8	0.7%	N17	MI-adpcm.e	1.01	0.0%	0.0
N5	MI-dijkstra	1.23	17.1%	18.9	0.5%	N18	MD-adpcm.e	0.86	0.0%	0.0

We use SimPoint 3.2 to select representative samples of each benchmark [7]. We warm the caches for 500 million instructions per core and then simulate 250 million instructions *per benchmark*, thus ensuring at least one billion committed instructions for our four-core evaluations.

When reporting performance results, we make use of three performance metrics: overall throughput (ΣIPC_i), weighted speedup ($\Sigma \frac{IPC_i}{SingleIPC_i}$) [20], and the harmonic mean of weighted IPC or *fair speedup* ($N/\Sigma \frac{SingleIPC_i}{IPC_i}$) [14], where IPC_i is the IPC of program$_i$ when running with the rest of the workload, and $SingleIPC_i$ is the IPC of program$_i$ when running on the processor *alone*.

2.2 Classification Results

We run each benchmark and observe the fraction of time each is classified as exhibiting thrashing behavior. These results are tabulated in Table 2 along with some other basic information such as the baseline IPC, cache access frequency, and the performance difference between providing a 4MB cache versus only a 1MB cache. The list is sorted from the most-frequently thrashing to the least. Note that due to the simplicity of our classification scheme, we do not distinguish between applications that are moderately thrashing (e.g., ϵ more misses than θ_{miss}) and extremely thrashy (e.g., much more misses than θ_{miss}). Likewise, this classification does not differentiate between thrashing behavior caused by large working sets versus those exhibiting streaming behaviors. Figure 2(a) shows one example of two different benchmarks running together and how they exhibit different thrashing phases during their execution.

We then created several workloads with different combinations of thrashing (T) and non-thrashing (N) applications, listed in Table 3. For the sake of workload creation, we consider any benchmark that spends >50% of the time exhibiting thrashing behavior as thrashing. In addition to the one thrasher with three non-thrasher (1T3N) workloads listed above, we also evaluated several more 1T3N workloads (F–I) that incorporate a few applications with small working sets to ensure that the proposed technique does not inadvertently hurt performance in such a situation. These additional "small" applications are taken from the MediaBench and MiBench suites which are more geared toward embedded environments and tend to have smaller working sets.

For each workload, we observed the performance for an LRU-based 4MB 16-way L2 cache and the same again with a UCP-managed cache. Figure 2(b) shows the performance for the LRU cache and the UCP cache for the T:N, T:T and N:N workloads. These results show that the only situation where UCP consistently provides a strong performance benefit is for the T:N workloads. UCP effectively "quarantines" the thrashing application into a relatively small partition that provides performance isolation for the other non-thrashing program.

For the N:N workloads, UCP is still able to find partitions that do not harm performance. The reason why there is no significant performance *benefit* over

Table 3. Multi-programmed workloads used in this paper. Refer to Table 2 for individual benchmark names.

Dual-Core		Dual-Core		Dual-Core		Quad-Core		Quad-Core	
Name	Apps	Name	Apps	Name	Apps	Name	Apps	Name	Apps
T:N-A	T3,N11	T:T-A	T3,T1	N:N-A	N13,N14	1T3N-A	T3,N11,N13,N18	2T2N-A	T0,T2,N8,N9
T:N-B	T1,N5	T:T-B	T0,T4	N:N-B	N0,N12	1T3N-B	T1,N5,N14,N17	2T2N-B	T0,T3,N2,N11
T:N-C	T0,N3	T:T-C	T5,T2	N:N-C	N9,N8	1T3N-C	T0,N0,N3,N16	2T2N-C	T1,T4,N5,N10
T:N-D	T4,N7	T:T-D	T0,T3	N:N-D	N5,N11	1T3N-D	T4,N6,N7,N12	2T2N-D	T0,T6,N8,N9
T:N-E	T5,N7	T:T-E	T4,T6	N:N-E	N5,N0	1T3N-E	T5,N4,N7,N15	2T2N-E	T1,T2,N1,N9
T:N-F	T2,N9	T:T-F	T0,T2	N:N-F	N3,N12	F–I	see text		
		T:T-G	T3,T4	N:N-G	N11,N2				

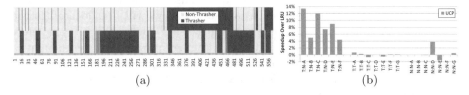

Fig. 2. (a) Timing example of two programs from SPEC2006 and their time-varying thrashing behaviors (top: cactusADM, bottom: soplex). Each sample point covers one million cycles, (b) Speedup of UCP over LRU on dual-core workloads.

LRU for these cases is that the combined access patterns of these applications is such that LRU's replacement decisions do not systematically punish one program over the other. For the T:T workloads where both programs are thrashing consistently, partitioning generally provides little help because both workloads have so many misses that even the best partitioning only increases the number of hits by a small amount relative to the total number of accesses. In this case LRU works about just as well as the partitioning approach.

The main observation that we make here is that the only benchmarks that appear to cause any major problems with respect to the shared cache resources are those that exhibit thrashing behaviors. Our hypothesis is that one does not need to conduct completely general partitioning of the cache among all cores, but instead one only needs to control or contain the thrashing subset.

3   Containing Thrashing Workloads

In this section, we present a simple yet effective cache management scheme that scales gracefully with both the number of cores and the cache's set associativity, and in the process also completely eliminates the need for *all* of UCP's shadow tag overhead *and* partitioning logic.

3.1   Thrasher Caging

From our experiments that evaluated UCP applied to a workload consisting of one thrasher and one non-thrasher (T:N), we observed that in most cases, the thrashing application is only allocated a small number of ways. The idea is that instead of attempting to explicitly compute the optimal partition size for all threads, we can instead simply assign a fixed-sized partition, or *cage*, for each thrashing application. This *Thrasher Caging* approach is very similar to traditional way-partitioned cache schemes, except that only thrashing applications get sequestered away. Any non-thrashing cores will continue to share all of the remaining cache capacity.

More precisely, for N cores and a w-way set-associative cache, each thrashing core receives a fixed allocation of c ways; no more, no less. The cage size c is typically less than a "fair" allocation where every thread receives the same amount of space, i.e., $c < \frac{w}{N}$. Most of our results make use of $c=2$. If there are T thrashing applications, then a total of Tc ways will be allocated to the T separate partitions or cages. The remaining $w - Tc$ ways will be completely shared by the remaining $N - T$ cores. This caging approach can be thought of as a partial-partitioning where some cache space is explicitly managed (i.e., the cages) while the remaining space is unmanaged (i.e., the other ways are regulated by traditional LRU). This is a very simple mechanism, but it also turns out to be very effective. If there are no thrashing applications present, then the entire cache is treated as a conventional LRU cache. If all threads are thrashing, then each program receives $\frac{w}{N}$ ways so as not to waste any of the cache space.

From an implementation perspective, this Caging approach is much more lightweight than the UCP approach. The complex partitioning mechanism can effectively be *completely eliminated* as the partition sizes are a fixed function of the programs' thrashing classifications. As a result, all of the UMON counters can also be eliminated, too. The only significant remaining overhead are the per-core shadow tags used for classifying whether a program exhibits thrashing behavior. Note that the partitioning mechanism is where most of the complexity lies when the number of cores or the set-associativity increases. Thrasher Caging reduces the number of operations from $O(w^2 N)$ (for Lookahead) to effectively zero regardless of the number of cores or the cache's set associativity.

3.2 Approximate Thrasher Detection (ATD)

The Thrasher Caging approach's only substantial overhead is from the per-core shadow tags used for the Thrasher classification. Note also, that the only role served by the shadow tags for Thrasher Caging is to identify when programs exhibit thrashing behaviors. One would suspect that the fine-grained per-way marginal utility-tracking capabilities of the per-core shadow tags is an overkill. This is in fact the case, and we describe a simple alternative to approximate this information, which we call Approximate Thrasher Detection (ATD).

Our approach is simple: we only track the absolute number of misses such that if a core causes more than $\tilde{\theta}_{miss}$ misses, then the core is considered to be thrashing.[1] Considering only misses without considering hits could potentially lead to cases where an application is unfairly punished (i.e., it has a high average hit rate over many memory accesses, but it still results in more than $\tilde{\theta}_{miss}$ misses). Our intuition is that counting only misses should still work for the *aggregate* system performance (as measured by, for example, overall throughput or weighted speedup) because whatever benefit those misses provide for the one application, the remaining $> \tilde{\theta}_{miss}$ misses would still wreak havoc for the other non-thrashing programs. The selection of the exact values for these thresholds are discussed in Section 4. We also considered a version where we use the miss *rate* rather than the absolute number of misses, but it turns out that tracking only misses performs better while being easier to implement.

Note that for our ATD, we only track the miss statistics on the actual misses observed on the real cache contents, independent of whether these accesses would have been hits in an unshared cache. The intuition for why this is still accurate is that for a thrashing workload, whether it receives a few ways or the entire cache, the majority of its accesses will be misses and therefore the number of misses observed in the real cache or an unshared cache will still be very similar (i.e., providing the entire cache for this application still will not significantly increase the number of hits). ATD completely removes *all* shadow tags, rendering the total storage overhead for our simplified partitioning scheme to only one counter per core to track per-core misses. Figure 3(b) illustrates the final design of Thrasher Caging with ATD.

---

[1] We use the notation $\tilde{\theta}$ instead of θ to emphasize that this threshold corresponds to an approximation of the previous classification approach.

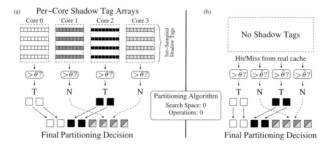

Fig. 3. (a) Shadow tag, thrasher detection logic, and example partitioning for the Thrasher Caging approach, and (b) hardware changes when using Approximate Thrasher Detection

3.3   Performance of TC and ATD

We evaluated Thrasher Caging (TC) on a variety of four-core workloads listed in Table 3. We simulated workloads with 4T0N (four thrashing programs, no non-thrashing), 3T1N, 2T2N, 1T3N, and 0T4N. Figure 4 only shows the results for 1T3N and 2T2N; the other workloads showed very little benefit from the baseline UCP, and so they are omitted for brevity. We also considered dual-core 1T1N applications with similar results [24]. Figure 4 shows the performance of these approaches compared to an LRU-based unmanaged cache for four-core workloads, with sub-plots (a), (b) and (c) showing the results for the weighted speedup, IPC throughput, and harmonic mean fairness metrics, respectively. Figure 4 also includes the performance results for TADIP-F, another recently proposed cache management scheme that does not explicitly partition the shared cache but instead dynamically adjusts per-thread insertion policies [9]. Across our simulated workloads, TADIP performs slightly better than UCP (with a lower implementation overhead). On average, our TC approach performs better than both UCP and TADIP, although there are individual workloads where UCP or TADIP is the best approach. Only for the fair speedup metric does TC not perform as strongly as the other approaches, but it still achieves fair speedup results close to the others and significantly better than an unmanaged LRU cache.

While TC was proposed to simplify/eliminate the complex partitioning decision logic, Figure 4 shows that TC also provides a slight performance improvement over UCP. At first, this may seem counter-intuitive that an approximation to optimal partitioning may perform better, but the optimal partitioning approach (UCP) assumes *disjoint* partitions for each thread. In TC, all of the non-thrashing threads share the same cache space without any further enforcement. As a result, threads may "steal" capacity from other threads in the sense that at any given moment, a thread may occupy more space than it would otherwise be allowed in a strictly partitioned approach. The benefits of relaxing the strict partitioning requirement have also been demonstrated in other studies [19, 25].

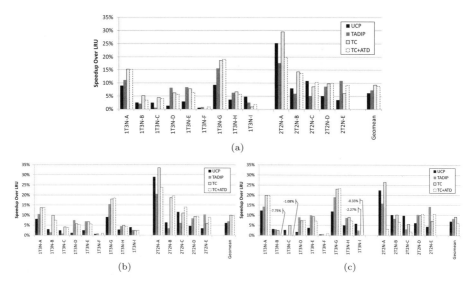

Fig. 4. Performance comparisons of Thrasher Caging (TC) and TC with Approximate Thrasher Detection. All results are speedups over an unmanaged LRU cache, using the (a) weighted speedup, (b) IPC throughput and (c) harmonic mean of weighted IPC metrics.

TADIP and TC actually provide similar benefits in different guises. When a thrashing application is present, TADIP effectively isolates this thread by forcing the thread's cache lines to be inserted at the LRU position. The non-thrashing threads will be inserted at the MRU position, and as a result, the overall scheme behaves similar to thrasher caging where the cage size is one, and all thrashing programs share the same cage. There are a few scenarios where TADIP's approach may break down. First, TADIP does not perform strict LRU insertion, but rather performs a probabilistic insertion where MRU insertion occurs with a probability $p = \frac{1}{32}$ and LRU insertion otherwise. For an application with extreme thrashing that inserts lines into the cache at a very high rate relative to the access frequencies of other cores, even the one out of 32 lines being inserted at the MRU position is enough to cause many other lines to be evicted. Second, there are some cases where maintaining some level of isolation, even between thrashing applications, is still beneficial. For example, many thrashing applications simply stream through memory in a sequential access pattern. For such programs, hardware prefetchers can easily predict the pattern and prefetch data into the cache. If these are inserted at the LRU position, however, the prefetched lines may be evicted before the corresponding core even has a chance to make use of the line. With separate per-thrasher partitions, TC avoids this situation. This may be part of the reason why the relative benefits of TADIP are reduced in a environment where prefetching is enabled [9].

Figure 4 includes the performance of TC with approximate thrasher detection (ATD). For the majority of benchmarks, the absolute number of misses serves as an accurate proxy for thrasher detection. There are a few individual workloads where the ATD approach actually performs better than shadow-tag-based TC. The reason for this is that the thrasher-classification criteria is itself a heuristic where the best threshold for thrasher classification will vary from one workload to the next (but we use a fixed threshold for all workloads). The "error" introduced by ATD could in fact push the effective thrasher classification to more closely mimic the classification results that would occur for a better selection of the threshold *for that workload.*

The performance results for TC+ATD are very positive; they demonstrate that the benefits of UCP for managing a shared cache can be obtained with a hardware implementation that is much simpler and scalable. Table 4 summarizes the storage overheads required to implement different cache management schemes. In particular, note that for most of the approaches, the storage overhead is measured in kilobytes (KB), whereas for TC+ATD, the storage overhead is only a few *bytes.* It is also important to point out that the overheads in Table 4 do not account for the logic and state required to implement the partition-decision logic (e.g., the Lookahead algorithm) where necessary, i.e., UCP. While TADIP's storage overhead is the same as TC+ATD's, our proposed approach appears to perform slightly better according to our simulations.

Table 4. Summary of overheads for different cache management schemes. Example storage overhead assumes s=4096 sets, w=16 ways, N=4 cores, t=36 bits per shadow tag entry, $\alpha=\frac{1}{128}$ (DSS sampling rate), m=2 (Way Merging rate), UMON counters, ATD miss counters and TADIP PSEL counters are b=10 bits each.

	Shadow Tag Storage	Counters (UMON/miss ctrs/PSEL)	Search Space Size	Storage 4MB/16-way L2, 4 cores
UCP (*no DSS*)	$swtN$	wNb	$O(w^N)$	1.1 MB
UCP (*w/ DSS*)	$\alpha swtN$	wNb	$O(w^N)$	9.1 KB
Thr. Caging (*w/ DSS*)	$\alpha swtN$	0	0	9.0 KB
TADIP	0	Nb	0	5.0 B
TC+ATD	0	Nb	0	5.0 B

4 Scaling and Sensitivity Analysis

4.1 Scaling to More Cores

Figure 5(a) shows the weighted speedups for 8-core configurations using an 8MB, 32-way LLC (the other metrics show similar trends and are omitted for brevity). The workloads feature different mixes of the same thrashing and non-thrashing applications from Table 2, although the specific workload compositions are omitted due to space constraints. The overall results are similar to the four-core results presented earlier in that TC provides some performance gain primarily due to allowing non-thrashing applications to share the same partition. In these workloads, the ATD approach introduces more performance degradation than before. It is important to note that we have *not* re-optimized the $\tilde{\theta}_{miss}$

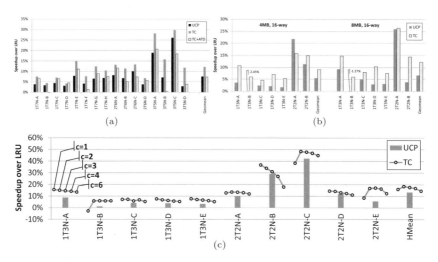

Fig. 5. (a) Weighted speedup results for 8-core workloads, (b) Weighted speedup results for smaller and lower-associativity caches, (c) Thrasher Caging performance for different cage sizes.

threshold for these simulations (i.e., this uses the threshold optimized for the four-core case). Overall, Thrasher Caging is an effective approach to managing a shared cache among many cores. With ATD, TC can on average still provide the performance benefits of UCP but with a trivial hardware overhead.

4.2 Sensitivity to Cache Configurations

Our results thus far have shown that Thrasher Caging with ATD works well for 4 and 8 cores on a processor with a shared 8MB, 32-way LLC. This cache configuration may be somewhat aggressive compared to current processors, so we also present results with 8MB/16-way and 4MB/16-way LLC's. Figure 5(b) shows the weighted speedup results for the four-core workloads. The overall results are similar to the earlier 8MB/32-way results, showing that our approach is also effective for less aggressive cache organizations.

4.3 Parametric Sensitivity

Our Thrasher Caging approach makes use of a few parameters that need to be tuned. In particular, the size of the per-thrasher cage and the various thrasher-detection thresholds all need to be chosen appropriately. Figure 5(c) shows the weighted speedup of TC (without ATD) for various cage sizes, along with the performance of UCP for reference. While we have used a cache size of $c=2$ throughout this paper, choosing a cage size of three or four does not have much impact on per-workload and overall performance. For a few workloads, having a cage too small ($c=1$) or too large ($c=6$) does adversely affect the performance. For the four-core results in this section, we have only conducted the sensitivity analysis on a subset of our workloads due to the large number of simulations required as well as to reduce problems associated with over-tuning.

The original thrasher classification criteria described in Section 4 uses two thresholds: θ_{miss} and $\theta_{MissRate}$. For our four-core workloads with a 8MB/32-way cache, we found that the best values for these thresholds were $\theta_{miss}=100$ and $\theta_{MissRate}=0.5\%$ (accounting for DSS). While these values may seem low, we found that for this cache size, program behaviors were very bimodal in that they either exhibited many misses or very few misses, but seldom had behaviors in between. Note also that this is a dynamic metric in that we collect these based on the number of *cycles* of execution rather than the number of instructions executed. That means a program could have a high MPKI rate, but a low IPC rate could still result in few observed misses within a fixed time interval. We experimented with a wide range of threshold values, and even using $\theta_{miss}=4000$ and $\theta_{MissRate}=6.0\%$ we achieved average weighted speedups within 1.8% of those achieved with the best threshold values. So while the thresholds might be viewed as somewhat arbitrary, the performance results are not very sensitive to the exact choices.

For the approximate thrasher detection threshold $\tilde{\theta}_{miss}$ we used a value of 2000 misses. Changing the threshold by ±1000 results in less than 2.4% loss in the performance benefit over LRU. Overall, the proposed technique does not exhibit any exceptional negative sensitivity to the exact threshold value.

5 Conclusions

In this work, we have shown that cache sharing problems are generally caused by a few applications that generate a large number of misses that end up displacing the cachelines used by the other programs. By simply containing and controlling these few programs, our Thrasher Caging technique can achieve better performance than UCP with a simpler implementation, and using Approximate Thrasher Detection we can *completely* eliminate all of the shadow tag, utility monitor and partitioning logic overheads. Finding simple, low-overhead mechanisms is critical for the adoption of such techniques in more constrained embedded multi-core processor designs. Modern processors contain other shared resources such as off-chip bandwidth and power; a possible avenue for future research is to explore whether simple management schemes similar in spirit to the techniques proposed in this paper can also provide most of the benefits of more complex approaches.

Acknowledgments

This research is supported by the National Science Foundation under Grant No. 0702275.

References

1. Bader, D.A., Li, Y., Li, T., Sachdeva, V.: BioPerf: A Benchmark Suite to Evaluate High-Performance Computer Architecture of Bioinformatics Applications. In: Proc. of the IEEE Intl. Symp. on Workload Characterization, Austin, TX, USA, October 2005, pp. 163–173 (2005)

2. Chandra, D., Guo, F., Kim, S., Solihin, Y.: Predicting Inter-Thread Cache Contenton on a Chip Multi-Processor Architecture. In: Proc. of the 11th Intl. Symp. on High Performance Computer Architecture, February 2005, pp. 340–351 (2005)

3. Chang, J., Sohi, G.: Cooperative Cache Partitioning for Chip Multiprocessors. In: Proc. of the 21st Intl. Conf. on Supercomputing, June 2007, pp. 242–252 (2007)

4. Dybdahl, H., Stenström, P., Natvig, L.: A Cache-Partitioning Aware Replacement Policy for Chip Multiprocessors. In: Proc. of the Intl. Conf. on High Performance Computing, Bangalore, India (December 2006)

5. Fritts, J.E., Steiling, F.W., Tucek, J.A.: MediaBench II Video: Expediting the Next Generation of Video Systems Research. In: Embedded Processors for Multimedia and Communications II, Proceedings of the SPIE, March 2005, vol. 5683, pp. 79–93 (2005)

6. Guthaus, M.R., Ringenberg, J.S., Ernst, D., Austin, T.M., Mudge, T., Brown, R.B.: MiBench: A Free, Commerically Representative Embedded Benchmark Suite. In: Proc. of the 4th Workshop on Workload Characterization, Austin, TX, USA, December 2001, pp. 83–94 (2001)

7. Hamerly, G., Perelman, E., Lau, J., Calder, B.: SimPoint 3.0: Faster and More Flexible Program Analysis. In: Proc. of the Workshop on Modeling, Benchmarking and Simulation (June 2005)

8. Hsu, L., Reinhardt, S., Iyer, R., Makineni, S.: Communist, Utilitarian, and Capitalist Cache Policies on CMPs: Caches as a Shared Resource. In: Proc. of the 15th Intl. Conf. on Parallel Architectures and Compilation Techniques, September 2006, pp. 13–22 (2006)

9. Jaleel, A., Hasenplaugh, W., Qureshi, M., Sebot, J., Steely Jr., S., Emer, J.: Adaptive Insertion Policies for Managing Shared Caches. In: Proc. of the 17th Intl. Conf. on Parallel Architectures and Compilation Techniques (September 2007)

10. Kim, S., Chandra, D., Solihin, Y.: Fair Cache Sharing and Partitioning in a Chip Multiprocessor Architecture. In: Proc. of the 13th Intl. Conf. on Parallel Architectures and Compilation Techniques, September 2004, pp. 111–122 (2004)

11. Lee, C., Potkonjak, M., Mangione-Smith, W.H.: MediaBench: A Tool for Evaluating and Synthesizing Multimedia and Communication Systems. In: Proc. of the 30th Intl. Symp. on Microarchitecture, Research Triangle Park, NC, USA, December 1997, pp. 330–335 (1997)

12. Lin, J., Lu, Q., Ding, X., Zhang, Z., Sadayappan, P.: Gaining Insights into Multicore Cache Partitioning: Bridging the Gap between Simulation and Real Systems. In: Proc. of the 14th Intl. Symp. on High Performance Computer Architecture, February 2008, pp. 367–378 (2008)

13. Loh, G.H., Subramaniam, S., Xie, Y.: Zesto: A Cycle-Level Simulator for Highly Detailed Microarchitecture Exploration. In: Proc. of the Intl. Symp. on Performance Analysis of Systems and Software, Boston, MA, USA (April 2009)

14. Luo, K., Gummaraju, J., Franklin, M.: Balancing Throughput and Fairness in SMT Processors. In: Proc. of the 2001 Intl. Symp. on Performance Analysis of Systems and Software, Tucson, AZ, USA, November 2001, pp. 164–171 (2001)

15. Moreto, M., Cazorla, F., Ramirez, A., Valero, M.: Explaining Dynamic Cache Partitioning Speed Ups. Computer Architecture Letters 6 (2007)
16. Narayanan, R., Ozisikyilmaz, B., Zambreno, J., Memik, H., Choudhary, A.: MineBench: A Benchmark Suite for Data Mining Workloads. In: Proc. of the IEEE Intl. Symp. on Workload Characterization, October 2006, pp. 182–188 (2006)
17. Qureshi, M., Lynch, D., Mutlu, O., Patt, Y.: A Case for MLP-Aware Cache Replacement. In: Proc. of the 33rd Intl. Symp. on Computer Architecture, June 2006, pp. 167–178 (2006)
18. Qureshi, M., Patt, Y.: Utility-Based Cache Partitioning: A Low-Overhead, High-Performance, Runtime Mechanism to Partition Shared Caches. In: Proc. of the 39th Intl. Symp. on Microarchitecture, December 2006, pp. 423–432 (2006)
19. Rafique, N., Lin, W.-T., Thottethodi, M.: Architectural Support for Operating System-Driven CMP Cache Management. In: Proc. of the 15th Intl. Conf. on Parallel Architectures and Compilation Techniques, September 2006, pp. 2–12 (2006)
20. Snavely, A., Tullsen, D.: Symbiotic Job Scheduling for a Simultaneous Multithreading Processor. In: Proc. of the 9th Symp. on Architectural Support for Programming Languages and Operating Systems, November 2000, pp. 234–244 (2000)
21. Srikantaiah, S., Kandemir, M., Irwin, M.J.: Adaptive Set-Pinning: Managing Shared Caches in Chip Multiprocessors. In: Proc. of the 13th Symp. on Architectural Support for Programming Languages and Operating Systems, Seattle, WA, USA (March 2009)
22. Stone, H., Tuerk, J., Wolf, J.: Optimal Paritioning of Cache Memory. IEEE Transactions on Computers 41(9), 1054–1068 (1992)
23. Suh, G.E., Rudolph, L., Devadas, S.: Dynamic Partitioning of Shared Cache Memory. Journal of Supercomputing 28(1), 7–26 (2004)
24. Xie, Y., Loh, G.H.: Dynamic Classification of Program Memory Behaviors in CMPs. In: Proc. of the Workshop on Chip Multiprocessor Memory Systems and Interconnects, Beijing, China (June 2008)
25. Xie, Y., Loh, G.H.: PIPP: Promotion/Insertion Pseudo-Partitioning of Multi-Core Shared Caches. In: Proc. of the 36th Intl. Symp. on Computer Architecture, Austin, TX, USA (June 2009)
26. Yeh, T.Y., Faloutsos, P., Patel, S.J., Reinman, G.: ParallAX: an Architecture for Real-Time Physics. In: Proc. of the 34th Intl. Symp. on Computer Architecture, June 2007, pp. 232–243 (2007)

SRP: Symbiotic Resource Partitioning of the Memory Hierarchy in CMPs*

Shekhar Srikantaiah and Mahmut Kandemir

Department of Computer Science and Engineering
Pennsylvania State University, University Park PA 16802, USA
{srikanta,kandemir}@cse.psu.edu

Abstract. There have been many recent works in the context of Chip Multi-processors (CMPs) investigating the need of intelligent shared cache partitioning which is believed to reduce the pressure on the off-chip bandwidth. Management of the off-chip memory bandwidth to improve system performance and/or mitigate performance volatility of applications has itself received considerable attention. Coordinated resource management schemes treat the interactions between cache allocation and bandwidth management as a black-box. This hinders the ability of these schemes from exploiting the intricate inter-relationships between the resource management strategies. In a multiprogrammed scenario, given the limited availability of the on-chip cache, it is not feasible to entirely eliminate off-chip accesses. However, it is possible to mitigate the impact of additional queueing delays associated with the memory controller by avoiding multiple applications from exercising the off-chip bandwidth simultaneously. Therefore, from the point of view of improving system performance, it is more important to have a symbiotic resource partitioning scheme that performs partitioning of each resource based on feedback it receives from the partitioning of the other.

Symbiotic resource partitioning (SRP) proposed in this paper avoids the scenarios of multiple applications exercising the off-chip memory bandwidth simultaneously by appropriately controlling the cache partitioning. In order to control the cache partitioning, SRP employs an empirical model that relies on a metric (last level cache misses per cycle) that represents the off-chip memory bandwidth demand of the applications and models the impact of cache partitioning on bandwidth demand by representing the last level cache misses per cycle metric as a function of the cache allocation per application. This model is dynamically updated to account for the phase behavior of the applications. Moreover, SRP is an iterative approach wherein each iteration of the approach consists of an update to the model, cache partitioning and bandwidth partitioning with a feedback from bandwidth partitioning that updates the model. Extensive simulations with a full system simulator and applications from the MiBench benchmark suite shows that SRP leads to a significant overall improvement in system performance as compared to a state-of the-art cache and bandwidth management schemes.

* This research is supported in part by NSF grants CNS #0720645, CCF #0811687, CCF #0702519, CNS #0202007 and CNS #0509251, a grant from Microsoft Corporation and support from the Gigascale Systems Research Focus Center, one of the five research centers funded under SRC's Focus Center Research Program.

Y.N. Patt et al. (Eds.): HiPEAC 2010, LNCS 5952, pp. 277–291, 2010.

1   Introduction

As the performance imperative of Moore's Law is approaching an upper limit for increasing processing power simply by increasing clock speeds, all major chip manufacturers have turned to chip multiprocessors (CMPs) to boost performance and improve thermal characteristics while reducing area and power requirements. Consequently, almost all computer systems today, from embedded devices to petascale computing systems, are being constructed using CMPs. Advancing into the CMP era has elevated the importance of the performance of the shared memory hierarchy in CMPs. Contention for resources in the shared memory hierarchy with limited resources like on-chip cache [1], [2], [3] and off-chip bandwidth [4] can significantly hamper the performance of applications resulting in degradation of the overall system throughput and fairness. Ideally, a CMP would perform off-chip communication as rarely as possible as off-chip memory accesses are not only slower but are also more energy consuming compared to on-chip accesses. Further, increasing number of cores would only exacerbate the problem of managing the limited off-chip bandwidth.

There have been many recent works investigating the need of intelligent shared cache partitioning [2], [5], [6], [7], [8], [9], [10], which is believed to reduce the pressure on the off-chip bandwidth. Management of the off-chip memory bandwidth [11], [12], [13], [14], [15], [16] to improve system performance and/or mitigate performance volatility of applications has itself received considerable attention due to the growing significance of the problem. Coordinated resource management schemes [17], [18] treat the interactions between cache allocation and bandwidth management as a black-box. This hinders the ability of these schemes from exploiting the intricate inter-relationships between the resource management strategies. In a multiprogrammed scenario, given the limited availability of the on-chip cache, it is not feasible to entirely eliminate off-chip accesses. However, it is possible to mitigate the impact of additional queueing delays associated with the memory controller by avoiding multiple applications from exercising the off-chip bandwidth simultaneously. Therefore, from the point of view of improving system performance, it is more important to have a *symbiotic resource partitioning* scheme that performs partitioning of each resource based on feedback (reinforcement) it receives from the partitioning of the other.

Modeling the interaction between cache partitioning and off-chip memory bandwidth demand can take us a long way in implementing such a symbiotic resource partitioning scheme. Although some previous works [4], [19] have indicated that metrics like cache miss rates, instructions per cycle (IPC) and misses per instruction (MPI) are not good metrics for measuring the system performance, many shared cache management approaches proposed in the literature [2], [7], [8], [9] continue to use them. Partitioning the off-chip memory bandwidth has an influence on the system performance and therefore influences the last level cache misses per cycle (MPC) as observed by the application. Therefore, the model also needs to be reinforced through feedback from bandwidth partitioning.

In order to address the above mentioned problems, in this paper, we propose such a symbiotic partitioning for resource partitioning across the memory hierarchy as an important step towards transcending the everlasting memory wall problem. Symbiotic resource partitioning (SRP) avoids the scenarios of multiple applications exercising the off-chip memory bandwidth simultaneously by appropriately controlling the cache partitioning. In order to control the cache partitioning, SRP employs an empirical model that relies on a metric (last level cache misses per cycle) that represents the off-chip memory bandwidth demand of the applications and models the impact of cache partitioning on bandwidth demand by representing the last level cache misses per cycle metric as a function of the cache allocation per application. This model is dynamically updated to account for the phase behavior of the applications. Moreover, SRP is an iterative approach wherein each iteration of the approach consists of (i) an update to the model (modeling the impact of cache partitioning on bandwidth demand); (ii) cache partitioning in order to reduce the overall demand on off-chip memory bandwidth; (iii) bandwidth partitioning based on the cache partitioning to improve overall system performance; and (iv) feedback from the bandwidth partitioning that reinforces the model used for cache partitioning.

The rest of the paper is structured as follows. The motivation for a symbiotic resource partitioning scheme is presented in Section 2. We describe the symbiotic resource partitioning approach including modeling and the iterative partitioning approach in Section 3. Our experimental setup is described in Section 4 followed by results in Section 5. The related work is described in Section 6, followed by our conclusions in Section 7.

2   Motivation

2.1   Choice of an Observable Metric

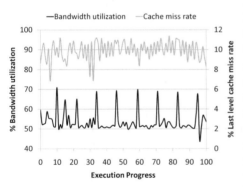

Many emerging CMPs employ shared last level caches which can be partitioned among concurrently executing applications. It is not very hard to see that the memory bandwidth requirement of an application depends on its shared cache allocation. To a certain extent, it is true that an increase in the cache allocation of an application results in a decrease in its off-chip bandwidth requirement (until the working set size completely fits in the cache). An increased cache space allocation can be used to retain additional memory blocks required by the application in the future on-chip, leading to reduced off-chip accesses. An increased cache space allocation also leads to re-

Fig. 1. Variations of percentage of peak-bandwidth demanded by *adpcm* with the last level (L2) cache miss rates

duction in the cache miss rate. Therefore, it is tempting (for optimization schemes that target to reduce the off-chip memory bandwidth) to assume that a reduction in cache miss rate is a good optimization metric to be targeted, *i.e.*, to assume that minimizing the last level cache miss rate would minimize the off-chip bandwidth demand and thereby improve system performance.

Figure 1 shows a dual-axes graph that plots the percentage of the peak off-chip memory bandwidth demanded by application adpcm (from MiBench [20]) on the primary y-axis along with the last level cache miss rates on the secondary y-axis with execution progress on the x-axis. Two important observations can be made from this plot. Firstly, the bandwidth demand is not uniform and the peak bandwidth demand of an application is significantly higher than the average bandwidth demanded. The maximum demanded bandwidth by adpcm is 70.8%, while the median bandwidth demand is 51.2% of the peak available bandwidth. Such peaks in the bandwidth demand increase the queuing delays in the memory controller. Therefore, it is important to address the peaks in bandwidth demands along with reducing the average bandwidth demand. Secondly, and more importantly, there is no correlation between the variations in the bandwidth demand and the variations in the last level cache miss rate. To quantify the relationship between the two metrics, we compute the statistical correlation between the bandwidth demand ($\mathcal{B}$) of an application and the last level cache miss rates ($\mathcal{M}$) as:

$$Corr(\mathcal{B}, \mathcal{M}) = \frac{Cov(\mathcal{B}, \mathcal{M})}{\sigma(\mathcal{B})\sigma(\mathcal{M})},$$

where $\sigma(\mathcal{B})$ and $\sigma(\mathcal{M})$ are the standard deviations of $\mathcal{B}$ and $\mathcal{M}$, respectively. $Cov(\mathcal{B}, \mathcal{M})$ is the covariance defined as:

$$Cov(\mathcal{B}, \mathcal{M}) = E(\mathcal{B}.\mathcal{M}) - E(\mathcal{B}).E(\mathcal{M}),$$

where $E(\mathcal{B})$ and $E(\mathcal{M})$ denote the expected values of $\mathcal{B}$ and $\mathcal{M}$, respectively. The value of $Corr(\mathcal{B}, \mathcal{M})$ ranges from -1 to 1, where 1 indicates a perfect correlation, 0 indicates no correlation, and -1 indicates negative correlation. A small correlation between $\mathcal{B}$ and $\mathcal{M}$ indicates that last level cache miss rates cannot be used as a measure of the reduction in the off-chip memory bandwidth. The correlation coefficient for adpcm (from Figure 1) is 0.12 which is a small value. This small correlation can be explained by noticing that cache miss rate is the ratio of number of cache misses to the number of accesses, while bandwidth is only dependent on the rate at which misses occur and not the accesses. Consequently, in programs where the number of accesses per unit time varies a lot, the correlation between miss rate and bandwidth demand is poor. Therefore, cache miss rate is not always a good indicator of the bandwidth demands of an application. A system's internal state (bandwidth demand) is said to be *"observable"* by a metric (like cache miss rate) if it is possible to infer (determine) the system state by measuring the metric alone. As seen from Figure 1, cache miss rate is clearly not an observable metric. Ideally, we can infer the extent to which we can improve the off-chip memory bandwidth demand from a metric like *"traffic inefficiency"* proposed in [4]. Traffic inefficiency is defined as the ratio of traffic produced by the cache (usually managed using a policy like LRU) to that of a perfectly managed cache. However, it is hard to measure such a metric online in real systems. A more measurable and observable metric for inferring the off-chip memory bandwidth demand (in unit time) is the average number of last level cache misses per cycle (MPC). As the bandwidth demand is proportional (linearly related) to the average MPC of the last level cache and the cache line size (assumed to be a constant for a specified architecture), MPC can be used as an observable metric for symbiotic resource partitioning.

2.2   Bandwidth Awareness of State-of-the-art Cache Partitioning

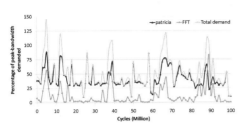

Fig. 2. Variations of percentage of peak-bandwidth demanded by *patricia* and *FFT* as the execution progresses. The two benchmarks are executed along with *susan* and *basicmath* on a 4 core CMP (see Section 1 for details).

A significant consequence of using non-observable metrics in cache partitioning schemes is that they are oblivious to bandwidth demand. As shown above, focussing on improving non-observable metrics like cache miss rate, IPC or MPI does not necessarily translate to reducing off-chip memory bandwidth. Specifically, such approaches do not address the problem of excessive queuing delays in the memory controllers due to multiple applications exercising the off-chip memory bandwidth simultaneously leading to contention in the memory controller queues.

Figure 2 plots the variations in percentage of peak bandwidth demanded by two applications, patricia and FFT, for a duration of 100 Million cycles. We use a state-of-the-art cache partitioning scheme (similar to utility cache partitioning [8]) with a total of four applications (patricia, FFT, susan, and basicmath) running on a 4-core CMP with our baseline configuration (details in Section 4). We plot the bandwidth demand of only the two most bandwidth-sensitive applications for the sake of clarity along with the total bandwidth demanded by the two applications. As we can see from Figure 2, the total demanded bandwidth by only two of the four applications exceeds the available peak bandwidth (100%) five times within an interval of 100 Million cycles. Note that the maximum demand that can be satisfied is 100% and each time this is crossed, it leads to significant queuing delays. An important observation that can be made from this plot is that the total demanded bandwidth increases to more than 100% of the peak available bandwidth mostly when individual application's peaks overlap on one another. A cache partitioning scheme that manages the cache in a bandwidth oblivious manner can result in such simultaneous increases in the demanded bandwidth. However, a more intelligent cache partitioning scheme can address the problem in two ways: (i) We can displace or control the peaks in demanded bandwidth by allocating additional cache space to an application that reduces its bandwidth demand by a greater degree; and (ii) We can utilize bandwidth partitioning in order to guarantee additional bandwidth to an application that is penalized in its cache allocation. Symbiotic resource partitioning performs both the above mentioned functions with an objective of improving the overall system performance.

3   Symbiotic Resource Partitioning

Symbiotic Resource Partitioning (SRP) determines per-application resource quotas in terms of the last level cache allocation and the off-chip memory bandwidth allocation, on the fly, in a transparent manner. Towards this objective, we use an online bandwidth estimation algorithm to dynamically determine the mapping between any given cache allocation and the corresponding application bandwidth requirement. While designing and implementing a symbiotic model for guiding the resource partitioning search is non-trivial, our key insight is to design a model with sufficient expressiveness to incorporate (i) tracking of dynamic memory access patterns, and (ii) minimal assumptions about the inner mechanisms of the the system as a whole, i.e., not assuming the interactions between shared cache partitioning and bandwidth partitioning to be a black box. In order to achieve this, we use a bandwidth-aware cache model based on minimal statistics collection in order to approximate a near-optimal allocation of resources to applications, and an online sampling and statistical interpolation technique that refines the initial model. In the following sections, we first introduce the bandwidth aware cache model and provide an overview of how we fine-tune the model based on online sampling (measurements of the effectiveness of the cache and bandwidth partitioning).

3.1 Bandwidth Aware Cache Model

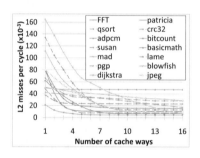

Fig. 3. Variations in misses per cycle (measure of off-chip bandwidth demand) with allocation of different ways of a shared cache

Partitioned shared cache lends itself to accurate and better modeling (over an uncontrolled shared cache) as cache behavior of each application can be modeled independently in the absence of inter-thread interferences. Figure 3 plots the variations in the measured misses-per-cycle (MPC) of various applications on our baseline processor configuration (details in Section 4) by varying the number of cache ways allocated to the application in a 16-way associative shared cache. The generic shape of the curves clearly shows the non-linear dependence of the bandwidth demand of applications measured in MPC on the number of cache ways allocated to it in the way-partitioned shared cache. The saturating non-linear behavior of the MPC of each benchmark (φ_i) observed in the plot can be modeled as a function of the number of cache ways (ω_i) allocated to it in the following general form:

$$\varphi_i = \varphi_i^\infty + \varphi_i^\circ . e^{-\alpha_i . \omega_i}, \tag{1}$$

where φ_i^∞, φ_i°, and α_i are the model parameters. Specifically, φ_i^∞ is the misses per cycle (MPC) of the application i when it is allocated maximum number of cache ways (theoretically, $\omega_i = \infty$). α_i is a parameter that roughly determines the utility of each additional cache way that may be allocated to application i. Also, φ_i° is the difference in MPC of the application when it is allocated no cache and φ_i^∞ (MPC with maximum cache). Note that, the model given in Eq. (1) very well captures the initial exponential decrease and the saturating behavior of the decrease in MPC with the increase in the number of cache ways.

It is important to emphasize that symbiotic resource partitioning can be extended to handle any irregularities in applications response to increasing cache (ways) by increasing the number of parameters in our model (by having a vector of parameters for each

---

Algorithm 1: SYMBIOTIC_PART(C, B, k, QoS_{Th})

comment: Partitions C cache ways and peak bandwidth B among k applications.

//Main iteration performing symbiotic partitioning

while $true$ do
$\left\{ \begin{array}{l} B\_C\_Enf\_Ratio \leftarrow \frac{Bandwidth\_EnforcementInterval}{Cache\_EnforcementInterval} \\ \textbf{for } i \leftarrow 1 \textbf{ to } B\_C\_Enf\_Ratio \\ \quad \textbf{do} \left\{ \begin{array}{l} \text{COLLECT\_NEW\_BANDWIDTH\_DEMAND\_SAMPLES}(Current\_partition) \\ \text{RECALIBRATE\_MODEL}(New\_bandwidth\_demand\_samples) \\ \text{CACHE\_PART}(C, k, model) \\ //\text{minimizes the total demanded bandwidth} \\ \text{SLEEP}(Cache\_EnforcementInterval) \end{array} \right. \\ \text{BANDWIDTH\_PART}(P, k, QoS_{Th}) \end{array} \right.$

---

concave curve). The model needs periodic recalibration in order to account for phase changes in application behavior. This recalibration involves taking new samples of the off-chip memory bandwidth demand for each application in a few cache configurations. We enhance the accuracy of the model through statistical regression to re-approximate the model by interpolating between the pre-computed and experimentally gathered sample points. A recalibration is necessary only if the application access pattern changes. If a new application is co-scheduled on the same infrastructure, we need to sample and compute the model parameters only for the new application. We have thoroughly analyzed the accuracy of the model. The average error between the predicted MPC and the observed MPC is less than 1.4% during multiple recalibrations through the execution across all applications.

3.2 Iterative Bandwidth Aware Symbiotic Resource Partitioning Algorithm

Based on the per-application cache model described above, we find the resource partitioning setting which gives the optimum, i.e., lowest combined bandwidth demand in our case. The symbiotic resource partitioning approach is *iterative* in nature. The partitioning of cache and bandwidth happens in a series of iterations as shown in Algorithm 1. Cache partitioning at the end of one iteration influences the bandwidth partitions in the same iteration and the bandwidth partitioning at the end of the current iteration influences the cache partitions to be selected dynamically in the following iteration. This iterative execution of our approach enables (i) adaptive behavior of both bandwidth and cache partitioning approaches; and (ii) inter-adaptability between bandwidth and cache partitioning. The statistical regression based bandwidth predictor described in the previous section is used to perform cache and bandwidth partitioning. Each cache partitioning iteration collects new samples of bandwidth usage for a given cache allocation. These new samples are used to recalibrate the prediction model as described in the previous section. The cache partitions determined are enforced for an interval of $Cache\_EnforcementInterval$. This is lesser than the duration for which each bandwidth partition is enforced ($Bandwidth\_EnforcementInterval$) due to the coarser phases observed in changes in the bandwidth demands.

This brings us to the important topic of overheads involved in symbiotic resource partitioning. There are perceivably two kinds of overheads involved with our approach: (i) The cost of regression analysis based prediction and search of the configuration to

Table 1. Baseline configuration

Processor Cores	2 GHz, 4/8 cores with private L1 data and instruction caches
Private L1 D–Caches	Direct mapped, 16KB, 64 bytes block size, 3 cycle access latency
Private L1 I–Caches	Direct mapped, 16KB, 64 bytes block size, 3 cycle access latency
Shared L2 Cache	16–way set associative, 512KB per core, 64 bytes block size, 15 cycle access latency
DRAM controller	on-chip; 128-entry req. buffer, FR-FCFS/open-page policy, 32-entry write data buffer, reads prioritized over writes
DRAM chip parameters	based on Micron DDR2-800 timing parameters [21]
DIMM configuration	single-rank, 8 DRAM chips put together on a DIMM (dual in-line memory module) to provide a 64-bit wide data interface to the DRAM controller
Round-trip L2 miss latency	For a 64-byte cache line, uncontended: row-buffer hit: 150 cycles, closed: 200 cycles, conflict: 300 cycles
DRAM channels	Scaled with cores: 1, 2 parallel lock-step 64-bit wide channels for respectively 4, 8 cores (each channel has 6.4 GB/s peak bandwidth)

be enforced and (ii) The cost of repartitioning either the bandwidth or the cache. We use a simple iterative search algorithm that moves towards the direction of increasing combined utility value for all valid configurations at each iteration. To avoid reaching a local optimum, we conduct searches from different points chosen randomly until each search reaches an optimum. We use the best result obtained from all searches. This low overhead method costs around 2400 cycles for our experiments, which is an insignificant fraction (0.024%) of the interval at which it executes. In general, the model has complexity that is proportional to the number of resources and number of applications. The overheads due to system calls to modify bandwidth partitions is minimal due to coarser granularity of bandwidth partitioning (comparable to scheduler time slice). Our OS interface for enforcement of cache partitioning is similar to that in [9]. A detailed discussion about timing and area overheads of the necessary hardware implementation can be found in [9]. We would like to emphasize here that all the experimental results discussed in Section 5 includes each of these overheads as we perform our simulations on a full system simulator.

4 Experimental Setup

4.1 Base System Configuration

We evaluate the proposed SRP on 4-core and 8-core CMPs. The first-level instruction cache and data cache are private to the processor core. All the cores share a level-two data cache with LRU replacement. We simulate the complete system using Simics full-system simulator augmented with accurate timing models similar to RUBY module of GEMS [22]. As our study deals with the memory bandwidth, we model the memory system in detail. DRAM bank conflicts and bus queuing delays are modeled. The DRAM parameters are modeled to resemble the Micron DDR2-800 [21]. The baseline configuration of our target CMP and the parameters used for the simulated memory hierarchy is as shown in Table 1.

4.2 Benchmarks

To quantitatively evaluate the effectiveness of our symbiotic resource partitioning approach on CMPs, we used multiprogrammed workloads of programs consisting of

Table 2. Benchmarks and their characteristics. MCPI stands for Memory Cycles Per Instruction (the number of cycles spent waiting for memory divided by number of instructions), L2MR(%) stands for the percentage L2 cache miss rate, and L2MPKI stands for Misses per Kilo Instructions in the L2 cache.

Benchmark	Category	MCPI	L2MR(%)	L2MPKI	Type
FFT (F)	Telecomm	1.22	5.46	19.06	II
patricia (P)	Network	1.17	6.5	12.38	IV
qsort (Q)	Auto/Industrial	1.12	9.55	31.36	IV
crc32 (C)	Telecomm	1.12	12.58	25.79	IV
adpcm (A)	Telecomm	1.09	18.75	51.41	IV
bitcount (B)	Auto/Industrial	1.08	7.16	4.77	III
susan (S)	Auto/Industrial	0.99	6.82	7.69	III
basicmath (H)	Auto/Industrial	0.96	4.02	6.64	I
mad (M)	Consumer	0.94	2.8	9.29	I
lame (L)	Consumer	0.91	3.45	11.86	II
pgp (G)	Security	0.86	5.92	14.76	II
blowfish (W)	Security	0.81	8.28	8.76	III
dijkstra (D)	Network	0.74	1.31	5.30	I
jpeg (J)	Consumer	0.66	2.47	6.25	I

applications (from the MiBench benchmark suite [20]) with diverse computational and memory access characteristics. MiBench is a set of commercially representative embedded programs from many different categories of application domains. All fourteen benchmarks used in our evaluation along with the categories to which they belong and their L2 cache and memory access characteristics are shown in Table 2. In particular, the characteristics presented include the memory cycles per instruction (MCPI) which is a measure of the program's memory intensiveness, the L2 miss rate (L2MR), and Misses per Kilo Instructions in the L2 (L2MPKI). Our applications are ordered based on their memory intensiveness in Table 2. Further, we divide the applications into four categories based on their (L2MR, L2MPKI) characteristics. The four types represent I(low, low), II(low, high), III(high, low), and IV(high, high). The classification of the applications into these four types is also shown in Table 2. We evaluate combinations of multiprogrammed workloads running on 4-core, and 8-core CMPs. Obviously, evaluating each combination of 4 benchmarks on a 4-core system requires an enormous amount of simulation time. Therefore, we have evaluated combinations of benchmarks from different categories. The alphabet next to each application in the table indicates a unique identifier used to represent the application in a multiprogrammed workload. In all our experiments, all the benchmark programs use the large input set. We warm up caches for approximately 100 Million cycles before collecting any statistics.

5   Experimental Results

5.1   Schemes for Comparison

Cache Only. In this scheme, only the shared last level cache is managed using a partitioning scheme similar to utility cache partitioning [8], while the bandwidth is shared among the cores with a conventional first-ready first-come-first-serve scheme [23].

Bandwidth Only. This scheme employs an un-partitioned (shared) last level cache while memory bandwidth management is performed using a scheme similar to stall-time fair memory scheduler [13].

Fair Share. This scheme tries to improve the fairness among applications by managing both the shared last level cache and the off-chip memory bandwidth. We use a cache management scheme similar to that proposed in [7] for partitioning the L2 cache among applications and use a fair memory bandwidth management scheme proposed in [15] for managing the scheduling of off-chip memory accesses.

5.2   Performance Metrics

The Fair Speedup metric (FS) of a workload using a partitioning scheme is defined as the harmonic mean of per application speedup using the scheme with respect to a baseline equal share case. We use equal sharing of cache ways and memory bandwidth for the base case. Fair speedup achieved by a scheme can be expressed as $FS(scheme) = N/\sum_{i=1}^{N} \frac{Execution\_Time_{app_i(scheme)}}{Execution\_Time_{app_i(base)}}$, where N is the number of applications in the workload, i.e., the set of applications that execute together. Note that FS is an indicator of the overall improvement in execution time gained across the applications. It is also a metric of fairness.

The Weighted Speedup metric (WS) of the workload using a partitioning scheme is defined as the sum of per application speedups using the scheme with respect to the baseline equal resource share case, i.e., $WS(scheme) = \frac{1}{N}\sum_{i=1}^{N} \frac{Execution\_Time_{app_i(base)}}{Execution\_Time_{app_i(scheme)}}$, where N is the number of applications in the workload.

5.3   Comparison of Fair Speedup Metric

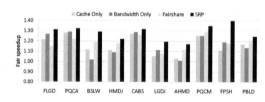

Fig. 4. Fair speedup results for the different mixes of applications. Each application mix is represented by a set of four alphabets, each representing one application (see Table 2).

Figure 4 plots the fair speedup metric of various schemes with respect to the Equal share partitioning scheme on different workloads. We observe that in all cases, the SRP scheme performs better than all the other schemes. The base case partitioning statically enforces equal sharing of the cache and bandwidth across applications with varying demands. The Cache only scheme, on the other hand, dynamically adapts to varying cache demands and partitions the shared last level cache of a CMP with the objective of reducing cache misses. We can observe from the figure that application mixes with applications that have a high cache miss rate (like PQCA, CABS, and PQCM) achieve significant benefits with the cache only scheme. But, as shown in Figure 2, this can still lead to excessive queuing delays in the memory controller. SRP avoids such delays and therefore performs better than cache only scheme. Similarly, many application mixes with applications that are memory bandwidth intensive (like FLGD, PQCA, LGDJ, and FASH) achieve a significant benefit with the bandwidth only scheme. The remaining application mixes that have a relatively more uniform mix of application characteristics (like HMDJ, AHMD, FPSH, and PBLD) tend to benefit more from the fair share scheme as this scheme manages both cache and bandwidth. However, the fair share scheme lacks coordination between the two management schemes, and therefore, SRP outperforms the fair share scheme in all cases. Overall, SRP achieves an average of 29.1%, 12.9%, 11.8%, and 10.3% improvement over the equal share, cache only, bandwidth only, and fair share schemes respectively, on the fair speedup metric.

5.4 Comparison of Weighted Speedup Metric

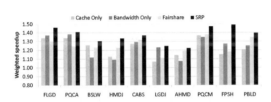

Fig. 5. Weighted speedup results for the different mixes of applications. Each application mix is represented by a set of four alphabets, each representing one application (see Table 2).

Figure 5 plots the normalized weighted speedup metric of various schemes with respect to the equal share partitioning scheme. One of the important problems addressed by symbiotic resource partitioning is the simultaneous increase in bandwidth demands of multiple applications in a multiprogrammed workload. Therefore, as seen from Figure 5, the maximum benefits from SRP are obtained in case of FPSH, which is constituted of benchmarks that are relatively more bandwidth sensitive. We observed that this is due to the increased number of conflicting (simultaneous) increases in bandwidth demand by the applications involved, which SRP is able to address that no other scheme can. Another important observation from Figure 5 is that the fair share scheme does not even perform as well as processor partitioning or cache partitioning alone in some cases, while SRP outperforms all the other schemes. Therefore, it is not only important to adopt an integrated cache and memory bandwidth partitioning scheme in order to adapt to changing demands of applications, but also to have a symbiosis between them. Overall, SRP achieves an average of 37.4%, 15.6%, 14.1%, and 12.9% improvement over the equal share, cache only, bandwidth only, and fair share schemes respectively, on the weighted speedup metric.

5.5 Discussion

The results so far clearly show that our approach is able to improve overall system performance. To study the reason for this in more detail, we also collected some more statistics. As we observed in Section 2 (Figure 2), the total demanded bandwidth by only two of the four applications (in the FPSH workload) exceeded the available peak bandwidth (100%) five times within an interval of 100 Million cycles when executed with a state-of-the-art cache partitioning scheme. The maximum demand that can be satisfied is 100% and each time this is crossed, it leads to significant queuing delays.

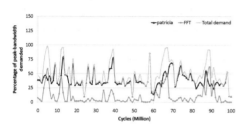

Fig. 6. Variations in percentage of peak-bandwidth demanded by *patricia* and *FFT* as the execution progresses with our symbiotic resource partitioning scheme. The two benchmarks are executed along with *susan* and *basicmath* on the baseline 4 core CMP (see Section 1).

Figure 6 plots the variations in percentage of peak-bandwidth demanded by *patricia* and *FFT* as the execution progresses with our symbiotic resource partitioning scheme. In order to make the comparison easier, we plot the same two applications as in Figure 2. Note that, the bandwidth demand of the other two applications (susan and basicmath) are negligible in comparison in both cases. As can be observed from Figure 6, the total demanded bandwidth by *patricia* and *FFT* is always below the peak available bandwidth. The bandwidth-aware nature of cache partitioning performed by symbiotic resource partitioning reduces the total bandwidth demanded by the applications. For instance, careful observation of the behavior of applications in the interval 60-70 Million cycles in Figure 2 and Figure 6 shows that, the peaks of the bandwidth demand of the two applications do not overlap. Although in some instances, the bandwidth demand of one application increases it results in a much larger decrease in the bandwidth demand of the other. This results in overall reduction in the queuing delays faced by the application resulting in an improvement in overall system performance.

5.6   Sensitivity Analysis

Sensitivity to enforcement interval. Recall that both cache partitioning and bandwidth partitioning are enforced dynamically for a duration of EnforcementInterval. This interval parameter decides the frequency at which partitions are reconfigured. We studied the impact of varying this parameter from its default value of 10 Million cycles used for cache partitioning and 50 Million cycles used for bandwidth partitioning in all our results. The results of varying the EnforcementInterval for the bandwidth partitioning of the workloads are presented in Figure 7(a). It is observed that we obtain better improvements as we reduce the reconfiguration interval from 100 Million to 50 Million cycles, as seen from Figure 7(a), as this provides a finer grain control on partitioning. However, further decreasing the interval (to 10 Million cycles) does not lead to additional benefits due to overheads involved in repeated reconfigurations. In a similar manner, Figure 7(b) plots results of varying the EnforcementInterval for cache partitioning of the same application mixes in the range of 1 Million - 100 Million cycles. It can be observed that the best trade-offs between repartitioning overheads and performance improvements are achieved at 10 Million cycles interval.

Sensitivity to number of cores. The ability of symbiotic resource partitioning approach to scale to higher number of cores and larger caches (higher associativity for a

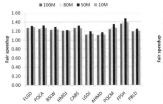

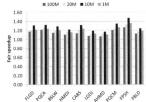

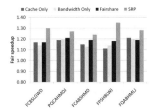

(a) Sensitivity to enforcement interval of bandwidth partitioning

(b) Sensitivity to enforcement interval of cache partitioning

(c) Improvements in the fair speedup metric with 8 core CMP.

Fig. 7. Results of sensitivity analysis

way partitioned cache) is critical for its success and needs to be evaluated. Note that the per-application model used in SRP is highly scalable and can easily scale to higher number of processors and cache sizes. We evaluated the performance of our SRP approach with a 8 core system against that obtained on our default configuration of 4 cores (see Table 1). The results with respect to fair speedup metric are plotted in Figure 7(c). Note that the fair speedup metric is computed with equal partitioning on the respective systems. We observe that SRP performs better with respect to the equal share case on an 8 core CMP than that achieved on an 4 core CMP. On an average, in the 8 core case, we see an improvement of 28.8% on the fair speedup metric over the equal share case as opposed to a 29.1% improvement obtained averaged across the workloads in the 4 core case.

6   Related Work

Recently, many researchers have explored CMP cache partitioning designs that attempt to alleviate inter-thread conflicts at the shared last level cache [3], [5], [7], [8], [9], [10], [17], [24]. Suh et al. [10] proposed a dynamic partitioning technique that partitions the last level cache at the granularity of cache ways to improve system throughput. Later, Qureshi and Patt [8] proposed a utility based cache partitioning scheme where the share received by an application was proportional to the utility rather than its demand. Our approach can be viewed as a utility based approach, where the relative utility of cache/bandwidth is directly measured based on the feedback from performance counters after bandwidth partitioning. Chang and Sohi [5] have proposed cooperative cache partitioning, wherein they use multiple time sharing partitions to resolve cache contention. They use similar metrics as ours (fair speedup and QoS metric) to quantify the benefits from their approach. All these studies are oblivious to bandwidth partitioning and thereby susceptible to suffering from excessive queuing delays due to multiple applications simultaneously exercising the off-chip memory bandwidth.

Nesbit et al. [15] showed that the commonly used FR-FCFS memory scheduling can lead to QoS and fairness problems if used in the context of multiprogrammed workloads, and propose the Fair Queueing Memory Scheduler (FQMS) to address these limitations. FQMS partitions a available off-chip DRAM bandwidth of a CMP among applications by providing an OS-specified minimum service guarantee to each thread. Policies for allocating the off-chip bandwidth to meet system level performance objectives are not explored, and allocation decisions are left to the OS. Mutlu et al. [13] proposed stall time fair memory scheduling (STFM), a technique that provides QoS to applications sharing the DRAM by equalizing the slowdowns that are observed by equal-priority threads. Later, the same authors improve upon STFM via batch scheduling [14], in which groups of outstanding DRAM requests from a given thread form the fundamental unit of scheduling. Neither of these works addresses the dynamic partitioning of off-chip bandwidth, and similar to FQMS, they leave allocation decisions to the OS. None of these schemes consider the impact of cache partitioning on the bandwidth demand of applications.

Bitirgen et al. [18] propose a framework that manages multiple shared CMP resources in a coordinated fashion to enforce higher-level performance objectives. Resource allocation is modeled as a machine learning problem and it treats the relationship between cache partitioning and off-chip memory bandwidth as a black box. In contrast, SRP exploits this relationship by modeling it to reduce excessive queuing delays in the memory controller.

7   Conclusion

The proposed symbiotic resource partitioning achieves significant improvements over partitioning of either the shared L2 cache or the off-chip bandwidth in isolation. We proposed a statistical regression based prediction model to predict the bandwidth demand of applications and techniques to find the most suitable bandwidth and cache partitions to reduce the total bandwidth demand. Extensive simulations using a full system simulator and a set of diverse multiprogrammed workloads show that our symbiotic resource partitioning approach performs, on an average, 28.8% and 29.1% better than equal partitioning on the fair speedup metric on 4-core and 8-core CMP systems respectively.

References

1. Chandra, D., Guo, F., Kim, S., Solihin, Y.: Predicting inter-thread cache contention on a chip multi-processor architecture. In: Proc. of the 11th International Symposium on High-Performance Computer Architecture (2005)
2. Srikantaiah, S., Kandemir, M., Irwin, M.J.: Adaptive set pinning: managing shared caches in chip multiprocessors. In: Proc. of the 13th International Conference on Architectural Support for Programming Languages and Operating Systems (2008)
3. Hsu, L.R., Reinhardt, S.K., Iyer, R., Makineni, S.: Communist, utilitarian, and capitalist cache policies on CMPs: caches as a shared resource. In: Proc. of the 15th International Conference on Parallel Architectures and Compilation Techniques (2006)
4. Burger, D., Goodman, J.R., Kägi, A.: Memory bandwidth limitations of future microprocessors. In: Proceedings of the International Symposium on Computer Architecture (1996)
5. Chang, J., Sohi, G.S.: Cooperative cache partitioning for chip multiprocessors. In: Proc. of the 21st Annual International Conference on Supercomputing (2007)
6. Guo, F., Solihin, Y., Zhao, L., Iyer, R.: A framework for providing quality of service in chip multi-processors. In: Proceedings of the 40th Annual IEEE/ACM International Symposium on Microarchitecture (2007)

7. Kim, S., Chandra, D., Solihin, Y.: Fair cache sharing and partitioning in a chip multiprocessor architecture. In: Proc. of the 13th International Conference on Parallel Architectures and Compilation Techniques (2004)

8. Qureshi, M.K., Patt, Y.N.: Utility-based cache partitioning: A low-overhead, high-performance, runtime mechanism to partition shared caches. In: Proc. of the 39th Annual International Symposium on Microarchitecture (2006)

9. Rafique, N., Lim, W.T., Thottethodi, M.: Architectural support for operating system-driven CMP cache management. In: Proc. of the 15th International Conference on Parallel Architectures and Compilation Techniques (2006)

10. Suh, G.E., Rudolph, L., Devadas, S.: Dynamic partitioning of shared cache memory. J. Supercomput. 28(1) (2004)

11. Ipek, E., Mutlu, O., Martínez, J.F., Caruana, R.: Self-optimizing memory controllers: A reinforcement learning approach. In: Proceedings of the 35th International Symposium on Computer Architecture (2008)

12. Lee, C.J., Mutlu, O., Narasiman, V., Patt, Y.N.: Prefetch-aware DRAM controllers. In: Proceedings of the International Symposium on Microarchitecture (2008)

13. Mutlu, O., Moscibroda, T.: Stall-time fair memory access scheduling for chip multiprocessors. In: Proceedings of the 40th Annual IEEE/ACM International Symposium on Microarchitecture (2007)

14. Mutlu, O., Moscibroda, T.: Parallelism-aware batch scheduling: Enhancing both performance and fairness of shared DRAM systems. In: Proceedings of the 35th International Symposium on Computer Architecture (2008)

15. Nesbit, K.J., Aggarwal, N., Laudon, J., Smith, J.E.: Fair queuing memory systems. In: Proceedings of the International Symposium on Microarchitecture (2006)

16. Rafique, N., Lim, W.T., Thottethodi, M.: Effective management of DRAM bandwidth in multicore processors. In: Proc. of the 16th International Conference on Parallel Architecture and Compilation Techniques (2007)

17. Iyer, R., Zhao, L., Guo, F., Illikkal, R., Makineni, S., Newell, D., Solihin, Y., Hsu, L., Reinhardt, S.: QoS policies and architecture for cache/memory in CMP platforms. SIGMETRICS Perform. Eval. Rev. 35(1) (2007)

18. Bitirgen, R., Ipek, E., Martinez, J.F.: Coordinated management of multiple interacting resources in chip multiprocessors: A machine learning approach. In: Proceedings of the International Symposium on Microarchitecture (2008)

19. Alameldeen, A.R., Wood, D.A.: Ipc considered harmful for multiprocessor workloads. IEEE Micro 26(4) (2006)

20. Guthaus, M.R., Ringenberg, J.S., Ernst, D., Austin, T.M., Mudge, T., Brown, R.B.: Mibench: A free, commercially representative embedded benchmark suite. In: Proceedings of the IEEE International Workshop on Workload Characterization (2001)

21. Micron: 1GB DDR2 SDRAM component: MT47H128M8HQ-25 (May 2007),
http://download.micron.com/pdf/datasheets/
dram/ddr2/1GbDDR2.pdf

22. Martin, M.M.K., Sorin, D.J., Beckmann, B.M., Marty, M.R., Xu, M., Alameldeen, A.R., Moore, K.E., Hill, M.D., Wood, D.A.: Multifacet's general execution-driven multiprocessor simulator (gems) toolset. SIGARCH Comput. Archit. News 33(4) (2005)

23. Rixner, S., Dally, W.J., Kapasi, U.J., Mattson, P., Owens, J.D.: Memory access scheduling. SIGARCH Comput. Archit. News 28(2) (2000)

24. Iyer, R.: CQoS: a framework for enabling QoS in shared caches of CMP platforms. In: Proc. of the 18th annual International Conference on Supercomputing (2004)

DIEF: An Accurate Interference Feedback Mechanism for Chip Multiprocessor Memory Systems

Magnus Jahre, Marius Grannaes, and Lasse Natvig

Norwegian University of Science and Technology

Abstract. Chip Multi-Processors (CMPs) commonly share hardware-controlled on-chip units that are unaware that memory requests are issued by independent processors. Consequently, the resources a process receives will vary depending on the behavior of the processes it is co-scheduled with. Resource allocation techniques can avoid this problem if they are provided with an accurate interference estimate. Our Dynamic Interference Estimation Framework (DIEF) provides this service by dynamically estimating the latency a process would experience with exclusive access to all hardware-controlled, shared resources. Since the total interference latency is the sum of the interference latency in each shared unit, the system designer can choose estimation techniques to achieve the desired accuracy/complexity trade-off. In this work, we provide high-accuracy estimation techniques for the on-chip interconnect, shared cache and memory bus. This DIEF implementation has an average relative estimate error between -0.4% and 4.7% and a standard deviation between 2.4% and 5.8%.

1 Introduction

Chip Multi-Processors (CMPs) commonly share parts of the memory system. While some CMPs have private caches and only share off-chip bandwidth, other CMPs share an on-chip interconnect and cache space between cores. This resource sharing is often beneficial since it can improve resource utilization compared to a private design and facilitates efficient inter-core communication. However, sharing may also adversely affect performance when the system resources are insufficient for co-scheduled processes. This is due to the use of rudimentary hardware policies like First Come First Served (FCFS) and Least Recently Used (LRU) which were primarily designed for use in single-core processors. These policies do not provide predictable resource allocations because processes with higher access frequencies receive a larger part of the shared resource [1,2]. Since CMPs often run multiprogrammed workloads, the performance of a single process can be heavily influenced by the processes it is co-scheduled with.

Resource allocation techniques that attempt to alleviate interference problems, commonly aim their effort at improving *fairness* and/or *Quality of Service (QoS)*. A memory system is fair if the performance reduction due to interference between threads is distributed across all processes in proportion to their

Y.N. Patt et al. (Eds.): HiPEAC 2010, LNCS 5952, pp. 292–306, 2010.

priorities [3]. QoS is provided if it is possible to put a limit on the maximum slowdown a process can experience when co-scheduled with any other process [4]. Nesbit et al. [5] propose a high-level architecture for resource allocation systems which divide the system into three independent, cooperating modules. Here, the *feedback mechanisms* provide measurements of the current resource utilization and/or the performance of the running programs. Then, the *allocation policy* decides on a new and improved resource allocation and implements this with the *allocation mechanisms*. Since resource allocations do not change very often, allocation policies should be implemented in software to achieve flexibility. On the other hand, allocation and feedback mechanisms that interact closely with the hardware resources, must be implemented in hardware for efficiency.

In this work, we provide the first detailed implementation of a unified feedback mechanism for the hardware-managed, shared memory system called the Dynamic Interference Estimation Framework (DIEF). DIEF dynamically estimates the average memory latency a process would experience if it had exclusive access to all shared resources. In addition, DIEF measures the actual shared memory latency to establish the relative latency impact from sharing effects. Choosing average memory latency as the interference metric has the advantage that the total interference latency is the sum of the interference latency of each shared unit. Consequently, the system designer can choose interference estimation techniques that achieve the appropriate accuracy/complexity trade-off. Since processing cores can hide latency, an allocation policy needs a performance-oriented feedback mechanism to complement DIEF which can be provided by well-known techniques like performance counters [6].

In this work, we aim our efforts at providing an accurate DIEF implementation. To accomplish this, we develop interference measurement mechanisms for ring and crossbar interconnects, shared caches and a multi-channel DDR2 memory bus. These mechanisms are tested on a variety of CMP architectures with 4, 8 or 16 cores, 2 or 3 cache levels and 1, 2 or 4 memory bus channels. DIEF is very accurate for these architectures and has an average relative estimate error between -0.4% and 4.7% and a standard deviation between 2.4% and 5.8%.

2   Background

2.1   Interference Definition and Metrics

When evaluating CMP memory system fairness, it is convenient to compare to a baseline where interference does not occur. One way of creating such a baseline is to let the process run in one processing core of the CMP and leave the remaining cores idle [7,8]. Consequently, the process has exclusive access to all shared resources, and we will refer to this configuration as the *private mode*. Conversely, all processing cores are active and the processes compete for shared resources in the *shared mode*. We refer to a baseline created in this way as a *Single Program Baseline (SPB)*.

It is also possible to create a fairness baseline by statically partitioning all shared resources equally among the processors [4]. We refer to this baseline type as a *Multiprogrammed Baseline (MPB)*. The main advantage of MPB is that it exists in the shared mode. Consequently, it is easy to ensure that a fairness technique does not perform worse than the baseline. However, MPB also has three major disadvantages. Firstly, it only accounts for interference in the resources that have been statically and equally partitioned. This can lead to erroneous results if important interference sources are missed. Secondly, static and equal division of DRAM bandwidth does not lead to a static and equal division of latency [1]. The reason is that the latency of a request depends heavily on which requests was issued before it. Consequently, it may be difficult to implement a good static and equal sharing baseline for the memory interface. Finally, the relationship between performance and resource allocation is rarely linear [2]. Consequently, a process may experience severe performance degradation in the statically shared baseline. If a fairness technique then removes this degradation, one might be lead to believe that the technique also improves throughput when the degradation in fact was due to the baseline's suboptimal resource allocation.

These problems can be avoided by using the Single Program Baseline (SPB). Unfortunately, SPB does not exist in the shared mode. By definition, it requires that the performance in the shared mode is compared to the interference-free private mode. In this work, we provide a feedback mechanism that estimates SPB latency at runtime. We define the interference I_i experienced by a request i as the difference between the shared mode latency L_i and private mode latency $\mathcal{L}_i$ (i.e. $I_i = L_i - \mathcal{L}_i$). This definition is an extension of the interference definition by Mutlu and Moscibroda [1].

The shared mode estimate of the private mode latency $\hat{\mathcal{L}}_i$ may be different from the actual private mode latency $\mathcal{L}_i$. Consequently, it is important that a feedback mechanism minimizes the difference between these values. We define the measurement error for request i to be $E_i = \hat{\mathcal{L}}_i - \mathcal{L}_i$. Since the interference estimate $\hat{I}$ is related to the private mode latency estimate $\hat{\mathcal{L}}$ by the formula $\hat{\mathcal{L}}_i = L_i - \hat{I}_i$, the feedback mechanism can choose to estimate either $\hat{\mathcal{L}}_i$ or $\hat{I}_i$ and compute the other. A dynamic resource allocation technique will use $\hat{\mathcal{L}}$ to establish the relative impact of interference on the different running processes. Consequently, the impact of the error depends on the shared mode latency L. To account for this we define the relative error $\mathcal{E}_i = E_i / L_i$. We aggregate multiple errors by using the arithmetic mean, standard deviation and root mean squared error of E and $\mathcal{E}$.

2.2   Modern Memory Bus Interfaces

Memory bus scheduling is a challenging problem due to the 3D structure of DRAM consisting of rows, columns and banks. Commonly, a DRAM read transaction consists of first sending the row address, then the column address and finally receiving the data. When a row is accessed, its contents are stored in a register known as the row buffer, and a row is often referred to as a *page*. If the row has to be activated before it can be read, the access is referred to as a *row miss* or *page miss*. It is possible to carry out repeated column accesses to an open page, called *row hits* or *page hits*. This is a great advantage as the latency of a

Table 1. Memory System Latency Taxonomy

Module	Type	Description	SM	PM	Int.
Interconnect	Entry (ie)	The number of cycles a request is kept in the private cache MSHR before it is accepted into an interconnect queue	L_i^{ie}	$\mathcal{L}_i^{\mathrm{ie}}$	I_i^{ie}
Interconnect	Queue (iq)	The number of cycles spent in the interconnect queue	L_i^{iq}	$\mathcal{L}_i^{\mathrm{iq}}$	I_i^{iq}
Interconnect	Transfer (it)	The number of cycles spent on transferring the request from source to destination	L_i^{it}	$\mathcal{L}_i^{\mathrm{it}}$	I_i^{it}
Interconnect	Delivery (id)	The number of cycles a request was delayed because a shared cache bank could not accept requests due to insufficient buffer space	L_i^{id}	$\mathcal{L}_i^{\mathrm{id}}$	I_i^{id}
Shared Cache	Capacity (cc)	The number of cycles used to service a miss that would not occur if the process had exclusive access to the shared cache	-	-	I_i^{cc}
Memory Controller	Entry (me)	The number of cycles a request was delayed in a shared cache MSHR before it was accepted into a memory controller queue	L_i^{me}	$\mathcal{L}_i^{\mathrm{me}}$	I_i^{me}
Memory Controller	Queue (mq)	The number of cycles a request spent in the memory controller queue	L_i^{mq}	$\mathcal{L}_i^{\mathrm{mq}}$	I_i^{mq}
Memory Controller	Transfer (mt)	The number of cycles the request occupied the memory data bus	L_i^{mt}	$\mathcal{L}_i^{\mathrm{mt}}$	I_i^{mt}
Shared Memory System	Total	The total number of cycles a request uses through the entire hardware-controlled, shared memory system	L_i	$\mathcal{L}_i$	I_i

row hit is much lower than the latency of a row miss. The situation where two consecutive requests access the same bank but different rows is known as a *row conflict* and is very expensive in terms of latency. DRAM accesses are pipelined, so there are no idle cycles on the memory bus if the next column command is sent while the data transfer is in progress. Furthermore, command accesses to one bank can be overlapped with data transfers from a different bank.

Rixner et al. [9] proposed the First Ready - First Come First Served (FR-FCFS) algorithm for scheduling DRAM requests. Here, memory requests are reordered to achieve high page hit rates which result in increased memory bus utilization. This algorithm prioritizes requests according to three rules: prioritize ready commands over commands that are not ready, prioritize column commands over other commands and prioritize the oldest request over younger requests.

3 Shared Memory System Latency Taxonomy

The main advantage of measuring interference in terms of average round trip latency through the shared memory system is that the total interference of a single request is the sum of the interference it experiences in each of the shared units. Consequently, it is possible to independently implement and validate the feedback mechanism for each source of interference. In this work, we develop a comprehensive view of memory system interference which is shown in Table 1.

The hardware-controlled, shared memory system commonly consists of three types of units. Firstly, an interconnect is needed to connect the private caches to one or more shared caches. Secondly, there can be one or more levels of shared caches with varying sharing degrees. Finally, off-chip bandwidth can be shared between cores. Although the organization of these shared units will vary from CMP to CMP, we believe that this model captures the essential types of interference in the hardware-controlled, shared memory system.

Within these units, the shared resources are either *bandwidth* or *capacity*. In the memory bus and interconnects, bandwidth is the main shared resource. However, memory requests are kept in finite buffers while waiting for access to the shared transmission channels. Consequently, there are also different forms of capacity interference in these units. We divide the latency through the units where bandwidth is the main shared resource into four parts. The *entry* latency is the latency the request experiences while waiting to be accepted into the input queue. Then, the *queue* latency is the number of cycles it spends in the queue before it is granted access to the resource. The next latency type is the *transfer* latency which is the number of cycles it takes to transfer the request from source to destination. Finally, it might not be possible to deliver the request if the destination lacks sufficient buffer space. In this case, the request experiences an additional *delivery* latency. There is no delivery latency in the memory bus since the last level cache must be able to receive responses to avoid deadlocks.

To provide system-wide, latency-based interference measurements, the latency cost of shared cache interference misses must be established. This problem can be solved by observing that interference misses are associated with the latency penalty of retrieving the data from the next cache level or memory. If we assume one level of shared caches, the cache capacity interference experienced by request i is the sum of request i's memory bus entry, queue and transfer latency ($I_i^{cc} = L_i^{me} + L_i^{mq} + L_i^{mt}$). For convenience, we use the first letter of the shared unit (i.e. i, c or m) and the first letter of the latency type (i.e. e, q, t, d or c) to produce a two-letter identifier (e.g. **interconnect entry** is **ie**).

4   The Dynamic Interference Estimation Framework

The purpose of a dynamic interference estimation technique is to provide a reliable measure of how memory system interference affects the running processes. In this work, we propose the Dynamic Interference Estimation Framework (DIEF) that continuously monitors all shared units to provide accurate interference estimates. Figure 1 shows DIEF's high-level architecture where each shared unit is augmented with extra functionality (not on the unit's critical path) that measures interference and/or latencies at runtime. These measurements are continuously communicated to the Interference Manager which uses it to measure the shared mode average round trip latency L and create an estimate $\hat{\mathcal{L}}$ of the private

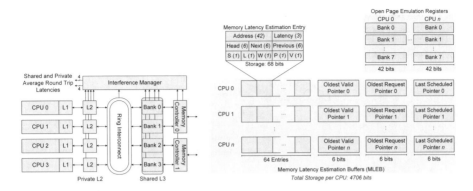

Fig. 1. Dynamic Interference Estimation Framework (DIEF) Architecture

Fig. 2. Private Memory Bus Emulation

mode latency $\mathcal{L}$. Since memory bus interference is the interference type with the largest impact, most of our efforts are directed at estimating this latency type [10]. The operating system must inform DIEF of context switches to ensure that the measurements are not polluted by the actions of other processes. In the case of multi-threaded applications, the operating system also needs to instruct DIEF to treat the application's set of processing cores as one entity. Without loss of generality, we consider the situation where each core runs one single-threaded application in the remainder of this work.

4.1 Estimating Private Memory Bus Latency ($\hat{\mathcal{L}}^{mt}$, $\hat{\mathcal{L}}^{mq}$ and $\hat{\mathcal{L}}^{me}$)

Estimating Transfer and Queue Latencies ($\hat{\mathcal{L}}^{mt}$ and $\hat{\mathcal{L}}^{mq}$). Modern memory bus scheduling algorithms reorder requests to improve memory bus throughput [9]. Therefore, the *execution order* of memory requests depend on the memory bus queue contents and can be very different in the shared and private modes. However, the *arrival order* of requests is very similar. Consequently, it is possible to estimate the private mode *execution order* by emulating the private scheduling algorithm on the shared mode requests. Then, the private *execution order* and bank state determine the transfer latency estimate $\hat{\mathcal{L}}^{mt}$. The queue latency $\hat{\mathcal{L}}^{mq}$ can be estimated by following the private *execution order* and accumulating transfer latencies.

Figure 2 shows the hardware support needed to emulate a private memory bus. This hardware is not on the critical path and consists of n *Memory Latency Estimation Buffers (MLEB)* (one for each processor). Each time the memory controller receives a request from a certain CPU, it is added to the corresponding MLEB. When the request is serviced by the memory controller, the state stored in this buffer is used to estimate its private mode queue latency $\hat{\mathcal{L}}^{mq}$ and transfer latency $\hat{\mathcal{L}}^{mt}$. This calculation can be allowed to take on the order of tens of processor cycles since the memory bus is commonly clocked at a much lower frequency than the processing core.

Table 2. Status Bits

S	Transfer latency estimation $\hat{\mathcal{L}}^{mt}$ is valid
L	$\hat{\mathcal{L}}^{mq}$ and $\hat{\mathcal{L}}^{mt}$ has been computed
W	The request is a write
P	Entry is private mode only
V	Entry is valid

Table 3. $\hat{\mathcal{L}}^{mt}$ Estimates

	Next State	
Prev. State	Read Bank i	Write Bank i
Hit (any bank)	40	40
Miss (any bank)	120	110
Conflict Read Bank i	200	190
Conflict Write Bank i	260	250
Conflict Read Bank j	170	160
Conflict Write Bank j	260	250

Each estimation entry has a head pointer, a next pointer and a previous pointer. The previous/next pointers store the private *execution order* by pointing to the element that was scheduled before/after the request in the private mode. The head pointer points to the estimation entry that was the next to be serviced when the request was added, and it is used to estimate queue latency. Furthermore, each entry contains five status bits: S, L, W, P and V. These are explained in Table 2. Finally, the *Oldest Valid Pointer* points to the oldest valid MLEB entry, the *Oldest Request Pointer* points to the oldest non-serviced entry and the *Last Scheduled Pointer* points to the most recently scheduled entry.

To improve estimation accuracy, we add the Open Page Emulation Registers. These where originally proposed by Mutlu and Moscibroda [1] and are used to estimate whether a request is a page hit, miss or conflict. Here, each register holds the address of the last accessed memory page. These registers are also used to schedule requests according to the FR-FCFS scheduling algorithm [9].

Generally, there are more queued requests in the MLEB than in the private mode memory bus queue since competition for the bus is more severe in the shared mode. This can result in overestimating the number of page hits if the process has sufficient page locality. To account for this, we add a parameter called the *Page Locality Factor*. This factor determines the number of estimation entries that should be examined while looking for a page hit. Setting the page locality factor to 1 assumes no reordering in the private memory system.

If we ignore the effects of shared cache interference, the requests that reach the memory bus are the ones that are not filtered out by the on-chip caches. Since we use the same cache hierarchy in the shared configuration and the baseline, the order of the memory request are nearly identical but their timing will be different. However, there may be differences resulting from the interleaving of writebacks and reads since the memory controller may reorder requests differently in the two configurations. When cache interference is taken into account, the request stream can be very different. Consequently, the shared cache interference technique should identify both private- and shared-only requests and communicate this information to the memory bus interference technique.

Finally, we need to produce estimates of the shared mode queue latency. This can be accomplished by adding a register for all queue entries and incrementing it with the memory bus transfer latency every time a request is finished.

Algorithm 1. Private Memory Bus Queue and Transfer Latency Estimation

procedure ESTIMATEPRIVATELATENCIES(Memory request r)
    while r not serviced **do**
        Emulate FR-FCFS scheduling of elements within horizon given by the Page Locality Factor
        Initialize request pointer c to point to head(r) and queue latency $\hat{\mathcal{L}}_r^{mq}$ to 0
        while c is not equal to r **and** c is scheduled before r **do**
            Increment queue latency $\hat{\mathcal{L}}_r^{mq}$ with the transfer latency $\hat{\mathcal{L}}_c^{mt}$ of request c
            Update c by following the next pointer of c
        Invalidate any entries that are no longer needed to compute queue and transfer latencies
    return transfer latency $\hat{\mathcal{L}}_r^{mt}$ **and** queue latency $\hat{\mathcal{L}}_r^{mq}$ of request r

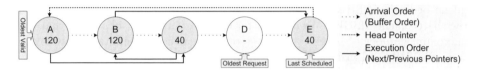

Fig. 3. Memory Bus Queue and Transfer Latency Estimation Example

Alternatively, a request can be assigned a timestamp on arrival and this timestamp can then be compared to the value of a counter when the request is issued.

The Latency Estimation Algorithm. Algorithm 1 summarizes the estimation algorithm for the private memory bus transfer latency $\hat{\mathcal{L}}^{mt}$ and queue latency $\hat{\mathcal{L}}^{mq}$. We illustrate the estimation procedure with the example in Figure 3. There are five queued requests, and request E has just been serviced by the shared mode memory controller. To determine the transfer latency $\hat{\mathcal{L}}_E^{mt}$ of E, the estimation algorithm emulates scheduling requests within the limit given by the Page Locality Factor. In this example, request A is serviced first and its transfer latency is estimated. Then, request C is serviced before B since it is a private mode page hit. Finally, request E is serviced before D since it accesses the same page as B which gives $\hat{\mathcal{L}}_E^{mt} = 40$. Then, we can estimate $\hat{\mathcal{L}}_E^{mq}$ by following E's head pointer to A and accumulating the transfer latencies of all elements between A and E in the private execution order. Consequently, the queue latency estimate for E is $\hat{\mathcal{L}}_E^{mq} = \hat{\mathcal{L}}_A^{mt} + \hat{\mathcal{L}}_C^{mt} + \hat{\mathcal{L}}_B^{mt} = 120 + 40 + 120$.

There are a number of possible transfer latencies due to different active pages, overlapping of commands with data transfers from other banks and timing constraints regarding when a bank can be precharged. However, we observed that only a small number of these possible latencies occur frequently in the private mode. Consequently, it is possible to store the most common transfer latencies in a lookup table. Then, the latency is determined by whether the previous and next requests are to the same bank and whether they are reads or writes. This lookup table is created at design time by analyzing the private mode access behavior for the chosen memory bus type. Table 3 shows the lookup table of the DDR2 memory bus used in this work.

A private-only entry (P bit set) can be invalidated when its latency is not needed to compute the queue latency of any other element. For shared mode entries, the latency of the entry must also be computed before it can be deleted. In addition, we require that the most recently scheduled element is not invalidated. The deletion algorithm is based on the observation that the head pointer of the oldest undeletable element e in the *arrival order* will point to the oldest head element h in the *arrival order*. Consequently, we know that all elements after h in the *execution order* are needed to compute the queue latency for e. If an entry has been removed due to insufficient buffer space, we use the last computed transfer and queue latency.

Estimating Memory Bus Entry Interference $\hat{I}^{\mathrm{me}}$. When the memory bus queue becomes full, the memory controller blocks and the requests remain in the shared cache MSHRs. We account for this interference by observing that the maximum number of requests a processor core can issue simultaneously is the sum of MSHRs and writeback buffers in the last-level private cache. Furthermore, the shared buffers will be dimensioned to handle roughly c times this number of requests (c = number of cores) since too few buffers will lead to frequent performance bottlenecks. The effect of this observation is that a single core will not be able to fill the buffers in the shared part of the memory system. Consequently, any shared mode latency due to memory bus blocking is interference.

4.2 Estimating Cache Capacity Interference $\hat{I}^{\mathrm{cc}}$

To identify shared cache interference misses, we use an Auxiliary Tag Directory (ATD) [11,12] per core. Each time a request is received in the shared cache, the request is inserted into the ATD belonging to the processor that sent the request. Consequently, the ATD contains the tags the processor would have had in the shared cache if it was running alone. On each access, we compare the output from the ATD with the output from the actual cache. If the request is a hit in the ATD and a miss in the real cache, we store a timestamp and tag the request as a shared mode only cache miss. This bit is used to keep the request out of the memory bus private mode latency estimation. When the request has been serviced in the memory bus and returned to the cache, we retrieve its latency and communicate it to the Interference Manager as cache capacity interference. We also record if an ATD entry would have been written to in the private mode. In this case, a replacement would have triggered a writeback in the private mode. When this happens, we insert a private mode only writeback request into the memory bus private mode latency estimation.

In this work, our aim is to accurately measure interference. Consequently, we are willing to invest a fair bit of area into making the estimates accurate. We use CACTI version 5.3 [13] to establish that the size of each ATD is roughly 4% of the shared cache area. Qureshi et al. [11] showed that sampling as few as 16 to 32 sets can be sufficient to represent cache behavior. With 32 sets, the area of each ATD is reduced to around 0.01 % of the shared cache area. In DIEF, using set sampling is not straight forward since the memory bus interference estimation mechanism needs to know which misses are shared-only interference misses. This problem can likely be avoided at the cost of reduced accuracy by

Table 4. CMP Models

Interconnect	#CPUs	Process	Private Cache	Shared Cache	Memory Bus
Crossbar, 8/16/30 cycles end-to-end transfer latency, 32 entry queue	4	65 nm	2-way 64KB L1 Data, 2-way 64KB L1 Inst.	16-way 8MB L2	DDR2-800, 4-4-4-12 timing, 8 banks, 1KB pages, 64 entry read queue, 64 entry write queue, FR-FCFS, Open Page Policy
	8	45 nm		16-way 16MB L2	
	16	32 nm		16-way 32MB L2	
Ring, 4/4/8 cycles per hop transfer latency, 32 entry queue	4	65 nm	2-way 64KB L1 Data, 2-way 64KB L1 Inst., 4-way 1MB Unified L2	16-way 8MB L3	
	8	45 nm		16-way 16MB L3	
	16	32 nm		16-way 32MB L3	

using an estimated interference miss probability to select requests for the memory bus interference estimation. The area overhead can be further reduced at the cost of accuracy and measurement latency by time multiplexing the ATDs. Work in this direction is underway.

4.3 Estimating Interconnect Interference ($\hat{I}^{ie}$, $\hat{I}^{iq}$, $\hat{I}^{it}$ and $\hat{I}^{id}$)

The main component of interconnect interference is due to requests having to wait for access to the shared transmission medium ($\hat{I}^{iq}$). It is easy to measure interference in the ring and crossbar interconnects used in this work since latency is independent of access order. If a processor i is not able to issue a request because a request r from processor j is being transferred, we add the number of cycles request r occupied the transmission medium for each delayed request from processor i to the interference estimate. Since the interconnects may be pipelined, the number of cycles a processor delays another processor may be less than the transfer latency. In the ring interconnect, the transfer latency depends on which core the process is scheduled on and this needs to be taken into account when estimating interference. Again, we assume that all blocking due to full buffers is interference.

5 Methodology

We use the system call emulation mode of the cycle-accurate M5 simulator [14] for our experiments and have extended M5 with crossbar and ring interconnects as well as a detailed DDR2-800 memory bus and DRAM model [15]. We model two CMP architectures that are similar to current general-purpose, high-performance CMP implementations and identify these models by the name of the on-chip interconnect (i.e. crossbar or ring). Table 4 summarizes the CMP models used in this work, and a further discussion of the models is provided by Jahre et al. [10]. The only difference between Jahre et al.'s configuration and ours is that we use an open page policy in the memory controller. We also use Jahre et al.'s 40 4-core workloads, 20 8-core workloads and 10 16-core workloads that were generated by picking benchmarks at random from the full SPEC

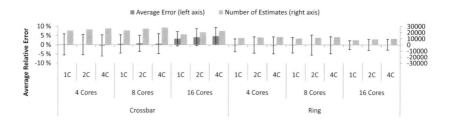

Fig. 4. Relative Estimation Errors and Number of Estimates

CPU2000 benchmark suite [16]. The only requirement given to the random selection process is that a benchmark can only appear once in each workload. These workloads are fast-forwarded for 1 billion clock cycles before we run detailed simulation for 100 million clock cycles. To achieve synchronized measurements of L and $\mathcal{L}$, it is critical to minimize the difference between the memory requests in the shared and private modes. To ensure this, we use static cache partitioning and an infinite bandwidth interconnect and memory bus during fast forwarding such that the simulation sample starts on a similar instruction in both modes. Furthermore, we run the shared mode experiments first and then retrieve the number of instructions the benchmark committed. Then, we run the private mode simulation for the exact same number of instructions.

6   Results

In this section, we present the results from our experiments with DIEF. When not otherwise stated, we use our best performing configuration with 8192 requests per sample, a page locality factor of 3 and a 64 entry bus estimation buffer. These values were found empirically by extensive simulation.

6.1   Estimation Accuracy

Figure 4 shows the average relative error and one standard deviation of all estimates produced by DIEF. In addition, Figure 4 contains the number of estimates used to compute these statistics. We use the abbreviations 1C, 2C and 4C to represent 1 memory bus channel, 2 memory bus channels and 4 memory bus channels, respectively. The main observation is that the average error is close to zero in all cases. Furthermore, the standard deviation is at most 5.8%.

Figure 5 breaks down the average root mean squared (RMS) error for all architectures used in this work. We have removed all interference types where the average RMS error is less than 2 clock cycles to improve readability. Furthermore, cache capacity interference is not included since it has no corresponding private mode latency. Figure 5 shows that most of the measurement error is due to the memory bus queue estimate $\hat{\mathcal{L}}^{\mathrm{mq}}$. This is not surprising as our queue latency estimation model does not cover the case where a request is delayed

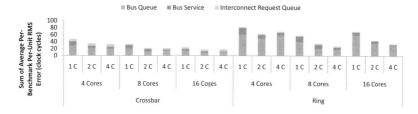

Fig. 5. Interference Estimation Error Breakdown

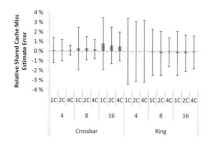

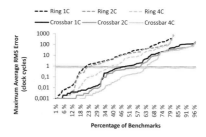

Fig. 6. ATD Estimation Error   **Fig. 7.** 4-core Bus Queue Error

by page hits that arrive after it. Furthermore, our model does not accurately predict the difference between the number of simultaneously queued requests in the two models. However, given the good average accuracy shown in Figure 4, the measurements are likely accurate enough to be used by a dynamic fairness technique. Another observation is that the absolute measurement error is larger in the ring architectures. This is due to poor utilization of the L3 cache because the private L2 caches reduce the access frequency. Consequently, a cache thrashing process is able to evict a larger amount of the data needed by a less cache intensive thread which in turn puts a larger strain on the memory bus.

To quantify the accuracy of the ATD interference miss estimates, we count the number of actual misses and the number of interference misses. Here, the shared mode miss count estimate is computed by subtracting the number of additional shared cache misses identified by the ATD from the shared mode miss count. Then, we adapt the relative error metric to cache misses by using the estimated number of misses $\hat{\mathcal{M}}$, the actual private mode number of misses $\mathcal{M}$ and the shared mode number of misses M ($\mathcal{E} = (\hat{\mathcal{M}} - \mathcal{M})/M$). Figure 6 shows that our ATD-based interference miss estimation has an average relative estimation error of at most 0.8% and maximum standard deviation of 3.4%.

Figure 7 shows the distribution of the memory bus queue RMS errors for the 4-core CMP models. Here, we represent the measurement error for each instance of a benchmark by the average RMS error of the estimates for this benchmark. Then, we sort the average RMS errors such that each point in the figure represents the maximum average RMS error observed for a certain percentage of benchmarks. Figure 7 shows that the memory bus queue estimates are very

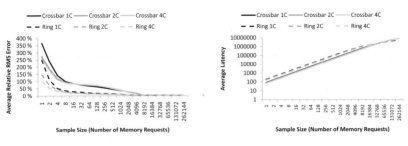

(a) Root Mean Squared Error   (b) Average Latency Between Estimates

Fig. 8. 8-core CMP Sample Size Accuracy Impact

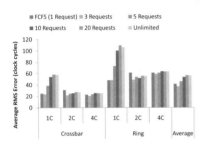

Fig. 9. 4-core Page Locality Factor

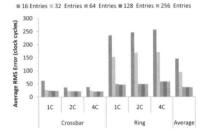

Fig. 10. 4-core Bus Buffer Size

accurate. When 60% of the benchmarks are taken into account, the worst average RMS error observed for any architecture is 20 clock cycles. However, there is a short tail where the measurement error is significant. Since the average round trip memory latency is high in these cases, the values are most likely good enough to be used by dynamic resource allocation techniques. Finally, the lines stop at 82% for the ring architecture and 97% for the crossbar architecture because some benchmarks have too few memory requests to produce any estimates.

6.2 DIEF Parameters

In this section, we provide an empirical analysis of DIEF's main parameters: sample size, page locality factor and memory bus estimation buffer size. The choice of sample size is a trade-off between achieving low variability and receiving new estimates often enough to make high quality resource allocation decisions. Figure 8 shows the average relative RMS error and average latency between estimates for the 8-core architectures. Our choice of 8192 requests per sample is on the flat part of the error plot and has an acceptable average latency.

Figure 9 shows the average RMS error for different page locality factors. The general trend is that the page locality factor should be low because there is usually more locality in the shared mode estimation buffer than in the private memory bus queues. This is because a larger number of requests are available to the scheduler in the shared mode due to more competition. A page locality factor of 3 is the best overall. Finally, Figure 10 shows the error resulting from varying the memory bus estimation buffer size. Here, 64 entries are necessary to achieve low error for the ring architecture.

7   Related Work

A few researchers have addressed the issue of dynamic interference measurement in CMPs. Cache Scouts [17] is a shared cache interference measurement technique that estimates interference by counting the number of cache blocks that are evicted by different processors. Consequently, they assume that all blocks evicted by a different processor would have been reused which may lead to measurement errors. Mutlu and Moscibroda [1] propose a run-time interference measurement technique that they use to guide a memory bus scheduling algorithm in a system with private caches.

Most previous studies that aim to improve resource sharing in CMP memory systems, have focused on a single component of the entire system. For example, techniques have been proposed to reduce cache capacity interference (e.g. [3,4]), cache bandwidth interference [18] and memory bus interference [1,8,19]. In addition, a few researchers have investigated how a chip-wide resource management technique can be designed. Iyer et al. [20] proposed a high-level framework for implementing a QoS-aware memory system, while Nesbit et al. [5] proposed the Virtual Private Machines framework where a private virtual machine is created by dividing the available physical resources among applications. In addition, Bitirgen et al. [21] showed how machine learning can be applied to the resource allocation problem.

8   Conclusion

Accurate feedback mechanisms are needed to implement robust resource allocation systems in future CMPs. In this work, we propose the Dynamic Interference Estimation Framework (DIEF) which is the first detailed implementation of a unified feedback mechanism for CMP memory systems. DIEF is a collection of techniques that cooperate to estimate the average memory latency a process would experience if it had exclusive access to all shared resources. Choosing the average memory latency as the unit of interference has the advantage that the total memory latency is the sum of the latency in each shared unit. Consequently, CMP designers can choose estimation techniques that achieve the desired accuracy/complexity trade-off for each shared unit. In this work, we describe a high accuracy DIEF implementation which has an average relative estimate error between -0.4% and 4.7% and a standard deviation between 2.4% and 5.8%.

Acknowledgments. This project was supported in part by the Norwegian Metacenter for Computational Science (NOTUR). Lasse Natvig is a member of HiPEAC2 NoE.

References

1. Mutlu, O., Moscibroda, T.: Stall-Time Fair Memory Access Scheduling for Chip Multiprocessors. In: MICRO 40: Int. Symp. on Microarchitecture (2007)
2. Qureshi, M.K., Patt, Y.N.: Utility-Based Cache Partitioning: A Low-Overhead, High-Performance, Runtime Mechanism to Partition Shared Caches. In: MICRO 39: Proc. of the 39th An. IEEE/ACM Int. Symp. on Microarch., pp. 423–432 (2006)
3. Kim, S., Chandra, D., Solihin, Y.: Fair Cache Sharing and Partitioning in a Chip Multiprocessor Architecture. In: PACT 2004: Proc. of the 13th Int. Conf. on Parallel Architectures and Compilation Techniques, pp. 111–122 (2004)
4. Chang, J., Sohi, G.S.: Cooperative Cache Partitioning for Chip Multiprocessors. In: ICS 2007: Proc. of the 21st Annual Int. Conf. on Supercomputing, pp. 242–252 (2007)
5. Nesbit, K., Moreto, M., Cazorla, F., Ramirez, A., Valero, M., Smith, J.: Multicore Resource Management. IEEE Micro 28(3), 6–16 (2008)
6. Sprunt, B.: The Basics of Performance-Monitoring Hardware. IEEE Micro 22(4), 64–71 (2002)
7. Eyerman, S., Eeckhout, L.: System-Level Performance Metrics for Multiprogram Workloads. IEEE Micro 28(3), 42–53 (2008)
8. Mutlu, O., Moscibroda, T.: Parallelism-Aware Batch Scheduling: Enhancing both Performance and Fairness of Shared DRAM Systems. In: ISCA 2008: Proc. of the 35th An. Int. Symp. on Comp. Arch., pp. 63–74 (2008)
9. Rixner, S., Dally, W.J., Kapasi, U.J., Mattson, P., Owens, J.D.: Memory Access Scheduling. In: ISCA 2000: Int. Symp. on Comp. Arch., pp. 128–138 (2000)
10. Jahre, M., Grannaes, M., Natvig, L.: A Quantitative Study of Memory System Interference in Chip Multiprocessor Architectures. In: HPCC 2009: 11th IEEE Int. Conf. on High Performance Computing and Communications, pp. 622–629 (2009)
11. Qureshi, M.K., Lynch, D.N., Mutlu, O., Patt, Y.N.: A Case for MLP-Aware Cache Replacement. In: ISCA 2006: Int. Symp. on Comp. Arch., pp. 167–178 (2006)
12. Dybdahl, H., Stenstrom, P., Natvig, L.: An LRU-based Replacement Algorithm Augmented with Frequency of Access in Shared Chip-Multiprocessor Caches. In: MEDEA 2006: Proc. of the 2006 workshop on MEmory performance, pp. 45–52 (2006)
13. Thoziyoor, S., Muralimanohar, N., Ahn, J.H., Jouppi, N.P.: CACI 5.1. Technical report, HP Laboratories Palo Alto (2008)
14. Binkert, N.L., Dreslinski, R.G., Hsu, L.R., Lim, K.T., Saidi, A.G., Reinhardt, S.K.: The M5 Simulator: Modeling Networked Systems. IEEE Micro 26(4), 52–60 (2006)
15. JEDEC Solid State Tech. Association: DDR2 SDRAM Specification (May 2006)
16. SPEC: SPEC CPU (2000), http://www.spec.org/cpu2000/
17. Zhao, L., Iyer, R., Illikkal, R., Moses, J., Makineni, S., Newell, D.: CacheScouts: Fine-Grain Monitoring of Shared Caches in CMP Platforms. In: PACT 2007: Proc. of the 16th Int. Conf. on Parallel Arch. and Comp. Tech., pp. 339–352 (2007)
18. Nesbit, K.J., Laudon, J., Smith, J.E.: Virtual private caches. In: ISCA 2007: Proc. of the 34th An. Int. Symp. on Comp. Arch., pp. 57–68 (2007)
19. Nesbit, K.J., Aggarwal, N., Laudon, J., Smith, J.E.: Fair Queuing Memory Systems. In: MICRO 39: Int. Symp. on Microarchitecture, pp. 208–222 (2006)
20. Iyer, R., Zhao, L., Guo, F., Illikkal, R., Makineni, S., Newell, D., Solihin, Y., Hsu, L., Reinhardt, S.: QoS Policies and Architecture for Cache/Memory in CMP Platforms. In: SIGMETRICS 2007, pp. 25–36 (2007)
21. Bitirgen, R., Ipek, E., Martinez, J.F.: Coordinated Management of Multiple Resources in Chip Multiprocessors: A Machine Learning Approach. In: MICRO 41: Proc. of the 41th IEEE/ACM Int. Symp. on Microarchitecture (2008)

Tagged Procedure Calls (*TPC*): Efficient Runtime Support for Task-Based Parallelism on the Cell Processor

George Tzenakis*, Konstantinos Kapelonis, Michail Alvanos*,
Konstantinos Koukos*, Dimitrios S. Nikolopoulos*, and Angelos Bilas*

Institute of Computer Science (ICS)
Foundation for Research and Technology - Hellas (FORTH)
100 N. Plastira Av. Vassilika Vouton, Heraklion, GR-70013, Greece
{tzenakis,kkapelon,alvanos,koukos,dsn,bilas}@ics.forth.gr

Abstract. Increasing the number of cores in modern CPUs is the main trend for improving system performance. A central challenge is the runtime support that multi-core systems ought to use for sustaining high performance and scalability without increasing disproportionally the effort required by the programmer. In this work we present *Tagged Procedure Calls* (*TPC*), a runtime system for supporting task-based programming models on architectures that require explicit data access specification by the programmer. We present the design and implementation of *TPC* for the Cell processor and examine how the runtime system can support task management functions with on-chip communication only. Through minimizing off-chip transactions in the runtime, we achieve sub-microsecond task initiation latency and minimum null task initiation/completion latency of 385 ns. We evaluate *TPC* with several kernels and applications, demonstrating that *TPC* achieves scalable on-chip execution of codes previously parallelized and optimized for shared-memory multiprocessors, can exploit additional fine-grain parallelism in codes previously parallelized at coarse levels of granularity, and performs competitively to existing task-based parallel programming frameworks that statically optimize data layout and task placement.

1   Introduction

Technology trends dictate that future high-performance, general-purpose and embedded systems will be built using heterogeneous chip multi-processors (CMPs) with many cores and tightly-coupled interconnects. Heterogeneous many-core CMPs require a large degree of parallelism in applications as well as dealing with heterogeneity, without significantly increasing programming effort.

For this reason, the role of the programming model is significant for future CMPs. The two main, explicitly parallel programming models used today are

---

* Also, with the Department of Computer Science, University of Crete, P.O. Box 2208, Heraklion, GR 71409, Greece.

Y.N. Patt et al. (Eds.): HiPEAC 2010, LNCS 5952, pp. 307–321, 2010.

shared memory and message passing. Shared memory requires programs to specify synchronization information for memory accesses. Message passing on the other hand requires programs to deal with data placement and communication buffer management. In both cases, application and system designers have been tantalized by the effort required to program and debug such systems for over two decades. The main issue appears to be drawing a different balance between the mechanisms that are available in the underlying system and the abstraction that is exposed to the applications.

We believe that task-based programming models have the potential to achieve this balance. At a high level, explicitly parallel, task-based programming models have two advantages: On one hand they force the programmer to consider code complexity and data transfers at design time without worrying about the underlying mechanisms for communication and synchronization. On the other hand they provide the underlying system (runtime and architecture) with extensive information for efficient execution and runtime optimization. Thus, tasks as an abstraction, present the potential for achieving efficient execution and reducing programmer effort.

Although task-based programming models have been proposed in the past, modern CMPs present new opportunities. Previous efforts with task-based programming models had to deal with coarse-grained tasks due to task management overhead. Task management operations, such as initiation, completion, queuing, and scheduling, in traditional parallel systems cost in the order of tens of thousands of cycles, relative to the clock cycle time of modern processors, due to communication and memory management overheads [14]. In turn, coarse-grained tasks make it hard for the programmer to identify and delineate tasks and, even more so, task and data dependencies. In contrast, fine-grained tasks are easier to identify in sequential codes by inspection as they require analyzing and resolving fewer data and control dependencies. Modern CMPs have the potential of significantly reducing the required task size and achieve efficient execution while reducing the associated effort to identify parallelism.

In this paper we introduce a runtime system for the Cell processor [8], *Tagged Procedure Calls (TPC)*, that aims at supporting task-based programming models. The notion of a task is general and can be interpreted in various ways. In our work we consider a task to be a piece of code that can execute in parallel *as well as* the data that will be accessed by the code. Despite their advantages, fine-grained tasks impose significant challenges for the runtime system. They require efficient basic mechanisms for task management, in particular, task initiation and completion that now become common-path operations. In this work we focus on better understanding and minimizing these basic overheads associated with task management.

We first examine the overhead associated with task management operations on a real system. We focus on task initiation, task completion, task queuing, and task data transfer. Our implementation of *TPC* achieves null task initiation latency from 180 to 380 cycles on the 3.2 GHz Cell processor, depending on the size of the argument list. This represents a significant improvement over task initiation latencies reported in earlier work on task-level parallel execution systems on the Cell [14]. The null task round-trip overhead in *TPC* is about 385 ns, when the ideal DMA round-trip latency of the Cell is just under 312 ns [2].

We examine the performance of *TPC* using both kernels and real applications. We port two applications from the SPLASH-2 [18] suite (FFT and LU) and demonstrate that porting applications written and optimized for shared-memory multiprocessors to *TPC* requires mostly simple and mechanical code changes. *TPC* achieves nearly perfect scaling of these codes on the Cell cores. We further port two applications written previously to exploit coarse-grain parallelism on multi-processors and clusters, PBPI [7] and an H.264 video encoder [17]. We demonstrate that *TPC* enables the exploitation of further fine-grain on-chip parallelism in these applications, with manageable programming effort. Lastly, we port and evaluate several benchmarks distributed with the Sequoia programming language [6]. This effort demonstrates that *TPC* performs competitively to existing task-based parallel programming models for the Cell.

The rest of this paper is organized as follows. Section 2 presents the design and implementation of *TPC* and its runtime system on the Cell processor. Section 3 presents the hardware and software environment we used for our performance evaluation. Section 4 presents our experimental results. In Section 5 we discuss the advantages of *TPC* over previous efforts and related work. Finally, we draw our conclusions in Section 6.

2 *TPC* Design and Implementation

The Cell processor contains a general purpose PowerPC Processing Element (PPE) and eight special purpose Synergistic Processing Elements (SPEs) with their own instruction set. Each SPE has 256 KBytes of local memory without any other cache between this memory and the SPE core. The PPE has a coherent memory hierarchy with two levels of cache prior to the single global external memory. DMAs in the Cell are capable of scatter/gather functions and can have multiple (16 per SPE) outstanding transfers. Moreover, the PPE can access the local memories of SPEs with remote load/store operations as they are mapped to the main memory address space (MMIO). The PPE and SPEs can also communicate with messages via small mailbox registers. These options create trade-offs that need to be understood before the runtime system is able to take advantage of them. Finally, all communication in the Cell processor happens over an on-chip element interconnect bus (EIB) that consists of four bi-directional rings.

TPC uses program annotations to identify certain procedure calls as concurrent tasks. Currently, annotations occur at the procedure level. Programmer can encapsulate blocks of code or groups of loop iterations in *TPC* procedures. *TPC* procedure calls execute in the same or another core, as asynchronous tasks, with the current core continuing execution. In this work, procedure arguments can be *in*, *out*, or *inout*. The issuing task can wait for tasks using point-to-point or barrier synchronization. When issuing an asynchronous task, the runtime returns a handle that can be used later for managing the specific *instance* of the issued task, while the issuing task continues with program execution. When a task completes, it notifies the issuer for its completion. *TPC* procedures have no return values and all arguments are passed by reference. *TPC* arguments and their sizes are determined at runtime before task initiation. *TPC* supports continuous and fixed-stride arguments. We expect that programming interface extensions for specifying memory layout for task arguments will play an important role on programmer effort.

The *TPC* runtime library consists of two main parts, the *initiator* and the *target*. Although any core can play the role of the initiator or target, currently, and due to the Cell architecture, we only support task initiation from the PPE. Similarly, only SPEs can execute tasks as targets. Each task consists of a descriptor. Task descriptors are prepared by the initiator and they are placed in task queues for execution. There is one task queue per target, located in its local storage. The task descriptor contains the function id and the list of arguments. For every argument, the descriptor specifies the argument's address in main memory, the argument size, a flag indicating if it is *in*, *out*, or *inout*, and for stride arguments the stride between the elements.

TPC uses a private task queue for each SPE. The task queue itself is an array of task descriptors. Since our goal is to eliminate off-chip operations, we place each task queue in the local storage of the corresponding SPE. In addition to the task queue, the runtime maintains a completion queue for each SPE (Figure 1(a)). The PPE polls each completion queue for task status notifications from the SPEs. When a completion is received the task entry in the corresponding task queue is released. Since tasks run to completion in each SPE, tasks complete in order. The task completion status consists of a flag and a task id.

An important architectural aspect for implementing a task-based runtime is the available mechanisms for communication among different memories and cores. Although DMA performance on the Cell has been thoroughly analyzed in previous work [2], low-latency control transfer mechanisms have not been fully explored. In this work we examine PPE to SPE round-trip latency with various mechanisms. We use the PPE as initiator, so the available options are: mailbox messages, remote stores to SPE's local store (MMIO), and PPE-initiated DMAs.

SPEs can communicate with the PPE via mailbox messages, DMA, or a variant of DMA using the Atomic Cache Unit (ACU). A simple, non-atomic DMA transfer writes results to main memory and invalidates the PPE's cache, thus requiring off-chip accesses. The ACU is intended for implementing high-performance atomic synchronization primitives between SPEs and the PPE in the global address space, using direct cache-to-cache transfers that remain on-chip. This mechanism supports reserve-line (load-locked), conditional-store, and unconditional-store operations.

Task initiation. Mailboxes are not appropriate mechanisms for initiating tasks. First, the mailbox register resides in the SPE's MFC. Sending mailbox messages incurs in the PPE the same cost as a remote store operation because the SPE mailbox register is memory mapped to the PPE in the same way as the SPE local memory. In addition, to safely use the mailbox register a remote load is required first to check the status of the mailbox register and to ensure that previous mailbox messages have been consumed by the SPE. This introduces a network round-trip latency before posting the mailbox message. Using PPE-initiated DMA requires five remote store operations to special SPE registers. Then, the DMA controller of the SPE performs the actual DMA from main memory to the local SPE memory. Thus, after preparing a task descriptor in (cached) memory, the only two realistic options for the PPE to initiate a task are: (a) issuing remote stores to post the descriptor to the SPE task queue or (b) issuing fewer stores to indicate the existence of a new task descriptor, which then the SPE can pull using DMA. Note that the first approach requires a number of MMIO stores from the PPE that depend on the size of the task descriptor for each task. The second approach requires a fixed number of remote stores at the PPE but introduces an additional DMA transfer in the SPE. Assuming the task descriptor is not evicted from the PPE cache, both approaches result in on-chip traffic only. In all cases, PPE stores to SPEs are cache inhibited and complete in program order. The PPE can use vector store instructions to reduce the number of stores required to post a single task descriptor. The final store instruction sets the active flag of the task descriptor in the task queue to notify the SPE of a new task arrival, while the SPE polls its local memory. In our evaluation we examine both options for task initiation.

Task pre-fetching and execution. Once a new task has been posted to the SPE's task queue, the SPE extracts the task descriptor, fetches *in* arguments, executes the designated function, and writes back *out* arguments. The main challenge in executing these steps is to maximize overlapping of data transfers with task execution. To achieve this, *TPC* pipelines the different stages of task execution and uses pre-fetching to overlap argument transfers and task execution.

Each task can be in one of the states ACTIVE, FETCH, READY, WRITE-BACK, COMPLETE. Before executing a task that is ready, the SPE prepares and issues the DMA commands for as many active tasks as possible from its task queue, depending on the available space in the local storage, and places these tasks in the fetch state. Then, it turns to executing the first task in the queue whose arguments are available. When a task is done executing, the SPE will initiate the write-back of *out* arguments and task completion status. Write-back is asynchronous; The SPE places the task in write-back state and during write-back it tries to pre-fetch data for the next active tasks in the queue. When write-back finishes, the task turns to the complete state. If there are no more active tasks in the task queue or the data of the next task has arrived, the next task starts execution. Multiple write-backs and pre-fetches might be outstanding and being overlapped with task execution.

Task completion. When a task completes, the SPE sends its completion status to the SPE's completion queue that is placed in main memory. The transfer of the completion status is ordered with respect to the write-back of the task's results. The PPE polls these queues for completed tasks from each SPE. A task completion informs the PPE that an entry in the corresponding task queue is now free and that it can issue a new task. Thus, the PPE polls the completion queue when: (a) there is no more space in the task queues (b) the application waits on task completion for synchronization purposes. We indicate the first type of wait as *queue stall* time and the second as *synchronization wait* time.

The SPE can signal completion via a mailbox register or DMA transfer. Although the writing of the mailbox register incurs very low overhead in the SPE, it requires the PPE to poll the status of the register via remote loads that generate unnecessary EIB traffic. Thus, it is preferable for the SPE to use a DMA transfer to a memory location. Then the PPE can poll using cached loads. In this case, to avoid the cache invalidation and the resulting off-chip transfer, we use the "putqlluc" atomic DMA command to unconditionally update the PPE's cache. Finally, each completion queue entry is padded and aligned to cache line boundaries (128-bytes) for optimal DMA performance.

Based on these observations the main task management operations in *TPC* are shown in Figure 1(a). Overall, task management operations in *TPC* require only on-chip transfers. Next, we discuss our evaluation methodology and the applications we use.

3   Experimental Platform and Methodology

In our experiments we use a Playstation3 (PS3) game console system, equipped with a 3.2 GHz Cell processor and 256 MBytes of main memory. On the PS3, applications are allowed to access only six of the eight SPEs in the Cell processor.

In our evaluation we use both application kernels as well as full applications. The applications we use are: FFT and LU from SPLASH-2 [18], PBPI [7], and an H.264 Encoder [1]. We re-implemented LU and FFT with single precision floating point arithmetic, replacing the original double precision version, because the SPEs exhibit significantly higher performance with single precision floating point operations. Using single-precision floating point arithmetic requires higher communication to computation ratios and results in a more realistic evaluation.

LU. We maintain the original algorithm [18] and modify the execution control structure of LU to employ a single *master* and multiple *worker* cores. Phases between barriers in the original code are translated to tasks, with the master core waiting between phases for all tasks to complete. Porting LU to *TPC* essentially involves converting three compute-intensive functions to *TPC*: bdiv(), bmod(), and bmodd(). The main modification to these functions is the identification of shared memory accesses in their body and conversion of these updates to a task argument list. We use the contiguous blocks version of LU from the SPLASH-2 suite, therefore we avoid stride arguments.

FFT. The SPLASH-2 version of FFT uses a six-step algorithm that involves alternating phases of transpose and FFT calculations. In our porting, we reorganize the code as follows: We merge steps two and three in a single asynchronous call to reduce data transfers, as both steps modify the same data. We modify the transpose step to transpose the matrix in place. We split the original matrix into blocks in a similar way as the original SPLASH-2 FFT but we use the local storage of SPEs as an intermediate buffer to transpose each block. Although certain aspects of porting FFT to *TPC* require understanding the existing code beyond syntactic modification, eventually the changes required are simple structural changes that do not require modifying data structures or re-writing the code. Similarly to LU, this is because FFT has been optimized to avoid fine-grain accesses to shared memory, which hinder scalability in traditional shared memory multiprocessors.

PBPI. Parallel Bayesian Phylogenetic Inference [7] constructs phylogenetic trees from aligned homologous DNA sequences. The original code is implemented in MPI. The TPC version of PBPI aims at exploiting fine-grain parallelism in each MPI process by using TPC tasks. We use TPC tasks to parallelize three loops that compute the likelihood on each node of the phylogenetic tree. The three loops are separated by barriers. Each node has enough data to produce tasks for all SPEs with argument sizes that result in efficient DMA transfers. Additionally, loop portions that each task executes are unrolled and vectorized. We introduce a user-defined parameter that specifies task size in terms of loop iterations. We implement a static load balancing scheme to ensure that all SPEs execute the same number of tasks, while adjusting their size to be as close as possible to the user-defined size.

H.264 Encoder. A typical H.264 video encoder consists of three components: prediction, transformation, and entropy encoding [17]. We port an existing parallel encoder, x264 [1], originally written for shared-memory multiprocessors, to the Cell using *TPC*. Although parallelization of x264 can occur at different granularities, the limited on-chip memory leads to parallelization at the macro-block level, which allows a single frame to be processed in parallel by all SPEs. This requires satisfying macro-block dependencies in an antidiagonal-based manner [16]. We port the analyze, encode and Context-based Adaptive Variable Length Coding phases to the SPEs, leaving the rest of the code on the PPE. This allows for parallelizing about 85% of the serial execution time. Finally, we vectorize certain kernels of motion estimation for the SPEs: sum of absolute differences, sum of absolute transformed differences, and pixel average. The remaining application code that runs on the PPE is vectorized using the PowerPC Altivec extensions.

Kernels. We port SAXPY, SGEMV, and CONV2D directly from their original implementation in Sequoia [6] to *TPC*, with no structural or algorithmic modifications in the kernel code. SAXPY and SGEMV are communication bound. CONV2D is computation bound. CONV2D uses convolution to apply a mask to a 2D image. The initial image of size $M \times N$, is decomposed into a set of parallel 2D convolution subproblems, each computing a non-overlapping region of the output image of size $S \times T$.

For each application, we present execution time breakdowns for both the PPE and the SPEs. We break down the execution of the PPE in three parts: time spent in the *TPC* runtime, time waiting for SPEs to complete, and time spent

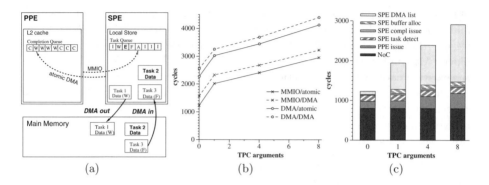

Fig. 1. (a) *TPC* runtime operations. (b) Null task latency for the different initiation and completion mechanism. (c) Null task round-trip breakdown for MMIO initiation and atomic DMA completion.

in application code. SPE breakdowns consist of task compute time, library time (including data transfer time), and idle time. Also, as a reference point, we show application execution time for a single PPE, where this is possible. Finally, in this work we assume that the code to be executed by each task is already present on the target SPE and PPE distributes tasks round-robin across SPEs.

4   Experimental Results

4.1   Basic Task Overheads

In this section we examine the basic overheads associated with task operations in *TPC* using null tasks, which perform no computation. Furthermore, we set the task queue size to a single entry to avoid overlapping of runtime overheads.

In Figure 1(b) we see the total latency for initiation and completion of a null task. We evaluate two methods for initiation and two methods for completion. The PPE can initiate a *TPC* task with remote stores directly to an SPE's local storage. We refer to this mechanism as MMIO initiation. Alternatively, the PPE can build the task descriptor locally in its L2 cache and initiate a DMA command in the SPE's DMA controller to fetch the descriptor to the local storage of the SPE. We refer to this mechanism as DMA initiation. Completion status from SPE can be sent with a simple DMA command or an atomic DMA command. We refer to these methods as DMA and atomic (ACU) completion respectively. We use zero-byte arguments to show how the overhead of the runtime varies with the number of *TPC* arguments without including the DMA transfer costs that are not affected by the design of the runtime system. First, we see that minimum round-trip latency is about 1230 cycles or 385 ns. Second, we note that using MMIO for task initiation and the ACU for task completion results in the lowest overhead. Using DMA instead of MMIO for task initiation adds about 1000 cycles, whereas replacing the ACU with regular DMA for task completion adds about 200 cycles.

Figure 1(c) shows the breakdown of null-task latency in the best case, when using MMIO and atomic DMA, for a varying number of zero-byte arguments. PPE initiation includes building the task descriptor and issuing the remote stores. The PPE initiation overhead increases slowly with the number of arguments from 180 to 380 cycles. The EIB round-trip latency is about 800 cycles. We should note that both PPE and SPE are dual-issue, in-order processors. This makes them vulnerable to register dependencies and poor instruction scheduling. For this reason, in the PPE, we use a separate `tpc_callN()` function for tasks with N arguments. In these versions of `tpc_callN()` functions, as the number of *TPC* arguments is fixed, we perform loop-unrolling and appropriate instruction scheduling to help the compiler produce more efficient code. However, we can not apply the same method for run-time operations in the SPE as they depend not only on the number of *TPC* arguments but also on the types of these arguments. We expect that compilers will be able to deal with these issues when generating code for the TPC runtime.

The SPE portion of the round-trip overhead, excluding DMA transfers for task data, involves four steps: SPE task detection recognizes the user function to be invoked and sets up internal structures; SPE DMA list builds the DMA list elements for input and output arguments, as described in the task descriptor; SPE buffer allocation allocates the required space for task data in the local storage; SPE completion builds the completion status and issues the atomic DMA command to signal completion. The processing of tasks in the SPE is dominated by the time needed to create the DMA list for fetching inputs and writing back results. The cost for a single argument is 650 cycles and increases to 1450 cycles for eight arguments. On the other hand, the time needed for task detection, buffer allocation, and issuing the DMA for the completion status is about 280 cycles and is not affected by the number of *TPC* arguments.

4.2   Impact of Queue Size

Figure 2 shows the impact of task queue size on null task latency and throughput, when using a single argument of varying size, with the generic version of the `tpc_call()` function. The minimum average latency for null task with a zero-byte argument is about 900-1000 cycles, when using more than two SPEs and queue size of two or four, due to overlapping of tasks on multiple SPEs. Larger queue sizes increase the average latency to about 1100 cycles when using more than one SPEs. We observe similar behavior in the case of non-zero arguments for null tasks. However, latency increases when queue size increases above four.

When looking at throughput in Figure 2, we see that a single argument of 8 KBytes or more can reach maximum throughput with queue sizes of two or more on three or more SPEs. A queue size of one can reach maximum throughput only when using all six SPEs. An argument size of 4 KBytes approaches half of the maximum throughput for two SPEs and a queue size of four. The maximum throughput achieved with a single 1-KByte argument is about 3 GBytes/s (12% of the theoretical peak of 25.6 GBytes/s) with four SPEs and a queue size of two or four.

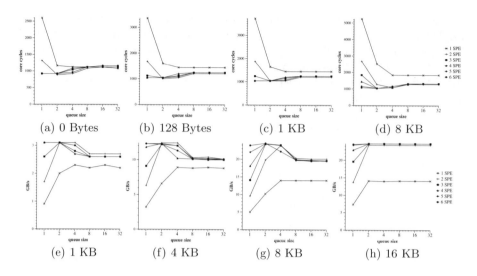

Fig. 2. Impact of queue size on null-task latency (top) and throughput (bottom) for different number of *TPC* arguments

Overall, we expect that a small task queue size of up to four will be enough for achieving all possible overlap of communication and computation in the SPEs.

4.3   Application Scaling

LU. Figure 3 shows LU execution time breakdowns for both PPE and SPEs with a $4K \times 4K$ input matrix, using 64×64 and 16×16 blocks. LU, though a shared memory application has already been optimized to avoid scattered, fine-grain accesses to shared data structures. For both block sizes, execution time scales with the number of SPEs. Maximum speedup for six SPEs is 5.98 and 5.87 for 16×16 and 64×64 blocks respectively. However, note that using 16×16 blocks is about 105% slower than using 64×64 blocks when using one SPE. With 64×64 blocks compute time dominates, as there are significantly fewer and larger DMA transfers and the larger task compute time allows the runtime to effectively pre-fetch future tasks.

FFT. Figure 3 shows the execution time breakdowns for the PPE and SPEs for 4M and 64K elements. The larger FFT problem size of 4M complex reals requires about 64 MBytes of memory. FFT exhibits good performance and scalability. For 4M FFT, *TPC* achieves speedup of 5.05 in 6 SPEs and for 64K FFT *TPC* achieves speedup of 5.1. The number of *TPC* tasks depends only on the problem size, as the task granularity is fixed to a single row of the matrix. For the 4M problem size there are enough tasks to fill the task queue of every SPE. On the other hand, the 64K problem size does not create enough tasks to take advantage of task pre-fetching and incurs higher sync wait times on the PPE for more than four SPEs. On the SPE side, compute time dominates the total execution time,

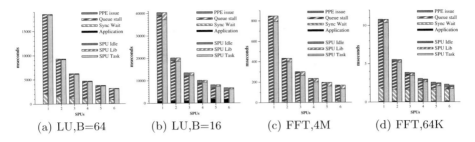

(a) LU,B=64   (b) LU,B=16   (c) FFT,4M   (d) FFT,64K

Fig. 3. LU and FFT execution times. LU uses $4K \times 4K$ matrix, with block sizes 64×64 and 16×16. FFT computes 4M and 64K complex elements respectively.

whereas argument transfer overheads are less than 4% and 7% for the 64K and 4M problem sizes respectively. Overall, scalability of FFT is currently limited mainly by the transpose steps of the algorithm. Table 1 shows that for 4M FFT the computation and transpose times scale differently. Computation time alone scales by a factor of 5.98 over 6 SPEs while the transpose time scales only by a factor of 1.93 because memory throughput is saturated for more than two SPEs. However, the time of the transpose step varies between 8.8% and 23% of the total execution time and has a lower impact on scalability.

H.264 Encoder. In our experiments we use a number of full high definition (1920×1088) video inputs taken from the HD-VideoBench [3]. Although the size of a single macro-block is the same for every task, the amount of computation involved in processing is different. Figures 4(a) and 4(b) present execution time breakdowns for both PPE and SPEs for two different videos. Each video has different computational complexity. We have set the queue size to two slots for this application due to the high memory requirements for code in the SPEs (about 150 KBytes of code). In our experiments we use three B-frames and one reference frame with 128×128 motion vector search window. The achievable speedup depends on the complexity of the input video sequence, since the input stream affects the required computations. Overall, using 6 SPEs results in a speedup of up to 5.0 compared to the initial version of the encoder running on the PPE.

4.4 Comparison to Sequoia

Finally, we compare *TPC* to Sequoia using the SAXPY, SGEMV, and CONV2D kernels that come with Sequoia. We port them to *TPC* using the same computation functions and the same data partitioning schemes. We also port PBPI to *TPC* and compare with its Sequoia implementation [15]. SAXPY and SGEMV are both communication bound kernels and saturate memory bandwidth with more than two or three SPEs. For CONV2D, in order to achieve better DMA performance, we split the $4K \times 4K$ image into 32×64 blocks where each task processes one block. The matrix is constructed in row-wise form, therefore we

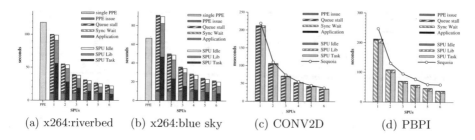

(a) x264:riverbed   (b) x264:blue sky   (c) CONV2D   (d) PBPI

Fig. 4. *TPC* execution time breakdowns for x264, 2D convolution and PBPI

Table 1. FFT speedup

	Speedup			
SPEs	Trans-pose fraction	Compu-tation	Trans-pose	Total
1	08.8%	1.00	1.00	1.00
6	23.0%	5.98	1.93	5.05

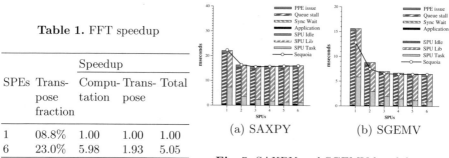

(a) SAXPY   (b) SGEMV

Fig. 5. SAXPY and SGEMV breakdowns

use stride arguments. Computation time dominates the SPE execution time in CONV2D. Figures 5 and 4(c) show that *TPC* and Sequoia scale similarly with both communication bound and compute bound kernels. The performance difference between *TPC* and Sequoia for SAXPY and SGEMV when the kernels use more than one SPEs is about 3%. *TPC* performs about 5% better than Sequoia in CONV2D due to better overlapping of DMA transfers in the *TPC* runtime.

For PBPI we use various task sizes in *TPC*. We find that tasks with argument sizes larger than 4 KBytes reach almost maximum speedup at queue sizes of 4 or higher. Figure 4(d) shows that with 6 SPEs we achieve a maximum speedup of 5.6 while Sequoia achieves a maximum speedup of 4.2 with the same setup. *TPC* benefits from dynamic task execution and better load balancing in PBPI.

5   Related Work

The introduction of multi-core processors in mainstream computing environments has given rise to numerous proposals and associated research efforts on parallel programming models. We concentrate our discussion of related work on task-level parallel programming models targeting heterogeneous multi-core processors with explicitly managed local memories and cover briefly other related work due to space considerations.

Sequoia [6] is a programming language which relies on explicit data accesses and is similar to *TPC* in that locality is exploited through annotation of data with in-out clauses. Sequoia follows a static execution model where the programmer statically optimizes the mapping of data and tasks relatively to the memory hierarchy. *TPC* implements a dynamic execution model where the programmer expresses parallelism and locality without considering the mapping of tasks and data to cores. *TPC* is optimized towards achieving low-overhead dynamic task management mechanisms in order to exploit fine-grain task-level parallelism, whereas Sequoia is optimized for explicit, static locality management.

CellSs [13] is a programming model for expressing task-level parallelism with code annotations. Contrary to *TPC*'s RPC-style programming model, CellSs uses compiler directives to annotate tasks and data with in-out clauses. The distinguishing feature of CellSs is the use of a helper thread that dynamically analyzes dependencies between tasks and schedules tasks dynamically after resolving their input dependencies. Dynamic dependence analysis incurs high overhead, which can be amortized if the analysis can increase the degree of available parallelism. *TPC* does not perform runtime dependence analysis although this is not precluded by its design. *TPC*'s task queues enable aggressive lookahead optimizations, such as pre-fetching via multi-buffering, similarly to CellSs. On the other hand, CellSs's scheduling model assumes coarse task granularity to mask the overhead of runtime data dependence analysis, whereas *TPC* targets fine-grain task-parallel execution. *TPC*'s measured task initiation/completion times are one order of magnitude lower than those currently reported for CellSs.

OpenMP has been extended to support task parallelism [12]. OpenMP tasks require the programmer to specify only the code region that will execute in parallel as a task. Instead, *TPC* requires specification of both code and data accessed by the task. The *XLC* [11] compiler for the Cell offers an OpenMP abstraction for loop level parallelism, using *DBDB* [9]. XLC splits loop iterations across SPEs and predicts statically the ideal number of grouped iterations in order to overlap communication with computation. On the other hand, *TPC* generates tasks dynamically and uses task queues to overlap DMA transfers of upcoming tasks with current task execution. Our evaluation shows that *TPC* is successful in hiding DMA latencies. Furthermore, *TPC* maps non-contiguous accesses always to DMA-list elements to minimize DMA initiation overheads in the runtime. On the other hand, DBDB uses an analytical model to predict whether those accesses should be mapped to a single DMA, including unnecessary data, multiple individual DMAs, or a single DMA list. The authors of DBDB find that DMA lists offer the best performance in most applications. Overall, *TPC* aims at minimizing the *runtime overhead* for preparing and initiating task and data transfers on both the PPE and SPEs, whereas DBDB aims at optimizing data transfer *time*.

Related work targeting heterogeneous multi-core architectures outside the context of task-level parallel programming models includes data-parallel programming models, such as RapidMind [10], and libraries for expressing and managing communication between heterogeneous components, such as IBM ALF and DaCs [5]. Other commonly used programming models for shared-memory multiprocessors, such as Cilk [4], do not provide support for heterogeneous systems with explicitly managed local memories, although there are ongoing efforts for extending these models to support heterogeneous systems in the future.

6 Conclusions

We present *Tagged Procedure Calls* (*TPC*) a programming model for the Cell processor, designed to exploit fine-grain parallelism and reduce programmer effort for scaling to large numbers of cores. *TPC* requires the programmer to annotate programs at the procedure level for specifying parallel tasks and their data accesses.

TPC implements task management using only on-chip operations for task creation, initiation, assignment, and completion. *TPC* achieves null task initiation and completion in 385 ns on the Cell, which is close to the round-trip DMA latency. We find that applications previously implemented and optimized for shared-memory multiprocessors can be ported with manageable effort that involves mostly mechanical code changes and achieve high parallel efficiency using *TPC*. In addition, our results show that *TPC* enables the exploitation of additional fine-grain parallelism on-chip in applications parallelized previously at coarse granularity. Through a comparison with the Sequoia programming language and its runtime we demonstrate that *TPC* performs competitively to existing task-level parallel programming frameworks.

Finally, based on our experience with *TPC*, runtime support for future CMPs will need to deal with three additional, broad issues: Mapping of the natural task sizes of applications to fine-grained tasks for memory efficiency, scheduling of fine-grained tasks, and code management. We believe that addressing these issues at the runtime and architectural levels can result in efficient and scalable task-based programming models for future CMPs.

Acknowledgments. We would like to thank Manolis Katevenis for discussions at early stages of the work. We are thankful to the Barcelona Supercomputing Center (BSC) and the Polytechnic University of Catalonia (UPC) for making available the QS21 boards for performance debugging experiments. Finally, we thankfully acknowledge the support of the European Commission through the SARC IP (Contract No. SARC-27648), HiPEAC NoE (Contract No. IST-004408 and IST-217068) and the MCF IRG project I-Cores (Contract No. IRG-224759).

References

1. VideoLAN - x264, http://www.videolan.org/developers/x264.html
2. Abellán, J., Fernández, J., Acacio, M.: Characterizing the Basic Synchronization and Communication Operations in Duall Cell-Based Blades. In: Proc. of the 8th International Conference on Computational Science, June 2008, pp. 456–465 (2008)

3. Alvarez, M., Salami, E., Ramirez, A., Valero, M.: HD-VideoBench. A Benchmark for Evaluating High Definition Digital Video Applications. In: Proceedings of the IEEE Workload Characterization Symposium, pp. 120–125 (2007)
4. Blumofe, R.D., Joerg, C.F., Kuszmaul, B.C., Leiserson, C.E., Randall, K.H., Zhou, Y.: Cilk: An Efficient Multithreaded Runtime System. In: PPOPP 1995: Proceedings of the Fifth ACM SIGPLAN Symposium on Principles and Practice of Parallel Programming, pp. 207–216 (1995)
5. Crawford, C.H., Henning, P., Kistler, M., Wright, C.: Accelerating Computing with the Cell Broadband Engine Processor. In: CF 2008: Proceedings of the 5th ACM Conference on Computing frontiers, Ischia, Italy, pp. 3–12 (2008)
6. Fatahalian, K., Knight, T.J., Houston, M., Erez, M., Horn, D.R., Leem, L., Park, J.Y., Ren, M., Aiken, A., Dally, W.J., Hanrahan, P.: Sequoia: Programming the Memory Hierarchy. In: Proceedings of ACM/IEEE Supercomputing 2006 (2006)
7. Feng, X., Cameron, K.W., Sosa, C.P., Smith, B.E.: Building the Tree of Life on Terascale Systems. In: Proceedings of the 21st International Parallel and Distributed Processing Symposium, mar 2007, pp. 1–10 (2007)
8. Hofstee, H.P.: Power Efficient Processor Architecture and The Cell Processor. In: Proceedings of the 11th International Symposium on High-Performance Computer Architecture, pp. 258–262 (2005)
9. Liu, T., Lin, H., Chen, T., O'Brien, K., Shao, L.: DBDB: Optimizing DMA Transfer for the Cell BE Architecture. In: ICS, pp. 36–45 (2009)
10. McCool, M.D.: Data-Parallel Programming on the Cell BE and the GPU using the RapidMind Development Platform. In: GSPx Multicore Applications Conference, Santa Clara, CA (October 2006)
11. O'Brien, K., O'Brien, K., Sura, Z., Chen, T., Zhang, T.: Supporting OpenMP on Cell. International Journal of Parallel Programming 36(3), 289–311 (2008)
12. OpenMP Architecture Review Board. Draft version 3.0 for public comments (January 2008), http://www.openmp.org/mp-documents/spec30_draft.pdf
13. Perez, J.M., Bellens, P., Badia, R.M., Labarta, J.: CellSs: Making it easier to program the Cell Broadband Engine processor. IBM Journal of Research and Development 51(5), 593 (2007)
14. Rico, A., Ramirez, A., Valero, M.: Available Task-level Parallelism on the Cell BE. Scientific Programming 17, 59–76 (2009)
15. Schneider, S., Yeom, J.-S., Rose, B., Linford, J.C., Sandu, A., Nikolopoulos, D.S.: A Comparison of Programming Models for Multiprocessors with Explicitly Managed Memory Hierarchies. In: PPOPP 2009: Proceedings of the 14th ACM SIGPLAN Symposium on Principles and Practice of Parallel Programming, pp. 131–140 (2009)
16. van der Tol, E., Jaspers, E., Gelderblom, R.: Mapping of H.264 Decoding on a Multiprocessor Architecture. In: Image and Video Communications and Processing (2003)
17. Wiegand, T., Sullivan, G.J., Bjontegaard, G., Luthra, A.: Overview of the H.264/AVC Video Coding Standard. Circuits and Systems for Video Technology, July 2003, vol. 13, pp. 560–576 (2003)
18. Woo, S.C., Ohara, M., Torrie, E., Singh, J.P., Gupta, A.: The SPLASH-2 programs: Characterization and methodological considerations. In: Proceedings of the 22nd International Symposium on Computer Architecture, pp. 24–36 (1995)

Analysis of Task Offloading for Accelerators

Roger Ferrer[1], Vicenç Beltran[1], Marc Gonzàlez[1,2], Xavier Martorell[1,2], and Eduard Ayguadé[1,2]

[1] Barcelona Supercomputing Center, Jordi Girona, 29
[2] Departament d'Arquitectura de Computadors, Univ. Politècnica de Catalunya, Jordi Girona, 1–3, Barcelona, Spain
{roger.ferrer,vbeltran,marc.gonzalez,xavier.martorell, eduard.ayguade}@bsc.es

Abstract. As an answer to the forthcoming heterogeneous multicore and accelerator–based architectures, we have proposed some syntactic extensions to C in the form of C pragmas, based on OpenMP, that make easier for programmers to offload parts of their applications to the auxiliary processors. Offloaded tasks can be made more profitable using a simple blocking strategy. And the runtime system is used to better support computation and communication overlap, while moving data to and from accelerators.

In order to prove the feasibility and usefulness of our proposal, we have considered the IBM Cell architecture. The performance of the whole system has been evaluated using HPCC STREAM Triad and several NAS benchmarks. We present their evaluation and a detailed performance breakdown at the level of parallel regions. We also classify the parallel regions according to their suitability to be exploited in accelerators. Overall, our performance is better compared to the results obtained from the IBM compiler for the Cell processor.

1 Introduction

Heterogeneous multicore architectures available today add an extra difficulty to programming. The process of writing or porting applications has to take into account that the algorithms must be thought or adapted to use the new architectural features and accelerators. Otherwise, the performance obtained is far from the peak performance offered by the hardware.

Programmers have been struggling to achieve high performance in heterogeneous multicore architectures. For that, they have to write code in different ways, with respect to what they are used to. It is common now to program on top of a vendor provided SDK on various architectures, like the Cell BE processor[1] and the NVIDIA GPU cards[2,3].

In this work, we are taking a higher–level approach, also thought to overcome the limitations of current compiler technology, while more powerful compilers are developed. We propose to extend the OpenMP[4,5] annotations to provide the compiler with more information about how the program can be transformed[6].

Y.N. Patt et al. (Eds.): HiPEAC 2010, LNCS 5952, pp. 322–336, 2010.

The main contributions of this paper are:

- The ability of defining parallel tasks that can be offloaded to accelerators. The approach allows for incremental parallelization as OpenMP supports. In this work we have focused on the Cell BE processor, although we believe that the approach is general enough and can be applied to other sorts of heterogenous multicore architectures.
- The automatic generation of DMA transfers guided by the annotations inserted by the programmer. In addition, double buffering techniques are implemented and demonstrated by means of the CellMT library, supporting threaded execution inside the Cell SPUs.
- Provide the parallelization of three NAS benchmarks[7,8] (CG, FT, and BT) using the extensions proposed in the SARC programming model, including the analysis of the performance obtained in the individual parallel regions in these benchmarks, determining which are good characteristics of parallel regions to be exploited in such heterogeneous environments.

We have developed the SARC transformations in the Mercurium C/C++ compilation infrastructure[9]. Results show that the transformations are feasible, and the performance reaches close to peak when using optimized kernels and is also better compared to the performance obtained by the IBM compiler.

The rest of the paper is structured as follows: Section 2 presents relevant related work. Section 3 presents our proposal. Section 4 presents the porting of applications and their evaluation. Finally, Section 5 outlines the conclusions and our future work.

2 Related Work

New processor designs based on heterogeneous multicores have raised the question about their programmability. General purpose computation on graphics processors has received a lot of attention as it delivers high performance computing at rather low cost. Major processor vendors have shown their intent to integrate GPUs as a GPU–core in the CPU chip [10,11]. CUDA [2], Compute Unified Device Architecture, proposed by the GPU vendor NVIDIA, is a programming model based on C and C++ for General Purpose Graphic Processor Units (GPGPU) computing. It is based on *kernels* that are run n times in parallel by n CUDA threads. Brook for GPUs [12] is a compiler and runtime implementation of the Brook [13] stream programming language that runs on GPUs. The Khronos group is developing a new standard, OpenCL [14], to take the power of GPUs and make it available for general–purpose computing. OpenCL standardizes the characteristics of various heterogeneous architectures, from GPUs to the Cell/B.E. processor. Compared to them, our approach can be used to automatically obtain the kernels from the applications source code, and OpenCL will give the low–level support to efficiently execute them in the accelerators.

Many programming models suitable for heterogeneous multicores express some form of task based parallelism. OpenMP 3.0 [4], introduces a `task` suitable for parallelization of irregular applications [15]. Cell Superscalar [16] is a programming model based on dependences among tasks designed to ease Cell programming. Recently, in [17], expressing dependences has also been proposed for OpenMP 3.0 tasks.

The CAPS HMPP [18] toolkit is a set of compiler directives, tools and software runtime that supports multi–core processor parallel programming in C and Fortran on Unix platforms. HMPP works based on *codelets*, that define functions that will be run in a hardware accelerator. These codelets can either be hand–written for a specific architecture or be generated by a compiler.

IBM provides the IBM XL C/C++ for Multicore Acceleration [19] (formerly known as Octopiler [20]). It is composed of a single source compiler, and its associated runtime environment. The compiler takes OpenMP applications, and transforms the code accordingly to the parallelization pragmas to be exploited in the Cell SPUs. When the compiler can determine that the data access pattern is regular, it uses a tiling transformation to inject the DMA transfers embedded in the code. For regions in which regularity cannot be established, the compiler code generation falls back on the use of a software cache [21], whose performance is lower than the tiling transformations. We have used the IBM compiler to compare some of our results to a commercial platform.

The PGI compilers [22] support regions of code to be outlined to accelerators, and `copyin` and `copyout` clauses to indicate data movement hints to the compiler.

Techniques such as double–buffering or multi–buffering have been widely used in the Cell BE to hide DMA latencies. Although both techniques are very effective, they must be used on a case–by–case basis, because these techniques require non–trivial code modifications. In [23], authors propose a prefetching technique for I/O intensive applications which is effective for applications with huge working sets that do not fit in main memory. In [24] a software cache is proposed for irregular accesses. The SPENK [25] nano–kernel provides a micro–threading model to increase the utilization of the Cell/B.E. resources. The SPENK kernel implements a preemptive threading model that allows the execution of complex multithreaded applications inside the SPUs. In this work, we have used the CellMT library [26] because it uses a highly optimized cooperative multi-threading model that provides a low context switch overhead mechanism that can overlap even small DMA transfers with computation.

3   Proposal

Our proposal is an extension to the OpenMP `task` construct[4] so we can express work to be offloaded to the accelerators. Besides of the part of the code we want to run in the accelerator, and since most of accelerators feature disjoint memories, expressing the flow of data going in and coming out to/from the accelerator is also required, specifically for those situations where the current compiler analysis technology is unable to determine accurately such flow of data.

3.1   Program Annotations

In this subsection we describe the program annotations that we use to better express data usage and work coarsening for the tasks outlined to accelerators.

Task outlining. In the context of a parallel region, OpenMP 3.0 allows to define a deferrable unit of work by means of `#pragma omp task`. This `task` can be executed at any time but OpenMP defines several synchronization points where task finalization is guaranteed.

Since accelerators may provide better performance for some specific codes, we may be interested in specifying that the task be run in one kind of accelerator. As an extension to current `task` syntax, we introduce the clause `device(accelerator-kind-list)`, where `accelerator-kind-list` is a comma-separated list of accelerator kinds feasible to execute the task.

Listing 1 shows a simple vector addition suitable for running in a SPU of the Cell.

Listing 1. Simple example of a task feasible for a SPU

```
#pragma omp task device(spu)
{
    int i;
    for (i = 0; i < N; i++)
    {
        a[i] = b[i] + c[i];
    }
}
```

Data movement hints. Accelerators often have their own memory banks, disjoint to the main memory of the processor. Data used in tasks that run in accelerators must be transferred from the main memory to the accelerator memory and viceversa.

In order to express this data movement we introduce `#pragma omp data` directive. This directive is paired with two clauses `copy_in(data-variable-list)` and `copy_out(data-variable-list)` which express the flow of data going to and coming from the accelerator respectively. Argument `data-variable-list` is a comma-separated list of variable names or *array-sections*[1] of the form `data-variable[lower:upper]`, meaning all elements from *lower* to *upper* (both included).

Listing 2 shows an example where we copy to the accelerator the two added arrays and we copy out the resulting array of the addition.

Listing 2. Moving data to and from the SPU

```
#pragma omp task device(spu)
{
#pragma omp data copy_in(b[0:N-1], c[0:N-1])
    int i;
    for (i = 0; i < N; i++)
    {
        a[i] = b[i] + c[i];
    }
#pragma omp data copy_out(a[0:N-1])
}
```

---

[1] This is a concept borrowed from Fortran 90.

Blocking hint. Accelerators not only feature disjoint memories, they are also much smaller than the main memory. This poses a problem when the data used by the task does not fit wholly in the accelerator memory. While we could always reduce the amount of data used in each task, like in Listing 3, this results in low performance caused by a low ratio between computation and number of data transfers.

Listing 3. Inefficient data transfer

```
int i;
for (i = 0; i < N; i++)
{
#pragma omp task device(spu)
{
#pragma omp data copy_in(b[i], c[i])
    a[i] = b[i] + c[i];
#pragma omp data copy_out(a[i])
}
}
```

Blocking loops can be a simple way to allow loops to run in accelerators with small memories, but it requires a manual transformation by the programmer. In order to alleviate all the problems related with handmade transformations, we provide a hint to the compiler to block the loop. The compiler will adjust appropriately all #pragma omp data when performing the blocking. To achieve this effect, we use #pragma omp for loop_blocking factors($factor_1, \ldots, factor_N$) in the outermost body of a N-depth perfect loop nest (see Listing 4).

Listing 4. Simple loop blocking

```
int i;
#pragma omp for loop_blocking factors(BlockSize)
for (i = 0; i < N; i++)
{
#pragma omp task device(spu)
{
#pragma omp data copy_in(b[i], c[i])
    {
        a[i] = b[i] + c[i];
    }
#pragma omp data copy_out(a[i])
}
}
```

4   Evaluation

In this section, we present the results obtained in the Cell/B.E. architecture, from the HPCC STREAM Triad, and a subset of the NAS benchmarks. The goal is to show how flexible the program transformations, and runtime optimizations are. As a case study, a Cell/B.E. blade has been used for the evaluation, with no loose of generality.

4.1   Execution Environment

The Cell Broadband Engine Architecture[1] (CBEA) is a heterogeneous multi-core processor designed by IBM, Sony and Toshiba, see Figure 1. The Cell is

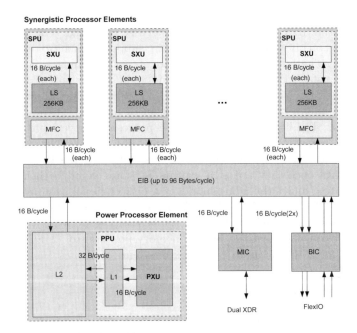

Fig. 1. Architecture of Cell Broadband Engine Architecture

built on top of a Power processor element (PPE). The PPE consists of a Power Processor Unit (PPU) and it is connected to a 512 KBytes L2 cache. The PPU is a dual issue in-order PowerPC64[27] with dual-thread support. Cell BE also features eight Synergistic Processor Elements (SPEs). Each SPE is composed of a Synergistic Processor Unit (SPU) and a Memory Flow Controller (MFC), the latter being a programmable memory controler of each SPE. SPEs have a local storage of 256 KBytes for data and code. An element interconnect bus (EIB) is used to interconnect all elements.

For this evaluation, we have used the Cell machines available at the Barcelona Supercomputer Center. They are QS20 blades powered with two Cell processors clocked at 3.2 GHz with 1 GB of RAM memory. They have the IBM Cell SDK 3.0 installed. In this environment, we have up to 16 SPUs available. All experiments have been done within the default Linux (version 2.6.24.7-92.fc8) execution environment, with the default virtual page size of 4096 bytes. All experiments have been executed 4 times and means and standard deviations calculated. We present the resulting means of the results, and we have ensured that the standard deviation of the experiments is very low. The machines were used in a dedicated mode.

We have extended the Mercurium C/C++ source-to-source compiler to implement the constructs presented in Section 3 and in [9,6]. Mercurium is an extensible source–to–source compiler targeted at code transformations. This compiler supports multiple file generation, making it suitable for multiple architecture compilation. After getting the transformed source code, we compile the PPU/SPU sides, each with the corresponding GCC 4.1.1, from the toolchain coming with the SDK 3.0, except when otherwise indicated. The parallel code generated runs on our CellMP runtime system, supporting such extensions in the Cell processor. The runtime system takes care of task spawning, synchronization, and DMA transfers. Besides, we address the issue of overlapping computation and communication with the use of the CellMT[26] threading library. This user level library enables the concurrent execution of multiple threads inside each SPE processor. The library allows each SPE processor to overlap the task computation and transfer times in a natural way. The CellMT library provides a cooperative multi-threading model, so it relies on the threads themselves to relinquish control once they are at a waiting–for–data point in their execution. This cooperative multi–threading model is a perfect fit for any processor with a managed local store, such as the Cell processor, because the context switch points are easily identified. In fact, all applications written for the Cell have these points explicitly identified by the memory flow control (MFC) operations used to wait for DMA request or mailbox messages.

4.2 Selected Applications

We have selected to evaluate our approach with several parallel applications exploiting regular and some irregular memory accesses. In the first place, we have taken the HPCC STREAM Triad benchmark to show the performance obtained in regular applications. Then, we have also selected three of the NAS benchmarks (CG, FT and BT). In the case of CG and FT, both benchmarks exhibit irregular memory accesses in one of their parallel regions. This is useful to see how our proposal behaves in these situations. In the following sections we explain how we have done the evaluation on all these applications, and what is the performance obtained.

4.3 Results Obtained from the HPCC STREAM Triad

We have coded the HPC Challenge STREAM benchmark [28] with our OpenMP extensions. In this section, we present the results obtained in the Triad algorithm. Listing 4.3 shows the code annotated. Observe the blocked parallel loop in lines 4–5, and how the tasks are labeled to be exploited in the Cell SPUs (line 7). Each task is getting a block of vectors b and c (line 9), computing, and putting the results (c) back to memory (line 11).

Figure 2 shows the results. It presents the GBytes per second obtained when STREAM Triad runs from 1 to 16 SPUs, and when using 1 memory module (sets of bars on the left hand side) and 2 memory modules (sets of bars on the right hand side). We reach 22.2 Gbytes/s on 8 SPUs, and 40.8 Gbytes/s on 16 SPUs when running with 2 SPU threads (thus fully exploiting double buffering), using one and two memory modules respectively. We exploit double buffering in the application code by using threading in the SPUs [26]. With this configuration, our numbers are equivalent to 86% of peak (25.6 Gbytes/s) on 8 SPUs and 79% of peak (51.2 Gbytes/s) on 16 SPUs.

```
1   void tuned_STREAM_Triad(double scalar)
2   {
3       int j;
4   #pragma omp parallel for loop_blocking factors(2048)
5       for (j=0; j<N; j++)
6       {
7   #pragma omp task device (spu)
8       {
9   #pragma omp data copy_in(b[j], c[j])
10          a[j] = b[j]+scalar*c[j];
11  #pragma omp data copy_out(a[j])
12      }
13      }
14  }
```

It is interesting to comment that the performance on 1 to 4 SPUs is better when using a single memory module (bars on the left hand side of the figure). This is because our SPU allocation algorithm starts at SPU 0 and continues sequentially up to SPU 15. This means that when using up to 8 SPUs we are using the SPUs in the Cell chip number 0. At 8 SPUs, the pressure on the memory module has gone too high and it is worthwhile to use the two memory modules to hold the data. In this case, it is noticeable the difference from 22.2 Gbytes/s using a single memory module, to 29.8 Gbytes/s when using the two memory modules. When running on 12 and 16 SPUs, the performance is also better when using the two memory modules. The reason why when using two memory modules, the performance with 12 SPUs is reduced compared to that of running on 8 SPUs needs to be further investigated. At this point, we attribute it to the fact that some of the SPUs in the Cell chip number 0 are accessing the memory module close to Cell chip number 1, and this causes conflicts in the interconnection network between the chips. This is something that does not happen when running on 16 SPUs and the two memory modules, as in this case the memory accessed is perfectly split between the two Cell chips.

If we compare these results with recently published results from the Intel Xeon 5500 Nehalem processor family, we can see that currently we are still competitive with our results on the Cell blade. A box with two Intel Xeon 5570 processors (for a total of 8 cores) achieves in this same benchmark 37.12 Gbytes/s [29,30].

4.4   Results Obtained from NAS CG

We have annotated NAS CG with the proposed extensions. All parallel loops expose regular accesses, except the one shown (annotated) in Listing 5.

In this loop, the inner–most `copy_in` directive in line 11 cannot be issued before the array section from `colidx` has been transferred, and accessed, getting the irregular index (`irreg_index`).

We have experimented with two different transformations for such irregular accesses. First, the naive translation to a DMA transfer initiated when the `copy_in` directive is found. A second transformation consists of generating an inspector[31] code that builds a DMA list (a feature of the Cell SPUs), then issuing the DMA list transfer to collect the irregular data, and finally, doing the computation on the collected data.

Listing 5. Annotated loop with an irregular data access in CG

```
1   #pragma omp for loop_blocking factors(block_size)
2       for (j = 1; j <= lastrow-firstrow+1; j++) {
3   #pragma omp task device(spu)
4       {
5           double sum = 0.0;
6   #pragma omp data copy_in (rowstr[j:j+1])
7           int lowk = rowstr[j], upk = rowstr[j+1];
8   #pragma omp data copy_in (colidx[lowk:upk], a[lowk:upk])
9           for (k = rowstr[j]; k < rowstr[j+1]; k++) {
10              int irreg_index = colidx[k];
11  #pragma omp data copy_in (p[irreg_index])
12              sum = sum + a[k]*p[irreg_index];
13          }
14          w[j] = sum;
15  #pragma omp data copy_out (w[j])
16      }
17      }
```

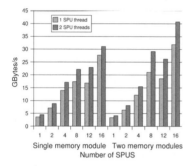

Fig. 2. Performance reported by STREAM Triad in a Cell blade

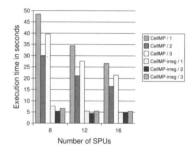

Fig. 3. Benefits of the irregular access transformation ans use of CellMT in NAS CG

Figure 3 shows the evaluation of the CG CLASS A benchmark from 8 to 16 threads when using both transformations, and from 1 to 3 CellMT threads per SPU. It can be observed that the transformation of irregular accesses to DMA lists (labelled *CellMP-irreg*) is very effective, and also that the best results are achieved when using 2 CellMT threads. The reason why 3 CellMT threads are not giving better results is that the DMA transfer times are shorter than the computation times across most of the parallel regions, as in the STREAM Triad case. In this situation, an extra thread is only adding overhead.

We have compared these results with the ones obtained with the IBM cbexlc compiler[32,20], version 1.0, for CLASS A in Figure 4, and CLASS B in Figure 5. The speedup shown is measured against the serial execution of the benchmark in the PPU, to have a common reference for all experiments. As a result, our program transformations and runtime system optimizations give better results than the IBM compiler, showing that the techniques used in the transformations are interesting to achieve better performance in this kind of accelerator–based architectures. Notice that the scalability of CG Class B is higher than that of Class A, similarly to what happens in plain SMP machines. This is because

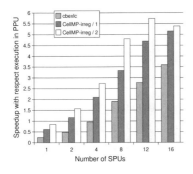
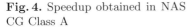

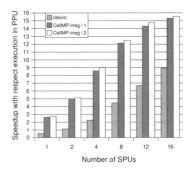

Fig. 4. Speedup obtained in NAS CG Class A

Fig. 5. Speedup obtained in NAS CG Class B

the higher the Class, the higher the data structures in the NAS benchmarks. Although each task DMA transfers have the same size, each task has also more work to do, it transfers-computes more times, and the overhead of spawning and joining parallel regions has less impact on the overall performance. In any case, for small tasks, we also notice that our CellMP execution environment still has some overhead, as it does not scale beyond 12 SPUs for CG Class A. This will be investigated in our future work.

4.5 Results Obtained from NAS FT

We have also used our OpenMP extensions to annotate the NAS FT benchmark. There are 4 main loops to be annotated. With this benchmark we do not see benefits from using CellMT threads. The reason is that in order to exploit 2 threads, the block size in which the benchmark operates has to be reduced. This causes an extra overhead to spawn parallelism from the PPU, and it is not worthwhile.

We present the results obtained in each individual parallel loop in the Class A of the FT benchmark in Figure 6. Class B gives similar results. Observe that loops scale well. Also, it is noticeable the benefit of the irregular support in the performance of the loop in function `evolve`, referred to as `evolve-lists` in the graph. Figure 7 shows the execution times obtained in the execution of NAS FT using the `cbexlc` compiler and our CellMP environment without (label *CellMP*) and with the irregular transformation (label *CellMP-irreg*). Notice also that in the three executions with a single SPU (and also in 2 SPUs), the performance obtained is worse than that obtained in the PPU. The fact that no parallel loop has been vectorized by the SPU compiler can be a good reason for this effect, but further investigation needs to be done to better determine the reasons of such poor performance of the FT code on the SPU.

4.6 Results Obtained from NAS BT

We have also annotated NAS BT with our OpenMP extensions. In this application we have faced a new issue: the code size outlined for the SPUs does not fit

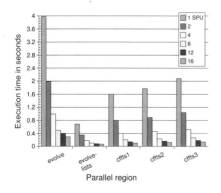

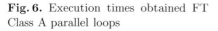

Parallel region

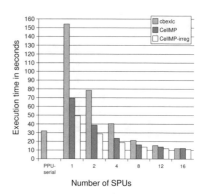

Number of SPUs

Fig. 6. Execution times obtained FT Class A parallel loops

Fig. 7. Execution time obtained in FT Class A

in their local store. To solve this, we have used the IBM compiler (through the *spuxlc* driver) to compile the code outlined for the SPUs, with overlay support.

We have annotated the 18 parallel loops offering better performance. They have been outlined by the Mercurium compiler automatically. The IBM compiler has generated the overlays, and we have obtained detailed timings for each of them. As with NAS FT, we have not seen benefits from using CellMT threads, as the block sizes are then reduced. Also, NAS BT has no irregular memory accesses that could be improved by using the irregular support in CellMP.

Figure 8 shows the evaluation of the NAS BT (Class A) application when executed in the PPU, and from 1 to 16 SPUs. As it can be observed, the application suffers a loose in performance when going from the PPU to 1 or 2 SPUs. With 4 SPUs, the performance is mostly equivalent to the PPU. For 8 and 16 SPUs, a slight increase in performance is still achieved.

Evaluated independently, we have found the following types of loops in NAS BT, with these characteristics:

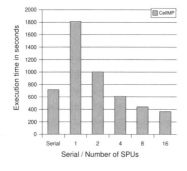

Serial / Number of SPUs

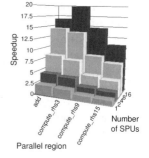

Fig. 8. Execution time obtained in NAS BT (Class A)

Fig. 9. Scalability of parallel regions with good properties in NAS BT

- Parallel regions fitting in the local store and with good DMA properties. Regions Add, compute_rhs3, compute_rhs9, and compute_rhs15 have the nice properties of having their code fitting well in the local store, and having large consecutive DMAs of more of 2 Kbytes per DMA transfer. Because of this, their performance in a single SPU is already comparable to the performance on the PPU. And when going to multiple SPUs, their scalability is very good, achieving speedups of above 12 in 16 SPUs (see Figure 9).
- Parallel regions fitting in the local store, with short DMA transfers. Regions identified by lhsx, lhsy, and lhsz still have their code fitting in the local store, but they do short DMA transfers. Such short DMA transfers are caused by convolution-like memory accesses, where in some transfers less elements than the full inner dimensions are moved. This way, data is transferred in small chunks, and the cost of the initiation of the DMAs is the penalty that reduces performance (see regions labeled as lhsan in Figure 10). Their speedup compared to the execution in the PPU does not go over 4.5.
- Parallel regions that do not fit in the local store and with short DMA transfers. The rest of regions shown in Figure 10 (labeled x_solven, y_solven, and z_solven) have very limited performance caused by a large penalty of overlay replacement during execution. All of them have a call to a large function (binvchrs) that goes to a different overlay section. In addition, their DMA transfers are short, due to the same reasons than in the previous case. In this case, their performance in a single SPU is much worse (3 to 4 times worse) than in the PPU, so the performance in 8 SPUs cannot be more than an speedup of 1.5 or 2. In addition, due to the extra DMA transfers caused by the overlay management, their scalability from 8 to 16 SPUs is very limited.

We think that future development, and porting, of applications for heterogeneous multicore processors will need to achieve a large portion of code fitting in the first category. Otherwise, the performance obtained will be severely limited, as it happens with the overall performance of NAS BT.

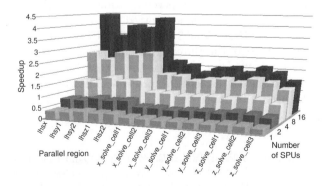

Fig. 10. Scalability of parallel regions with bad properties in NAS BT

5   Conclusions and Future Work

We have shown the feasibility of defining tasks to be offloaded to accelerators and the generation of automatic DMA transfers. By means of annotations in the source code the programmer defines those tasks and specifies the intended data movement. Blocking, also specified by directives, can be used as way to overcome the local storage limitations of heterogeneous multicore processors with local stores, allowing to increase the granularity of offloaded tasks.

Our evaluation has used the Cell/B.E. processor as a case study. We show that our transformations effectivelly allow to exploit the computation and communication resources of the Cell using the CellMT SPU threading library. We have presented the evaluation of STREAM Triad and the NAS benchmarks CG, FT, and BT. With STREAM Triad we show how we can obtain 79% of peak bandwidth when using 16 SPUs, and 86% of peak when running on 8 SPUs. A detailed analysis of the parallel regions in CG, FT, and BT shows that it is important to have them fit in the local stores of the SPUs, and to have DMA transfers of consecutive data, and as large as possible. Our overall performance is competitive with the IBM compiler for the Cell/B.E.

We have observed that our CellMP runtime system has some overhead, specially when running on a large number of SPUs. As future work, we will investigate what are the sources of such overhead, and better tune the runtime system to support fine–grain tasks. We will continue coding applications with our OpenMP extensions, in order to further demonstrate their usability, and also trying to influence comercial compilers to incorporate some of the techniques to improve the static analysis of the compilers to be able to generate better code automatically.

Our long term plan includes extending this model also to FPGAs and GPUs as well. For FPGAs, our idea is to use the same task annotations to describe which is the code that should be implemented in the FPGA. In this context, data movement coul d be automatically generated from the `copy_in` and `copy_out` directives.

Acknowledgements

We would like to thank the Barcelona Supercomputing Center (BSC) for the use of their machines. This work has been supported by the Ministry of Education of Spain under contracts TIN2007-60625 and CSD2007-00050, the Generalitat de Catalunya (2009-SGR-980), the European Commission in the context of the SARC integrated project #27648 (FP6), the HiPEAC-2 Network of Excellence (FP7/IST-217068), and the Mare Incognito project under the BSC-IBM collaboration agreement.

References

1. Chen, T., Raghavan, R., Dale, J., Iwata, E.: Cell Broadband Engine Architecture and its first implementation. IBM Developer Works (November 2005)
2. NVIDIA corporation: NVIDIA CUDA Compute Unified Device Architecture Version 2.0 (2008)

3. NVIDIA corporation: NVIDIA Tesla GPU Computing Technical Brief (2008)
4. OpenMP Architecture Review Board: OpenMP Application Program Interface. Version 3.0 (May 2008), http://www.openmp.org
5. Ayguadé, E., Copty, N., Duran, A., Hoeflinger, J., Lin, Y., Massaioli, F., Teruel, X., Unnikrishnan, P., Zhang, G.: The Design of OpenMP Tasks. IEEE Transactions on Parallel and Distributed Systems 20(3), 404–418 (2009)
6. Ayguadé, E., Badia, R.M., Cabrera, D., Duran, A., Gonzalez, M., Igual, F., Jimenez, D., Labarta, J., Martorell, X., Mayo, R., Perez, J.M., Quintana-Orti, E.: A Proposal to Extend the OpenMP Tasking Model for Heterogeneous Architectures. In: Fifth International Workshop on OpenMP, IWOMP (2009)
7. Jin, H., Frumkin, M., Yan, J.: The OpenMP Implementation of NAS Parallel Benchmarks and Its Performance. Technical Report NAS-99-011, NASA Ames Research Center (1999)
8. Kusano, K., Satoh, S., Sato, M.: Performance evaluation of the Omni OpenMP compiler. In: Third International Symposium on High Performance Computing, pp. 403–414 (2000)
9. Ferrer, R., Gonzalez, M., Silla, F., Martorell, X., Ayguadé, E.: Evaluation of Memory Performance on the Cell BE with the SARC Programming Model. In: Proceedings of the 9th Workshop on Memory Performance: Dealing with Applications, systems, and architecture (MEDEA 2008) (October 2008)
10. Intel Corporation: Intel Corporation's Multicore Architecture Briefing (March 2008), http://www.intel.com/pressroom/archive/releases/20080317fact.htm
11. AMD Corporation: AMD 2007 Technology Analyst Day, http://www2.amd.com/us-en/assets/content_type/DownloadableAssets/FinancialA-DayNewsSummary121307FINAL.pdf
12. Stanford University: BrookGPU, http://graphics.stanford.edu/projects/brookgpu/
13. Stanford University: Brook Language, http://merrimac.stanford.edu/brook/
14. Group, K.O.W.: The OpenCL Specification (February 2009), http://www.khronos.org/registry/cl/
15. Ayguadé, E., Copty, N., Duran, A., Hoeflinger, J., Lin, Y., Massaioli, F., Su, E., Unnikrishnan, P., Zhang, G.: A Proposal for Task Parallelism in OpenMP. In: Chapman, B., Zheng, W., Gao, G.R., Sato, M., Ayguadé, E., Wang, D. (eds.) IWOMP 2007. LNCS, vol. 4935, pp. 1–12. Springer, Heidelberg (2008)
16. Perez, J.M., Bellens, P., Badia, R.M., Labarta, J.: CellSs: Making it easier to program the Cell Broadband Engine processor. IBM Journal of Research and Development 51(5), 593–604 (2007)
17. Duran, A., Pérez, J.M., Ayguadé, E., Badia, R.M., Labarta, J.: Extending the OpenMP Tasking Model to Allow Dependent Tasks. In: Eigenmann, R., de Supinski, B.R. (eds.) IWOMP 2008. LNCS, vol. 5004, pp. 111–122. Springer, Heidelberg (2008)
18. Dolbeau, R., Bihan, S., Bodin, F.: HMPP: A Hybrid Multi-core Parallel Programming Environment. In: Workshop on General Processing Using GPUs (2006)
19. IBM Corporation: XL C/C++ for Multicore Acceleration (January 2009), http://www-01.ibm.com/software/awdtools/xlcpp/multicore/
20. O'Brien, K., O'Brien, K., Sura, Z., Chen, T., Zhang, T.: Supporting OpenMP on Cell. International Journal of Parallel Programming (2008)
21. Balart, J., Gonzalez, M., Martorell, X., Ayguadé, E., Sura, Z., Chen, T., Zhang, T., O'Brien, K., O'Brien, K.: A Novel Asynchronous Software Cache Implementation for the CELL/BE Processor. In: Adve, V., Garzarán, M.J., Petersen, P. (eds.) LCPC 2007. LNCS, vol. 5234, pp. 125–140. Springer, Heidelberg (2008)

22. Group, T.P.: PGI Fortran & C Accelerator Programming Model (December 2008), http://www.pgroup.com/lit/whitepapers/pgi_whitepaper_accpre.pdf
23. Rafique, M.M., Butt, A.R., Nikolopoulos, D.S.: Dma-based prefetching for i/o-intensive workloads on the cell architecture. In: CF 2008: Proceedings of the 2008 conference on Computing frontiers, pp. 23–32. ACM, New York (2008)
24. Chen, T., Zhang, T., Sura, Z., Gonzalez, M.: Prefetching irregular references for software cache on cell. In: CGO 2008: Proceedings of the sixth annual IEEE/ACM international symposium on Code generation and optimization, pp. 155–164. ACM, New York (2008)
25. Ahmed, M.F., Ammar, R.A., Rajasekaran, S.: SPENK: Adding Another Level of Parallelism on the Cell Broadband Engine. In: IFMT 2008: Proceedings of the 1st international forum on Next-generation multicore/manycore technologies, pp. 1–10. ACM, New York (2008)
26. Beltran, V., Carrera, D., Torres, J., Ayguadé, E.: CellMT: A Cooperative Multi-threading Library for the Cell/B.E. In: HiPC 2009: Proceedings of the 16th Annual IEEE International Conference on High Performance Computing. IEEE Computer Society, Los Alamitos (2009)
27. Weltzer, J., Silha, E., May, C., Frey, B., Furukawa, J., Frazier, G.: PowerPC Architecture Book V. 2.02. IBM Corporation (2005)
28. McCalpin, J.D.: STREAM: Sustainable Memory Bandwidth in High Performance Computers (2008), http://www.cs.virginia.edu/stream
29. Corder, S., Sheumaker, K.: STREAM Benchmarking: Intel Xeon 5500 Nehalem vs AMD Opteron 2400 Istanbul (2009), http://www.advancedclustering.com/company-blog/stream-benchmarking.html
30. Corporation, I.: Intel Xeon Processor 5000 Sequence (2009), http://www.intel.com/p/en_US/products/server/processor/xeon5000
31. Balart, J., Gonzalez, M., Martorell, X., Ayguadé, E., Labarta, J.: Runtime Address Space Computation for SDSM Systems. In: Almási, G.S., Caşcaval, C., Wu, P. (eds.) LCPC 2006. LNCS, vol. 4382, pp. 330–344. Springer, Heidelberg (2007)
32. Chen, T., Sura, Z., O'Brien, K., O'Brien, J.K.: Optimizing the Use of Static Buffers for DMA on a CELL Chip. In: Almási, G.S., Caşcaval, C., Wu, P. (eds.) LCPC 2006. LNCS, vol. 4382, pp. 314–329. Springer, Heidelberg (2007)

Offload – Automating Code Migration to Heterogeneous Multicore Systems

Pete Cooper[1], Uwe Dolinsky[1], Alastair F. Donaldson[2], Andrew Richards[1], Colin Riley[1], and George Russell[1]

[1] Codeplay Software Ltd., Edinburgh, UK
[2] Oxford University Computing Laboratory, Oxford, UK

Abstract. We present *Offload*, a programming model for offloading parts of a C++ application to run on accelerator cores in a heterogeneous multicore system. Code to be offloaded is enclosed in an *offload* scope; all functions called indirectly from an offload scope are compiled for the accelerator cores. Data defined inside/outside an offload scope resides in accelerator/host memory respectively, and code to move data between memory spaces is generated automatically by the compiler. This is achieved by distinguishing between host and accelerator pointers at the type level, and compiling multiple versions of functions based on pointer parameter configurations using *automatic call-graph duplication*. We discuss solutions to several challenging issues related to call-graph duplication, and present an implementation of Offload for the Cell BE processor, evaluated using a number of benchmarks.

1 Introduction

In this paper, we contribute towards the goal of programming heterogeneous multicore processors like the Cell Broadband Engine (BE) [1] using a familiar threading paradigm. To this end, we present Offload, a programming model and implemented system for offloading portions of large C++ applications to run on accelerator cores. Code to be offloaded is wrapped in an *offload* block, indicating that the code should be compiled for an accelerator, and executed asynchronously as a separate thread. Call graphs rooted in an offload block are automatically identified and compiled for the accelerator; data movement between host and accelerator memories is also handled automatically. The Offload approach allows the development of portable multi-threaded applications for homogeneous *and* heterogeneous platforms: the language extensions we propose are minimal, and preprocessor macros can be used to select between, for example, a POSIX thread and an Offload thread on a homogeneous or heterogeneous platform respectively. The advantages to this approach are evident: large source bases can be incrementally migrated to heterogeneous platforms with relatively little change; portability across heterogeneous and homogeneous platforms is possible, and the burden of writing data movement and accelerator start-up and clear-down code is lifted from the programmer.

After discussing the challenges of heterogeneous multicore programming we make the following contributions. We present the Offload language extensions, and describe

Y.N. Patt et al. (Eds.): HiPEAC 2010, LNCS 5952, pp. 337–352, 2010.

automatic call-graph duplication, where multiple versions of a function[1] are compiled for an accelerator, based on the contexts in which the function is called. We then discuss our solutions to challenging problems associated with call-graph duplication in the presence of pointer types for separate memory spaces, function pointers and virtual methods, and multiple compilation units. Finally, we present experimental results for a Cell BE implementation of Offload, evaluated using several benchmarks.

2   Programming Heterogeneous Multicore Processors

Processor manufacturers are increasingly opting to deliver performance improvements by implementing processors consisting of *multiple* cores due to problems in obtaining further performance increases from single core processors. Multicore processors may be *homogeneous*, consisting of n identical cores, or *heterogeneous*, where some or all of the cores differ in specialisation. In principle, a homogeneous multicore processor with n cores connected to shared memory can offer a factor of n-times execution speedup over a single-core processor at the same clock rate. However, contention for access to shared memory may lead to a performance bottleneck, known as the *memory wall*, where adding further cores quickly leads to diminishing returns.

The memory wall problem has led to a recent mainstream shift towards *heterogeneous* multicore processors in the *host with accelerators* pattern, where a host core connected to main memory coordinates a number of possibly diverse processing element (PE) cores each equipped with private "scratch-pad" memory. Independent calculations can be processed in parallel by separate cores with reduced contention for shared memory. The PE cores need only access shared main memory via direct memory access (DMA) to read input data, write results, and communicate with one another. The Cell BE [1] is one such processor design, consisting of a Power Processor Element (PPE) host with 8 Synergistic Processor Element (SPE) accelerator cores.

The use of scratch-pad memories can boost performance, but increases the complexity of concurrent programming. The programmer can no longer rely on the hardware and operating system to seamlessly transfer data between levels of the memory hierarchy, and must manually orchestrate data movement using DMA. Experience writing and debugging industrial software for heterogeneous multicore processors has identified the following key problems:

Separate programs are required for different cores. Distinct cores may have entirely different instruction set architectures, making it necessary to write, compile and maintain separate versions of functions for each type of core, as well as platform-specific "glue" code, to start up and clear down accelerator threads.

Data movement is untyped and unsafe. Low level data movement primitives operate on untyped bytes and data words. Mistakes in interpretation of untyped data or misuse of DMA primitives can lead to nondeterministic bugs that are hard to reproduce and fix.

Furthermore, many large applications have already been successfully parallelized for homogeneous multicore processors using POSIX or Windows threads. In this case the problem is not to find potential parallelism, but rather exploit already identified potential

---

[1] We use *function* to refer to functions and methods in general.

by offloading threads to accelerator cores with minimal disruption to an existing code-base. The Offload approach aims to ease the programming of heterogeneous multicore systems via a *conservative* extension to the C++ language.

We focus on systems where there is one type of accelerator core, equipped with a small scratch-pad memory, and with sufficient functionality to be programmed in C. The approach could be naturally extended to support multiple types accelerator.

3   Offload Language Extensions

3.1   Offload Scopes

The central construct of the Offload system is the *offload block*, a block prefixed by the **offload** keyword. Code outside an offload block executes on the coordinating host core; code inside an offload block executes on an accelerator core in a separate thread.

Offload blocks extend the syntax of C++ expressions as follows:

$Expr$ ::= ... | **offload** $Domain?$ $Args?$ { $Compound\text{-}Stmt$ }

$Args$ ::= (list of variable names) $Domain$ ::= (list of function names)

An offload block evaluates to a value of type `offload_handle_t`, an opaque type defined in header files supplied with the Offload system. The expression has the side-effect of launching a thread on an accelerator core. This *offload thread* executes *Compound-Stmt*, with standard sequential semantics. Host execution continues in parallel. The host can wait for the offload thread to complete by calling library function `offload_join`, passing as an argument the handle obtained on creating the offload thread. Multiple offload threads can be launched to run in parallel, either via multiple offload blocks, or by enclosing an offload block in a loop.

An offload thread can access global variables, as well as variables in the scope enclosing the associated offload block. Additionally, an offload block may be equipped with an argument list – a comma-separated list of variables names from the enclosing scope. Each variable in this list is copied to a local variable in the offload thread with the same name; references to this name inside the offload block refer to the local variable. An offload block may also be equipped with a *domain*, which we discuss in §5.2.

These concepts are illustrated by the following example:

```
int main() {
  int x = ...;
  int y = ...;
  offload_handle_t handle = offload(y) {
    // runs on accelerator, 'y' passed by value
    ... = x; x = ...; // 'x' accessed in enclosing scope
    ... = y; y = ...; // local copy of 'y' accessed
  };
  ...         // host runs in parallel with accelerator
  y = ...; // changes to 'y' do not affect offload thread
  ...
  offload_join(handle); // wait for offload thread
}
```

For brevity, we omit details of parameters and handles in the examples that follow.

The **offload** keyword can also be used as a function qualifier. A function with the **offload** qualifier is called an *offload function*, and function names can be overloaded using **offload**. We refer to offload functions and offload blocks as *offload scopes*. Offload functions can only be called from offload scopes, but it is permissible to call a non-offload function from an offload scope; this is discussed in detail in §4. We illustrate offload functions using the following example:

```
void f() { ... }              // (1)
offload void f() { ... } // (2)
offload void g() { ... } // (3)
void h() { ... }              // (4)

int main() {
  f();     // calls (1) on host
  g();     // error, 'g' is an offload function
  offload {
    f(); // calls (2) on accelerator
    g(); // calls (3) on accelerator
    h(); // calls (4) on accelerator
  }
}
```

3.2 Outer Pointers and Data Movement

Data declared inside an offload scope resides in accelerator memory. We distinguish pointers to local memory from pointers to host memory, referring to the latter as *outer pointers*. An additional qualifier for pointers and references,[2] the **outer** qualifier, specifies that a pointer refers to host memory. Pointers outside an offload scope have the **outer** qualifier by default. Assignment between outer and non-outer pointers is illegal; this ensures that an outer/non-outer pointer does not refer to data residing in accelerator/host memory.

Dereferencing an outer pointer in an offload scope causes data to be moved between host and accelerator memory. Data movement may be achieved via direct memory access (DMA). However, unless synchronization primitives are used to guard access to host memory, non-volatile data can be cached locally, so data movement may be implemented using a software cache, or via double-buffered streaming DMA if accesses have a regular pattern. Our Cell BE implementation (see §6) uses a software cache by default, and provides library functions to flush or invalidate the cache. These functions can be used in conjunction with mutexes to allow sharing of data between host and offload threads.

Consider the following listing, where a -> b indicates data movement from a to b:

```
offload void f(outer float * p) {
  *p = *p + 42.0f; // host -> accelerator, accelerator -> host
}
```

---

[2] Henceforth we will only talk about pointers; everything we say about pointers applies to references also.

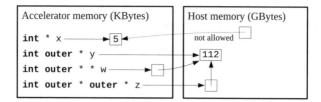

Fig. 1. Examples illustrating the **outer** qualifier for pointers

```
float a;

int main() {
  offload {
    outer float * p = &a;
    float b = *p;        // host -> accelerator
    *p = b + 42.0f;      // accelerator -> host
    float c = a;         // host -> accelerator
    a = c;               // accelerator -> host
    p = &b;              // error! '&b' is not outer
    f(p);                // legal function call
    f(&b);               // error! '&b' is not outer
  }
}
```

Taking the address of global variable a obtains an outer pointer p, through which data can be transferred between host and accelerator memory. Accessing host variable a directly from an offload scope also results in data movement. The listing illustrates illegal assignment between outer and non-outer pointers.

Outer pointers allow data transfers to be expressed without exposing the programmer to low-level, non-portable operations. By regarding outer and local pointers as incompatible, the compiler is able to ensure that transfers are well typed. Fig. 1 provides further illustration of the use of outer pointers in memory-space separation.

C++ permits overloading on the basis of **const** and **volatile** qualifiers. The Offload language extends this to the **outer** qualifier, allowing functions to be overloaded with different combinations of outer pointers. For an instance method on a class, the **outer** qualifier can be applied to the **this** pointer by placing **outer** after the closing bracket of the parameter list for the method; an example of this is given in §4.1.

4   Call-Graph Duplication

Suppose we require that *only* offload functions can be called from offload scopes. We call this the *strict* requirement. In this case, the compiler knows exactly which functions to compile for the accelerator (the offload functions) and host (the non-offload functions). Furthermore, the pointer signature for an offload function specifies exactly those pointers for which dereferences correspond to data movement operations (the outer pointers). The drawback is that the programmer may have to manually duplicate functionality to match the contexts in which a function is called. We illustrate the process of manual function duplication with the *strict* requirement, then show how automatic call-graph duplication can be used to handle programs that do not satisfy this requirement.

4.1 Manual Function Duplication

Consider the following class:

```
class SecretKeeper {
  int[SIZE] secrets;
public:
  int getSecret(int * p) const { return secrets[*p]; }
};
```

Listing 1. A simple C++ "secret keeper" class.

The following listing declares a SecretKeeper object both outside and inside an offload block, and calls the getSecret method on each object with a combination of outer and local pointers:

```
int main() { ...
  SecretKeeper outKeeper;
  int x; ...
  // normal method call on host
  int secretSum = outKeeper.getSecret(&x);
  offload {
    SecretKeeper inKeeper;
    int y;  ...
    secretSum +=
      inKeeper.getSecret(&y)  // (1) local 'this', local 'p'
    + inKeeper.getSecret(&x)  // (2) local 'this', outer 'p'
    + outKeeper.getSecret(&y) // (3) outer 'this', local 'p'
    + outKeeper.getSecret(&x) // (4) outer 'this', outer 'p'
  }; ...
}
```

Listing 2. Calling getSecret with various pointer configurations.

To satisfy the *strict* requirement, the programmer must define additional offload versions of getSecret for the four contexts in which the method is called inside the offload block:

```
class SecretKeeper {
  // as before, with additional methods:
  offload int getSecret(int * p) {
    return secrets[*p]; // matches context (1)
  }
  offload int getSecret(outer int * p) {
    return secrets[*p]; // matches context (2)
```

```
    }
    offload int getSecret(int * p) outer {
        return secrets[*p]; // matches context (3)
    }
    offload int getSecret(outer int * p) outer {
        return secrets[*p]; // matches context (4)
    }
};
```

Listing 3. Manually duplicating the getSecret method.

Although the bodies of these methods are syntactically identical, their compilation results in different data movement code. For example, in case (2), dereferencing outer pointer p results in a host-to-accelerator data movement operation, while indexing into local member secrets is a normal array lookup; in case (4) both dereferencing p and indexing into secrets require host-to-accelerator data movement operations: the outer **this** pointer means that the secrets member is located in host memory.

Manual function duplication with the *strict* requirement is time-consuming and results in many similar versions of the same function, which must all be maintained. However, when a program satisfies the *strict* requirement it can be compiled appropriately for the host and accelerator cores. We now show how a program that does *not* satisfy the *strict* requirement can be automatically translated into a form where the *strict* requirement is satisfied, from which it can be successfully compiled.

4.2   Automating the Duplication Process

Suppose a function f has been declared with the following signature:

$$T_0 \; f(T_1 \; p_1, \ldots, T_n \; p_n) \; \{ \; body \; \}$$

Note that f is *not* an offload function. Now suppose f is invoked from an offload scope, violating the *strict* requirement, in the following context:

$$e_0 \; = \; f(e_1, \ldots, e_n);$$

For $0 \le i \le n$, let U_i denote the type of expression e_i (where e_0 evaluates to an lvalue), and suppose that U_i and T_i are identical if **outer** qualifiers are ignored. In other words, the function application is well-typed if we ignore outer pointers. Then we can generate an overloaded version of f as follows:

offload $U_0 \; f(U_1 \; p_1, \ldots, U_n \; p_n) \; \{ \; body \; \}$

Let f' denote the newly generated version of f. Functions f and f' are identical, except that f' has the **offload** qualifier, and pointer parameters of f' may have the **outer** qualifier if they are passed outer pointers as actual arguments. The call to f from the offload scope now obeys the *strict* requirement, since it refers to the offload version of f, *i.e.* f'.

If *body* itself contains calls to non-offload functions then function duplication will be applied to these calls, with respect to the version of *body* appearing in f', so that f'

only calls offload functions. This process continues until function duplication has been applied to all call-graphs rooted in offload scopes, hence the term automatic *call-graph* duplication. The result is a program which obeys the *strict* requirement, and can thus be compiled appropriately for the host and accelerators. Compilation may fail if duplicated functions misuse outer pointers, as in the following example:

```
void f(int * x, int * y) { x = y; ... }

int main() {
   int a = 5;
   offload {
      int b; f(&a, &b); // '&a' is outer, '&b' is not
   }
}
```

Function duplication produces a duplicate of f where the first parameter is an outer pointer. However, this duplicate is not well-typed as it makes an assignment between an outer pointer and a non-outer pointer:

```
offload void f(outer int * x, int * y)
{   x = y; ... } // type error!  'x' is outer, 'y' is not
```

If outer pointers are used correctly then, in the absence of other general errors, all duplicated functions can be compiled for the accelerators, with data movement code generated corresponding to accesses via outer pointers.

Note that a function is only duplicated with a given signature at most once, meaning that call-graph duplication works in the presence of recursion. Also note that duplication is performed on demand: although a function with n pointer parameters has 2^n possible duplicates, only those actually required by an application will be generated. The above discussion explains how call-graph duplication works for functions; the approach easily extends to instance methods with a **this** pointer. In particular, the code of Listing 1 can be compiled with respect to the class definition of Listing 2; the duplicated methods of Listing 3 are generated automatically.

We have presented call-graph duplication as a source-to-source translation, followed by regular compilation. In a practical implementation the technique would most likely be implemented at the call-graph level – this is the case with our implementation (§6). In particular, the programmer never needs to see the duplicated functions generated by the compiler.

4.3   Offload Functions Are Still Useful

If a function should behave differently on the accelerator with a particular configuration of outer pointers, the required variant can be explicitly overloaded using the **offload** keyword. Suppose the getSecret method of §4.1 should return a pre-defined error constant when called on an outer **this** pointer with an outer pointer parameter. This can be specified by adding an offload version of getSecret to the secretKeeper class of Listing 1:

```
offload int getSecret(outer int * p) outer { return ERR; }
```

This version of getSecret will be called whenever the method is invoked on an outer object with an outer pointer parameter; otherwise call-graph duplication will be used to compile the standard version of the method appropriately.

A common use of offload functions is to allow specialised versions of performance-critical functions to be tuned in an accelerator-specific manner, *e.g.* to exploit accelerator features such as SIMD instructions.

5   Issues Raised by Call-Graph Duplication

While call-graph duplication is conceptually simple, its implementation is challenging in the presence of the full complexity of C++. We discuss the way type inference can increase the extent to which call-graph duplication can be automatically applied (§5.1) and our solutions to the issues raised by function pointers and virtual methods (§5.2), and multiple compilation units (§5.3).

5.1   Type Inference for Outer Pointers

The driving factor in the design of Offload is the extent to which existing code can be offloaded to an accelerator without modification. Disallowing assignments between inner and outer pointers in the type system provides a useful degree of type-checking across the host/accelerator boundary. However, when applying call-graph duplication to large examples, it is convenient to design the type system so that the **outer** qualifier is automatically applied in two circumstances:

– When a pointer variable p is initialised upon declaration to an outer pointer, p is given the **outer** qualifier
– If a cast is applied to an outer pointer then the destination type in the cast is automatically given the **outer** qualifier

We present two small examples to illustrate why these methods of inferring outer pointers are useful. The following example finds the smallest element in a list of non-negative integers, where the list is terminated by the value -1:

```
int findMin(int * intList) {
  int result = *intList;
  for(int * p = intList+1; *p != -1; p++)
    if( *p < result ) result = *p;
  return result;
}

int arrayOfIntegers[100] = { ... };

offload { int smallest = findMin(arrayOfIntegers); ... }
```

Because findMin is invoked with the outer pointer arrayOfIntegers, the compiler will attempt to compile a version of findMin which accepts an outer pointer. Without type inference, the compiler would reject the input program for attempting to assign an outer pointer intList+1 to an inner pointer p and the call-graph duplication attempt would fail. With type inference, the initialisation of p to an outer pointer means that p is given the **outer** qualifier implicitly.

The following function, which returns the floating point number corresponding to a machine word given by a pointer, illustrates type inference with casts:

```
float reinterpretInt(int * i) { return *((float *)i); }
```

Without type inference, if `reinterpretInt` is called from an offload scope with an outer pointer, the program would be rejected for attempting to cast an outer pointer into an inner pointer. Automatically adding the **outer** qualifier to the cast means that the code compiles un-problematically.

Inference of outer pointers minimizes the extent to which the **outer** keyword propagates throughout a large base of source code; in many practical examples, code can be enclosed in an offload block with no **outer** annotations whatsoever.

5.2   Function Pointers and Virtual Methods

Consider the following type definition for functions which accept an integer argument and return no value:

```
typedef void (* int_to_void) (int);
```

Assuming multiple functions have been declared with this type, consider a function pointer variable in host memory, followed by an offload block which makes a call via the function pointer:

```
int_to_void f_ptr;
...
offload { f_ptr(25); }
```

The problem is that, assuming `f_ptr` has been initialised to a valid address, the call via `f_ptr` invokes *some* function matching the function type `int_to_void`, but we do not know which one until run-time. For the call to succeed, it is necessary for a version of the function to which `f_ptr` is assigned to have been compiled for the accelerator, and loaded into local store. A similar problem applies when virtual methods are invoked from an offload scope.

In general, statically determining the precise set of functions to which a given function pointer may refer is intractable. A safe over-approximation would be to compile *all* functions matching the `int_to_void` signature for the accelerator. This would, however, significantly increase compile time and accelerator code size.

Our solution is to use *function domains* – annotations to an offload block listing the names of functions that the block may invoke via function pointers or virtual calls. A domain for an offload block may be specified immediately following the **offload** keyword, as shown in the grammar of §3.1.

Function domains are implemented on the accelerator by a lookup table. The value of the function pointer is used to obtain the address of the corresponding duplicated routine on the accelerator, which is then invoked in place of the host routine whose address was taken by the function pointer. An attempt to invoke a function not specified in the domain results in a run-time error and diagnostic message. There is scope for extending the compiler with heuristics to deduce domains automatically in many practical cases.

The following games-related example (derived from industrial source code) uses an array of function pointers for collision response between game entities, and illustrates that domains occur naturally in practical examples:

```
typedef void (* collisionFunction_t) (Entity *, Entity *);
collisionFunction_t collisionFunctions[3][3] =
```

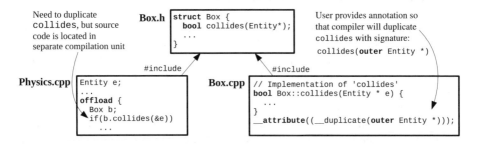

Fig. 2. Example of call-graph duplication over multiple compilation units

```
    { fix_fix, fix_mov, ..., dead_dead }; // 2d function table
...
// domain annotation on offload block
offload [ fix_fix, fix_mov, ..., dead_dead ] {
  for(...i, j...)
    // apply appropriate function according to status
    collisionFunctions [status[i]] [status[j]] (...);
}
```

Each entity has a status: `fix`, `mov` or `dead`, for fixed, moving or dead entities respectively. The array `collisionFunctions` provides a collision response function for each combination of object statuses, *e.g.* function `fix_mov` is invoked for collision response between a fixed and a moving object. By equipping the offload block with a named list of collision functions, the call via the `collisionFunctions` array will succeed.

5.3   Multiple Compilation Units

Automatic call-graph duplication depends on the compiler having access to the source code for all invoked functions. For large applications this is not the case, as source code is split into multiple files for separate compilation. Suppose source code is not available for method `collides`, called from an offload scope in compilation unit `Physics.cpp`. The compiler cannot perform call-graph duplication and simply generates code to call `collides` with the pointer signature required by the call site. Suppose `collides` is implemented in compilation unit `Box.cpp`. The programmer must mark the implementation with a *duplication obligation*, so that when `Box.cpp` is processed the compiler will duplicate the required version of `collides`, even if `collides` is *not* called from an offload scope in `Box.cpp`. This is illustrated in Fig. 2.

Annotating source code with duplication obligations is not too onerous – if the `collides` method of `Box` calls other functions that *are* defined in `Box.cpp` then since `Box::collides` is marked for duplication, these functions will be automatically duplicated appropriately. Thus, programmer annotations for duplication obligations are restricted to the boundaries of compilation units.

6   A Cell BE Implementation of Offload

We have implemented Offload for the Cell BE processor under Linux.[3] A C++ application with offload blocks is compiled to intermediate C program text targeting the
PPE and SPE cores. A makefile and linker script are also generated; these use the PPE
and SPE GCC compilers to generate a Cell Linux PPE executable with embedded SPE
modules, one per offload block.

A small run-time system implements the target-specific glue code required to use
an accelerator, such as handling the transfer of parameters from the host and setup
of a software cache through which access to the host memory is provided. The runtime also permits offloaded code to invoke routines on the host, *e.g.* to call malloc/free
on host pointers, and for mutex-based synchronization via the POSIX threads API.
Our implementation includes header files with definitions of SPE-specific intrinsics,
allowing their use in programs where some SPE hand-tuning is desired.

Given a multi-threaded C++ application, we propose the following method for offloading threads to run on SPEs:

1. Profile application to identify a computationally expensive host thread
2. Replace this thread with an offload block, adding outer pointer annotations, function domains and duplication obligations where necessary for correctness
3. Replace performance-critical functions with offload functions, specialised with
   SPE-specific optimizations where necessary for performance
4. Repeat this process until all appropriate host threads are offloaded

By (2) we mean that a call to create a thread running function f should be replaced with
an offload block which calls f. It is straightforward to define thread creation macros that
allow an application to use either POSIX or offload threads, depending on the available
support for a particular platform.

Basic offloading achieves the goal of getting code to run on SPEs, freeing the PPE to
perform other useful work. This can provide a performance benefit even if performance
of offloaded code is non-optimal. To achieve higher performance, it may be necessary
to write offload versions of performance-critical functions, hand-optimized for SPEs.
The main barrier to performance for the Cell BE is data movement. The Offload system
includes a set of header files to optimize access of contiguous data in host memory.
These header files define templated iterator classes, to be used in offload functions,
that optimize reading/writing of data from/to host memory using double-buffering. The
compiler generates advice messages, based on static analysis, to guide the programmer
towards refactorings to improve performance.

7   Experimental Results

We have developed a set of examples to investigate the performance improvement over
serial code which can be achieved using Offload for the Cell BE processor, and the ease
with which the language extensions can be applied:

---

[3] In addition, an implementation of Offload for Sony PlayStation 3 consoles is available to SCE-
licensed game developers.

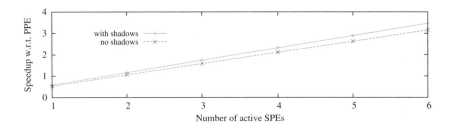

Fig. 3. Scaling of SphereFlake offload across multiple SPEs

- A Mandelbrot fractal generator, generating a 640×480 pixel image
- SphereFlake: a ray tracer generating a 1024×1024 pixel image [2]
- A set of five image processing filters operating on a 512×512 pixel image, performing: embossing, noise reduction, sharpening, Laplacian edge detection, and greyscale conversion

Experiments are performed on a Sony PlayStation 3 console, for which 6 SPEs are available to the programmer. We compare the performance of the computations as follows. The original code executing on a single hardware thread of the Cell PPE is used as a baseline against which to compare successive versions where computation is offloaded to between 1 and 6 SPEs. For a configuration with N SPEs, the benchmarks are multi-threaded to spawn N offload threads, each of which computes $1/N$ of the problem size.

Mandelbrot. The generator computes the Mandelbrot set value for each pixel using scalar operations. Offloading this sequential computation on to a single SPE yields a $1.6\times$ performance increase over the PPE baseline. When 6 SPEs are utilised the performance increase is $13.5\times$. By hand-optimizing the offloaded code to buffer output pixels, writing back to the host a line at a time, a performance increase of $14\times$ over the serial baseline is achieved. This modest improvement over the non-optimized case indicates the program is compute bound.

SphereFlake. SphereFlake [2] is a fractal ray tracer for generating and ray tracing a procedural model of spheres. We have applied Offload to this third party application, offloading parts of the ray tracer to run in parallel across Cell SPEs. Thanks to automatic call-graph duplication, it was possible to use the core of the ray tracer without modification. We applied some modest refactorings to improve performance, ensuring that procedural model generation is performed in SPE local store, and buffering output pixel values in local store, to be written to main memory by DMA a row at a time.

We benchmark the ray tracer with and without support for shadows. Performance scales linearly with the number of SPEs used, as shown in Fig. 3. With one SPE, performance is around $0.5\times$ that of the PPE baseline; with two SPEs, performance slightly exceeds that of the PPE. Maximum performance is achieved with six SPEs, with speedups of $3.47\times$ and $3.16\times$ PPE performance with and without shadows respectively.

Image processing filters. Fig. 4 shows the performance of our image processing filters, offloaded using either a single SPE, or all six available SPEs. For each offloaded

| Filter | Emboss | Noise | Sharpen | Laplacian | Greyscale |
	no manual opt.	no manual opt.	buffered output	buffered I/O	fully optimized
Speedup: 1 SPE	0.6×	0.85×	0.76×	3.13×	3.06×
Speedup: 6 SPEs	3.27×	2.76×	2.96×	6.51×	3.44×

Fig. 4. Speedups for offloaded image processing filters, with one and six SPEs

benchmark, the figure indicates whether we have performed no additional manual optimization, optimizations to buffer output, input and output, or extensive manual optimizations, including vectorization.

For the Laplacian filter, which computes output pixels using a 5×5 kernel, we find significant improvements can be gained by avoiding use of the software cache via explicit pre-fetching of input data. By using explicit DMA intrinsics to maintain a copy of five rows of input pixels in SPE local store, and buffering output for transfer to main memory a row at a time, offloading to a single SPE out-performs the PPE version by $3.13\times$. The price for this is increased source code complexity, and loss of portability. However, we were able to apply these manual optimizations incrementally, starting with a simple, non-optimized offload and gradually working towards a finely tuned version.

Performance scales only modestly for the greyscale benchmark as SPEs are added, due to the lightweight nature of the computation. This is an example where offloading a *single* thread to an accelerator can provide a useful speedup.

Discussion of performance. Our investigation of the performance of offloaded code identifies three categories of benchmarks, distinguished by the ease with which performance increases are obtained, and the steps required to achieve such increases. Computationally intensive algorithms, such as Mandelbrot and SphereFlake, result in increased performance by offloading, requiring little programmer effort, as execution times are dominated by computation rather than data access. Less straightforward are applications such as our image filter examples, that perform relatively little computation per data item on a large volume of data, but access contiguous data using a regular stride. In this case, basic offloading typically results in a performance decrease, which can easily be ameliorated using simple DMA operations which can be hidden in templated classes. A third category of applications, for which we do not present results, access large volumes of input data in an unpredictable manner, or in a manner not amenable to efficient DMA operations. This type of application may require significant restructuring for high performance to be achieved.

8   Related Work

Programming models. Of the recent wealth of programming models for multicore architectures, closest to Offload are Sequoia [3] and CellSs [4]. The Sequoia language abstracts both parallelism and communication through side-effect free methods known as tasks, which are distributed through a tree of system memory modules. When a task is called on a node, input data is copied to the node's address space from the parent's address space, and output is copied back on task completion. This provides a clean way to distribute algorithms that operate on regularly-structured data across heterogeneous multicore processors. However, tasks to be accelerated must be re-written using the bespoke Sequoia language, and the approach is only applicable when the data required by a task (its *working set*) is known statically. The latter requirement has its advantages, allowing aggressive data movement optimizations. CellSs is similar to Sequoia, involving the identification of tasks to be distributed across SPEs, and requiring the working set for a task to be specified upfront.

The idea of optimizing data movement based on regularly structured data is the basis for stream programming languages such as StreamIt [5] and Brook [6], and more recently HMPP [7] and OpenCL [8]. These models encourage a style of programming where operations are described as kernels – special functions operating on streams of regularly structured data – and are particularly suitable for programming compute devices such as GPUs. As with Sequoia and CellSs, exploiting regularity and restricting language features allows effective data movement optimizations. The drawback is that these languages are only suitable for accelerating special-purpose kernels that are feasible to re-write in a bespoke language. In contrast, Offload allows portions of general C++ code to be offloaded to accelerator cores in a heterogeneous system with few modifications. The flexible notion of outer pointers does not place restrictions on the working set of an offload thread. The price for this flexibility is that it is difficult to automatically optimize data movement for offload threads.

Call-graph duplication.   Our notion of call-graph duplication is related to function cloning [9], used by modern optimizing compilers for inter-procedural constant propagation [10], alignment propagation [11], and optimization of procedures with optional parameters [12]. Automatic call-graph duplication applies function cloning in a novel setting, to handle multiple memory spaces in heterogeneous multicore systems. Call-graph duplication is related to C++ template instantiation, and faces some of the same challenges. Call-graph duplication across compilation units (§5.3) is similar to template instantiation across compilation units, which is allowed in the C++ standard via the **export** keyword, but supported by very few compilers.

Memory-space qualifiers.   The idea of using qualifiers to distinguish between shared and private memory originated in SIMD array languages [13], and is used in PGAS languages such as Titanium [14], Co-array Fortran and Unified Parallel C [15]. Similar storage qualifiers are used by CUDA and OpenCL to specify data locations in accelerators with hierarchical memory.

9   Conclusions and Future Work

Our experimental evaluation with a Cell BE implementation of Offload give a promising indication that the techniques presented in this paper allow performance benefits of accelerator cores to be realised with relative ease, requiring few modifications to existing code bases.

While Offload is more flexible than alternative approaches for programming heterogeneous systems, this flexibility means data movement for offload threads is hard to optimize. We plan to extend Offload with facilities for annotating an offload block with information about expected data usage, which the compiler can use to apply more aggressive optimizations.

Call-graph duplication can potentially lead to a significant blow-up in code size, if a function with several pointer arguments is called with many configurations of local/outer pointers. This can be problematic when accelerator memory is limited. We plan to investigate tool support for providing feedback as to the extent to which call-graph duplication is required, and opportunities for reducing duplication.

Acknowledgements

We are grateful to Anton Lokhmotov, Paul Keir, Philipp Rümmer, and the anonymous reviewers, for their insightful comments on an earlier draft of this work. Alastair F. Donaldson is supported by EPSRC grant EP/G051100.

References

1. Hofstee, H.P.: Power efficient processor architecture and the Cell processor. In: HPCA, pp. 258–262. IEEE, Los Alamitos (2005)
2. Hoines, E.: A proposal for standard graphics environments. IEEE Comput. Graph. Appl. 7, 3–5 (1987)
3. Fatahalian, K., Horn, D.R., Knight, T.J., Leem, L., Houston, M., Park, J.Y., Erez, M., Ren, M., Aiken, A., Dally, W.J., Hanrahan, P.: Sequoia: programming the memory hierarchy. In: Supercomputing, p. 83. ACM, New York (2006)
4. Bellens, P., Perez, J.M., Badia, R.M., Labarta, J.: CellSs: a programming model for the Cell BE architecture. In: Supercomputing, p. 86. ACM, New York (2006)
5. Thies, W., Karczmarek, M., Amarasinghe, S.P.: Streamit: A language for streaming applications. In: Horspool, R.N. (ed.) CC 2002. LNCS, vol. 2304, pp. 179–196. Springer, Heidelberg (2002)
6. Buck, I.: Brook specification v0.2., http://merrimac.stanford.edu/brook/
7. CAPS Enterprise: HMPP, http://www.caps-entreprise.com/hmpp.html
8. Khronos Group: The OpenCL specification, http://www.khronos.org/opencl
9. Cooper, K.D., Hall, M.W., Kennedy, K.: A methodology for procedure cloning. Comput. Lang. 19, 105–117 (1993)
10. Metzger, R., Stroud, S.: Interprocedural constant propagation: An empirical study. LOPLAS 2, 213–232 (1993)
11. Bik, A.J.C., Kreitzer, D.L., Tian, X.: A case study on compiler optimizations for the Intel Core 2 Duo processor. International Journal of Parallel Programming 36, 571–591 (2008)
12. Das, D.: Optimizing subroutines with optional parameters in F90 via function cloning. SIGPLAN Notices 41, 21–28 (2006)
13. Lokhmotov, A., Gaster, B.R., Mycroft, A., Hickey, N., Stuttard, D.: Revisiting SIMD programming. In: LCPC, Revised Selected Papers, pp. 32–46. Springer, Heidelberg (2008)
14. Yelick, K.A., Semenzato, L., Pike, G., Miyamoto, C., Liblit, B., Krishnamurthy, A., Hilfinger, P.N., Graham, S.L., Gay, D., Colella, P., Aiken, A.: Titanium: A high-performance Java dialect. Concurrency - Practice and Experience 10, 825–836 (1998)
15. Coarfa, C., Dotsenko, Y., Mellor-Crummey, J.M., Cantonnet, F., El-Ghazawi, T.A., Mohanti, A., Yao, Y., Chavarría-Miranda, D.G.: An evaluation of global address space languages: Coarray Fortran and Unified Parallel C. In: PPOPP, pp. 36–47. ACM, New York (2005)

Computer Generation of Efficient Software Viterbi Decoders*

Frédéric de Mesmay, Srinivas Chellappa,
Franz Franchetti, and Markus Püschel

Electrical and Computer Engineering
Carnegie Mellon University
Pittsburgh PA 15213, USA
{fdemesma,schellap,franzf,pueschel}@ece.cmu.edu

Abstract. This paper presents a program generator for fast software Viterbi decoders for arbitrary convolutional codes. The input to the generator is a specification of the code and a single-instruction multiple-data (SIMD) vector length. The output is an optimized C implementation of the decoder that uses explicit Intel SSE vector instructions. At the heart of the generator is a small domain-specific language called VL to express the structure of the forward pass. Vectorization is done by rewriting VL expressions, which a compiler then translates into actual code in addition to performing further optimizations specific to the vector instruction set. Benchmarks show that the generated decoders match the performance of available expert hand-tuned implementations, while spanning the entire space of convolutional codes. An online interface to the generator is provided at www.spiral.net.

Keywords: Library generation, high performance software, vectorization, domain-specific language, Viterbi algorithm.

1   Introduction

The Viterbi algorithm is a maximum likelihood sequence decoder introduced by Andrew Viterbi [1], and finds wide usage in communications, speech recognition, and statistical parsing. In the past, the high throughput requirements for decoding demanded dedicated hardware implementations [2]. However, the dramatically growing processor performance has started to change this situation: intensive processing is now often done in software for reasons of cost and flexibility. A prominent example is software defined radio [3].

Unfortunately, developing a generic high-throughput software Viterbi decoder is difficult. The reason is that the best performance can only be achieved by using vector instructions (such as Intel's Streaming SIMD Extensions, SSE), which most modern processors provide. To take advantage of these instructions, the programmer has to explicitly issue them using an intrinsics interface or directly

---

* This work was supported by NSF through awards 0325687 and 0702386, and by DARPA through the Department of Interior grant NBCH1050009.

Y.N. Patt et al. (Eds.): HiPEAC 2010, LNCS 5952, pp. 353–368, 2010.

write assembly code. Achieving performance gains with these instructions first requires proper restructuring of the dataflow of the decoder with respect to the vector length. Then, the programmer must deal with the intricacies of the instruction sets as the available instructions differ between platform vendors and vector lengths. Finally, because the total vector length in bits is fixed, there is a degree of freedom arising from the tradeoff between speed and precision (e.g., 4-way vectorization implies 32 bits per element while the faster 16-way vectorization implies only 8 bits per element).

Because of the difficulty in handling these issues, existing approaches are based on manually writing specific assembly routines for each decoder (e.g., [4]), which involves considerable effort given the large set of different codes and platforms used in real-world applications.

Contribution of this paper. In this paper, we present a method to automatically generate fast implementations of software Viterbi decoders. Our generator takes as input, a specification of the convolutional code and the vector length to be used. The output is a C program for the corresponding Viterbi decoder implemented using SSE. Note that the methods presented in this paper are generic enough to apply to other instruction sets. Only the performance critical forward pass of the decoder is actually generated – the infrastructure and the traceback stages are reused from the high-performance decoders by Karn [4].

Our generator consists of three components:

1. A domain specific language, called VL, to describe the forward pass at a high level of abstraction. The language is a generalization of the Kronecker product formalism used to describe fast Fourier transforms [5].
2. A VL rewriting system that restructures the forward pass depending on the target vector length.
3. A compiler that takes VL as input, outputs C code including SSE intrinsics, and performs various low level optimizations.

As we will show, our generator can handle arbitrary convolutional codes, arbitrary vector length, and produces decoders with excellent performance. It is implemented as part of the Spiral program generation system [6]. An online interface is provided at www.spiral.net/software/viterbi.html.

Related work. Our approach is similar to the one taken by Spiral to generate programs for linear transforms [6]. Spiral uses the domain-specific language SPL [7] to explore alternative algorithms for a given transform, and vectorize and parallelize fast Fourier transform algorithms (FFTs) [8,9]. While our VL is closely related to SPL due to the inherent similarities between Viterbi decoding and FFTs (which were already noted in [10,11]), a significant difference with previous work is that the selection between alternative algorithms is not present. However, the wide range of convolutional codes that one would want to generate still offers a compelling case for on-demand generation of high-performance code.

VL is a subset of the Operator Language (OL) that aims at generalizing SPL to capture more general computations. [12] presents the general OL framework while this this paper focuses on issues specific to Viterbi decoding.

To achieve high performance, other decoding algorithms for convolutional codes also exist. Examples include the lazy Viterbi (efficient for long constraint lengths) and the Fano algorithm (efficient for good signal-to-noise ratios) [13,14]. This paper only considers "standard" Viterbi decoders.

Organization of this paper. In Section 2 we provide background on convolutional codes and the Viterbi decoding algorithm. In Section 3, we introduce the language VL to describe the forward pass of Viterbi decoding and explain how to generate scalar code. Vectorization through VL rewriting is covered in Section 4. In Section 5, we benchmark the performance of our generated decoders, and conclude in Section 6.

2 Background: Viterbi Decoders

In this section, we provide background on convolutional codes and Viterbi decoders. We then introduce the butterfly representation for Viterbi decoders.

2.1 Encoding Convolutional Codes

The purpose of forward error-correcting codes (FEC) is to prevent corruption of a message by adding redundant information before the message is sent over a noisy channel. At the receiving side, the redundant data is used to reconstruct the original message despite errors. In this paper, we focus only on a single type of FEC, namely convolutional codes. These codes are heavily used in telecommunications standards such as GSM and CDMA.

A convolutional encoder takes as input a bit stream and convolves it with a number of fixed bit sequences to obtain the output bit stream. Since convolution is equivalent to polynomial multiplication, each of these fixed bit sequences is called a (binary) *polynomial* although it is represented by a single integer.

Formally, a convolutional code is specified by N integers smaller than 2^K, denoted with $p_1, \ldots, p_N$. Such a code is said to have a *constraint length* K and a *rate* $1/N$, i.e., for each input bit, the encoder produces N output bits.

Finite State Machine (FSM) representation.. The encoding process can be described using a FSM with 2^{K-1} states that outputs N bits on each transition (Fig. 1). The precise layout depends on the convolutional code itself but each state always has a 0-transition (input bit is 0) and a 1-transition (input bit is 1) to other states. The initial encoding state is assumed to be 0 and the input stream is padded with $K - 1$ trailing zeros which guarantees that the final state is also 0.

More precisely, there exists a 0-transition between states n and m if $m \equiv 2n \mod 2^{K-1}$. Similarly, there exists a 1-transition between states n and m if $m \equiv (2n + 1) \mod 2^{K-1}$. Denoting the bit-wise AND as &, the bit-wise XOR as $\oplus$ and the XOR on all bits by $\bigoplus$, the output bit $b_{n \to m}^\ell$, corresponding to the polynomial p_ℓ when transitioning from state n to state m is computed as

$$b_{n \to m}^\ell = \bigoplus \left(p_\ell \& \left(2n \oplus (m \& 1) \right) \right) .$$

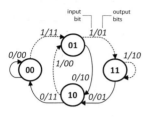

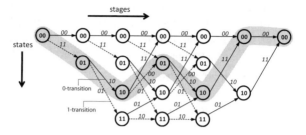

Fig. 1. FSM representation of the encoder $r = 1/2$, $K = 3$ with polynomials 7 and 5

Fig. 2. Viterbi trellis corresponding to the encoder of Fig. 1. The highlighted path shows that the message 1010_2 (first padded to 101000_2 to guarantee that the final state is 0) is encoded as $11\,10\,00\,10\,11\,00_2$.

Viterbi trellis. An equivalent representation of the encoding process "unrolls" the finite state machine in time to yield the Viterbi *trellis*, as shown in Fig. 2. Each path from the initial state to the final state represents a possible message. Note that the number of vertical stages, called the *frame length* F, is independent of the convolutional code but agreed upon by the two communicating parties.

The different states of the encoder are placed vertically, the different time steps, or *stages* are placed horizontally. The initial state (first stage) when starting a frame is 0. The zero padding explained previously implies that the last $K - 1$ transitions are 0-transitions, guaranteeing that the final state is also 0.

2.2   Viterbi Decoding

The Viterbi algorithm is a dynamic programming method that performs maximum likelihood sequence decoding (MLSD) on a convolutionally encoded stream. Intuitively, the decoder receives a bit stream and has to find the path in the Viterbi trellis that best corresponds to it, which would ideally be the same path the encoder originally took. The best visualization of the Viterbi algorithm again uses the Viterbi trellis but its purpose is now reversed: the incoming message is fixed and the path is to be found. It is composed of three phases, the *branch metric* computation, the *path metric* computation, and the *traceback*.

Branch metrics computation. In the first phase, the Viterbi algorithm assigns a cost, called the *branch metric*, to each edge in the trellis. This value represents how well the received bits would match if we knew the encoder took the transition corresponding to a given edge. It is computed by taking the Hamming distances between the bits the transition should output and the actually received ones (Fig. 3).

Path metrics computation. After the previous phase, the problem is equivalent to finding the shortest path between the entry and the exit vertices on a directed acyclic graph with weighted edges. Therefore, the second phase is a breadth-first forward traversal of the graph. It progressively computes the *path*

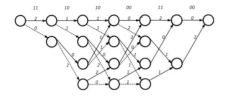 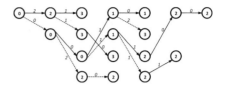

Fig. 3. Branch metrics computation. Assuming the decoder just received the message 11 10 10 00 11 00 $_2$ which is the previous example message with two bit flips (corresponding to injected errors), the Hamming distance between the bits actually received and the output bits corresponding to each arrow (shown in Fig. 2) is computed.

Fig. 4. Path metrics computation and traceback. Using the branch metric, the shortest path from the initial state to all states is computed, leaving only one predecessor for each node. Finally, only one complete path remains: it can be simply read off by starting in the final state and going backwards. Here, this path corresponds to the original message: 101000 $_2$.

metric, which is the shortest path to get from the root to each vertex. If a state has the path metric π, there exists one message that ends in the state with π corrupted bits and this message is less or equally corrupted than all other possible messages. While computing this, the predecessor of each node is remembered as a *decision bit*[1] (Fig. 4).

Traceback. The decision bits describe the ancestor of each vertex. Given this information and the final state, one can reconstruct the shortest path, called the *survivor path* by reading off predecessors.

In a software Viterbi decoder, it is important to perform branch and path metrics computations simultaneously to improve the ratio of operations over memory accesses. The fusion of these two phases is called the *forward pass*.

2.3 Viterbi Butterflies

The trellis shown on Fig. 2 has a regular structure except for the initial and final stages. The initial stage can be handled like all other stages by inserting prohibitively high path metrics as appropriate. Handling the final stage like all other stages simply involves computing all path metrics—the useless ones are automatically discarded.

Closer inspection of the trellis structure now shows that each stage of the forward pass can be decomposed in two phases: a fixed permutation called a *perfect shuffle* and a parallel operation on 2^{K-2} 2-by-2 substructures called *butterflies* (Fig. 5). In the following, we denote the states of a butterfly as shown below:

---

[1] The structure of the FSM guarantees that there are exactly two incoming edges into each vertex, except for the leftmost nodes in the trellis where there is only one.

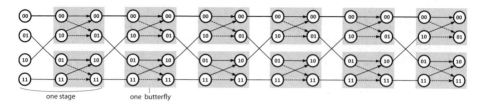

one stage   one butterfly

Fig. 5. Each stage in the Viterbi trellis consists of a perfect shuffle and 2^{K-2} parallel butterflies (here $K = 3$ and $F = 6$)

During the path metric computation, each butterfly does two *Add-Compare-Select* operations to compute the path metrics π_U and π_V from the path metrics π_A and π_B and the branch metrics $\beta_{A \to U}$, $\beta_{A \to V}$, $\beta_{B \to U}$ and $\beta_{B \to V}$:

$$\begin{cases} \pi_U = \min_{d_U}(\pi_A + \beta_{A \to U}, \pi_B + \beta_{B \to U}) \\ \pi_V = \min_{d_V}(\pi_A + \beta_{A \to V}, \pi_B + \beta_{B \to V}) \ . \end{cases} \tag{1}$$

Note that the minimum operator $\min_d(a, b)$ actually performs both the compare and select operations simultaneously. It returns the actual minimum of a and b and stores the binary decision in the decision bit d.

Simplification. Other effects, notably polynomial symmetries and soft decisions, actually modify the above expression. However, for reasons of brevity, we will not elaborate on them here.

3   Generating Scalar Code

The goal of this paper is to enable computer generation of efficient software implementations of the Viterbi decoder for arbitrary convolutional codes. To achieve this, we introduce a domain-specific language, called Viterbi language (VL), to concisely describe the (most critical) forward pass of the decoder and its associated compiler that translates the description into actual C code. Both are described in this section.

There are two main reasons for using a domain-specific language. First, it structures and simplifies the implementation of our software generator. Second, it enables the SIMD vectorization of the forward pass through rewriting VL expressions rather than optimizing C code. The vectorization is explained in Section 4.

For reasons that will become clear, VL is closely related to the signal processing language (SPL), a domain-specific language that was designed to generate high performance implementations of linear transforms [6,7]. We start with a brief introduction to SPL, motivate VL and explain the compilation process.

3.1   Fast Transform Algorithms: SPL

Linear transforms in signal processing are usually presented as summations, but can be equivalently viewed as a matrix. A linear transform computes $y = Tx$, where x is the complex input vector, y the complex output vector, and T the fixed transform matrix. For example, the n-point Fourier and Walsh-Hadamard transforms are defined by the following $n \times n$ matrices [5]:

$$\mathbf{DFT}_n = [e^{-2\pi kl\sqrt{-1}/n}]_{0 \leq k,l < n} \, ,$$

$$\mathbf{WHT}_n = \begin{bmatrix} \mathbf{WHT}_{n/2} & \mathbf{WHT}_{n/2} \\ \mathbf{WHT}_{n/2} & -\mathbf{WHT}_{n/2} \end{bmatrix}, \quad \mathbf{WHT}_1 = [1] \, .$$

A fast algorithm for a transform T reduces the number of operations required for computing Tx and can be viewed as a factorization of T into a product of sparse structured matrices.

SPL. SPL is the language used to describe such algorithms. It is based on matrix algebra and captures structured matrices. Parametrized symbols are used to represent frequently occurring matrices:

- The $n \times n$ identity matrix is denoted with I_n.
- The *stride permutation* matrix L_k^n reads the input at stride k and stores it at stride 1. In particular $L_{n/2}^n$ is the *perfect shuffle* that interleaves the first half of a vector with the second half.
- The *butterfly*[2] matrix F_2 corresponds to a DFT on two points: $F_2 = \begin{pmatrix} 1 & 1 \\ 1 & -1 \end{pmatrix}$
- The $n \times n$ *bit-reversal* permutation is denoted with R_n and the *twiddle* matrix T_i^n is a particular diagonal matrix. Their exact form is not important here.

Further, SPL uses matrix constructs to build matrices from other matrices. An example is the product AB which effectively composes two matrix vector multiplications: $(AB)x = A(Bx)$. The product can be indexed as in $\prod_{i=0}^{n} A_i = A_1 A_1 \ldots A_n$.

Finally, the *Kronecker product* (also called *tensor product*) of two matrices and its indexed variant are defined as

$$A \otimes B = [a_{k,l}B], \quad A \otimes_j B_j = [a_{k,l}B_j], \quad A = a_{k,l} \, .$$

Most importantly,

$$I_n \otimes A = \begin{pmatrix} A & & \\ & \ddots & \\ & & A \end{pmatrix} \, .$$

Pease algorithms. The SPL expressions for the Pease $O(n \log n)$ algorithms for the Fourier and Walsh-Hadamard transforms is shown below:

$$\mathbf{WHT}_{2^n} \rightarrow \prod_{i=0}^{n-1} \left((I_{2^{n-1}} \otimes F_2) \, L_{2^{n-1}}^{2^n} \right) \, , \tag{2}$$

$$\mathbf{DFT}_{2^n} \rightarrow R_{2^n} \prod_{i=0}^{n-1} \left(T_i^n (I_{2^{n-1}} \otimes F_2) \, L_{2^{n-1}}^{2^n} \right) \, . \tag{3}$$

The associated dataflow for the Pease WHT is shown in Fig. 6 (the Pease DFT is very similar). Note the similarity to the Viterbi trellis shown in Fig. 5, but remember that the butterflies operate differently. The resemblance between the DFT, the WHT and the Viterbi forward pass was already noted in [10,11]. Omega networks also share this dataflow [15].

---

[2] The Viterbi and DFT butterflies are different but related as we will see.

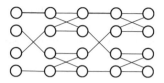

Fig. 6. Dataflow of the Pease algorithm for the $\mathbf{WHT}_4$

3.2 Representing the Viterbi Algorithm

The Viterbi algorithm is not a linear transform and therefore, does not fit the earlier framework. However, as discussed above, the forward pass (branch and path metric computation, excluding the traceback) is closely related to the Pease algorithms (2) and (3).

From now on, we will only consider the forward pass, excluding the traceback. The reason is that the traceback is both trivial and computationally much cheaper than the forward pass, requiring $O(F)$ operations versus $O(2^K F)$ for the forward pass. Hence, in practice, except for very short constraint lengths, a generic traceback is not the performance bottleneck.

Butterflies similarities. The DFT butterfly F_2 is an operator that takes two inputs x_0 and x_1 and produces two outputs y_0 and y_1:

$$\begin{cases} y_0 = x_0 + x_1 \\ y_1 = x_0 - x_1 \ . \end{cases}$$

Similarly, we view the j-th Viterbi butterfly decoding the i-th codeword as an operator $B_{i,j}$ that consumes and produces two path metrics as in (1). The difference between F_2 and $B_{i,j}$ is that, depending on its position, the Viterbi butterfly uses values from some external arrays to compute the branch metrics, and it also writes values to an external decision bit array (through the "select" part of the minimum operator).

Viterbi language (VL). In Table 1, we give the grammar in Backus-Naur form of a domain specific language called VL tailored to describe the operations performed during the forward pass of the Viterbi algorithm. VL uses parts of SPL but also includes the Viterbi butterfly. In SPL, the composition operation is equivalent to matrix multiplication, but this is not true of VL. We will occasionally refer to elements of VL as operators.

Forward pass algorithm. Using VL, The forward pass of a Viterbi decoder with constraint length K, frame length F, denoted $\mathbf{F}_{K,F}$ can be expressed in a way that is similar to the Pease algorithms (2) and (3):

$$\mathbf{F}_{K,F} \rightarrow \prod_{i=1}^{F} \left((I_{2^{K-2}} \otimes_j B_{F-i,j}) L_{2^{K-2}}^{2^{K-1}} \right) \ . \tag{4}$$

3.3 Compiler

The VL compiler is responsible for producing efficient code from an algorithm expressed in VL. By translating an operator A into code, we mean creating the

Table 1. Definition of the Viterbi Language in Backus-Naur form

$<$op$> ::= $	$\mathbf{F}_{K,F}$	*Viterbi forward pass*
	I_n	*identity*
	L_n^{mn}	*stride permutation*
	$B_{i,j}$	*Viterbi butterfly*
	$<$op$> <$op$>$	*composition*
	$\prod <$op$>$	*iterative composition*
	$<$op$> \otimes <$op$>$	*tensor product*

Table 2. Translating VL expressions to code. x denotes the input and y the output vector. C and D are generic operators optionally parametrized by their superscript and of domain and range optionally specified by their subscript. `x[b:e]` denotes the sub-vector of x starting at `b` and ending at `e`.

construct	code
$y = (CD)x$	```t = D(x);``` ```y = C(t);```

$y = \prod_{i=0}^{l-1} C^i x$	```y = C(l-1, x);```
	```for (i=l-2;i>=0;i--)```
	``` y = C(i, y);```

$y = (\mathrm{I}_m \otimes_j C_n^j)x$	```for (j=0;j<m;j++)```
	``` y[j*n:j*n+n-1] =```
	``` C(j, x[j*n:j*n+n-1]);```

$y = \mathrm{L}_m^{mn} x$	```for (i=0;i<m;i++)```
	``` for (j=0;j<n;j++)```
	``` y[i+m*j]=x[n*i+j];```

$y = B_{i,j}x$	*see equation (1)*

code for the function `A` that takes the input vector `x` and the output vector `y` as parameters and performs $y = A(x)$.

To generate the code, the compiler traverses the VL expression tree top-down, matching sub-trees with the templates shown in Table 2 and specializing them if needed. Plugging this code inside the generic traceback would yield a correct, albeit unoptimized implementation.

In practice, various optimizations are performed such as loop unrolling, array scalarization, strength reduction, copy propagation, precomputation and common sub-expression elimination. While some of these optimizations may be left to a C compiler, performing them inside the VL compiler typically yields better results, as C compilers generally have conservative aliasing assumptions. Most importantly, it also performs loop merging which means that perfect shuffles are never explicitly performed but merged (i.e., translated into readdressing) with the subsequent computation.

4   Generating Vector Code

The vast majority of current processors provide additional instructions working on vector registers, often branded as "multimedia" extensions like Intel's MMX and SSE or AMD's 3DNow!. The speedups for suitably structured applications like Viterbi decoders can be significant: for example, [4] achieves up to a 16x speedup using SSE. We first provide some background on these instructions, then show how to automatically take advantage of them by rewriting VL expressions. Finally we tackle overflows, a side effect of vectorizing the Viterbi algorithm.

4.1   Background: Short-Vector Instructions

Single-instruction multiple-data (SIMD) vector instructions instructions perform operations on short vectors in parallel. We call the length of the vector ν and the instructions ν-way. For instance, if $\nu = 4$, a point-wise addition of 4 scalars could be done with a single vector instruction instead of four *scalar* instructions. Also, vector instruction sets offer ways to reorganize (*shuffle*) the data within a short vector.

The *vector length* ν depends on the exact instruction set. The larger ν, the more operations can be performed simultaneously. In general, the expected speedup of efficiently *vectorized* code over its scalar counterpart can be up to the order of ν which makes it critical in high-performance applications. For example, Intel-compatible processors offer integer vector instructions for $\nu = 4 - 16$.

The drawback of these instructions is that they add complexity at various levels. First, they only operate on ν *contiguous* elements, which means algorithms have to be restructured to expose this parallelism. This step involves algorithmic knowledge, and compilers often fail at doing it automatically. Second, since compilers fail, it has to be done by hand which is complex and time-consuming. Third, vector instructions are processor specific, so using them requires precise knowledge and reduces portability.

4.2   Generating Vectorized Decoders: Overview

Fig. 7 gives an overview of our approach to generating a vectorized Viterbi decoder. The user specifies as input the convolutional code (i.e., the rate $1/N$, K, the polynomials p_ℓ and the frame length F) and the vector length ν. The generator outputs a ν-way vectorized Viterbi decoder, implemented using SSE.

As shown in Fig. 7, first, the generator instantiates the appropriate VL expression (4) and generates a scalar decoder (Section 3). This decoder is then executed to obtain the normalization factors needed to prevent overflows (Section 4.4). The ν-way vectorization is then performed by first rewriting the scalar VL algorithm. The result is then compiled into source code using the previous template matching system. Finally, a peephole optimizer ensures the features available in the instruction set are fully exploited. The resulting implementation of the forward pass is inserted into a generic framework to obtain the complete decoder.

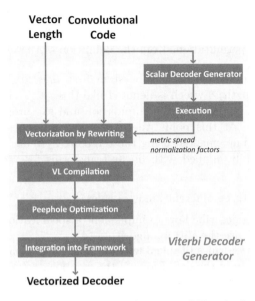

Fig. 7. Automatic generation of vectorized Viterbi decoders

Our implementation targets 4 to 16-way Intel SSE but the generic principles behind the generator makes it easy to retarget to another instruction set.

4.3   Vectorizing Rewriting System

In this section we explain how to automatically vectorize the forward pass of the Viterbi decoding using VL. First we identify some VL expressions, called vector base cases, that can directly be mapped into vector code. Vectorization is then achieved by rewriting the forward pass algorithm (equation (4)) into an equivalent VL expression that consists exclusively of vector base cases. This expression is then mapped into vector code and further optimizations are performed. The details are explained next.

Base cases. For the vectorization of the Viterbi algorithm, three types of base cases are required.

- One construct that can be implemented with all ν-way short vector instruction sets is $C \otimes I_\nu$ with C being any side-effect free VL operator. When implementing $C \otimes I_\nu$, the template system first implements C with its corresponding scalar template (Table 2) and then replaces all scalar variables and scalar operations inside the code by their ν-way vector counterparts. For instance, L_2^4 is a permutation of four elements whereas $L_2^4 \otimes I_\nu$ is a permutation of four vectors of ν elements each. To denote that the construct is a base case, we write $C\bar{\otimes}I_\nu$.
- The Viterbi kernel has side effects and thus does not fall into the previous category. We denote by $\vec{B}_{i,l}^\nu$ the vector code that executes ν Viterbi kernels over contiguous elements.

- Another class of vector base cases is the perfect shuffle of 2ν elements, written as $\vec{L}_{\nu}^{2\nu}$. We use the method in [16] to automatically generate efficient vector code for these permutations from the definition of the instruction sets.

Vector tags. The vectorization subsystem first *tags* a given VL expression with the vector length ν, which is denoted like this: $\underline{A}_{\nu}$. The full expression is then rewritten using algorithms, manipulation and tag propagation rules until all tags disappear. At this point, the expression only consists of vector base cases that can be implemented using the template system. The same approach has been successfully applied with linear transforms for vectorization [9] and parallelization[3] [8].

Rules. There are three different kinds of rules:

- The algorithms describe how to implement a specification using VL. In this paper, we only use the Viterbi algorithm (4).
- The manipulation rules (Table 3 left) are basic mathematical identities that can be proved from the definitions of the symbols.
- The tag propagation rules (Table 3 right) describe how the tags interact with the other symbols.

Viterbi vectorization. Using all the manipulation rules, the system automatically derives the following equality, which we call the *partial tensor flip*, that holds for any parametrized operator C^j and integers m, n and ν such that ν divides m:

$$\left(I_m \otimes_j C^j\right) L_m^{mn} = \left(I_{m/\nu} \otimes_{j_1} L_{\nu}^{n\nu} \left(C^{j_1\nu+j_2} \otimes_{j_2} I_{\nu}\right)\right) \left(L_{m/\nu}^{mn/\nu} \otimes I_{\nu}\right) .$$

Because of this transformation, the rewriting systems returns the following vectorized form of the algorithm in (4) and consists exclusively of base cases that can be mapped to code as explained above:

$$\mathbf{F}_{K,F}{}_{\nu} \rightarrow \prod_{i=1}^{F} \left[\left(I_{2^{K-2}/\nu} \otimes_{j_1} \vec{L}_{\nu}^{2\nu} \vec{B}_{F-i,j_1}^{\nu}\right) \left(L_{2^{K-2}/\nu}^{2^{K-1}/\nu} \otimes I_{\nu}\right)\right] .$$

In words, at each stage, this algorithm first permutes full vectors then iteratively ($i = 1, \ldots, F$) computes $2^{K-2}/\nu$ independent Viterbi butterflies and performs in-vector permutations $L_{\nu}^{2\nu}$ on each result. Remember that in the final code, the initial permutation in each i-step is never performed but merged with the subsequent butterfly computations.

Code generation. Using the previously explained template system, code can be generated for the algorithm above. In practice though, an additional pass with a peephole optimizer is inserted to handle the specifics of the instruction set which is unfortunately very irregular.

---

[3] This paper does not handle the parallelization of the Viterbi algorithm because, in traditional settings, it is not relevant. Even in multi-core systems, the cost of exchanging data over the interconnect is too high to split the trellis handling over multiple cores. It is more practical to parallelize by assigning different frames to different cores.

Table 3. Manipulation (left) and vectorization (right) rules. C and D are generic operators optionally parametrized by their superscript.

$$\mathrm{I}_{mk} \otimes_j C^j = \mathrm{I}_m \otimes_{j_1} (\mathrm{I}_k \otimes_{j_2} C^{j_1 k + j_2})$$

$$\mathrm{L}_{km}^{kmn} = (\mathrm{I}_k \otimes \mathrm{L}_m^{mn})(\mathrm{L}_k^{kn} \otimes \mathrm{I}_m)$$

$$(\mathrm{I}_m \otimes C)(\mathrm{I}_m \otimes D) = (\mathrm{I}_m \otimes CD)$$

$$(\mathrm{I}_m \otimes_j C_n^j)\,\mathrm{L}_m^{mn} = \mathrm{L}_m^{mn}(C_n^j \otimes_j \mathrm{I}_m)$$

$$\underline{CD}_\nu \to \underline{C}_\nu\,\underline{D}_\nu$$

$$\underline{\prod C}_\nu \to \prod \underline{C}_\nu$$

$$\underline{I_m \otimes_j C^j}_\nu \to I_m \otimes_j \underline{C^j}_\nu$$

$$\underline{C \otimes \mathrm{I}_\nu}_\nu \to C \bar{\otimes} \mathrm{I}_\nu$$

$$\underline{B_{i,l\nu+j} \otimes_j \mathrm{I}_\nu}_\nu \to \vec{B}_{i,l}^{\nu}$$

$$\underline{\mathrm{L}_\nu^{2\nu}}_\nu \to \vec{\mathrm{L}}_\nu^{2\nu}$$

4.4 Overflows

The path metrics increase on average with the stage number. For implementation however, they must stay within a finite window of representable values. The precision offered by short vector instructions might not be sufficient to guarantee the absence of overflows so the algorithm must sometimes be slightly modified.

For instance, with Intel's SSE, all vector operations are performed in 128 bits vector registers. Therefore, in 4-way mode, elements are 32-bits long whereas in 16-way mode, elements are 8-bits long. In this last case, metrics are likely to overflow the window of 256 "legal" values.

There are known methods to help rescaling these metrics (see [17]) but they are based on empirical properties of the code which is why we need to first generate a scalar version of the decoder (i.e., in which overflows will not occur) and only then generate the vectorized version once these properties are determined. We will not detail this process further even though it is fully automated.

5   Results

In this section, we analyze the performance of our generated Viterbi decoders. We compare against existing optimized implementations, show the generality of our generator, and show the speedup obtained by vectorization.

Experimental Setup. All experiments are performed on an Intel Core 2 Extreme X9650. All code is compiled using the Intel Compiler (icc) 10.1 with performance flags (-fast -fomit-frame-pointer -fno-alias). The performance in each case is measured by entirely decoding (forward pass and traceback) multiple frames. Initialization and precomputation (one time costs) are excluded.

Our generator supports any valid combination of rate, polynomials, frame length, and constraint length $K \geq 6^4$. Vectorization is available for all convolutional codes and for processors that are SSE-compatible through 4-way, 8-way and 16-way intrinsics.

---

[4] The limitation is an artifact of the actual implementation. The methods presented in this paper are applicable for all constraint lengths.

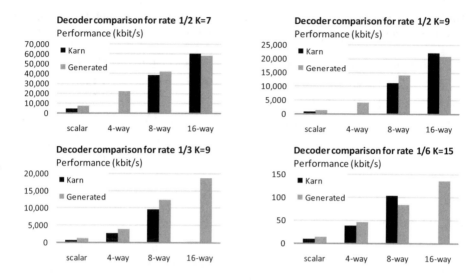

Fig. 8. Performance comparison between the generated and hand-optimized decoders

Benchmarking. We first compare our generated decoders against Karn's hand-written decoders [4]. Karn's forward error correction software supports four codes $(1/2, K = 7$ nicknamed "Voyager", $1/2, K = 9, 1/3, K = 9$ and $1/6, K = 15$ nicknamed "Cassini") available for different vector lengths. Not all vector lengths are supported for all codes. The forward pass in [4] is written separately in assembly for each combination of code and vector length.

In Fig. 8, we show the performance results for these four codes and for all vector lengths. A missing bar signifies that the implementation is not provided by Karn. Analysis of the plots shows that our generated decoders have roughly equal performance compared to Karn's software.

Performance of supported codes. To show the generality of our generator and the consistent performance, we generated decoders for known "good" codes (see [18]) of rate $1/2$ collected and all four vector lengths 1, 4, 8, 16. Fig. 9a shows the performance results and, as expected, the lines show the exponential decay in performance when the constraint length increases. Similar graphs are observed for other rates.

Quality of Vectorization. Fig. 9b shows the speedup achieved by vectorization in Fig. 9a. The baselines are the non-vectorized scalar decoders. We observe a consistent speedup of about 3.5 for 4-way, 6 for 8-way, and 10 for 16-way vectorization. The smaller gains for longer vectors is expected since they require more involved shuffle operations. The peak for both 16-way and 8-way with short constraint length is caused by the reduction of the memory footprint due to the use of shorter data types.

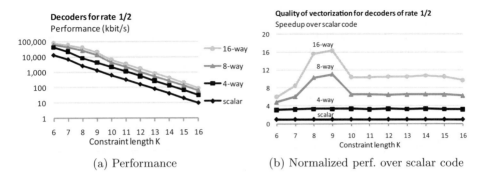

(a) Performance   (b) Normalized perf. over scalar code

Fig. 9. Performance of various generated decoders for rate 1/2. Note that each point on these graphs actually replace one manually tuned assembly code.

Code Generation Time. Note that, in the previous graphs, we present 40 different optimized decoders, all of which were generated in less than one hour. We estimate that it would take an expert more than a day to produce each one of the forward passes in assembly, which implies an improvement in the development time in the range of three orders of magnitude.

6 Conclusion

We presented a framework and its implementation that completely automates the implementation of fast software Viterbi decoders for modern computing platforms with SIMD instruction sets by generating the performance critical forward pass. The basic idea is to construct a domain specific mathematical language to express the forward pass, to vectorize by rewriting in this language, and to use a backend for low level optimizations. The same approach could be used for parallelization but it is more efficient (and trivial) to parallelize across frames.

Our framework enables the instant generation of any decoder across a wide spectrum of parameters. The generated decoders' performance is on-par with specialized expert implementations. Further, it enables fast porting to new architectures as only small changes are needed to support a new instruction set.

We invite the reader to visit the online interface to our generator at `www.spiral.net/software/viterbi.html`.

References

1. Viterbi, A.: Error bounds for convolutional codes and an asymptotically optimum decoding algorithm. IEEE Transactions on Information Theory 13(2) (April 1967)
2. Gemmeke, T., Gansen, M., Noll, T.: Implementation of scalable power and area efficient high-throughput viterbi decoders. Solid-State Circuits 37(7) (July 2002)
3. Mitola III, J.: Software Radio Architecture. John Wiley & Sons, Chichester (2002)

4. Karn, P.: FEC library version 3.0.1 (August 2007),
   `http://www.ka9q.net/code/fec/`
5. Van Loan, C.: Computational frameworks for the fast Fourier transform. Society
   for Industrial and Applied Mathematics, Philadelphia (1992)
6. Püschel, M., Moura, J.M.F., Johnson, J., Padua, D., Veloso, M., Singer, B., et al.:
   SPIRAL: Code generation for DSP transforms. Proc. of the IEEE 93(2) (2005)
7. Xiong, J., Johnson, J., Johnson, R., Padua, D.: SPL: a language and compiler for
   DSP algorithms. SIGPLAN Not. 36(5), 298–308 (2001)
8. Franchetti, F., Voronenko, Y., Püschel, M.: FFT program generation for shared
   memory: SMP and multicore. In: Supercomputing, SC (2006)
9. Franchetti, F., Voronenko, Y., Püschel, M.: A rewriting system for the vectorization
   of signal transforms. In: Daydé, M., Palma, J.M.L.M., Coutinho, Á.L.G.A., Pacitti,
   E., Lopes, J.C. (eds.) VECPAR 2006. LNCS, vol. 4395, pp. 363–377. Springer,
   Heidelberg (2007)
10. Forney Jr., G.D.: The viterbi algorithm. Proc. of the IEEE 61(3) (March 1973)
11. Rader, C.: Memory management in a viterbi decoder. IEEE Transactions on Com-
    munications [legacy, pre - 1988] 29(9), 1399–1401 (1981)
12. Franchetti, F., de Mesmay, F., McFarlin, D., Püschel, M.: Operator language: A
    program generation framework for fast kernels. In: IFIP Working Conference on
    Domain Specific Languages (DSL WC). LNCS, vol. 5658. Springer, Heidelberg
    (2009)
13. Feldman, J., Abou-Faycal, I., Frigo, M.: A fast maximum-likelihood decoder for
    convolutional codes. In: Proc. of Vehicular Technology Conference, pp. 371–375
    (2002)
14. Fano, R.: A heuristic discussion of probabilistic decoding. IEEE Transactions on
    Information Theory 9(2), 64–74 (1963)
15. Lawrie, D.: Access and alignment of data in an array processor. IEEE Transactions
    on Computers C-24(12), 1145–1155 (1975)
16. Franchetti, F., Püschel, M.: Generating SIMD vectorized permutations. In: Hen-
    dren, L. (ed.) CC 2008. LNCS, vol. 4959, pp. 116–131. Springer, Heidelberg (2008)
17. Hekstra, A.: An alternative to metric rescaling in viterbi decoders. IEEE Transac-
    tions on Communications 37(11), 1220–1222 (1989)
18. Chambers, W.: On good convolutional codes of rate 1/2, 1/3, and 1/4. In: Singapore
    ICCS/ISITA 1992. Communications on the Move, November 1992, vol. 2, pp. 750–
    754 (1992)

Author Index

Printing: Mercedes-Druck, Berlin
Binding: Stein+Lehmann, Berlin